Southeast Asia in United States Policy

by RUSSELL H. FIFIELD

[•] • [•] [•] • [•] [•] • [•] [•] • [•] [•] • [•] [•] • [•] [•] • [•]

Southeast Asia
in United States Policy

[•] • [•] [•] • [•] [•] • [•] [•] • [•] [•] • [•] [•] • [•] [•] • [•]

Published for the
COUNCIL ON FOREIGN RELATIONS
by FREDERICK A. PRAEGER, *Publishers*
New York • Washington • London

FREDERICK A. PRAEGER, *Publishers*

111 Fourth Avenue, New York 3, N.Y., U.S.A.
77-79 Charlotte Street, London W.1, England

Published in the United States of America in 1963
by Frederick A. Praeger, Inc., Publishers

Third printing, 1965

SOUTHEAST ASIA IN UNITED STATES POLICY

FIRST EDITION

Library of Congress catalog card number: 63-20144
Printed in the United States of America
by Capital City Press, Inc., Montpelier, Vermont

Council on Foreign Relations

The Council on Foreign Relations is a non-profit institution devoted to study of the international aspects of American political, economic and strategic problems. It takes no stand, expressed or implied, on American policy.

The authors of books published under the auspices of the Council are responsible for their statements of fact and expressions of opinion. The Council is responsible only for determining that they should be presented to the public.

For a list of Council publications see pages 489 and 490.

To my mother

EMMA H. FIFIELD

Preface

What has been American policy in Southeast Asia? What is it today? What should it be in the coming years? Any meaningful analysis must consider carefully American national objectives and must reflect a realistic estimate of the ever-changing situation in that important part of the world. In circumstances where the United States is deeply involved, where its impact is considerable, and where the stakes are high, the alternatives to current policy merit particular attention. As for the countries of Southeast Asia, the decisions of Washington can obviously influence the range of selection in their own policies.

American policy in Southeast Asia at present and in the foreseeable future centers on the problems of security and stability in a divided world. Developments of the past can provide valuable perspective although the United States does not have the advantage of many years of direct contact throughout the area. Only in the last decade has the security of Southeast Asia—the maintenance of the political independence and territorial integrity of its states—become a major concern of policy-makers in Washington.

Security is a concept the dimensions of which are no longer primarily restricted to military and strategic considerations but embrace in varying degrees of importance diplomatic, political, economic, ideological, and cultural relationships. Broadly interpreted, aggression can range over an ascending scale from a diplomatic, economic, and propaganda offensive against the adversary to an all-out assault with thermonuclear weapons, while the response to it can be graduated to meet the needs of the deepening crisis. Security also blurs in many respects the distinction between domestic and foreign developments in an area of international turmoil.

The problems of stability for countries in the throes of nation-building are no less pressing than those of assuring security in a divided world. The many pressures for economic and social change need to be promptly recognized, evaluated, and constructively acted upon if Asians are to be helped in meeting their rising expectations through economic growth.

This book seeks to set forth current conditions and problems and develop a rationale for American policy in Southeast Asia in the years ahead, suggesting guidelines for making it applicable through different instrumentalities. Since specific policy goals will vary with time, the changing circumstances, and the countries involved, it examines the constants and variables, the continuities and the possible developments. If this study arouses a greater public interest in and understanding of the area and American policy there, the efforts in undertaking it will have been amply rewarded.

In the summer of 1959, the Council on Foreign Relations, mindful of international events of grave significance, established a Study Group on Southeast Asia in U. S. Policy. Harlan Cleveland ably served as chairman, skillfully bringing out the viewpoints of the participants, during the seven meetings from late 1959 to late 1960. David J. Padwa was an effective rapporteur. Participating in Study Group discussions were A. Doak Barnett, Alexander D. Calhoun, Lieutenant General Paul W. Caraway, USA, Christian G. Chapman, Melvin Conant, Harold C. Conklin, Colonel Donald J. Decker, USMC, Alexander Eckstein, F. Bowen Evans, William Henderson, Robert C. Herber, Alfred le S. Jenkins, George McT. Kahin, John Kerry King, Colonel William R. Kintner, USA, Hyman Kublin, Kenneth P. Landon, Henry R. Lieberman, John M. H. Lindbeck, Paul M. A. Linebarger, William P. Maddox, Walter H. Mallory, Lieutenant General Richard M. Montgomery, USAF, John D. Montgomery, Karl J. Pelzer, J. Morden Murphy, Robert R. Nathan, Philip E. Mosely, Lucian W. Pye, John D. Rockefeller, 3rd, G. William Skinner, Herbert D. Spivack, John Milton Steeves, Admiral Felix B. Stump, USN (ret.), Phillips Talbot, Frank N. Trager, Captain Alexander K. Tyree, USN, Allen S. Whiting, Kenneth Todd Young, and Robert W. Zimmermann.

A number of other people took out time from their busy schedules to comment on certain position papers in the early stages of the manuscript: Harry J. Benda, Lawrence S. Finkelstein, Colonel Amos A. Jordan, Jr., USA, Ernest K. Lindley, J. A. Modelski, Richard L. Park, Guy J. Pauker, Josef Silverstein, Robert E. Ward, David A. Wilson, and Charles Wolf, Jr. Individuals who kindly gave interviews on the project in the United States were Dean Acheson, Leland M. Goodrich, Paul H. Nitze, J. Graham Parsons, James Plimsoll, Walter S. Robertson, and Dean Rusk. To all these people the author expresses his gratitude for the consideration given him.

Participation in a Council Study Group on the politics of U. S. aid in Burma, Thailand, Viet-Nam, and Taiwan with Carter Goodrich as chairman and John D. Montgomery as research secretary and in a Council Discussion Group on government problems in newly independent countries with Robert Blum as chairman and a number of specialists in the role of discussion leaders was stimulating. As a Professor of Foreign Affairs at The National War College, 1958-1959, and a Visiting Research Fellow at the Council on Foreign Relations, 1959-1960, the author had an opportunity to profit from hearing authoritative speakers on the problems of foreign policy. He has been able to travel in Southeast Asia as a Fulbright Research Professor, a Guggenheim Fellow, and a faculty member of The National War College. To the individuals who made these opportunities possible, the writer expresses his appreciation.

Americans in Southern Asia and the Pacific, officials and private citizens alike, some in positions of great responsibility and others having less influential roles, military officers as well as civilian officials, have given the author many insights across a wide spectrum of opinion and outlook. And in Washington as well as London, though quite naturally on a more limited scale in the latter, Americans concerned with U. S. policy in Southeast Asia have been helpful. Mention should be made of Foreign Service officers Robert S. Lindquist and John I. Getz.

The writer desires to indicate his gratitude to individuals in the foreign offices of the European, Asian, and South Pacific members of the Southeast Asia Treaty Organization—Australia, New Zealand, the Philippines, Thailand, Pakistan, France, and Great Britain along with its Phoenix Park establishment at Singapore—who with others in those countries have assisted him at different times in the course of his travel and research. The same consideration holds true for various officials and other individuals in Japan, Taiwan, Indonesia, the Federation of Malaya, VietNam, Cambodia, Laos, Burma, and India. The British Crown Colony of Hong Kong, like the State of Singapore, is a valuable source of information relating to developments in the Far East. Persons associated with the Australian National University, the

Royal Institute of International Affairs, and the Centre D'Etudes de Politique Etrangère have been cooperative. A visit at SEATO Headquarters in Bangkok and interviews with a large number of officials were rewarding. Although the writer is not in a position to list by name the persons abroad who have assisted him, he owes a real debt to many of them.

The author also takes this occasion to express his appreciation to the University of Michigan which granted him a leave of absence to undertake this study and to Professor James K. Pollock, Chairman at the time of the Department of Political Science, who helped to facilitate it. Miss Ruth Savord and Donald Wasson with their staff at the library of the Council on Foreign Relations gave unstinted aid; assistance also came from librarians at Columbia University and the University of Michigan. Miss Lorna Brennan with her staff and Mrs. William Sprentall helped in various stages of the preparation and typing of the manuscript. To Philip E. Mosely, Principal Research Fellow at the Council, go thanks for encouraging the writer in his task.

Although the author of this book has profited from all the various sources mentioned, the conclusions are his own. This volume is not an example of group research; the writer accepts full responsibility for the work. Wide differences of opinion naturally existed among the members of the Study Group, in the comments by others on the position papers, and in the interviews at home and abroad. The value in the methodology of the policy studies under the Council on Foreign Relations lies in the perspective, depth, and versatility displayed by individuals who from their wealth of background and experience point out to a prospective author the wide horizons and specific limitations of his projected book.

R. H. F.

Contents

Southeast Asia in United States Policy

[ONE]

Dimensions of the Challenge

Southeast Asia presents a challenge of major proportions to the United States—a challenge that poses diverse and complex questions affecting the future of the American people. From Burma to the outermost islands of the Philippines and Indonesia, this spacious corner of the Asian continent extends more than 3,000 miles east and west and over 2,000 miles north and south. Its total land area is somewhat less than half that of the United States and supports a rapidly growing population, estimated at some 216 million in 1963. Its people are fragmented ethnically, culturally, religiously, and linguistically; they are divided politically.

The new political map of Southeast Asia perhaps points up most strikingly the rapid change which the area is undergoing. Within less than a dozen years after V-J Day, the Philippines acquired independence from the United States; Indonesia, from the Netherlands; the two Viet-Nams, Cambodia, and Laos, from France; Burma and Malaya, from Great Britain. When Singapore received self-government in 1959, the only remaining colonial areas were British Borneo, Portuguese Timor (technically an overseas province), and West New Guinea, governed by the Dutch but claimed by the Indonesians. In 1962 West New Guinea was turned over to UN administration, pending its transfer to Indonesia, and in the same year the foundations were laid for a Federation of Malaysia that would embrace the remaining British possessions. Thailand is the one country in the region which never lost its sovereignty to a Western power.

Newly independent except for Thailand, the nine states of the region are in the throes of nation-building. They are laboring under handicaps and problems common to all the economically less developed countries aspiring to a better life for their people. And looming over the region is the lengthening shadow of Communist China. These conditions define in the broadest of terms the challenge that Southeast Asia sets for U.S. policy: the promotion of stability to permit internal development, and the promotion of security to prevent a take-over by international communism.

The decline of Western colonial rule in Southeast Asia has greatly altered the power status of the area. In many respects it has returned to the precolonial era of weak and sometimes contesting states that are not often willing to work together. Whatever its precise meaning, the expression "power vacuum" is indicative of the situation prevailing among the states in this area of great strategic, economic, and demographic significance.

In addition to the mere size of the region, its geographical location gives it special significance in the world balance. Peninsular and insular Southeast Asia link continental China and Australia in a sort of causeway. At the same time the Strait of Malacca between Sumatra and Malaya and the Sunda Strait between Sumatra and Java provide water passageways, so necessary for trade and the use of naval power, through the Malay barrier between the Pacific and Indian oceans. Singapore's location off the tip of the Malay Peninsula and, 700 miles to the north, the narrow Kra Isthmus between the Gulf of Siam and the Andaman Sea figure prominently in the security of the area. Bangkok is a key center in the pattern of international air transport, with flights of only a few hours separating it from Calcutta, Darwin, or Hong Kong. And in the northeastern part of the region there is the Democratic Republic of Viet-Nam, a veritable Communist spearhead and a formidable threat in Southeast Asia.

Traditionally, the economy of the region has supplied the world with foodstuffs and raw materials, and among the exports rice, rubber, tin, and petroleum may be singled out as having particular significance in international politics. Before the Pacific war Burma, Thailand, and Indochina constituted the rice bowl of Asia, with the traditional markets in China, Japan, and India as well as in deficit areas within the region like Malaya, the East Indies, and usually the Philippines. Since the war's end the pattern of trade has varied, but the importance of the rice bowl remains. About 90 per cent of the world's production of natural rubber comes from Southeast Asia, especially from Indonesia and Malaya, as does about 60 per cent of the world's output of tin. Nor should other items, such as petroleum (the main sources in the Far East), bauxite, tungsten, iron ore, tea, sugar, coffee, spices, tobacco, abacá, copra, and coconut oil, be ignored. The development of synthetic products in the industrial countries, the practice of stockpiling, and the more efficient use of raw materials have affected the strategic importance of certain of the products of Southeast Asia, but the basic significance of many items in the world economy will remain for the indefinite future.

The markets of Southeast Asia, sure to grow in importance, are of interest not only to the Western powers, but also to Communist China, and to Japan and India. Economic ties between the new states and Western countries continue, for long-established patterns of trade, banking, and investment have not been destroyed in a number of cases; the Federation of Malaya, for instance, has been the largest dollar-earner among the Commonwealth members of the sterling bloc.

Although certain areas are heavily populated, Java and Madura having at least 1,200 people per square mile, the region as a whole is underpopulated. With a rate of population growth of about 2.0 per cent annually, Southeast Asia could still support many additional people. In contrast, Communist China has a population of over 670 million, increasing at an estimated annual rate of 2.3 per cent. Nationalistic governments, already generally critical of the existing Chinese minorities, do not want to open the doors to immigration; yet, even if Peking were able to regulate immigration into the area on its own terms, the dimensions of the population explosion on the Chinese mainland indicate that the region could only be a temporary safety valve.

THE COMMUNIST OFFENSIVE

In this area, so rich in resources and potentialities but weak in self-defense capabilities, the challenge of the Communist powers to free world and American interests is acute and unrelenting in the various pressures being exerted. Despite the Soviet Union's seniority in the Communist hierarchy and the resources at its command, Communist China is more influential in the region. As long as the ties of the Moscow-Peking alliance remain relatively firm, each is in a position to strengthen the other in Asia. But serious differences of opinion leading to greater competition for influence would, of course, have widespread ramifications for international communism in Southeast Asia. There are already signs that such competition may develop.

Meanwhile, the People's Republic of China gives evidence of probing more deeply and taking greater risks than the Soviet Union in sensitive Asian areas. The spectrum of activity available to the leaders in Peking is wide and diffuse, extending from subversion, through insurrection, to open attack. In Southeast Asia the possibility of war limited in terms of territory, weapons, and objectives is greater than in many other areas of Eurasia where the Communist and free worlds meet. "Aggression by proxy" could here produce a war of miscalculation. And in the years ahead the acquisition by Communist China of a sustained nuclear capability is certain to add to the hazards. Diplomatically, the Sino-Soviet challenge is constant and intensive, opposing not just the so-called "collective colonialism" of SEATO but exploiting almost all the intra-regional frictions and controversies. The economic challenge of the Communist bloc members is revealed in extensive programs of trade and aid and in the unflagging efforts of Communist China to create an image of itself as the model for Asian development.

Precedents exist for a pattern of relationships between Communist China and Southeast Asia, modified, of course, to meet the conditions of the twentieth century. Historically, the kingdoms and principalities of precolonial Southeast Asia reflected the vicissitudes of Chinese dynasties, particularly when the strong emperors of the Middle Kingdom tended to project their influence upon their weaker neighbors. Although the pattern was not uniform, the common practice was for a local ruler to recognize the suzerainty of the Emperor of China, become his vassal, and render tribute at certain intervals. (Only in Annam was the degree of Chinese influence so pronounced that the people actually became Sinified.) Even in the early years after V-J Day, before the Communist conquest of the mainland, the actions of Chiang Kai-shek raised apprehensions in some Western circles about China's ultimate posture in the area.

The immediate objective of Communist China in Southeast Asia is to create a buffer area for the security of its own territory. The evidence provided by the recent Korean and Indochinese wars and subsequent diplomacy suggests that the Peking regime is determined to keep the northern parts of Korea and Viet-Nam under Communist governments and outside the sphere of influence of any potentially hostile power. If it is not possible to have sympathetic Communist governments in other buffer areas, China seems prepared for the time being to settle for neutral regimes—a category into which Laos and Cambodia fall.

Another clear-cut Chinese objective is to compel the withdrawal of the power and influence of the United States not only in Southeast Asia, but throughout the entire Far East. SEATO is a particular target of Peking's efforts, with Great Britain, France, and Australia being disparately lumped with the United States in the Chinese Communist hostility to any Western influences in the area. Naturally, Communist China seeks to bring Taiwan under its domination; and it certainly does not favor the expansion of Japanese or Indian influence, whether economic or political, in Southeast Asia.

The ultimate objective of the People's Republic of China in the region is the establishment of paramountcy. Politically this objective means setting up Communist regimes amenable to the guidance of Peking. The model, in other words, is not the expansion of China in terms of new provinces, but the creation of Communist states which will recognize the leadership of their giant neighbor. By this means both its ideological and strategic objectives would be met: communism would expand its hold on millions of Asians while weak states, previously hostile or neutral, would be made allies. This would insure the end of the Western threat within the region, the strengthening of buffer areas, and the supremacy of the Chinese armed forces. Economically the paramountcy of the People's Republic of China would signify the control of the area's economy in the interests of Peking. A "Co-Prosperity Sphere," with China taking the place of Japan, is not outside the realm of possibility. Indeed, it is clear that the growing industrialization of Communist China would be complemented by the raw materials and markets of a dependent Southeast Asia. And culturally, the development of a favorable image of the People's Republic as a custodian of Asian culture would be avidly promoted.

So far as is known, Peking has no fixed timetable for establishing its paramountcy over Southeast Asia. The tactics used will vary from country to country, and advance and retreat will be likely. Communist China probably considers that time is on its side; after all, the Soviet Union was not able to establish the Communist regimes in Eastern Europe under its paramountcy until many years after the Bolshevik Revolution of 1917.

THE DYNAMICS OF CHANGE

Even if the Communist threat did not exist, the pressures for economic and social change in Southeast Asia would raise serious problems in American foreign policy. Pressures are building up that can produce considerable turmoil unless they are channeled by governments toward constructive ends. The achievement of national independence and the termination of Western colonial rule have not led to the green pastures of prosperity that many revolutionary leaders promised. At the same time the winning of national freedom has weakened the ties of unity that once marked the struggle for self-determination.

The "revolution of rising expectations," an expression that has caught the public imagination, does not lend itself to clear-cut definition. It arises from a growing discontent with existing economic and social conditions and focuses on the demand for a higher standard of living for the underprivileged millions of Asia. The revolution has the momentum to transcend the barriers of cultural and political diversity in Southeast Asia, so that many leaders from the area are now speaking the same language when economic questions arise in international discussions. The lethargy of the past is being shaken through the expansion of communications, the use of mass media, the employment of propaganda techniques, and the accomplishments in educational adaptation. New and unstable governments have to respond to these pressures. No longer, for example, can the *tao*, the common man in the barrios of the Philippines, be taken for granted by the officials at Malacañang, the presidential palace in Manila.

Central to this revolution is nationalism, the most dynamic force in Southeast Asia. Emotional rather than rational, abstract rather than concrete, nationalism embodies a deep-seated feeling of many Asians that under their own leadership and basically through their own efforts a better and more abundant life can be attained. To many Southeast Asian leaders nationalism is practically synonymous with anticolonialism, for, intensely absorbed in the revolutionary period, they have not been able to adjust to a new political environment. In a widespread anti-Western outlook, the former colonial powers are generally blamed for the underdevelopment of the area, and their remaining economic interests have often been under attack. Despite the need for private capital investment from abroad to help meet the growing demands of the people, confidence on the part of both Asian and Westerner is too frequently lacking.

Leaders in some states have been willing to join alliances with Western powers, but others profess to see in nonalignment or neutralism a way of assuring their independence and, at the same time, of getting assistance from the Communist as well as from the non-Communist world. Domestic considerations involving the balance of political forces sometimes buttress ideological outlook, for nonalignment may represent a compromise between pro-Western and pro-Communist factions in the body politic. Whatever the proportion of sincerity and opportunism in the neutralists' equating of the Sino-Soviet bloc and the Western coalition, all agree that another world war, whether or not Southeast Asia became a battlefield, would set back for a long time any real chance for economic development. Memories of the Japanese occupation, of the dislocation and destruction during the Pacific war, and of the conditions that prevailed after it, are still vivid in the minds of the older generation. Pacifism, in the strict sense of the term, is not widespread, but it colors attitudes in some countries where traditions of nonviolence have been associated with Theravada Buddhism and Gandhian philosophy. In many of the attitudes on pacifism or neutralism there is also noticeable a degree of Asian identification. Racialism may even take the form of a tinge of pride in the limited industrial achievements, despite the human cost incurred, of fellow Asians in the People's Republic of China.

Marxism appeals to certain intellectuals and politicians as a solution to the "revolution of rising expectations." Having studied its tenets as college students before the Second World War, they attempted to give practical application to theoretical concept after they came to power. Socialism was considered in some countries to be the best alternative to capitalism.

The Asian revolution has a momentum that waits for no leisurely analysis or tardy response. Domestic developments that often spanned many decades in Western Europe are being telescoped into far shorter periods of time in Asia today. It is all the more important, then, that in its policy the United States be associated with the constructive forces in Southeast Asia though, clearly, these forces are in process of evolution and require constant evaluation. Nationalism, for example, with its positive and negative aspects, can grow in intensity as its human base is being broadened from the elite in the cities to the peasants in the countryside. The association of nationalism with anticolonialism may acquire a different emphasis as the era of Western rule recedes

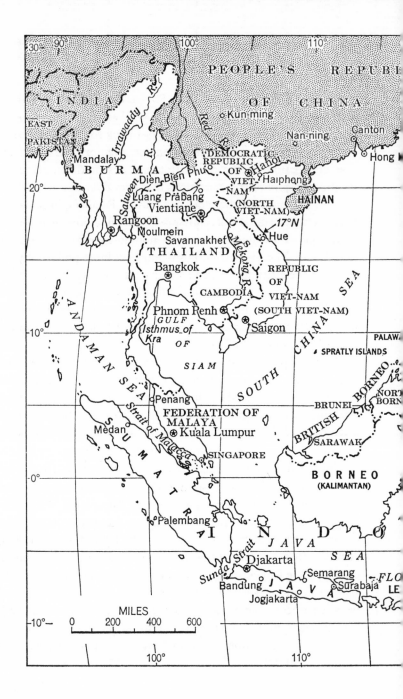

SOUTHEAST ASIA

⊕ Capital of country
⊙ Cities over 500,000 population
○ Other cities

Taipei
TAIWAN (FORMOSA)

LUZON

REPUBLIC
Manila OF THE
MINDORO PHILIPPINES
SAMAR
PANAY Cebu LEYTE
NEGROS
SULU
SEA
MINDANAO
Davao
Zamboanga

P A C I F I C

O C E A N

CELEBES
SEA
Manado

HALMAHERA

CELEBES
(SULAWESI)
E

CERAM
Ambon

B A N D A   S E A

SEA
LESSER SUNDAS

PORTUGUESE
TIMOR

A S I A

WEST
IRIAN

Kotabaru

NORTHEAST
NEW
GUINEA
(Aust.)
PAPUA
(Aust.)

A R A F U R A   S E A

A U S T R A L I A
Darwin   140°

130°   140°   30°

20°

10°

0°

10°

into history and the apprehension over the power and intentions of Communist China becomes more pronounced. At the same time neutralism may become somewhat less popular, for the boundary controversy between peace-minded India and an aggressive Communist China has weakened the faith of many in the Five Principles of Peaceful Coexistence. If these developments prove to be of more than transitory significance, how can the United States best take account of them over the next decade?

American objectives in Southeast Asia, as has been pointed out, center around the promotion of stability on the domestic front and security in the community of nations. To help the Asians meet their rising expectations through economic growth, American security policies have bought time for the weak countries by preventing international communism from taking over Southeast Asia. The specific policy goals vary in scope, in time, from country to country, and with changes in the local situation. It is the task of the following chapters to examine the constants and variables, the continuities and the possible developments, in these policies.

Priority in American efforts depends upon the international situation at a given time, the pressures being exerted, and the countermeasures that are needed. In the ultimate analysis, the tests of American national objectives are twofold: Are they sound in conception? Are they operationally attainable? Objectives may be limited by realism, but realism cannot exist without objectives. Moreover, what they should be as the decade unfolds, compared to what they are today, raises another set of questions.

[TWO]

Evolution of U.S. Policy

The present American goals in mainland Southeast Asia and in Indonesia have developed since the preliminaries of the Second World War. The United States does not have a long record of involvement in the region, and thus it is hard put to acquire those deeper perspectives which can be gained only from long experience. Apart from the acquisition of the Philippines in 1899 after the Spanish-American War, Washington's role in the entire region was limited until Imperial Japan began to acquire its first footholds in the late 1930s. At that time the United States was in the process of reducing its limited responsibilities still further, for in 1935 the Philippines had been given Commonwealth status, a major step on the road to independence. Japanese military inroads in French Indochina and economic penetration in the Netherlands East Indies became an increasing cause for American concern; yet, prior to the Japanese attack on Pearl Harbor, cooperation with the Dutch and the British in Southeast Asia was conditioned by technical American neutrality.

After December 7, 1941, the possibility of any sustained collective defense effort by the Americans, British, and Dutch was soon removed by the rapidity of the Japanese conquest. If the United States could have fought alongside the Dutch in what were then the East Indies, the British in Malaya, and even the French in Indochina, it would have done so. Loss of these strategic opportunities was most regrettable from the military standpoint, but at least Washington was spared from military action that in the postwar period might give the appearance of supporting colonialism.

In the immediate postwar years the United States continued to hold back from any actions which would seem to support the re-imposition of Western empires; indeed America's main intervention was on behalf of Indonesian independence. But the United States could no longer stand aloof when the armies of Communist China reached the borders of Burma, Laos, and Viet-Nam.

From the surrender of Japan on August 14, 1945, to the proclamation of the People's Republic of China in Peking on October 1, 1949, the United States had followed its traditional policy of deference to other powers in Southeast Asia. No careful plans had been made during the war about the future of the region, aside from considering the organization of a trusteeship for Indochina. Since the British, French, and Dutch obviously intended to return to power in their colonial possessions after the defeat of Japan, the United States could scarcely give priority to making political blueprints for the territories of its European friends. Furthermore, in the years right after V-J Day no outside state threatened the security of Southeast Asia. Japan had been occupied and disarmed, and its territory restricted to the home islands; Nationalist China, friendly but weak, ruled the Chinese mainland from the borders of peninsular Southeast Asia to the territory controlled by Mao Tse-tung, far to the north; and the Soviet Union was in no position at the time to bring pressure to bear along the boundaries of Southeast Asia. The United States was largely concerned in the Far East with the occupation of Japan and the Marshall Mission to strengthen China; and as the cold war developed American attention became more and more focused on Europe and the containment of the Soviet Union through the successive stages of the Truman Doctrine, the Marshall Plan, and the North Atlantic Treaty.

Sympathetic to the peoples of Southeast Asia, America supported the legitimate expression of nationalism during this period, granting sovereignty to the Republic of the Philippines on July 4, 1946, and giving prompt recognition to the new states in South and Southeast Asia—Burma, India, Pakistan, and Ceylon. During this period the United States had its most active role in Indonesia, where it sought to end the fighting between the Dutch and Indonesians both through its own influence and through the United Nations, and also helped to establish an independent Indonesia. With the liquidation of Thailand's position as an ally of Japan during the Pacific war, the United States (wanting to see the Thai friendly to the West and free of undue nationalistic pressure at home) quietly urged moderation on London in its peace negotiations with Bangkok. Americans were also active in trying to settle Thai-French differences.

Washington was fully aware of the attempts of international communism to capture the nationalist movements in Southeast Asia, and it soon became clear during the postwar period that the negotiations between the Communists and legitimate governments in the Far East were unproductive and coming to an end. After over a year of effort, the Marshall Mission in China collapsed in January 1947 against a background of mounting civil war between the Nationalists and the Communists. The previous month in Indochina saw the outbreak of hostilities between the French and the Vietnamese of Ho Chi Minh after a period of long negotiations. In the Philippines Luis Taruc, leader of the

Communist-infiltrated Hukbalahap forces, failed to reach any lasting settlement with the government authorities in Manila, despite intermittent efforts punctuated by bloodshed. The outbreak of Communist revolts in 1948 in Malaya, Indonesia, and Burma, following the meetings in Calcutta of a regional "youth" conference and of the Second Congress of the Indian Communist party early in the year, finally left Thailand as the only important country in Southeast Asia not subjected at one time or another to armed defiance inspired by the Communists. The United States was not directly involved in suppressing these Communist conspiracies, for the French in Indochina, the British in Malaya, and the Burmese, Philippine, and Indonesian authorities took primary responsibility. Nevertheless, the implications of the Communist bid for power caused growing concern in Washington for the future of the area.

THE KOREAN WAR

With the establishment of the People's Republic of China and the increasing evidence of Peking's aggressive, militant policy in the Far East, the United States took the leadership in efforts to provide a deterrent. Southeast Asia soon became a focal point in the rivalry of the two governments, which for different reasons had played a relatively passive role in the area from 1945 to 1949.

The Korean War which broke out in June 1950 had profound implications for the region. In the first place, the conflict demonstrated to the United States that a miscalculation on the part of the Soviet Union could bring war to this area. The entrance of Communist China into the Korean conflict indicated the willingness of Peking to take the risk of an all-out war at the possible expense of its own economic future, but, at the same time, the United States showed the Sino-Soviet bloc its determination to

fight, even under difficult conditions, in the event of naked aggression in an area where it had interests. Although the ending of bloodshed by the armistice of July 1953 left Korea divided almost along the same line as before the conflict, each side gained a better understanding of the other.

The Korean War bought time for American and other Western efforts, limited as they were, to cope with the growing threat of international communism in Southeast Asia. Because the Chinese Communist military resources were committed in Korea, the Peking government was not able to take full advantage of the opportunities open in Indochina. In his statement of June 27, 1950, on intervention in Korea President Harry S Truman announced, among other things, that military aid to the Philippines would be accelerated, American forces in the island republic would be strengthened, a military mission would be sent to Indochina, and the furnishing of military assistance to France and the Associated States of Viet-Nam, Cambodia, and Laos would be speeded. Headed by R. Allen Griffin, an American survey mission on the needs for economic and technical aid visited Southeast Asia earlier in the year, followed later by the Melby-Erskine Joint State-Defense MDAP Survey Mission, which made a somewhat less extensive trip through the area. Both missions visited Thailand, which was increasingly concerned over the menace of international communism, and in September 1950 the United States and Thailand signed an agreement on economic and technical aid, followed the next month by one on military assistance in services, arms, and equipment. Although the American government had followed since V-J Day a policy of diplomatic support for Thailand as the only country in Southeast Asia that had escaped colonization, relations between Bangkok and Washington now assumed the character of an *entente cordiale*.

The Korean War also affected Southeast Asia through American policy decisions regarding Taiwan, Japan, Australia, and

New Zealand. On June 27, 1950, Washington announced that the Seventh Fleet had been ordered to protect Taiwan from any attack and that the government of Chiang Kai-shek was being asked to stop sea and air operations against the Chinese mainland —an indication that the United States was not going to allow the fall of Taiwan to Communist China, at least for the duration of the Korean War. The growth of American support for Chiang Kai-shek and the subsequent entrenchment of the Nationalist cause brought the Overseas Chinese and the new governments of Southeast Asia to realize that two Chinas were in existence probably for some time to come.

Speeded by the United States as a consequence of the Korean War, the peace settlement with Japan helped to rehabilitate Nippon in Southeast Asia. Although the Philippines, Burma, and Indonesia were eligible to sign the peace treaty at San Francisco on September 8, 1951, Burma declined to attend the short conference, Indonesia signed but did not ratify the pact, and the Philippines, despite the advantage of getting a separate mutual defense agreement with the United States on August 30, signed the treaty but postponed ratification until after the conclusion of a much-delayed reparations settlement with Japan. Still under French influence, the Associated States of Indochina attended the peace conference and signed the pact. Despite the unenthusiastic reaction of countries in Southeast Asia, the San Francisco peace settlement paved the way for several reparations agreements in the region and facilitated the normalization of relations between Japan and a number of countries in the area.

Australia and New Zealand were influenced in their decision to approve the San Francisco peace treaty by the signing with the United States of a tripartite security pact on September 1, 1951, commonly called the ANZUS Treaty. Although the members of the British Commonwealth in the Southwest Pacific were largely motivated by memories of the Japanese occupation of

Southeast Asia or the "Near North" and by desires to create a common front against future Japanese militarism, the terms of the tripartite security pact were sufficiently broad to include concerted resistance to future Communist aggression in the Pacific area.

CRISIS IN INDOCHINA

After the Korean armistice the Peking government played an increasingly important role in the war in Indochina. The intimate relations between Mao Tse-tung and Ho Chi Minh, however, contrasted with those between Communist and non-Communist leaders in Asia. Despite a desire for international recognition after the establishment of the People's Republic, Peking had been publicly critical of prominent Asian nationalist leaders. For instance, in November 1949 Liu Shao-chi, one of the most influential figures in Communist China, criticized U Nu, Sukarno, and Nehru as puppets of Western imperialism. Propaganda organs of the People's Republic had not hesitated upon occasion to express open sympathy for the Communist rebels in Burma, Malaya, and the Philippines. Nevertheless, Burma under Premier U Nu became the first non-Communist country to recognize the Peking government, and Indonesia under President Sukarno followed. The decision of Washington not to recognize Communist China was very influential in the adoption of a similar attitude by the Philippines and Thailand.

The growing influence of the People's Republic of China in the government of Ho Chi Minh during the Indochina War arose from a number of interrelated factors. When Viet-Minh and Chinese Communist forces met at the northern Vietnamese frontier, Peking was able to give direct assistance to its friends in Indochina. Moreover, the common objectives of international communism in the area strengthened the position of the People's Republic as the leading Asian exponent of the world revolution. Ho Chi Minh was supported by Peking in his claims that he represented the personification of Vietnamese nationalism in the struggle against the French imperialists, that he was the true embodiment of Asian aspirations faced with the obstructionism of Western reactionaries, and that he stood for the real principles of Asian solidarity against the divide-and-rule tactics of the die-hard colonialists.

The battle of Dien Bien Phu in northwestern Viet-Nam marked the climax of the Indochina War, involving both the People's Republic of China and the United States in crucial policy decisions. Although Communist China did not openly intervene in the conflict as it had in Korea, it helped the Democratic Republic by granting supplies and providing training facilities. The arms, technicians, and advice provided by the Chinese Communists proved to be a telling factor in the victory of the Viet-Minh when the battle of Dien Bien Phu reached its turning point in April 1954.

Despite the growing concern of France over the outcome of that battle, voiced in an appeal for American help, the United States did not consider that conditions conducive to intervention existed. The specific prerequisites for Washington's willingness to consider military intervention in Indochina had once been defined by Secretary of State John Foster Dulles: the current lawful authorities would have to issue an invitation; assurance would have to be given of full independence to Viet-Nam, Cambodia, and Laos; France would have to promise not to relinquish the struggle until its successful conclusion; the United Nations would have to give evidence of concern; and some of the other states of the area would have to join in the collective attempt. If these conditions were met, the President would be prepared to go to Congress on the matter of intervention. But even then the

Congress would have been hesitant to commit the nation to a war in Southeast Asia unless convinced by overriding considerations of danger to American security. Obviously, direct military aggression by Communist China in the area would have presented the issue in clear terms; in fact, Peking had been warned over two years before.

When Indochina came under formal discussion at a plenary session of the Geneva Conference on May 8, 1954, not only was the military advantage on the side of the Communists, but the Viet-Minh also enjoyed a psychological boost from the fall of Dien Bien Phu the previous day. The conference had been called by the American, British, French, and Soviet foreign ministers, who at a session in Berlin early in the year had made arrangements for a meeting on Korea and Indochina. France, Great Britain, the United States, the Soviet Union, and the People's Republic of China, together with Cambodia, Laos, the State of Viet-Nam, and the Democratic Republic of Viet-Nam became the formal participants in the meetings concerned with Indochina—the first time that the five major powers of the world had attended a conference together.

The discussions at Geneva were long, difficult, and acrimonious. The Western powers differed in some of their attitudes while the Communist states presented a much more solid front despite evidence of some disagreement among themselves. The American delegation was eager to prevent the recognition of any extension of international communism into Southeast Asia. The French under Premier Pierre Mendès-France, who assumed office June 17, wanted to find a quick way out of the costly war while salvaging as much as they could of their position in Indochina. The British, represented by Foreign Secretary Anthony Eden, desired to put an end to the fighting lest it develop into a general war in the Far East or the world. The Russian, Chinese, and Vietnamese Communists wanted an Indochina in the hands of governments that were Communist or pro-Communist. Intense diplomatic activity, often far removed from Geneva, accompanied the proceedings of the conference.

The settlement reached on July 20 and 21 reflected a compromise among the opposing forces. Three armistice agreements were signed to bring to an end the fighting in Viet-Nam, Cambodia, and Laos. Viet-Nam was provisionally divided, roughly at the seventeenth parallel, with Ho Chi Minh's Democratic Republic being restricted to the north and the State of Viet-Nam to the south. General elections under conditions allowing the "free expression of the national will" were to be held in July 1956 under the supervision of India, Canada, and Poland for the purpose of bringing about the unification of the country. Neither North nor South Viet-Nam was to join a military alliance or allow foreign bases on its soil. The pro-Communist Pathet Lao forces in the Kingdom of Laos were temporarily permitted to regroup in the two provinces of Phong Saly and Sam Neua, and all citizens in Laos were to be allowed to participate freely in general elections by secret ballot leading to the political integration of the country. Although no Communist regroupment areas were established in Cambodia, provisions were made for general elections like those in Laos. The settlement also reflected the Communist desire to neutralize Cambodia and Laos, but during last minute negotiations the Khmer government managed to remove some of the restrictions on the kingdom and, as a consequence, on Laos. Three international supervisory commissions were established with India as chairman and Poland and Canada as members to superintend the execution of the armistices in Viet-Nam, Cambodia, and Laos. The members of the Geneva Conference agreed to respect the independence, sovereignty, territorial integrity, and unity of the three states and not to interfere in their domestic affairs.

For France, the Geneva settlement marked the end of its role as a great power in Southeast Asia. Despite the limited military rights in Laos granted at the conference, France soon saw its political influence in Indochina greatly reduced, its economic position substantially weakened, and its cultural influence declining, though at a much slower rate. After the Geneva Conference, Cambodia and Laos were accorded diplomatic recognition by many states which had previously refused to take the step.

The United States did not accept the terms of the Geneva settlement. In a unilateral declaration, however, Washington took note of the three armistice agreements along with certain other provisions and declared it would consider "with grave concern" the violation of the armistice through the renewal of aggression. It is estimated that the United States during the four years prior to the Geneva settlement had expended over $1,200 million in economic and military assistance in Indochina.

For Peking, the Geneva Conference and the resulting arrangements constituted a major achievement in its rising international stature. Premier Chou En-lai proved himself a tough negotiator, determined to advance the cause of international communism in Southeast Asia. Communist China's over-all position would have been much weaker, however, had it not been for the general support of the Soviet Union represented by Foreign Minister V. M. Molotov, acting as an ally under the Sino-Soviet pact of 1950.

In his final speech at Geneva Premier Chou En-lai not only reflected the Communist gains made at the meeting but also presaged a change of tactics to capitalize on those advances. He referred to the Five Principles of Peaceful Coexistence as the basis for the preservation of collective peace and to the expected support for the Geneva settlement by the Colombo Powers: India, Pakistan, Ceylon, Burma, and Indonesia. Written into the Indian-Chinese agreement on Tibet, on the previous April 29, as the foundation of relations between New Delhi and Peking, the Five Principles called for mutual respect for sovereignty and territorial integrity, nonaggression, noninterference in each other's domestic affairs, mutual benefit and equality, and peaceful coexistence. The result of long correspondence between Communist China and India, the principles can be accurately identified with no single person, although Prime Minister Nehru first called them the *Panch Shila* as a consequence of a later visit he made to Indonesia. While the Geneva Conference was technically in session, they had been embodied in a communiqué of Nehru and Chou En-lai on June 28 and of U Nu and Chou En-lai the following day. To the Western powers and their allies, the phrase "peaceful coexistence" in its Communist context meant a *détente* of a temporary nature while the Communist countries built up their power and weakened their adversaries. Chou En-lai's observations at Geneva on peaceful coexistence and neutralism were to bring dividends at the Asian-African Conference at Bandung the following April.

The Manila Conference

Viewed in Washington as advantageous to world communism at the expense of Western interests, the Geneva arrangements gave impetus to American efforts to establish a collective security system in Southeast Asia. Although the United States had for a while opposed a multilateral security pact in the Pacific as advocated by President Elpidio Quirino of the Philippines, Washington became more interested in some kind of collective security for the area as the aggressive intentions of international communism became more apparent in the Far East, especially with the outbreak of the Korean War. It had not been considered feasible to negotiate a broad multilateral treaty of this nature in connection with the Japanese peace settlement, but the ANZUS pact and the bilateral agreements made by the United States with the Philippines and Japan were cautious steps in that direction.

In an address on April 16, 1953, shortly after assuming office, President Dwight D. Eisenhower called for "united action" in Southeast Asia, and Secretary of State Dulles vigorously supported the cause of collective security in the area. On March 29, 1954, in a widely heralded speech Dulles observed that under current conditions "the imposition on Southeast Asia of the political system of Communist Russia and its Chinese Communist ally, by whatever means, would be a grave threat to the whole free community"; he called for "united action" even if it meant "serious risks."[1] The conflict in Indochina proved an obstacle to such action, for a number of prospective participants viewed a multilateral security pact or "united action" under the circumstances as a means of involvement in war rather than a deterrent to it. The United States believed a security treaty would strengthen the West in the coming negotiations with the Communists on Indochina, but Great Britain was convinced that such a pact should await the outcome of the Geneva Conference.

Although Secretary of State Dulles and Foreign Secretary Eden had disagreed on certain aspects of a possible collective security treaty during conversations in London, April 11-13, President Eisenhower and Prime Minister Winston Churchill affirmed on June 28 in a communiqué resulting from their discussions in Washington that plans for collective defense in Southeast Asia would be pressed regardless of the Geneva negotiations. Between June 2 and June 11 military staff discussions of a previously established Five-Power Staff Agency had already taken place in the American capital among the representatives of the United States, Great Britain, France, Australia, and New Zealand. After the visit of Prime Minister Churchill, an Anglo-American study group began to consider in detail the form of a defense agreement in Southeast Asia and the form of a possible

[1] "The Threat of a Red Asia," Address by Secretary Dulles, *The Department of State Bulletin*, April 12, 1954, p. 540.

guarantee of an Indochina settlement. London was especially interested in bringing the Colombo Powers into any security system relative to Southeast Asia; but despite British efforts they
proved unwilling to guarantee the Geneva settlement on Indochina, and most of them were opposed to participation in negotiations for a collective security pact. Australia and New Zealand, on the other hand, joined the United States in a communiqué on June 30 calling for the quick negotiation of a multilateral defense arrangement in Southeast Asia. Six days later
American, British, French, and Australian military officers began
discussions in Singapore on the practical aspects of collective security in the area.

The United States also gave thought to the Philippines' request for stronger assurances. In a speech on April 18, President
Ramón Magsaysay had urged the creation of a NATO-type security alliance, provided the right to self-determination of Asians
was respected and the Philippines was given a "plain and unequivocal guarantee" of American assistance under the mutual
defense pact in case of attack. On September 4, at a meeting in
Manila of the United States-Philippine Council, set up in 1954
for consultation under the alliance of 1951, Secretary Dulles gave
the Philippines further assurances of U.S. support if the republic
were the victim of armed aggression. In a joint communiqué
Dulles was quoted as having asserted: "If the Philippines were
attacked, the United States would attack immediately."[2] These
assurances were welcomed in Manila, for the government placed
more emphasis on its security ties with Washington than on
those with any possible combination of powers.

After some five months of negotiations, largely against the
backdrop of the Geneva Conference, the United States, Great

[2] Text of the Joint Communiqué Issued by the United States-Philippine
Council on September 4, 1954, Malacañang, Manila, *Department of Foreign
Affairs Review*, March 1955, p. 28.

Britain, France, Australia, New Zealand, the Philippines, Thailand, and Pakistan at last met in conference at Manila on September 6, 1954, to formulate the final terms of an alliance. Following the usual welcoming addresses and the ranking delegates' opening statements, the conference moved into closed session, producing for signature two days later the Southeast Asia Collective Defense Treaty with an "understanding" of the United States, a protocol to the Manila Treaty, and the Pacific Charter.

The opening addresses of the Asian participants are especially revealing since they tended to be more specific than most of the Western speeches. In the words of Senator Francisco A. Delgado the Philippines wanted an alliance where the members were bound "to act immediately in case of aggression, *one for all and all for one.*"[3] The planned organization should also provide for assistance in developing the economies of its Asian members, economic cooperation being considered just as important as military. The Philippines was eager to have stated in an article, not just in the preamble, the "unequivocal recognition of the principle of self-determination for Asian peoples and their right to self-government or independence."[4] It is clear that the draft treaty considered by the Working Group prior to the opening of the conference did not meet all the desiderata of Manila.

Thailand was also forthright in its viewpoints at the beginning of the meeting. Prince Wan Waithayakon, Minister of Foreign Affairs, wanted a security commitment "as near as possible to that of NATO" and insisted that subversion be dealt with in the pact. He was eager to have Laos, Cambodia, and Free Viet-Nam included in the treaty area, for they merited the protection and were neighbors of Thailand; and he offered Bangkok as the head-

[3] Address of Francisco A. Delgado, *The Signing of the Southeast Asia Collective Defense Treaty, the Protocol to the Southeast Asia Collective Defense Treaty and the Pacific Charter, Proceedings* (Manila: Conference Secretariat, 1954), p. 45.
[4] Same, p. 46.

quarters for the organization or Council seat under the pact. Stressing that the peace of the world was indivisible, the Thai delegate heartily welcomed the United States, Great Britain, and France in the alliance as "great powers with world interests." He carefully observed that Thailand had quickly and readily associated itself with the United States, which he singled out as the country taking the initiative in the negotiations without which the pact now contemplated would not have materialized. Prince Wan further noted that the security treaty would be within the framework of defense permitted under the United Nations Charter.

In his opening address Chaudhri Muhammad Zafrulla Khan, Pakistan's Minister for Foreign Affairs and Commonwealth Relations, stressed that his country opposed trying "to make provision against aggression only of a particular variety."[5] Divided into western and eastern parts, Pakistan had "vital interests" and "responsibilities" in both the Middle East and Southeast Asia. It was obvious that Karachi did not want to limit the "provision against aggression" to the Communist type alone.

For Australia and New Zealand the proposed alliance would mark their first treaty commitments to the security of Southeast Asia. Noting the discussion that had occurred over a NATO-type and an ANZUS-type treaty, R. G. Casey, the Australian Minister for External Affairs, believed the real test to be the purpose and the attitude of the participants. Although he advocated an increase in economic aid to Southeast Asia, he did not want the Colombo plan to be superseded. Mr. Casey thought the independence of the members should be supported against any foreign threat and stressed the sovereign equality of the signatories. He did not foresee the need for a large, complicated organization.

[5] Address of Chaudhri Muhammad Zafrulla Khan, *The Signing of the Southeast Asia Collective Defense Treaty*, p. 34.

Great Britain, through the Marquess of Reading, Minister of State at the Foreign Office, asserted that the purpose of the Manila gathering was to warn potential aggressors in advance that the participating states intended to remain free. He hoped other countries would voluntarily join in the effort for collective defense. Noting that a "prolonged period of quiet" was essential for economic development, Lord Reading concluded significantly that Great Britain did not want a "toothless treaty" but one that would "preserve the future safety and peaceful development" of the countries of Southeast Asia and the Western Pacific. Guy La Chambre, a Minister of State for France, also stressed the importance of promoting economic welfare, but he was not specific in his remarks.

The U. S. Secretary of State, John Foster Dulles, warned that the Communist gains in Indochina would be looked upon as bridgeheads for consequent victories. He believed it should be made clear that the reaction to "an attack upon the treaty area" would be "so united, so strong and so well placed" that the potential aggressor would know that it "would lose more than it could hope to gain."[6] The Secretary indicated that the United States did not favor tying down committed forces but rather advocated "the deterrent of mobile striking power, plus strategically placed reserves."[7] Calling attention to the dangers of subversion and indirect aggression, he observed that "no simple and no single formula" existed to cover them. He called for a protective mantle over Cambodia, Laos, and Viet-Nam and hoped the membership would be enlarged by the participation of others. Having noted the importance of trade among all the free states, Dulles stressed the role of the Western powers in meeting the yearning of Asians for freedom from "so-called 'colonialism'."

[6] Address of John Foster Dulles, *The Signing of the Southeast Asia Collective Defense Treaty*, p. 41.
[7] Same, p. 42.

Although the negotiations in the closed sessions at the Manila Conference were short, reflecting the effectiveness of previous spade work and the willingness to compromise on remaining issues, there was further frank expression of the differences in viewpoint evident in the opening speeches. The United States, for instance, wanted the Manila Treaty to be directed specifically at "Communist" aggression but agreed to the removal of the word "Communist" from Article IV, paragraph 1, on condition that a U.S. "understanding," qualifying aggression as Communist, be inserted above the signatures. Another difficulty arose in the final drafting of the Pacific Charter, a broad statement of principles strongly urged by President Ramón Magsaysay as an indication that the powers were not encouraging colonialism. The last version, found in the Charter, called for the signatories to "promote self-government and to secure the independence of all countries whose peoples desire it and are able to undertake its responsibilities," but the words "and are able to undertake its responsibilities" had not been included in the Philippine draft.[8] Senator Delgado later explained that the phrase had been added in the last draft as a compromise to prevent a deadlock between the Asian participants and Great Britain, France, Australia, and New Zealand.

The chief architect of the Southeast Asia Collective Defense Treaty was Secretary Dulles. Although it did not materialize as early as he had desired and although its final terms were modified by negotiation, the treaty reflected the approach to security favored by the American Secretary of State. His personal interest in the project bridged many difficulties in the course of the negotiations leading to its conclusion. The creation of a system of collective defense at the Manila Conference was a landmark for American policy in Southeast Asia.

[8] Text of the Pacific Charter, *The Signing of the Southeast Asia Collective Defense Treaty*, p. 88.

CONSISTENCY IN POLICY

From the annexation of the Philippines in 1899 to the conclusion of the Manila Pact in 1954 the United States was able to pursue a relatively consistent policy toward Southeast Asia. A number of common denominators help to explain the broad consistency of Washington's policy.

During this period Southeast Asia was generally an area of limited interests for the United States. For most of these years the flag waved only over the Philippines, a fairly well-defined insular area, raising few problems in the eyes of Washington with neighboring colonies. Militarily U.S. interests were limited to the defense of the archipelago, a requirement made difficult, if not impossible, by the Japanese acquisition and subsequent fortification of the Carolines, Marshalls, and Marianas, a mandate entrusted to Nippon under the League of Nations. Indeed, it was widely held that the Philippines and Guam were hostages to peace between Washington and Tokyo, for the mandated islands extended over a broad expanse of the Pacific between the principal American base at Pearl Harbor in Hawaii and the Philippines in the Far East.

During the Pacific war U.S. military interests in Southeast Asia were reflected in the creation of Mountbatten's South-East Asia Command (SEAC) which was approved by Roosevelt and Churchill at the Quebec Conference in August 1943. At first only Ceylon, Sumatra, Malaya, Thailand, and Burma were included, with Indochina as an "additional area in which guerrilla forces operated" and northeastern India "under temporary operational control." All Indonesia, the entire island of Borneo, and Indochina south of the sixteenth parallel were added to the Command on August 15, 1945; northern Indochina came under Chiang Kai-shek. Only the Philippines in Southeast Asia remained under General Douglas MacArthur's Southwest Pacific Command.

After the defeat of Japan the Pacific Ocean was in effect an American lake, both on the sea and in the air. The Carolines, Marshalls, and Marianas were organized as the Territory of the Pacific Islands, a U.S.-administered strategic trust area under the United Nations; Okinawa and the rest of the Ryukyus, the Bonins, and some other islands, once under Japanese administration, were now under American authority—though Tokyo retained residual sovereignty and resumed administration of the Amami-Oshima group of the northern Ryukyus in December 1953. Yet until the Manila Pact U.S. military commitments through treaty obligations were restricted in Southeast Asia, apart from the Philippines.

American political interests in the area were also limited between 1899 and 1954. At the outbreak of the Pacific war in 1941 the United States had only an office of a high commissioner and a consulate in Manila, a legation in Bangkok, consulates general in Batavia, Singapore, and Rangoon, and consulates in Saigon, Penang, Medan, and Surabaja. By late 1954, however, American representation had changed as a result of the emergence of new states and of increased U.S. political interests. Embassies were maintained in Manila, Djakarta, Saigon, Phnom Penh, Bangkok, and Rangoon; a legation in Vientiane; a consulate general in Singapore; and consulates in Kuala Lumpur, Hanoi, Chiengmai, Penang, Medan, and Surabaja. The expansion of the cultural, economic, and military components of the official American community indicated the increased political interests of the United States, which became more pronounced after Washington assumed commitments under the Manila Treaty.

American economic interests during the period were concentrated in the Philippines more than in any other country in Southeast Asia, although there were also a number of key imports like rubber and tin from the East Indies and Malaya and investments like those in Indonesian petroleum. In addition, the

United States had a stake in the maintenance of ocean shipping and air routes in Southeast Asia. American cultural interests in the region which had been extremely limited during the colonial era—apart from the Philippines and to a lesser extent Thailand—began to grow in the years after the emergence of the new nations.

Viewed from the perspective of Washington's limited interests in the area, it is not surprising to find that from 1899 to 1954 the United States reacted to events concerning Southeast Asia rather than attempted to shape them. The United States did not really engage in a long-range planning for the region until the menace of Communist China became acute. Although the criticism that Washington did not have a positive policy toward the area for a long time is well founded, it should be recalled that Southeast Asia, apart from the Philippines, was largely the colonial preserve of the British, French, and Dutch—even the Kingdom of Thailand was politically and economically influenced by London and Paris. Moreover, the collapse of the colonial structure after V-J Day came much faster than American planners had expected.

There were few occasions between 1899 and 1954 when Washington could have altered the course of events in Southeast Asia. During the war, when France and the Netherlands were dominated by Germany in Europe and by Japan in their Southeast Asian empires, President Roosevelt might have been able to secure clear-cut pledges for a truly liberal postwar approach by Paris to French Indochina and by The Hague to the Netherlands East Indies. Although he gave some attention to the problems, especially in regard to French Indochina, Roosevelt never seriously attempted to interfere; in fact, on occasion he discouraged subordinates from probing too deeply into the matter. Eager to win the global conflict with a minimum of friction with the allies of the United States, Roosevelt was aware of Churchill's opposition to developments that might imperil the British Empire in Malaya, Borneo, and Burma, not to mention India. When colonial wars erupted in Indonesia and Indochina after the defeat of Japan, Washington could no longer influence the train of events in terms of long-range policy.

Developments in Southeast Asia from 1899 to 1954 involved America with outside powers more than with the countries of the area itself. American policy was focused on London, Paris, and The Hague during the colonial era, then on Tokyo during Japan's New Order in Greater East Asia, and finally on Peking with the rising menace of the People's Republic of China. Although the emergence of new states in Southeast Asia has added an important element, the ultimate future of the area continues to rest in the hands of outside powers.

During the wars of the twentieth century, the United States has found it increasingly difficult to balance its responsibilities in Western Europe and in the Far East. Although President Woodrow Wilson fought a diplomatic battle to restrain Japan from an aggressive policy in China during World War I, he found it necessary to give priority to Allied harmony in Europe in the common effort to defeat Imperial Germany. In World War II President Roosevelt believed that Hitler's Reich must be crushed before full attention could be given to defeating Japan and its New Order in Greater East Asia. And in the subsequent cold war President Truman directed America's major effort into bolstering Western Europe, possibly at the expense of Nationalist China in Asia (or so said some of his critics). If a reverse policy had been followed and China had not passed under the control of the Communists, Southeast Asia might have been one of the beneficiaries. Yet the alternative in Washington's eyes was the more serious possibility that the industrialized countries of Western Europe might become satellites of the Soviet Union.

An extremely important element of U.S. policy in the period

from 1899 to 1954 was the absence of American military commitments to Southeast Asia, apart from the Philippines. None of the agreements made at the Washington Conference of 1921-22 involved America in a military alliance. Even in the period before Pearl Harbor, when Tokyo was infiltrating into French Indochina, putting pressure on the Netherlands East Indies and alarming Thailand, the United States did not guarantee any mainland country against Japanese expansion. Discussions were held with the British and the Dutch on ways of meeting Tokyo's pressure, but when the attack came there was very little coordinated effort to repel it.

After the collapse of Japan, the United States once more wished to restrict its military responsibilities in the Western Pacific. Nor did Washington favor the military commitment sought by Thailand's government for some time before the Manila Treaty. When Secretary of State Dean Acheson defined the U.S. "defensive perimeter" in January 1950, he specifically mentioned only the great chain of islands—the Aleutians, Japan, the Ryukyus, and the Philippines. The defense pact with the Philippines and the tripartite alliance among the United States, Australia, and New Zealand were as far as Washington was prepared to go in 1951. Conditions in Southeast Asia were not believed conducive to a NATO-like or ANZUS-like alliance, and the United States was reluctant to commit itself where it might not be able to meet its obligations. But the mounting crisis in Indochina produced a change in attitude; here, in fact, are found the real origins of SEATO and of U.S. military commitments in mainland Southeast Asia.

Throughout the history of American policy in the region a characteristic idealism has been evident, particularly in America's traditional opposition to colonialism. The acquisition of the Philippines by the United States was not generally accepted as permanent, and efforts were soon under way to prepare the Filipinos for self-government and eventual independence. In the weeks before Pearl Harbor when the British considered invading Thailand to establish a defense line across the Kra Isthmus, one reason for their hesitation was their understanding that the United States did not want to find itself supporting a colonial power's aggression in Southeast Asia. The American role in the conflict between the Dutch and Indonesians after V-J Day was substantially motivated by opposition to colonialism. And during the war in Indochina there was a continuing concern lest Washington be forced into backing French imperialism against Vietnamese nationalism.

The other elements of American idealism have been a consistent and growing concern for human betterment and a desire to see democracy flourish in the new states of Southeast Asia. Washington has hoped that the Philippines could become a show-window of democracy, and it was pleased to see the new nations of the region adopt at least a nominal commitment to democratic ideals. As experiments in constitutional democracy have not always been successful, however, the United States is becoming more realistic in its approach to government in the area.

American policy has sometimes suffered from the lack of authoritative information on the countries and problems of Southeast Asia, apart from the Philippines. Prior to the Pacific war, there were relatively few U.S. government officials in the area; businessmen were not numerous; missionaries were concentrated in certain areas; tourists rarely visited the countries; and few scholars were active in studying the region. Gaps in knowledge were reflected in government, in the press, in the universities, and in scholarly journals. But after the war many Americans came, through experience and through study, to learn more about the area.

Fortunately, U.S. policy in Southeast Asia has generally been bipartisan. Since the broad division between Republicans and Democrats on the annexation of the Philippines, no grave split has occurred and the controversy over China policy has not extended to Southeast Asia. The difficult question of intervention in Indochina in April 1954 did not become a partisan issue, although it is true that the Republican administration, taking office in 1953, was more prepared to make commitments to mainland Southeast Asia than President Truman and his advisers had been. Yet the decline of French power in Indochina and the growing influence of Communist China created conditions allowing the Manila Treaty to be approved in the U.S. Senate on a bipartisan basis. In fact, the pact was signed both by a prominent Republican Senator, H. Alexander Smith, and by a distinguished Democrat, Mike Mansfield. But as the United States became more and more involved in the domestic and international politics of Southeast Asia, the possibilities of partisan controversy grew greater.

[THREE]

Communist China in
Southeast Asia

The thrust of Communist China into Southeast Asia appears to
be motivated both by traditional reasons of state and by ideological ambition to spread its own version of revolutionary socialism.
In consequence, neither a reading of Chinese history nor a study
of Communist institutions and ideology is alone sufficient to interpret this finely woven blend of new visions and old memories.
Much of the area which the Chinese emperor once ruled as Annam, or the Pacified South, has already been occupied by a most
tangible representative of the Communist bloc, the Democratic
Republic of Viet-Nam, although there is still uncertainty regarding the relative influence of Peking and Moscow upon Ho Chi
Minh. But even if the North Viet-Nam regime did not exist, the
countries of Southeast Asia are so divided on foreign policy issues that Communist China and the Soviet Union have ample
opportunities for various kinds of intervention.

PEKING'S TACTICS

Although the long-range objective of the People's Republic is a Southeast Asia made up of Communist states subservient to its will, the tactics used to achieve this goal have not been consistent. The revolutionary posture characteristic of the period from the establishment of the Peking government in 1949 to the transition years of 1952-54 was followed by a phase of peaceful coexistence, which reached its zenith in 1955 and 1956. The last half of 1957 ushered in a period of intense championship of Chinese national interests at the expense of good relations with the leading neutralist governments in South and Southeast Asia—India and Indonesia—as well as with others who were indirectly affected. Although Peking eventually returned to a more conciliatory policy toward Djakarta, it became increasingly militant toward New Delhi. Even during the difficulties with India, the direct relations of Communist China and Cambodia were beyond reproach, at least in Phnom Penh's view, and they showed improvement with respect to Burma and Nepal. At any given time the tactics of Communist China presented elements of both attraction and coercion, with one or the other usually predominant.

In retrospect, the Bandung Conference from April 18 to 24 in 1955 can be considered a high point in Peking's policy of attraction. The most distinguished gathering of Asians and Africans ever assembled at the "summit" level, this meeting afforded Premier Chou En-lai an excellent opportunity to apply the politics of attraction. Convened by the premiers of the five Colombo. Powers: Jawaharlal Nehru of India, U Nu of Burma, Mohammad Ali of Pakistan, Ali Sastroamidjojo of Indonesia, and Sir John Kotelawala of Ceylon, the conference represented twenty-nine countries, cutting across Communist, uncommitted, and pro-Western orientations. In addition to the prime ministers of the sponsoring powers and the People's Republic of China, other prominent leaders were Pham Van Dong of the Democratic Republic of Viet-Nam, Prince Norodom Sihanouk of Cambodia, Prince Wan Waithayakon of Thailand, Carlos P. Romulo of the Philippines, Gamal Abdel Nasser of Egypt, and Kwame Nkrumah of the Gold Coast (later Ghana).

Aware of a chance to gain respectability in a large part of the world emerging from colonialism, Communist China quickly became a major contributor to the atmosphere of good will at the conference. Since the composition of the assembly had helped to prevent any strong pro-Communist or pro-Western viewpoints from gaining ascendancy, the People's Republic of China was able to join the twenty-eight other participants in the final communiqué which reflected common aspirations and evoked a sympathetic response in many countries. Colonialism was condemned "in all its manifestations." Each nation's right to "defend itself singly or collectively" as provided by the United Nations Charter was upheld, although arrangements for collective defense were not to "serve the particular interests of any of the big powers." The expression "peaceful coexistence" was not used in the declaration on the Promotion of World Peace and Cooperation, but it was stated that "nations should practice tolerance and live together in peace with one another as good neighbors and develop friendly cooperation. . . ."[1]

The Bandung spirit, as it was soon called, was not destined to endure. Even if Communist China had not torpedoed it by a change of tactics, it would have been difficult to give practical application to many of the conference recommendations for political, cultural, and economic cooperation. The diverse national interests and conflicting policies of the different participants

[1] "The Final Communiqué of the Asian-African Conference," Press Release, Permanent Mission of the Republic of Indonesia to the United Nations, *passim*. Reprinted in Russell H. Fifield, *The Diplomacy of Southeast Asia: 1954-1958* (New York: Harper & Brothers, 1958), pp. 512-519.

could not remain submerged, especially since the common denominator of opposition to colonialism became less effective as the era of winning independence receded. The complex problems of economic development brought up, through the need for foreign aid, the issues of the cold war; common opposition among Asians and Africans to the remnants of white racism did not provide a sufficiently broad base for cohesion. Peking's public desire for another conference at the Asian-African summit has not materialized; and if it should, the result might prove to be more divisive than unifying.

There were probably several reasons for Communist China's shift of tactics from peaceful coexistence to nationalist militancy in the latter part of 1957. Peking may have concluded that the maximum had been achieved through the Bandung spirit and that better opportunities now existed in truculent tactics. Perhaps the People's Republic believed that its increased power justified a stronger posture in South and Southeast Asia or that neutralism, conceived as an avenue to communism, could be encouraged more by fear than by kindness. Peking may also have become impatient and frustrated over the response to international communism in peripheral areas. Finally, there is the possibility of a miscalculation in judging the probable reactions to such aggressive tactics. Although the Bandung image of Communist China will be difficult to re-create in Asia, many avenues still remain, particularly political assurances, economic and technical assistance, and cultural exchange, should Peking desire to utilize them. And, as has been noted in cases like Burma and Cambodia, the People's Republic has been particularly careful to keep the diplomatic door open despite an over-all truculent posture. Each shift in Chinese Communist tactics has, however, tended to reduce the chances of flexible action.

The disputes among the non-Communist states of Southeast Asia have given the People's Republic of China an especially good opportunity to further its interests. In the controversies between Cambodia and the Republic of Viet-Nam and between Cambodia and Thailand, Communist China has not urged the three countries to compose their differences through quiet diplomacy or the machinery of the United Nations; Peking has rather staunchly supported Phnom Penh against Saigon and Bangkok and even indicated that military aid would be given to Cambodia upon request. In fact, Peking has supported Phnom Penh more openly than Washington has Bangkok and Saigon.

The outbreak of civil war in Indonesia on February 15, 1958, following the establishment of the Revolutionary Government of the Republic of Indonesia (PRRI) on parts of Sumatra and Sulawesi gave Communist China a chance to offer "volunteers" to President Sukarno, if necessary to help suppress the insurrection. It was widely held in Djakarta that the PRRI was aided by American arms and supplies through Taiwan and the Philippines, with the tacit support of the Taipei and Manila governments, and that SEATO was involved behind the scenes in efforts to assist the dissident cause. When a rebel bomber was shot down over Ambon, it proved to be piloted by an American citizen who had recently served in the U.S. armed forces. The military victories of the central government and the failure of the insurrectionists to receive substantial foreign aid made academic the Chinese Communist suggestions of military assistance. Yet it is quite possible that in the dire straits of another civil war Djakarta would accept offers of help from the People's Republic, however difficult to implement if only because of geographical factors.

Varying according to time and place, the diverse tactics of Peking include the protection of ethnic minorities related to those in Communist territory; the specific use of Overseas Chinese or North Vietnamese to subvert established governments; the resurrection or intensification of historic boundary disputes;

the support of local Communist parties or fronts, often through appeals to nationalism or to social and economic advancement; the establishment of dependence (military, economic, or both) upon the Communist bloc; and the employment of the classical technique of provoking a crisis to gain concessions and weaken the opposition. Through its overseas branches the Communist-dominated Bank of China has been influential in some countries; newspapers and businessmen sympathetic to the People's Republic have been able to obtain loans on easy terms, while certain overseas Chinese and some Communist parties have benefited by the careful use of its funds. The Chinese Chambers of Commerce are also favored instruments of infiltration, and possible profits from trade with Communist China provide tempting bait for merchants. Thailand has been especially subjected to this approach, but the government has banned commerce with the People's Republic. The All-China Federation of Trade Unions attempts to influence and control labor movements in Southeast Asia, Indonesia presenting an excellent target for this type of Communist subversion. An effective Pacific and Asian regional dockworkers organization under Communist domination could seriously affect shipping in the Pacific.

PEKING'S INSTRUMENTS OF POLICY

No state in Southeast Asia is beyond the influence of one or more of Communist China's instruments of policy, if only through the existence of Overseas Chinese in all the countries of the region. The diplomacy of the People's Republic has to be flexible, coping with countries of widely varying international outlook—a Communist friend like the Democratic Republic of Viet-Nam, allies of the United States like Thailand or the Philippines, and uncommitted nations like Cambodia or Indonesia. Peking's relationships in the region can be official or unofficial, open or covert, and conventional or "popular."

Among the non-Communist Southeast Asian states, Burma, Indonesia, Laos, and Cambodia have diplomatic relations with the People's Republic. Peking's embassies in Rangoon, Djakarta, Vientiane, and Phnom Penh provide notable examples of the strong influence that can be brought to bear by a Chinese Communist mission. Thailand, the Philippines, and the Republic of Viet-Nam maintain diplomatic relations with Taipei, while the Federation of Malaya has formal ties with neither Communist nor Nationalist China. The absence of Chinese Communist embassies in Bangkok, Manila, Saigon, and Kuala Lumpur has acted as a brake on Peking's official activities in these countries.

The failure of the People's Republic to be represented in the United Nations limits Peking's opportunities for contacts with delegates of member states that have refused recognition. The Southeast Asian members of the United Nations that favor the seating of the People's Republic are Burma, Indonesia, and Cambodia, while those opposed are the Philippines, Thailand, and on occasion the Federation of Malaya and Laos. Because of the absence of Communist China from the United Nations, the Economic Commission for Asia and the Far East (sometimes called "the economic parliament of Asia") has no representation from the Chinese mainland.

The most favorable opportunity Peking has had to participate in a large international conference outside the Communist grouping was clearly at Bandung. Although it was understood among the Asian and African participants that attendance did not necessarily imply recognition of other governments represented there, Premier Chou En-lai was able to have informal conversations with a number of prominent Southeast Asians whose governments did not recognize Peking. The Bandung Conference was a clear-cut triumph for the personal diplomacy of the

Chinese leader; the appeal of the Five Principles of Peaceful Co-existence, on which Chou En-lai based his approach, was enhanced by the Chinese premier's engaging personal contacts with Asian and African leaders.

After Bandung Premier Chou En-lai continued his campaign of personal diplomacy in South and Southeast Asia. Having previously visited New Delhi, Rangoon, and Hanoi in 1954 en route from Geneva to Peking, he made a grand tour of Afghanistan, Burma, Cambodia, Ceylon, India, Nepal, North Viet-Nam, and Pakistan in 1956-57, later making additional visits to many of these countries. In return, prominent leaders from the Southeast Asian states of Indonesia, Burma, Cambodia, and Laos have found that the People's Republic of China can stage a most impressive welcome for a state guest if the occasion demands. President Sukarno has never forgotten the shouting and the tumult he once received as a visitor to the twentieth-century heirs of the Mandate of Heaven.

"Popular diplomacy" or "people's diplomacy" refers to the efforts of Communist China to reach influential nonofficial individuals through a personal approach designed to build up attitudes favorable to "New China." When necessary, such sympathy can be used to strengthen domestic pressures in favor of cooperation with Peking. Standard in the program are guided tours in the People's Republic, tailored to the special interests of the visitors, and interviews with prominent Chinese leaders, scaled according to the occupations and influence of the guests. Communist China welcomes delegations of many kinds: youth groups, journalists, trade unions, women's organizations, and others, with many different interests, be they political, scientific, health and social welfare, religious, cultural, commercial, educational, athletic, agricultural, and so on. Chinese delegations in turn are sent abroad to represent a wide range of activities and to contribute to the image Peking wants to create. The countries of Southeast Asia, including some states with no formal relations with Peking, have been a special target for "popular diplomacy"; in particular, "Friendship Societies" or "Friendship Associations" have been active in Burma and Indonesia, in Cambodia and Laos. Peking's "popular diplomacy" is buttressed by subsidized publications which are sold cheaply or given away in many areas, by the Peking Radio which has numerous programs directed toward the Overseas Chinese and the peoples of Asia, and by the wide distribution of motion pictures produced on the mainland.

It is difficult to evaluate the effect in Southeast Asia of Communist China's diplomacy, whether conventional or "popular." During the high tide of "peaceful coexistence," when efforts were made to implement the Five Principles, Peking acquired a favorable image in the eyes of many leaders in the area, but the subsequent displays of militant nationalism have revived old memories and created new apprehensions. Many leaders of the area are beginning to realize that the People's Republic has little interest in the maintaining of the international *status quo* and favors any changes which may contribute to its triumph.

Trade and aid programs afford the policy-makers in Communist China an instrument of great potentiality. In addition to extensive economic and technical assistance to the Democratic Republic of Viet-Nam, Peking has provided aid to nonaligned Cambodia, Burma, and Indonesia in Southeast Asia. The latest recipient is Laos. Although the assistance sent abroad could well be used at home in Communist China's Herculean effort to develop its own economic potential, the economic considerations are outweighed by political ones, such as the element of national prestige, the opportunity for extending Communist influence (particularly Chinese), and the desire to challenge U.S. efforts. Well aware that commerce can be a sword with two cutting edges, benefiting Chinese interests and hurting those of Japan and India, Peking is encouraging trade in Southeast Asia, both within and without its circle of diplomatic relationships. Yet, although Communist China needs foreign exchange, its trade in Southeast Asia has been subject to marked and sudden fluctuations reflecting domestic developments in the Great Leap Forward.

Both the Overseas Chinese and the local Communist parties are used by the Peking government as agents of subversion, sources of intelligence and propaganda, and channels of communication. They can be helpful in the promotion of revolution, if other approaches to a Communist take-over do not promise success. Colonization, it should be noted, has long been associated with Chinese expansion. Numbering more than twelve million, the Overseas Chinese constitute an influential segment of the population of Southeast Asia. The State of Singapore is overwhelmingly Chinese (76.6 per cent of the population) and the Federation of Malaya has a huge Chinese "minority" (37.8 per cent) almost equal to the Malay population. More than one-fourth of the population of British Borneo is Chinese (27.0 per cent), and Thailand has a Chinese minority of great economic, if not numerical, strength (11.3 per cent). In the other areas of Southeast Asia the figure is less impressive: South Viet-Nam (6.2 per cent), Cambodia (5.5 per cent), Indonesia (2.7 per cent), Burma (1.6 per cent), the Philippines (1.2 per cent), Laos (0.6 per cent), and North Viet-Nam (0.4 per cent).

The Overseas Chinese play an important role in the economy of Southeast Asia, for, as already indicated, they are very influential in the commercial classes. Although in general they have not entered agriculture, they control a large amount of the retail trade throughout the countries and also many branches of foreign commerce which are not in European hands. They have been active in setting up large enterprises, especially commercial ones, and in the colonial period they ranked next only to the Europeans in facilitating the production and export of many key items, such as rubber and tin. They have long controlled the milling as well as the distribution of rice, an element of great economic power in countries where rice is the staple food. And in some areas Chinese now constitute the majority of the urban working class.

The rise to power of indigenous Southeast Asians following the withdrawal of most of the Western colonial rulers is having serious consequences for the Overseas Chinese who can no longer be certain of their future. Generally hostile to the economic power of the "aliens," the new political leaders are usually determined to break the strongholds of the Chinese and transfer their occupations to the hands of indigenous inhabitants. Even in Thailand, where assimilation has made considerable progress, certain forms of discrimination are common, and the possibility is always present that the Bangkok authorities will revert to the repressive policies pursued upon occasion under Premier Pibulsonggram. Yet the Chinese have shown considerable dexterity in coping with the discriminatory measures of the Asian governments; they are skillful in conforming to the letter of the law while evading its intent. Moreover, indigenous Southeast Asians, even some high in government circles, are often willing to help the "aliens" evade a measure if duly compensated in return.

Hardly more than one-fourth of the Chinese now living in major centers in Southeast Asia are China-born. Migration has practically ceased; only a relatively few individuals move to Southeast Asia through legal or illegal channels. Yet, for the most part, the Overseas Chinese in the region represent an unassimilated minority. Proud of being Chinese, they want their own customs, language, schools, newspapers, and organizations and often resist the efforts of local governments toward their integration or assimilation, voluntary or forced. Although they have welcomed the emergence of mainland China as a power in world affairs, and still have many personal ties there, they are not necessarily sympathetic to communism. The People's Republic encourages a number of Chinese and non-Chinese students from Southeast Asia to continue their higher education on the mainland, while the United States has assisted the Nationalists in providing education for a limited number of Overseas Chinese in Taiwan.

With their basic concern in making a living, the Chinese in the Nan Yang generally react to the contesting appeals of Nationalist and Communist China in terms of their economic future. When the People's Republic is making progress in its economic expansion and gaining stature abroad, the Overseas Chinese are more apt to be influenced by Peking; but when it suffers serious domestic or foreign setbacks, they are certain to be more cautious in their attitudes. Furthermore, the postures of the local Asian governments toward Taipei and Peking affect the reaction of the Chinese minorities. Overt attachment to either Chinese government can under certain circumstances bring repression. Pro-Kuomintang minorities predominate in the Philippines and South Viet-Nam, these governments having diplomatic relations with the Republic of China; but the Chinese minority in Thailand is considered more sympathetic to Peking than to Taipei— an exception to the generalization. Pro-Communist minorities in Indonesia, Cambodia, and Burma live under the watchful eye of Peking's embassies, and the new generation of Chinese is likely to attach even less importance to Taiwan than the present.

As an instrument of policy the Overseas Chinese are valuable to the People's Republic in only a few areas. Successful subversion of the Chinese majority in Singapore could turn the strategic island into an ally of Peking unless effective countermeasures were taken; and the large Chinese population could create chaos in the Federation of Malaya as a preliminary step toward overthrowing the government. Even within the present constitutional frameworks, the Chinese have become a major political force in Singapore and Malaya, and to the north the sizable Chinese minority in Thailand could influence the future of the kingdom in favor of the People's Republic.

On the other hand, the Overseas Chinese can be a source of ill will between Communist China and the states of Southeast Asia. Peking is often torn between the cultivation of friendly official relations and the protection of the Chinese minorities. Indonesia is a case in point. On April 22, 1955, the two countries signed a treaty agreeing on procedures for ending the dual citizenship of Chinese residents in the island republic, Peking relinquishing in this instance the traditional Chinese concept of citizenship based on *jus sanguinis*. Hailed at the time as a model for similar treaties between Communist China and other Southeast Asian countries, the agreement soon lost much of its luster when its implementation proved difficult, the exchange of ratification instruments being delayed until January 1960 and a protocol putting the treaty into effect until December.

Meanwhile, considerable resentment was aroused in Peking by Indonesia's action of May 14, 1959, banning aliens from business activities outside the larger cities of the archipelago (effective January 1, 1960), and by the further step, later in 1959, empowering regional army commanders to force aliens in certain rural areas to move to cities of permitted residence. When it gave strong support to the local Chinese in their opposition to the measures, the embassy of the People's Republic in Djakarta was charged by the Indonesian government with interfering in the internal affairs of the country. Additional ill will resulted from the harsh treatment of Indonesia's foreign minister Subandrio during a visit to Peking. By the end of 1959, relations between the two Asian states were severely strained, and the repatriation of some 7,000 Chinese by March 31, 1960, did not resolve the crisis. President Sukarno, however, did not want the controversy to interfere with future relations between Djakarta and Peking, and tension between the two capitals subsided in 1961.

Although identification with the states of the area would clearly benefit the long-range interests of the Overseas Chinese in Southeast Asia, integration and assimilation constitute a long process, especially in an atmosphere of widespread discrimination. The new governments of the region must become more sympathetic to the problems of the Overseas Chinese, but the latter must also develop a broader concept of loyalty. Meanwhile, Peking can be expected to champion the Chinese minorities, for it considers them important in advancing local Communist parties, in providing foreign exchange, in assisting economic penetration, and in furthering the ultimate goal of a Chinese-dominated Nan Yang.

Local situations of great complexity and of marked diversity have conditioned the impact of the People's Republic on the orthodox Communist parties of Southeast Asia. In fact, they appear to have considerable autonomy in local operations and may be more responsive to suggestions than to orders from the outside. Their propaganda, however, indicates a basic similarity in world outlook; their programs have responded to shifts in Communist tactics; and their goals are the same throughout Southeast Asia. Claiming by example to represent the best approach to revolution in the colonial and semicolonial world, Communist China has had an increasingly pronounced impact on the parties. Although it would still be a mistake to consider Peking the center of a closely knit web, organizational ties are becoming stronger. In addition to strong moral support, Communist China can give the political parties financial aid, supplies, and on occasion, arms, as well as training for party cadres and military personnel. If necessary, prominent refugees from Southeast Asian states can be sheltered in China for possible use at some favorable time.

Peking's influence on specific Communist movements in the region varies to a considerable extent. Where the Overseas Chinese are a particularly numerous minority or where a heritage of suspicion against China is pronounced, too close an identification with Peking might handicap the Communist parties. The closest ties with the Chinese Communists are those maintained by the party led by Ho Chi Minh, a relationship cemented by the aid which the Viet-Minh received from the People's Republic during and after the Indochina war. Despite the traditional dislike of China in Viet-Nam, the common bonds of ideology have proved strong. Moreover, Ho Chi Minh believes that his hopes for the unification of the Vietnamese people depend upon Peking's aid, direct or indirect. The Chinese Communists for their part appear to support Viet-Minh leadership in the Communist effort in Laos and Cambodia. In Laos, the Pathet Lao and its political arm, the Neo Lao Hak Xat (NLHX), and in Cambodia the Pracheachon (Nationalist) party claim to represent genuine nationalist movements, responsive to the aspirations of the people, but actually they reflect Viet-Minh influence. In 1958 the Neo Lao Hak Xat showed considerable strength at the polls in Laos while the Pracheachon party failed to gain any representation in Cambodia.

In Thailand, Singapore, and Malaya, Communist China has relied on the Overseas Chinese in attempting to win support through sympathetic political parties. For example, an outright orientation to Peking would have been a likely result in Singapore if the leftist People's Action party, which came to power in the election of 1959 by winning 43 of 51 Legislative Assembly seats, had lost its parliamentary majority chiefly because of the secession of its extreme left wing. Great Britain would have had the right—and, it might be added, the power—to intervene in an emergency; yet the Communists will remain a real threat as long as pro-Peking Chinese students and workers form a substantial part of the political support of the People's Action party, or of dissident groups.

In the Federation of Malaya, as in Singapore, the Communist movement has been overwhelmingly Chinese in composition and orientation. Although the Malayan Communists were not able to gain their objectives in their 1948 revolt against the government, they caused considerable bloodshed and destruction by means of guerrilla warfare. Isolated from the People's Republic of China, they received no material Chinese aid of any significance. The achievement of independence by the Federation in 1957 and the victory of the Alliance party of Malays, Chinese, and Indians at the polls in 1959 have contributed to the rebels' declining power. The hopes of Peking now probably lie in the possibility of friction between the Chinese and Malay elements of the Alliance, in the use of subversion to exploit the Chinese against the government, and in continuing attempts to destroy the foundations for an effective Federation of Malaysia consisting of Malaya, Singapore, Sarawak, North Borneo, and Brunei.

Prospects for the Communists to achieve power at the polls are extremely limited in Thailand, where there is no tradition of political parties and elections, and where regimes established by *coups d'état* have at times governed without them. Although its exact numbers are difficult to estimate, the Chinese Communist party in Thailand may have a membership of about 5,000 Chinese, while the Thai Communist party may have around 200 Thai. Operating underground, both groups are weak, though the former has a potential following among the Overseas Chinese; and both look to the People's Republic of China as a source of inspiration and direction.

The Communist movements in the Philippines, Burma, and Indonesia present different patterns in their relations with Peking. In 1950, when the Communist-led rebellion was at its height, the Hukbalahaps raised their greatest threat to the Manila government. Yet, even then, the isolation of the islands from the rest of the Communist world allowed the rebels to receive little more than ideological support, especially from Peking. The Communist party of the Philippines (CPP) is illegal, but beyond this consideration, there is strong opposition in the islands to the People's Republic of China and a local party sympathetic to its policies is certain to be at a marked disadvantage. A Chinese Communist party may have 300 to 400 members.

In Burma political fragmentation has both weakened and strengthened the Communists. The Burma Communist party now has about 2,000 members and constitutes the strongest underground nucleus of its kind in the Union. There are other Communist groupings, both above and below ground, but they are divided in outlook. In early 1962, for instance, the National United Front, operating above ground, included a Communist membership of around 3,000. In 1958 the split in the Anti-Fascist People's Freedom League (AFPFL), the governing coalition of Burma since independence, presented real opportunities for the Communists, but the subsequent regimes of General Ne Win checked their activities. Like other outside powers, the People's Republic may not have been certain of the real significance of many political developments inside Burma. At least it has shown remarkable restraint in its policy toward the country. Although the boundary controversy between the two neighbors has been serious and the Kuomintang troops in the Union presented real provocation on occasion, Peking has not given the Burmese Communists substantial aid. Yet the contacts and the program of the Burma Communist party and of the National United Front suggest a close, though circumspect, relationship between Peking and certain Burmese Communist leaders.

Although its original links were with Moscow, the PKI or Communist party of Indonesia has been influenced by Peking since 1949 and has accepted both ideological and certain financial aid from the People's Republic. After the failure of an armed revolt in 1948, the PKI was reorganized on a much more effective basis. When D. N. Aidit became Secretary-General in 1953, the importance of a broad united front and of mass organization, both reflecting a Maoist approach, was already being noted. In late 1957 the Indonesian Communist party was estimated to have over a million members; now with 1,750,000 it has surpassed the Italian party as the largest outside the Sino-Soviet bloc. In 1955 the PKI received six million votes in the national elections, and in 1957 it polled even more in local electoral contests. In view of the uneasy position of the Overseas Chinese in Indonesia, coupled with growing Indonesian apprehension over the power and intentions of Communist China, it is likely that the PKI, under Aidit's leadership, does not minimize the importance of Moscow in the world Communist movement. In 1962, however, the party's sympathy to Communist China seemed to be increasing, and it should be remembered that Peking has regularly given strong support to the PKI.

The Soviet Union and the Peking-Moscow Axis

The Soviet Union, like the People's Republic, has sought to profit from the international tensions of Southeast Asia. For example, its airlifting and airdropping of supplies and weapons contributed to the 1960-62 Laotian crisis. In the United Nations Moscow has strongly championed the claim of Indonesia to West New Guinea and has supported Burma's demands for the removal of Kuomintang forces from its territory. During the Indonesian insurrection of 1958, the Kremlin made clear its approval of the Djakarta government's efforts to suppress the revolt. Although somewhat less active than Communist China in supporting Cambodia in its disputes with Thailand and South

Viet-Nam, the Soviet Union has generally held to a similar attitude.

On the other hand, Moscow was not sympathetic to Peking's
position in the controversy with Indonesia over the status of the
Chinese minority in the archipelago. Apparently the Soviet
Union believed that in this case the interests of world communism were better served through cultivating the government of
President Sukarno. In February 1960, when relations between
Peking and Djakarta were at a low ebb, a well-timed visit to Indonesia by Premier Nikita Khrushchev strengthened the Soviet position in Djakarta. Although Khrushchev also hoped to improve
relations between Communist China and the island state, he deliberately snubbed Peking's ambassador at an official reception in
an effort to dissociate the U.S.S.R. from the recent policies of the
People's Republic in Indonesia.

The U.S.S.R. has more official channels to the states of Southeast Asia than does Communist China. In addition to ambassadors
accredited to Rangoon, Phnom Penh, and Djakarta, one has been
accredited to Bangkok and another to Vientiane. As could be expected, Moscow, like Peking, has extensive representation in
Hanoi. Membership in the United Nations gives Soviet diplomats numerous opportunities for personal contacts with Southeast Asian officials. In fact, the Russians were present at a meeting of ECAFE in Kuala Lumpur although the Federation of
Malaya declines to have diplomatic relations with the Soviet
Union.

Prominent Russian leaders, such as Khrushchev, Voroshilov,
and Mikoyan, have made frequent visits to countries in Southeast Asia, including Indonesia, Burma, and North Viet-Nam.
In turn, many of the leaders of the area have visited Moscow
and have been royally received. Though not in the proportions
of Communist China's efforts, "popular diplomacy" is also encouraged by the Soviets in their policy toward Southeast Asia;

nor has Moscow neglected the different media for propaganda.

The U.S.S.R. has its own aid programs in a number of Southeast Asian states, namely, Indonesia, Burma, Cambodia, Laos, and North Viet-Nam. Djakarta has increasingly become a major recipient of military and economic aid. Military assistance may eventually mount to a billion dollars while the Soviet military advisory group in the island republic may already be the largest in a non-Communist state. The efforts in aid and trade as an instrument of policy reflect the determination of the Soviet Union to maintain its own interests in the international Communist drive in the region.

The existence of the Peking-Moscow axis has very practical effects in Southeast Asia, for the two countries pursue basically complementary diplomatic policies in the area, the trade and aid programs are not competitive, and a degree of similarity exists between the Chinese and Russians in attitudes toward the local Communist parties. Although the Soviet Union is not able geographically to exert direct military pressure on the boundaries of Southeast Asia, it can contribute to the military actions of its ally, the People's Republic. By applying pressure at a number of places along the vast periphery of its own empire, the U.S.S.R. can create diversions favorable to the military gestures of Communist China. Moreover, as the leaders of Southeast Asia are well aware, Soviet planes and missiles represent a strategic threat. During the offshore island crisis involving Quemoy and Matsu in September 1958 Khrushchev, despite his desire not to get involved in a nuclear war with the United States, made the most sweeping pledge of support to his Asian ally, that had been given publicly up to that date.

The Peking-Moscow axis is affected by an unusually large number of variables influencing each ally and producing a complex pattern of dynamic relationships. Involved are such factors as: changes of power status, affecting one partner or their com-

bined posture; differences in targets and tactics, producing varying degrees of mutual support or restraint; badly coordinated
decisions by one ally upsetting the timing of the other's moves
on the world stage; and shifts within the governing elites of
either country, influencing axis relationships, the elites in the
satellite states, and the Communist parties in the outside world.
Under the circumstances, it is not surprising that axis policy is
sometimes ambivalent.

Tensions between the partners of the Peking-Moscow axis
cannot be kept beneath the surface, and their airing before the
outside world may help to provide an impetus for adjusting differences. In the early 1960s an ideological dispute of considerable
intensity between Khrushchev and Mao Tse-tung was raging
over whether or not war between the Communist and capitalist
worlds was inevitable. At stake was basic Communist strategy
toward the West. The Soviet Premier, fully cognizant of the
destructiveness of thermonuclear warfare, optimistic about the
growing economic strength of the Sino-Soviet bloc, and convinced that communism would triumph in the underdeveloped
areas, believed in peaceful competition, whereas the Chinese
leader was a fundamentalist in his interpretation of Leninism.
Although Khrushchev and Mao agreed that wars of "national
liberation" from colonialism were "just," a point of ominous significance for countries like the Republic of Viet-Nam in Southeast Asia, the Kremlin leader opposed not only total but also limited or "local" wars. His distinction between wars of "national
liberation" and limited ones appears artificial, however, since
either could spiral under conditions of escalation to all-out conflict. Contrary to Mao's interpretation, the Soviet Premier has
proclaimed that a Communist revolution in a country may be
achieved by parliamentary processes without the necessity of
war. The two leaders have also disagreed on economic assistance
to a state like India. Both consider the Indian government to be

bourgeois and nationalist, but Khrushchev is willing to take advantage of an "anti-imperialist" environment that might eventually favor a Communist orientation. Important in the ideological difference between Moscow and Peking is the conviction of the Chinese leader that he is the best interpreter of Marxism-Leninism, a contention not accepted by the Soviet Premier. Friction also arises from variations in the practical applications of Communist doctrine; for example, the Chinese, unlike the Soviets, consider the commune to be an essential institution for the development of true socialism.

Khrushchev is not a man to yield in his principles or intentions, and Mao Tse-tung is equally adamant. At Communist meetings in Bucharest and Moscow in 1960, efforts were made to reach a compromise on ideological disputes, but the basic difference in outlook remained. In 1961 the Peking regime refused to support the Soviet Union in its efforts to bar Albania from the Communist grouping. Charges of "left wing sectarianism" by the Russians and of "revisionism" by the Chinese are an indication of their divergent outlooks. Since the long-range strategy and tactics of the axis partners may vary to a greater extent in the years ahead, the effects upon the Communist parties of Southeast Asia could be substantial. In 1962 most of them were already sympathetic to Mao Tse-tung in his support of Albania, especially those in North Viet-Nam and Indonesia.

The national interests of the Soviet Union and Communist China differ in several areas of Eurasia. Moscow is paramount in Eastern Europe, save in Albania, although Peking's general impact on the area has at times increased since the death of Stalin. In Asia Communist China is more influential than the Soviet Union in North Korea and seeks to increase its voice in the affairs of the Mongolian People's Republic. Although the regime in North Viet-Nam might prefer guidance from Moscow rather than from Peking, Ho Chi Minh apparently tries to balance his relations with both. In the non-Communist states of Asia, the contrast between the more militant policy and doctrinaire outlook of the People's Republic and the more restrained attitude of the U.S.S.R. is apt to cause friction between different factions, possibly forcing Soviet-oriented groups to be more aggressive in order to compensate for Russia's apparent caution. In Africa and Latin America both Moscow and Peking are trying hard to make friends and gain influence.

As the People's Republic grows in power, the question of the degree to which Moscow can assume responsibility for Peking's international activities is highly debatable. In the years between 1956 and 1959 the imports of Communist China from the Soviet Union were on a pay-as-you-go basis, but in 1961 Moscow agreed to postpone payment of a 1960 trade deficit amounting to the equivalent of over $300 million. Long-term credits for economic purposes from the U.S.S.R. to the People's Republic have been minimized or stopped for some time, the equivalent of $430 million having been extended between 1949 and 1959. Nevertheless, Peking has continued to repay its Korean War debt to Moscow. Large numbers of Russian advisers have left China, and Mao Tse-tung has begun to look to Western powers for food and industrial goods. On the other hand, although Peking's military dependence upon Moscow is declining with the development of the Chinese Communist war potential, the People's Republic under the Russian shield will continue for several years to need military aid and tacit support from the U.S.S.R. in some of its objectives, and particularly in any major confrontation with the United States.

Many Kremlin leaders are well aware of the long-range implications of the rising power of Communist China. In his visit to the United States in 1959 Premier Khrushchev indicated that a *détente* between Washington and Moscow could accomplish much more for the peace of the world now than in the years ahead. At the time of the Vienna meeting between President John F. Kennedy and the Soviet leader in June 1961, Peking went out of its way to brand the American chief executive a greater threat to peace than President Eisenhower. In late 1962 Moscow, for its part, was critical of China's military offensive in India, while Peking condemned the Kremlin for withdrawing its offensive weapons from Cuba in the face of U.S. pressure. Russians are not unaware of the rapidly expanding population of China, which will probably exceed a billion some time in the 1970s, in comparison with their own moderately growing 221 million. The frontiers of the large, sparsely settled areas within the Soviet Union adjacent to China are not well defined in some sectors. Doubts have even been raised about the sincerity of the Kremlin's protestations that Peking should be in the United Nations. But despite such differences and apprehensions the Sino-Soviet alignment is sufficiently durable to prevent an open break in the foreseeable future. Over a longer time-span, the growing strength of the People's Republic and the increasing cooling of revolutionary ardor in the Soviet Union may lead some day to the dissolution of the alliance.

U.S. COURSES OF ACTION: EFFECTS IN SOUTHEAST ASIA

In the determination of American policy toward the People's Republic of China Southeast Asia occupies a high priority. The question of recognition is here, as elsewhere, crucial; and the refusal of the United States to recognize the legitimacy of the Peking regime constitutes a bulwark against recognition by a number of governments in the region. America's position also serves to maintain the diplomatic stature, restricted as it is, of the Republic of China on Taiwan. It is also asserted in Washington that the nonrecognition policy toward Peking helps restrict Communist inroads among the Overseas Chinese in Southeast Asia and inhibits local Communist parties in a number of countries.

As long as the United States holds the line against recognition, the Philippines and Thailand are likely to follow a similar policy, and the Federation of Malaya will be under less pressure to establish diplomatic ties with Peking. Since Communist China recognizes North Viet-Nam as the government of all Viet-Nam, the Republic of Viet-Nam constitutes a special case. American championship of Nationalist China will probably insure continued diplomatic relations between Taiwan and the Philippines and Thailand, although both Bangkok and Manila have their doubts about the long-range prospects of the Chinese Nationalists. Since the Federation of Malaya has diplomatic ties with neither Taipei nor Peking, it is difficult to foresee conditions leading to formal relations with Nationalist China. The absence of Chinese Communist missions in so many Southeast Asian states prevents Peking from using official channels, important in more ways than one, in its business both with the Overseas Chinese and with local Communist movements; yet the Chinese Communists have been able to establish covert channels throughout the Nan Yang.

In the event of U.S. recognition of Communist China without a caveat preserving Nationalist Taiwan, the diplomatic posture of Southeast Asia would undergo a significant alteration. Thailand, "bending like a bamboo before the wind," would be the country most likely to recognize Peking immediately after the American action. Although the Philippines might delay, a desire to be like other Asian states and not to be isolated in China policy would bring its government in the end to recognize the People's Republic. The Federation of Malaya would probably consider it desirable to exchange envoys with Peking unless the rebel activity in the country took a serious turn for the worse. At the same time, basic differences in China policy between the United

States and Indonesia, Burma, and Cambodia would be reduced, possibly leading to greater cooperation in Asia.

American withdrawal of diplomatic and material support from Taiwan would mean the isolation of the Nationalists from Southeast Asia. While, as an exception, the Republic of Viet-Nam might continue diplomatic relations, even this gesture is by no means certain. At any rate, the status of Nationalist China would not long be a subject of speculation, for the Chinese Communists would move to take over Taiwan and the Pescadores.

The acquisition of Formosa by the People's Republic would give the Overseas Chinese no outside alternative to Peking. Although Taiwan may now have the sympathy of only a significant minority of them, the fall of Nationalist China would obliterate the concept of Formosa as a custodian of traditional Chinese culture and as an area of possible self-sustaining economic growth outside the Communist framework. It is likely that American recognition of Communist China would be a matter of marginal importance for the Overseas Chinese, who for the most part are preoccupied with their daily problems; but if Washington's action involved the liquidation of Nationalist Formosa, the impact would be much more pronounced.

The Communist parties in Southeast Asia would certainly be strengthened by the American withdrawal of support for Nationalist China, a decision that would be interpreted as further evidence, in Mao's words, that "the east wind prevails over the west wind." The removal of Nationalist China from the scene would substantiate the Communist parties in their loudly stated predictions of Taipei's downfall and would give substance to their prophecies of an early American withdrawal of support from Southeast Asia. Moreover, because of its close association with the Nationalists, the United States would inevitably suffer a serious decline in prestige, and this in itself would advance the interests of the local Communist parties.

In the event American recognition was extended to Peking but present ties with Taipei were maintained, the reaction in Southeast Asia would be more qualified. Thailand, and possibly the Philippines, would recognize Communist China but would probably maintain missions in Taiwan. The Federation of Malaya would be under some pressure to exchange envoys with Peking, though not to the same extent as if no other Chinese government existed.

Although it would generally strengthen Peking's role in the activities of the Overseas Chinese and in local Communist parties in Southeast Asia, a "two Chinas" policy would not stifle the efforts of the Chinese Nationalists and their sympathizers in the region. Under certain circumstances, it might even contribute to their cause in the uncommitted countries. The effects of a "two Chinas" policy upon local Communist parties and the Overseas Chinese would greatly depend on whether the "new look" was permanent or only a temporary expedient working to the ultimate advantage of Peking.

If the United States should recognize the People's Republic of China, the future of SEATO would be a matter of special concern. American recognition of Peking would probably lead not only Thailand and the Philippines, but also Australia, New Zealand, and possibly France to exchange diplomatic missions with the People's Republic. Great Britain and Pakistan already recognize Peking, but it should be remembered that British recognition came at a critical time when London was trying to put down the Communist revolt in Malaya. In a broadcast on January 6, 1950, Malcolm MacDonald, the British Commissioner-General in Southeast Asia, significantly made a point of assuring the people of the Federation that recognition implied neither approval of communism nor weakening of the effort to quell the insurrection. If SEATO becomes an alliance like NATO, with most of its members having diplomatic relations with the very country whose aggressive activities led to its organization in the first place, Washington should be careful to assure allies and friends in Southeast Asia of the continuing strength of America's international commitments and its resolute opposition to Communist aggression.

The seating of the People's Republic of China in the United Nations would be less significant in Southeast Asia than American recognition of Communist China. Nevertheless, if the present U.S. position of resolute opposition to the representation of Peking in the world organization is rejected in one or more of its major bodies, Washington is certain to lose prestige in the area. If a country like Thailand sought an excuse to recognize Peking, the latter's representation in the world organization would afford an excellent occasion; and, of course, the seating of the People's Republic would enhance its world stature and redound to the advantage of the Communists in Southeast Asia. It is likely, however, that America's close alignment with some Southeast Asia states is more important to them than UN votes on the People's Republic of China. Although a "two Chinas" policy on representation in the United Nations would remove some of the difficulties, others would certainly be created; and anyway, it is clear that Washington, Peking, and Taipei are not currently prepared to accept such a solution.

FOUR

The American
Military Posture

In strictly military terms the United States constitutes almost the only major barrier to the accomplishment of Chinese Communist objectives in Southeast Asia. Before the Second World War the region was dominated by European fleets and armies, but today the power of Great Britain in the area has been greatly diminished while that of France has been virtually eliminated, and that of the Netherlands ended. A primary cause of this Western eclipse, of course, was the smashing series of military victories and diplomatic triumphs by which Japan imposed a short-lived unity upon Southeast Asia; but Japan in its turn was reduced to military impotence. For its part, India since independence has been occupied with serious defense problems along its frontiers; and the continental base of Australia is not yet sufficiently well developed to project substantial power into the "Near North." It is clear that the United States cannot escape the responsibilities which accompany its great power in the Pacific. If, in the fore-seeable future, American might were withdrawn from the Far East, Southeast Asia would almost certainly fall under the control of the People's Republic of China.

MILITARY CAPABILITIES OF PEKING

The Chinese Communists now have the military capabilities to overrun all the mainland and all the islands of Southeast Asia, unless local resistance be reinforced by powerful American intervention. If the United States did not interpose its armed forces, Peking could extend its military control to Taiwan and South Korea, and (perhaps in conjunction with Moscow) to the islands of Japan. Within the narrower compass of the Southeast Asian mainland, the armies of North Viet-Nam are the strongest indigenous land force and they could overrun South Viet-Nam, if the latter were not assisted from the outside.

For immediate deployment in Southeast Asia, Communist China is believed to maintain some 350,000 troops and about 600 planes (largely jet) along with a few submarines. These troops are, of course, only a fraction of the military forces of the People's Republic, estimated to have a total strength of some 2.5 million. The sinews of Chinese might are the ground forces organized in 150 divisions, each composed of 10,000 to 12,000 men with capable leadership, generally sound training, and high morale. Greater mobility and firepower have resulted from stress on new techniques and re-equipment with modern weapons. The army of the People's Republic of China, although basically conventional with increasing emphasis on specialization, is considered to have a high over-all operational capability. And it must never be forgotten that these formidable forces can be supplemented by over 500,000 public security troops and the seemingly inexhaustible (though only poorly trained) reserves of a paramilitary People's Militia estimated at 10 million. In terms of physically fit men between the ages of 15 and 49, the military manpower potential of Communist China is well over 40 per cent *of the total population* of Southeast Asia.

The Chinese Communist air force, which is now the third largest in the world, has approximately 2,500 planes organized into some 30 air divisions. Most of the aircraft are Soviet-constructed jet fighters, although there are some IL-28 jet bombers and possibly a small number of TU long-range bombers. In equipment, training, and mission, this air force is basically a tactical arm, but the creation of a real strategic capability is not impossible. The mobility and flexibility of Chinese air power between northern Manchuria and the South China Sea have been vastly increased through the construction of jet air bases. Although pilot training has apparently not reached an optimum, aircraft performance has been judged good.

Communist China's navy of over 240 vessels is, by a considerable margin, the biggest indigenous naval force in the Far East. At least 30 submarines, 1 light cruiser, 4 destroyers, 6 gunboats, 15 frigates, several torpedo boats, and other craft are included, although these are heterogeneous vessels ranging from old to new types. Nevertheless, these ships have extensive capabilities for amphibious attack, patrol, minelaying, and coastal escort, and the naval air support has modern jets. It can be easily seen that Peking's interest in increasing the number of submarines is of no little consequence to the United States. Finally, the Chinese Communists have neglected neither the construction and modernization of naval bases, nor the development of a merchant marine.

Within the mainland of Southeast Asia, the Democratic Republic of Viet-Nam has about 300,000 men in its armed forces plus a few aircraft and a very small navy of 20 vessels supported by miscellaneous patrol ships. Its military striking power is definitely found in the 15 divisions of ground forces. The conscription system is efficient, and it can select from about 1,560,000 physically fit men between 15 and 49 who constitute the military manpower potential. The army has had combat experience, is under capable leadership, and morale is considered high; soldiers are even entitled to a higher standard of living than the general civilian population. Strategically located in North Viet-Nam, these troops are in the process of being re-equipped with Soviet arms and possess a considerable degree of mobility. Their equipment and organization are planned to take advantage of the terrain of Southeast Asia where they might see action.

When the whole sweep of the Western Pacific is considered, the military forces of Communist China and North Viet-Nam must be judged to be strengthened by the presence in the Far East of some 500,000 Soviet troops, supported by large sea and air forces. Russian submarine strength (including a nuclear-powered component) is particularly notable; at Petropavlovsk in the peninsula of Kamchatka the Kremlin has its only submarine base that opens directly on the high seas, while the Kurile Islands between Japan and Kamchatka also have considerable strategic significance. Whether viewed from the non-Communist countries of Southeast Asia or from Taiwan, Japan, and Korea, the military posture of the Sino-Soviet bloc is formidable.

When the People's Republic of China and the Democratic Republic of Viet-Nam plan the logistics of possible operations in peninsular Southeast Asia, they have to reckon with rugged terrain, seasonal torrential rains, and inadequate transportation. These circumstances, however, could only hamper determined aggressors; they do not by themselves constitute a real deterrence. Transportation facilities, moreover, between Southern China and North Viet-Nam have now been improved to the point where they are considered relatively good. High priority was given to the rebuilding or construction of rail and road links.

Trains now run from Hanoi to Kunming in Yunnan and to Yungning (Nanning) in Kwangsi with further extensions into China. North Viet-Nam has around 7,500 miles of roads, some extending into Peking's territory, and Communist China's development of transportation facilities in the Luichow Peninsula and, immediately to the south, on the island of Hainan must also be noted. Air transportation facilities in southern China are considered adequate but, in spite of steady improvements, they are less advanced in North Viet-Nam; however, C-54-type planes can land on a number of North Vietnamese airfields, including Hanoi, and C-47s can use still others. From North Viet-Nam suitable invasion and supply routes lead into Laos and South Viet-Nam and on into Thailand and Cambodia. Peking can utilize the Burma Road from Kunming to Lashio in northern Burma, and then continue to Mandalay and Rangoon. From Kunming another possible route runs to Kengtung in Burma and southward to Thailand.

In the military build-up of the People's Republic of China the Soviet Union played an active role in the early years of the alliance. Russian advisers to the land, sea, and air forces of Communist China provided valuable expertise; and Soviet military loans and war matériel, especially heavy and complex equipment, contributed substantially to the power position of Peking. It is estimated, however, that 1957 was the last year when Moscow gave Peking substantial military aid.

With or without Russian assistance, Communist China can be expected to make every feasible effort to acquire its own nuclear technology and weapons. The military, diplomatic, political, and psychological advantages of membership in the club of nuclear powers are important in the thinking of the leaders of the People's Republic. Is China to be less proud than France? In 1958 the Soviet Union provided a nuclear research reactor and it has furnished a supply of enriched uranium. By now more reactors may well be in operation or under construction. Chinese nuclear testing of a token nature will probably occur between 1963 and 1965, although a stockpile of atomic weapons is not probable until late in the decade or early in the 1970s. It may well be that the U.S.S.R. has ceased its technical and material assistance to Peking's atomic effort.

Moscow has so far denied to its Chinese ally both nuclear weapons and long-range missiles, thus keeping it dependent upon the Soviet atomic shield. But it is possible that the U.S.S.R. has brought Peking's military facilities up to the point where, in some emergency, Russian atomic arms could be transferred to the latter. During the Quemoy crisis of 1958 it was not entirely ruled out that Communist China would receive nuclear weapons, if they were employed against it. At the present time any supply of such arms from Moscow would signify a much greater identity of political and military objectives than apparently exists.

When the People's Republic acquires a nuclear stockpile and delivery capability, the military and political implications for Southeast Asia are certain to be profound. The countries of the region will be subjected to greater pressure against allowing American bases or stockpiles of nuclear arms on their soil. Nuclear blackmail might even be attempted to prevent the United States from intervening in local wars inspired by international communism. Many of the states in Southeast Asia have only a few targets of major importance, and their cities could be destroyed in a few, medium-range nuclear strikes. Asians who have opposed the use of nuclear weapons, associating them with the U.S. bombing of Japan, would obviously not want to see their own countries suffer through such attacks. Tendencies toward neutralism are apt to receive even greater support when Communist China becomes an atomic power.

The leaders in Peking can probably be expected to weigh the use of atomic weapons with care and to employ their nuclear capability for political rather than military purposes. Yet they will, of course, be under far less restraint from Moscow when they control their own atomic arsenal. The Soviet Union for its part is apt to be concerned over American nuclear retaliation against the Chinese mainland should overconfidence in Peking lead to serious mistakes in Southeast Asia.

An international prohibition on the storing and use of nuclear weapons in the region is not currently feasible for the United States. The People's Republic has a number of advantages in Southeast Asian warfare which might be offset through the employment, or even the threat, of American tactical nuclear arms. Even when Peking acquires its atomic capability, it is obvious that a ban would still work to its advantage. As for any effective detection system associated with an international ban of nuclear weapons tests, Communist China's cooperation would be necessary. Meanwhile, the People's Republic may possibly launch an earth satellite in the 1960s, a development that would add to its military prestige and have considerable psychological impact upon the Afro-Asian world.

SOUTHEAST ASIA AS A POWER VACUUM

The military forces of the non-Communist states of Southeast Asia, when taken as a whole, are so limited that it is not surprising to hear the area described as a power vacuum. Perhaps it would be more revealing to visualize these local forces as different levels within a vast and irregular basin. The lowest point of this basin is the long valley of Laos from which the contours of force rise abruptly to the Chinese cliffs in the north and somewhat less steeply to the Viet-Minh heights. If one assumes that the strategic key to the area is the low plateau of Thailand just to the south of the Laotian "valley," the following account will begin there and traverse in order the bordering levels of Burma, Laos, and Cambodia. Outside this innermost ring of states are a series of disconnected military plateaus—the coastal plains of South Viet-Nam, the virtual island of peninsular Malaya, and the archipelagos of Indonesia and the Philippines. Finally, a brief account will be given of more distant Asian forces—those of Pakistan, India, the Republic of China on Taiwan, and Japan—which may prove relevant to any future crisis in Southeast Asia.

Thailand is currently able to maintain internal security and to defend itself against any one of the bordering states of Burma, Laos, Cambodia, or Malaya. The ground forces, adequately equipped but being strengthened, have had as their nucleus 33 battalions. The Royal Thai Navy of some 70 small vessels (of mixed American, Japanese, Italian, and British origin) can engage in small-scale patrol, minelaying or sweeping, antisubmarine, and amphibious operations. The expanding Royal Thai Air Force of 150 planes is able to conduct limited airlift operations for the national police and the army, and to render some air-ground support. The kingdom has an estimated 2,790,000 physically able men between 15 and 49 in age as compared with 2,650,000 for Burma.

To the immediate west, the Union of Burma has 60 battalions in its ground forces which can maintain internal security and offer some resistance to a Chinese invasion. The Burmese Navy of some 50 small vessels patrols the inland waterways and coastal areas, while the Burmese Air Force of around 70 planes can ferry soldiers and supplies and provide limited air-ground support to the Burmese Army.

Across the great Mekong which forms part of the frontier of Thailand is Laos, the weakest state in Southeast Asia, having virtually no capacity to resist any external aggression and only limited means for maintaining internal security. Above all, political divisions within this kingdom are reflected in the armed forces. In early 1963 the rightists had an army estimated at 70,000 men, the Pathet Lao one of 18,000, and the neutralists 12,000. Plans were made to integrate these armed groups into a single force of 30,000, and each faction was to provide one-third of this official army. It should be noted, however, that the estimated figures of the three armed factions are debatable. Laos has no navy and only a small air force.

Beyond the Cardoman mountains on Thailand's eastern frontier lies the Kingdom of Cambodia, militarily weaker than either Thailand or the Republic of Viet-Nam and stronger only than Laos, its other neighbor. Cambodia can, however, maintain internal security, improvement being noticeable since the early years of independence. The ground forces have 28 infantry battalions; the Royal Cambodian Navy possesses five small vessels for coastal and inland waterways patrols; and the Royal Cambodian Air Force of around 50 planes can provide limited liaison and transport support as well as aerial observation to the army. The nation's military posture is currently being strengthened.

The Republic of Viet-Nam, east of the Khmer kingdom, is building up its armed forces in the face of mounting Communist subversion. South Viet-Nam has a limited defensive capability against the Democratic Republic but is dependent upon foreign logistical support, a matter of considerable domestic and international significance. The army now consists of around 200,000 men supported by a civil guard of about 100,000 and a self-defense corps of 75,000. The Vietnamese Navy of over 100 small vessels has developed a degree of effectiveness in coastal and river patrol, while the Vietnamese Air Force of around 100 planes is able to furnish limited support to the army in aerial strikes, reconnaissance, troop transport, evacuation and supply. It is estimated that the military manpower potential of the state is

1,360,000 physically fit males between the ages of 15 and 49, in contrast to 230,000 for Laos and 535,000 for Cambodia.

After a long and costly struggle against Communist rebels the Federation of Malaya is now able to assure internal security. The country has its own capacity for limited defense, backed by the Commonwealth Strategic Reserve of British, Australian, and New Zealand forces. The Federation has the eight infantry battalions of the Royal Malay Regiment plus two reconnaissance units of battalion size. The Royal Malayan Navy of 12 vessels, chiefly engaged in coastal patrol, also has a small minesweeping capability while the Royal Malayan Air Force has one squadron. An estimated 810,000 physically able men between 15 and 49 in age make up the military manpower potential. The State of Singapore for its part has an infantry regiment of about battalion size.

In insular Southeast Asia the armed forces of Indonesia can now maintain internal security and, if invaded, offer modest to substantial resistance. The republic has 380,000 men in its infantry divisions and 20,000 in its paramilitary police; and in recent years Moscow has given the country an offensive capability in the air and on the sea. Because the extensive coastal areas of the vast archipelago call for adequate naval forces, the Indonesian Navy with more than 140 vessels and a personnel of over 15,000 is rapidly growing. Its older ships were for the most part acquired from the Dutch navy and were British in construction; Italian yards later provided a number of destroyer-and-escort-type ships; and in 1958, Indonesia acquired some vessels from Yugoslavia and the Soviet Union which included patrol, destroyer, and submarine types. Later came many other Russian ships of various categories, including a cruiser of the Sverdlov class. Over 200 aircraft and more than 15,000 men make up the Indonesian Air Force, engaged in helping the army preserve internal security. It is reported to have a good transport capability though, like the navy, its main limitations are shortages of adequately trained personnel and maintenance facilities. The air force has been and still is expanding; before 1961, about 100 jet fighters, light jet bombers, and trainers had been purchased from the Soviet bloc, and in subsequent years more planes, many of recent model, have come from Moscow. Since 1958 weapons and equipment have been bought from both West and East but with the mounting West New Guinea crisis the Communist bloc became by far the larger source. The estimated military manpower potential of the island republic is great: 11,630,000 physically fit men between 15 and 49 in age, ranking only behind Communist China, India, Japan, and Pakistan in Asia.

The Republic of the Philippines can maintain internal security but has no offensive capability. Its ground forces have one division and the Philippine Navy, almost all of whose 40-odd small vessels were formerly American, is really a coast guard. The air force has around 200 planes with a good capability in transport. It is partly equipped with jets and fairly well trained, being able to support the army and constabulary in preserving internal security. The estimated military manpower potential is small compared with Indonesia—3,020,000 physically fit men between 15 and 49.

The other non-Communist Asian forces relevant to the military situation in Southeast Asia are found in Pakistan, Taiwan, India, and Japan. As a member of SEATO, Pakistan has commitments to Southeast Asia. It has over 160,000 men in its ground forces, a navy of 25 vessels planned for operations in home waters, and an air force of about 200 planes, effective in ground support as well as internal security. The navy, primarily a coastal patrol, minesweeping, and light escort force, is improving. Its larger ships are for the most part British in origin, including the one light cruiser, but its newest units are coastal minesweepers obtained from the United States. Although Pakistan is militarily much weaker than India or Communist China, it is stronger than its other Asian neighbors.

The Republic of China on Taiwan has a total armed strength of 600,000 men with 21 divisions. It has a strong air force of 90,000 men with over 500 planes, the greater number representing late U.S. models, while the airfields are excellent. There are 50,000 men in the Chinese Nationalist navy which constitutes the smallest branch of the armed services. The actual combat forces number about 465,000, around a third of the combat ground troops being located on the offshore islands. Under certain circumstances Chinese Nationalist units might be used in Southeast Asia, but the political obstacles to their participation are formidable. Southeast Asian nationalists frequently have equivocal attitudes to any Chinese and may fear being dragged into the Communist-Kuomintang controversy. Much would depend upon the scope of Communist aggression, for states facing national survival are more apt to welcome assistance from any source and be less concerned with political implications. As a general principle, however, it would be unwise to count on Nationalist forces for the defense of Southeast Asia.

When all its land, sea, and air forces are considered, India is the strongest military power in Southern Asia. Its army of around 500,000 men is the largest located in the region, and the Indian Navy of over 45 vessels, the biggest in the Indian Ocean, is surpassed in the British Commonwealth only by the British, Canadian, and, for the present, the Australian. In recent years the navy's fighting capacity has been considerably increased; it now includes a small aircraft carrier, two light cruisers, and three destroyers. The Indian Air Force of more than 500 planes is diversified and can furnish tactical support for the army and contribute to air defense. New Delhi's military posture is being strengthened in the face of Chinese Communist aggression. The use of India's armed forces in Southeast Asia is at present un-likely, given the tensions with Communist China and with Pakistan.

Japan, once the conqueror of Southeast Asia, is not in a political or military position in the immediate years ahead to bring any military strength to bear in the region. Its armed might, significantly termed "Self-Defense Forces," of over 200,000 men consists in large part of ground troops. The Japanese air force of 24,000 men and navy of 30,000 are still weak; the latter has a few submarines, some 18 destroyers, well over 50 mine ships, and a number of other vessels. In the more distant future, however, a Nipponese military role in Southeast Asia should not be ruled out.

In view of the prevailing situation a number of defense con-cepts are theoretically possible for the Southeast Asian states although not necessarily practicable. Considerations of deter-rence, as well as combat effectiveness if deterrence fails, are involved. The countries could place their external security in the hands of outside powers through bilateral or multilateral treaties of alliance. If this concept is carried to its logical conclusion, domestic forces, perhaps only police, would be maintained solely for internal security. This scheme minimizes the need, should a nation be invaded, to gain time for effective diplomatic, political, and military action on the part of its allies and friends and to establish the existence and extent of the armed aggression, often so important in Communist warfare. The local forces necessary for these requirements, it should be added, can also serve to rally the indigenous population against the invader. At present the states of Southeast Asia give almost every indication of desiring to maintain or to build up armed strength beyond the minimum needs of internal security or even beyond a fire-alarm force in the event of external aggression. This attitude, in turn, is related to criticism in Washington that the United States in some cases is helping to establish and equip military forces beyond the actual requirements.

At the other end of the spectrum the countries of Southeast Asia could deliberately accept a defense concept, technically an option, based squarely upon neutrality in the event of future war. They might place complete confidence in the good faith of outside powers by having only police forces. Or, as in the case of Switzerland, they might build up their own military strength as a deterrent, limited though it would be. Under the latter alternative, the victim of armed aggression would be better able to delay the enemy and seek effective military aid from friends and the United Nations. Neutrality, as an approach to defense in Southeast Asia, places a high premium on the good intentions of Communist China and on the reliability of friends as compared with allies.

Another concept calls for a military role where the states of the region not only defend their own borders in time of war but also assist allies through deliberately creating diversions or dispatching expeditionary forces. Obviously this defense approach involves the real acceptance of the principles of collective security and implies the existence of a substantial military potential. Clearly, at the present time neither condition obtains throughout Southeast Asia. Even in the SEATO framework the principal task of the Southeast Asian members is to defend their own territory with possibly only token forces sent outside it.

A defense concept, increasingly out of date as a result of developments in military technology, calls for each state to defend its boundaries by fighting in line according to conventional patterns of defense. A maximum use is made of fortifications, if they exist, while mobile reinforcements are essential to strengthen weak positions. The cost in life and material could easily be so heavy as to be prohibitive, while a delaying action —not to mention a holding one—might not be effective. This defense concept is not generally applicable to Southeast Asia, even if it is elsewhere, because of the military weakness of the countries, the overwhelming power of Communist China in comparison, their exposed land frontiers, and the greater advantages of guerrilla warfare.

In contrast, a defense concept based upon actions to impede and delay the aggressor through mobile units, each one having a small number of highly trained men, would be more realistic. Time might be gained through selling space at a cost not prohibitive, while the indentity of the invader could be established and friendly powers might bring assistance. The mobile units would be able to capitalize on the rugged terrain, and the men on their kinship with or knowledge of the people. The tactics of guerrilla warfare could be effectively used to hinder and weaken the invader who might himself employ them in his operations. "Deterrence by denial" might be a factor of significance.

AMERICAN FORWARD STRATEGY

In the light of strong Communist military capability and pronounced Southeast Asian weakness, the United States has committed itself to a "forward strategy" in the Pacific. Standing in marked contrast to the "Fortress America" notion, this strategic concept requires the maintenance of substantial American forces in the western part of the ocean, on or adjacent to the coast of mainland Asia. The presence of armed forces of the United States along the Bamboo Curtain serves as a constant reminder to the People's Republic of China, as well as to the Soviet Union, that Washington is determined to preserve its forward strategy. At the same time American allies along the periphery of Communist China are reassured while the neutrals are encouraged to take a stronger stand of their own. So, continued reaffirmation of American capability through physical evidence and of American determination through resolute official statements is indispensable.

The Pacific Command of the United States is the largest in the world, extending from the western shores of the Americas to the coasts of Eastern Asia and halfway across the Indian Ocean, and from the Arctic to the South Pole. The Commander in Chief, Pacific (CINCPAC), whose headquarters is at Pearl Harbor, is charged with responsibility for the operations of the navy, marine corps, army, and air force in the vast area. His unified command is a means by which American military power can be coordinated and directed in the Pacific.

In line with the forward strategy, about one-half of the Pacific Fleet is either in the western part of the ocean or en route out or back. The Seventh Fleet operates in Far Eastern waters and the First Fleet along the western shores of the U.S. mainland. Naval bases or facilities used in the Western Pacific are in Japan, Taiwan, the Philippines, South Korea, Guam, and Okinawa, those in Japan and the Philippines being particularly important in the forward strategy. Units of the 3rd Marine Corps Division are based in Okinawa where they can be quickly moved into troubled areas. (For instance, 1,800 marines were sent to Thailand in May 1962.) A high degree of mobility and flexibility enables American naval forces in the Western Pacific to meet a variety of crises as they arise in the Far East. At present almost one-third of the manpower of the Department of the Navy is assigned to the Pacific area.

The location of the major elements of the United States Army, Pacific, also reflects the concept of forward strategy. In Korea is stationed the Eighth Army, with a subordinate command in Japan; on Okinawa in the Ryukyus is the IX Corps, with army air defense and special forces (airborne) groups and an added Battle Group; and in Hawaii, the 25th Infantry Division. Korea and Okinawa together have only some 80,000 troops, yet they represent the major U.S. combat ground forces in the Far East. Some 2,200 infantrymen were stationed in Thailand during part of 1962.

A posture of readiness for various possible situations necessitates a high degree of flexibility. It is important that the United States have combat units adept in guerrilla warfare in jungle territory and able to cooperate with local Asian organizations. The First Special Forces Group on Okinawa is specifically trained in guerrilla activities behind enemy lines, and many of the men acquire first-hand information by visiting possible targets of Communist attack. The 25th Infantry Division stationed in Hawaii is a strategic reserve available for quick use in the area of the Pacific Command. In the event of an emergency, elements of the Strategic Army Corps could be deployed in the theater.

The Pacific Air Forces of the United States have combat-ready bases in Guam, Okinawa, the Philippines, Taiwan, South Korea, and Japan. The 5th Air Force has headquarters in Japan and the 13th in the Philippines. A thousand airmen are now stationed in Thailand. In the American military posture Okinawa is one of the most important islands in the Western Pacific. Not only does it provide military facilities but it is also a key in the coastal radar screen. In other areas bases would be available, depending upon the scope and extent of the fighting. In effect, they already exist in South Viet-Nam and Thailand. Of course, the automatic use of the facilities of present bases located on the territory of allied countries cannot always be taken for granted. Nevertheless, the Pacific Air Forces have the capability of making the quickest significant retaliation to Communist aggression in Southeast Asia. Moreover, the mobility of the global U.S. Air Force is a factor of great significance in any theater. Tactical Air Force units can be quickly flown to U.S. bases near trouble spots in the Far East; in the spring of 1960 a composite air-strike force was sent on a training exercise to Southeast Asia across the Pacific from the United States. In view of the international situation, the Pacific Air Forces constantly maintain a high degree of combat readiness.

The total U.S. personnel now under CINCPAC in the Pacific and the Far East is said to be around 300,000. A mobile striking force, primarily of sea and air composition, armed with nuclear and conventional weapons, capable of quick and effective action when and where used, remains the cardinal element in the American military presence in the area. The Seventh Fleet with its amphibious potential is the largest mobile force, and it can be quickly augmented in time of emergency. During part of the offshore island crisis of 1958 it was expanded in the Taiwan Strait region to include 70,000 men and around 50 combat ships, among them 6 aircraft carriers, 3 heavy cruisers, and 40 destroyers. In August 1960 it was announced that a marine corps battalion landing team on a standing basis was being assigned to duty aboard ships of the Seventh Fleet. Jets of recent model are flown from Okinawa and the Philippines while the United States Strategic Air Force from bases in Guam and elsewhere can bomb targets in all the reaches of the Communist Far East. Matador missiles, which can use atomic or conventional warheads and have a range of more than 500 miles, have been installed in Taiwan and South Korea. Longer range missiles of 1500 miles were later to be deployed in Okinawa. Modernization of American arms and equipment along the periphery of the Far East can compensate with greater firepower for numerical disadvantages. At the same time the Asians must remain or be convinced that Washington can effectively counter Moscow's growing strategic threat.

The forward strategy of the United States in the Western Pacific involves long lines of communication; American forces have to be brought into the region from great distances. Bang-kok, for instance, is 9,000 miles (or 60 supply-ship days) from San Francisco. Quick access into crisis areas involves complex logistical arrangements, adequate airlift and sealift, heavy equip-ment stockpiling nearby, and rapidly available bases or facilities. Seaborne "pre-positioning" can contribute to flexibility and mobility. The speedy commitment of a large number of U.S. troops on the mainland of Asia obviously raises grave problems; in early 1961 the United States did not have available the ships and planes that could transport two divisions into Laos in 14 days. Japan has played an important role as the key supply base in the Far East, and its loss in this capacity would be a serious blow to American interests. From an operational viewpoint it is clear that a forward strategy is essential at present if U.S. weapons systems are to be utilized in time to cope with crisis.

The Western allies of the United States in SEATO can offer only limited military aid in Southeast Asia. Australia has some 21,000 men in its ground forces, an air force of over 200 planes, and a navy of over 70 vessels, including one small aircraft carrier, another converted in 1961 to a fast military transport, seven destroyers, and six antisubmarine frigates. Although two of these destroyers and one frigate are in reserve, the Australian navy can engage in antisubmarine and minesweeping activities as well as convoy escort in the South and Southwest Pacific. (As a relic of its former imperial might, Great Britain still has three submarines in Sydney.) The Royal Australian Air Force is small but well manned and has considerable light bomber and fighter strength. Canberra is increasing the strength of its armed forces, partly as a result of the Dutch withdrawal from West New Guinea and growing Indonesian might in the Near North.

New Zealand has some 4,900 men in its ground forces, over 30 vessels in its navy, and about 100 planes in its air arm. The navy is being modernized, and among its larger vessels are two light cruisers, one of which is in reserve. Planned for mine-sweeping and convoy escort, the navy could operate with an allied unit far from New Zealand. Size restricts the tactical capability of the air force though its personnel of over 4,200 is excellent.

The armed forces of Great Britain in Southeast Asia are limited, but, depending upon the world situation, reinforcements could be brought into the area. British planning today stresses the development of amphibious task forces with commando units. Singapore is the army, navy, and air force headquarters for the United Kingdom in the Far East. The British Far Eastern Fleet centers around one small aircraft carrier, several submarines, a force of destroyers, and a few other ships (including a number of attached Australian and New Zealand vessels—a light cruiser from the latter and destroyer-and-escort-type ships from the former). Apart from a squadron of mine sweepers in Hong Kong, the Fleet is based at Singapore, and it can undertake limited minesweeping, antisubmarine, and convoy-escort tasks in a large area of the Indian and Pacific Oceans.

Units of the Royal Air Force, as well as of the Australian and New Zealand air forces, operate from Singapore and Malaya. Although the total number is not large, many of the pilots and air crews there are experienced in close and general air support of ground troops fighting in a jungle environment, and are efficient in tasks related to supply, transport, and reconnaissance.

British ground forces in the Malaya-Singapore area are supplemented by troops from Australia and New Zealand. In the 17th Gurkha Division, the major land force, there are British, Australian, New Zealand, and Gurkha units organized into three infantry brigade groups which are stationed in Singapore, central Malaya, and north Malaya. The brigade group in the north helps Federation of Malaya forces to control Communist guerrillas along the Thai border. The United Kingdom also has in its

Far East Land Force a number of ground troops stationed in Hong Kong and the Maldives, although British Borneo had only a nominal military presence before the recent troubles. The Commonwealth Strategic Reserve of British, Australian, and New Zealand land, sea, and air forces, including Gurkha and Sarawak troops, constitutes a tangible element of Commonwealth military power in Southeast Asia.

The use of French forces in the region is dependent upon developments in Europe and Africa. France in early 1963 still had a base at Seno in Laos with 500 to 1,000 men chiefly from the army, and military missions in the kingdoms of Cambodia and Laos. The base, however, was scheduled to be relinquished. Three patrol ships comprise the French navy in Southeast Asia. As is clear, the military presence of France in the region at the present time is almost negligible.

General War

The United States seeks to deter the outbreak of a general war and to prevent local aggression from taking place. If deterrence fails, Washington wants to prove to the enemy that local aggression does not pay and that general war cannot result in victory. In local conflicts, American military objectives are confinement of the action and the swift defeat of the aggressor; in general war, national survival at the expense of the enemy. Politically, the United States seeks to weaken and render impotent the international Communist movement as a threat to the nation's security and at the same time to preserve the values and institutions cherished by the American people. As viewed from Moscow and Peking, the military power of Washington constitutes the essence of deterrence, with political, economic, and moral considerations being secondary.

Since both the Soviet Union and the United States have great strategic nuclear capabilities in atomic weapons and delivery systems, a nuclear stalemate has come into being, operating as a real deterrent to general war. But any marked weakening in the capability or determination of the United States to wage a general war if its survival or vital interests were at stake would increase the possibilities of an all-out conflict. In contrast, any weakening in Soviet power would not advance the chances of a general war as far as an American offensive is concerned, for Washington is basically committed to striking only in retaliation to Communist initiative.

With both the Soviet Union and the United States having the strategic nuclear capacity to devastate each other so that national survival is the issue, the degree of provocation must be raised to a high level before all-out war is accepted as a means of national policy. Had the current situation in military technology existed in 1914, it is doubtful that the assassination of the heir to the Austro-Hungarian throne would have led to the outbreak of the First World War. A Hitlerian dictator, however, might take the risks that others would avoid, and there is always the chance of an accident or mistake. Although the possibility exists that strategic atomic weapons might not be used in a general war, the chances of this are few; and, at any rate, the threat of nuclear warfare on an all-out basis would be a major consideration every minute of the conflict.

Nevertheless, the threat of local aggression by the Communists is not removed by the existence of strategic nuclear plenty in the Soviet Union and the United States. The weapons systems for deterring a general conflict are not so well adapted for preventing local aggression. Moreover, the international Communist movement is dynamic, seeking to capitalize on any military situation that provides opportunities without maximum risks. Depending upon the situation, the Communists might be prepared to fight a local war with conventional weapons, old or modern. If the Communist powers are convinced that the United States is not militarily prepared to defeat local aggression, it will occur at the time, place, and circumstances they choose.

As a result, the United States must possess the means of graduated deterrence, and in the event of local war must be able to make a choice of weapons (conventional or nuclear—perhaps on an escalation basis) to provide the suitable response. In many a local war situation the use of tactical atomic weapons by American forces may be essential to overcome Communist advantages. It is argued that the line between certain nuclear arms and certain conventional ones should not be drawn too arbitrarily and that the values of weapons be reassessed. The time factor is also important, for, unless aggression is quickly halted, the danger of its spiraling into a general war is enhanced. For the United States the alternative to defeating local aggression when it clearly involves American interests is to see its overseas positions destroyed piecemeal, the confidence of its overseas allies dissipated, its deterrent capacity greatly reduced, and its own ultimate survival placed in jeopardy.

All these considerations have a direct bearing upon American policy in Southeast Asia. In the event of a general war the area, as in the last global conflict, would have a secondary role. If an all-out war occurred, it must be assumed that the Soviet Union and the People's Republic of China would be fighting as allies. Peking would probably attempt to overrun peninsular Southeast Asia and, if it seemed possible, the insular part of the region. Although the United States with its allies does not presently have forces in place in the Far East for a general war, the Philippines, Indonesia, Malaya, and southern Thailand to the Kra Isthmus might well be kept from Communist control. More territory to the north in Thailand and even in southern Viet-Nam might be held, but with greater difficulty. As a last resort, the Philippines,

Australia, and New Zealand should be preserved from Communist occupation. In the event of an all-out war, Communist China would probably pay little attention to the neutrality of weak neighbors in Southeast Asia, and their invasion could lead to appeals for aid to the United States. America must plan to meet many possible diplomatic and military contingencies in the region.

In general war today the major American effort would be initially directed against the Soviet Union, and emphasis would be shifted to the People's Republic of China only when the military situation made it possible. In such a conflict Communist China could not be defeated just by driving it from Southeast Asia. This consideration is obviously significant in military planning for contingencies in the Far East.

Communist China's acquisition of nuclear arms in an all-out war is not beyond the realms of possibility, and it might resort to tactical atomic weapons in an invasion of Southeast Asia. Yet the use of strategic nuclear arms against China might produce less havoc than against the Soviet Union, for with its vast population of some 670 million people living in a large area far more rural than industrialized, China has a real survival potential. Mao Tse-tung himself, in stressing the importance of men over weapons, has indicated his belief that though a substantial portion of China's population could be decimated, the nation would still exist. Perhaps half the Chinese (a number greater than the current population in either the U.S.S.R. or the United States) could survive a nuclear holocaust and constitute the nucleus of future world power.

LIMITED WAR

In Southeast Asia the possibilities of local war far outweigh those of a general conflict. A local or bush-fire war limited in objectives, area, and weapons offers opportunities to Communist China that must not be underestimated. From the political standpoint, the instability of the countries of Southeast Asia and their differences of outlook on national security, together with problems of cohesion among the Western allies in their relations with the Asian states, all incline Peking toward taking calculated risks. And in contrast to Europe, where the international alignment has resulted in tightly drawn lines, the area of maneuverability is broad in Southeast Asia. From the military standpoint, Communist China and its North Vietnamese ally are in a position to take advantage of their location, the terrain, ill-defined boundaries, and interior communications despite the primitive characteristics of many facilities. In addition to their knowledge of guerrilla operations, the forces of Ho Chi Minh gained practical experience in certain other problems of warfare at Dien Bien Phu. Mao and Ho also expect sympathetic Asians to help in furnishing intelligence and in solving logistical problems. Above all, it should be stressed that the aggressive, militant, and revolutionary character of communism at its present stage of development in China greatly enhances the chances of calculated risks being taken in Peking.

Although limited wars in Southeast Asia can occur under a great variety of circumstances, certain common denominators could be present in all of them. It may prove illuminating to construct from some of these common factors the hypothetical course of an imaginary limited war. This hypothetical conflict takes the form of a possible extension of the Laotian crisis of 1960-62. This "typical" limited war is therefore deemed to have started in Laos as extensive guerrilla activity by local Communist or pro-Communist forces, aided and abetted by the North Vietnamese. Assume that Viet-Minh assistance consisted at first of training, furnishing arms, and giving central direction to the operations. Later, as the fighting continued, the Viet-Minh thought it necessary to support the guerrillas with regular forces whose disguise was possible in the beginning, but whose identification became more certain as the conflict widened.

The government of Laos, it is assumed, takes the step of formally appealing to the signatories of the Manila Treaty. SEATO, faced with a situation where it must take action or suffer serious consequences, accedes to the Laotian request for aid. America and Thailand send forces and supplies by land and air into the beleaguered kingdom, while the other members of SEATO adopt a sympathetic attitude. The Communist Laotian and Vietnamese forces are unable to overthrow the government of Laos and are forced to consider general retreat.

The People's Republic of China, which has been giving moral support to the Communist effort as well as advice, arms, and supplies to the Viet-Minh forces and through them to the Pathet Lao, sees in the intervention of the United States and SEATO a threat to its own security. In the guise of "volunteers," Chinese Communist forces come openly to the support of the Pathet Lao and Viet-Minh. The war in Laos is extended to a large part of Southeast Asia as North Vietnamese troops cross the seventeenth parallel into the Republic of Viet-Nam and Chinese Communist forces move into northern Thailand through Laos and northern Burma.

Land, sea and air forces of the United States are now engaged in a major attempt to stop the Chinese and North Vietnamese troops. Aware of the need to hold a line across the Kra Isthmus, if need be, Great Britain, Australia and New Zealand agree to the use in the common war effort of units of the Commonwealth Strategic Reserve based in Malaya, and they also make other forces available. Pakistan offers a limited contribution to the defense of Burma; the Philippines, with its important American bases, helps in the war effort through cooperation with the United States. The participation of France is minimal. South

Vietnamese, Thai, and Burmese forces, for their part, are attempting to defend their homeland. Cambodia proclaims its neutrality, waiting to jump on the winning side; and the Federation of Malaya prepares to defend itself in the event of invasion. Indonesia, furthest removed from the scene of hostilities, declares itself neutral and is beset by difficulties arising from internal Communist activity on the part of the Overseas Chinese and the Indonesian Communist party.

The forces of SEATO finally manage to stop the Communist invaders at a line running roughly through southern Viet-Nam, Laos, Thailand and Burma. Both sides are now faced with basic questions of objectives in continuing the war, of the means of doing so, and of localizing the conflict. The importance of agreement among the United States and other members of SEATO on objectives is evident, for only then can a sound strategy be formulated and realistic plans made. It has, of course, been easy in the past for the United States and its allies to agree on an objective of preventing a local war, but in a case where deterrence has failed it is not easy to decide what the continuing local conflict is to accomplish and how the goal can best be reached.

Along the range of possible objectives three alternatives should be examined more closely: the complete defeat and unconditional surrender of the People's Republic of China, the establishment of a new *status quo* in Southeast Asia as a result of the military operations, and Communist China's forfeiture of the fruits of aggression through forced withdrawal to its own territory without, however, undergoing total defeat.

First, if the complete defeat of the People's Republic is the objective, the war could easily become global in scope. Military operations would certainly extend well beyond Southeast Asia, and the American use of strategic atomic weapons might well become necessary. The Soviet Union at the present time would most likely go to war rather than see its major ally reduced to impotence. A general conflict would then ensue with the local war in Southeast Asia becoming a secondary theater. In fact, it is only through the active participation of the Soviet Union in a local conflict that any war is likely to become global in scope.

Even if Moscow did not come to the help of Peking, the total defeat of China would probably mean chaos in much of Eastern Asia. With the overthrow of the Chinese Communist regime, the Nationalist government on Taiwan would attempt to fill the vacuum and return to full power on the mainland, but it might prove inadequate to the situation. In the circumstances a future Chinese regime might even be as hostile to American interests as the Communist government of Mao Tse-tung, although the defeat and occupation of Japan serve as a reminder that military defeat can be turned into alliance between victor and vanquished.

If the total defeat of Communist China is the American and allied objective in the event of Peking's aggression in Southeast Asia, the fighting would not be restricted to the region, regardless of the attitude of the Soviet Union. As already indicated, China could not be brought to its knees just in Southeast Asia. Land, sea and air operations against the vast Chinese mainland would be necessary. Forces of the Republic of Korea and of Nationalist China would probably see action, and in the circumstances it would be extremely difficult for Japan to keep out of the hostilities. Even if the Philippines, Australia, and New Zealand were not members of SEATO, the first would be involved to some extent, if only through the implications of the mutual defense pact with the United States, and the two Southwest Pacific powers through the ANZUS Treaty. The American use of tactical and, quite possibly, strategic atomic weapons against Communist China, though probably necessary to bring about the total defeat of the government, would contribute immeasurably to the chaotic conditions in the country upon the end of the war.

To turn now to the second alternative. Should the conflict

in Southeast Asia be localized and the fighting reach a stalemate, the United States might in consequence decide that its objectives were so highly limited in the region it should agree to the *status quo* created by the hostilities. In this alternative there would figure considerations of the heavy cost in human and material resources necessary to force the withdrawal of the Chinese Communists. The situation here would differ from the Korean armistice, for it would mean a substantial extension of the Bamboo Curtain. Although the exact line where a stalemate might be reached is hard to determine, a settlement based on this alternative might well produce the partition of a number of Southeast Asian states. Moreover, SEATO would have proved its uselessness, and faith in American pledges and power would be shattered. A climate would be created in the rest of Southeast Asia in which Communist subversion would thrive, and a repetition of Chinese aggression could be expected.

Finally if the basic objective of the United States and its allies in a limited regional war is to force Communist China to forfeit its territorial gains, thus proving that aggression does not pay and reassuring weak allies and friends that their political independence and territorial integrity will be upheld, the military aim would be to inflict sufficient punishment to drive China back to its own soil and thereby cause it not to hazard placing its national survival in jeopardy. Under these conditions the war in Southeast Asia might well be localized. As indicated, it is doubtful whether the Soviet Union would openly intervene on Communist China's behalf, unless the complete defeat of its most important ally was the issue. Although Moscow would like to see its major rivals weakened and might create diversions elsewhere, its furnishing of technicians, arms and supplies to Peking might be limited to local needs. In fact, the Soviet Union might not want to supply the People's Republic of China to the extent that the latter might gain too powerful a military position in Southeast Asia.

The allies of the United States in SEATO would also want to localize the conflict. The metropolitan territories of the Western powers are not directly threatened and national survival is not yet at stake. The Asian members of SEATO realize that since they would not be the first concern of the United States in a global war, they would not have top priority in the allocation of reinforcements and supplies. In an all-out conflict Thailand might be completely overrun and the future of the Philippines and Pakistan placed in jeopardy. Both the United States and Communist China, aware of the dangers of a nuclear global war for themselves, though not concerned to the same degree, might not want to take the risk of extending the conflict outside Southeast Asia.

If only a local war is fought, land operations by regular forces would obviously be restricted to the area, but air combat and guerrilla actions might still spread to adjacent territory. For instance, southern China might be bombed but not the central and northern parts of the country. The Chinese Communists, for their part, might bomb allied installations outside the actual theater of land operations, thus making SEATO divert forces for their protection. An allied naval blockade might be put into effect, and here incidents might arise if Communist ships from the Soviet Union or Eastern Europe tried to violate it. Although the major Chinese operations would be by land, supplemented by air power, Chinese Communist mining and submarine activity could cause some havoc. Seaborne invasion is unlikely, for the command of the South China Sea would be in allied hands. The SEATO powers would also have air superiority, reducing the possibilities of airborne attack and enemy paratroopers to limited objectives.

SOUTHEAST ASIA IN UNITED STATES POLICY

[98]

The American use of strategic atomic weapons would probably not be necessary, though the aggressor should know that
they might be used as a last resort to compel a return to Chinese
territory. But tactical atomic arms might be employed early in
the hostilities if the situation necessitated it. Considerable destruction by allied forces in territory being defended by the
SEATO powers could occur, raising a serious problem. The circumstances of the outbreak of war and the course of the hostilities would be very important in the specific Asian reaction to the
use of tactical atomic weapons. The early commitment of U.S.
ground forces might serve to minimize the territorial loss, and if
tactical nuclear arms are employed, the destruction at first might
be nearer the often sparsely populated borders of the invaded
countries and at a later stage along the frontiers of the aggressor's
homeland. In short, to halt a Chinese Communist invasion in
Southeast Asia and force the aggressor back to his home territory
would necessitate substantial and coordinated effort on land, sea
and in the air by the allied powers.

American Military Assistance

The forward strategy of the United States in the Western Pacific, from Northeast Asia to Southeast Asia, is strengthened by
the armed forces of its Asian allies. Taken together, these forces
contain the impressive total of almost two million men, but they
are divided among many sovereign states over a very wide area.
Even when taken singly, however, each of these free Asian armies constitutes a limited deterrent to an attack by Communist
China or Communist Viet-Nam. Fighting on their own soil, the
Asian armies can, it is hoped, at least conduct a holding operation which will give Washington time to determine appropriate
diplomatic and military action. Without American military aid

these forces would not possess their present limited strength; without their existence the United States might not want to assume the higher costs of alternatives. The Joint Chiefs of Staff have stated that not a single dollar should be added to American defense expenditures if it has to come from the military assistance program. Such aid, furthermore, is an important factor in developing ties between Asian recipients and both the United States and the Western alignment.

Although the Communists accuse Washington of training and equipping Asians to fight Asians from Korea to Southeast Asia, the decision to request or to terminate American military assistance rests with the local governments. It is true that the cost per man of maintaining Asian forces is far below that of American forces and that the former often occupy strategic territory where a build-up of U.S. forces is not politically or practically feasible, yet there are strong elements of mutual interest in American military aid to Southeast Asian states.

In addition to the basic mutual interest in deterring aggression, Washington's military assistance wherever given in the region helps to promote internal security and a general feeling of confidence. All elements of progress, it needs to be emphasized, depend upon the maintenance of civil order, for the Communists profit from chaotic conditions where they can publicly pose as saviors of the people while secretly working to impose their own version of order. In a general effort to prevent chaos and encourage national morale, American military aid is given not only to a formal ally like Thailand but also to a neutral like Cambodia. Mutuality of purpose, of course, is easier to achieve when the donor and the recipient share a common evaluation of Communist intentions and pursue similar foreign policies. In some cases American aid also serves to forestall or limit a neutral's dependence on arms and supplies from the Sino-Soviet bloc.

Critics have often argued that American military assistance

may have the unintentional effect of supporting unpopular regimes or clearing the way to power for authoritarian military leaders. American-equipped paratroopers can even overthrow a regime sympathetic to the United States, as happened in Vientiane in 1960 and almost in Saigon. The political situation is highly complex in Southeast Asia, for standards of leadership and understanding of the people's role in the state are in flux. American military assistance cannot avoid supporting the leaders of the recipient government and their supporters. But if the United States distributed some military aid through opposition parties, it would open itself to grave charges of intervention in internal politics. American military aid is not *designed* to prevent change in the *status quo*; a general concern for order surely includes concern for orderly transitions between different administrations. In the event that a new government comes into power, it is quite possible that its leaders, like the former ones, will see the mutual advantages of continuing American military aid.

Although Washington wishes to promote regional cooperation and an awareness of mutual dependence in Southeast Asia, U.S. military assistance programs are based on bilateral agreements. Given the differences among the states of the region in their relations to each other and to the Communist powers, the chances for organizing military assistance on a truly multilateral basis are slight. It is always necessary to bear in mind that two countries receiving aid might even use it against each other, contrary to the American desire of promoting responsible international conduct and good will in the area. Even in the case of SEATO, American military assistance to the Asian members is channeled through bilateral aid agreements. Although a modest level of regional cooperation has been achieved in SEATO training exercises, efforts to establish a Pacific Defense College at Baguio for both members and nonmembers of the organization have not yet brought tangible results.

In planning allocations of American military aid the establishment of force levels and the supply of weapons are tied to regional considerations where feasible. A possible ideal, not capable of attainment under current conditions, would be the creation of joint task forces from different countries in the region that could be used wherever and whenever necessary for its defense. As it is, the force levels are related as far as possible to the assumed degree of threat to each country. Furthermore, the United States cannot encourage the development of balanced land, sea, and air forces, for these are very expensive. The Southeast Asian states could scarcely maintain them, and American sea and air support is expected to be available. Yet for reasons of national prestige and freedom of action, the countries would find it difficult (even if all were firm military allies) to accept the principle of comparative advantage; that is, where each country capitalizes on its particular assets in building a balanced military establishment for the entire alliance. Under the current conditions, appropriate weapons supplied to the local Asian forces may be less expensive, simpler, and easier to maintain and use than the sophisticated tools of war turned over by the United States to many of its NATO allies. Some of the military forces in Southeast Asia being built up by American aid are too costly for the local governments now, or perhaps ever, to support. Apart from this budgeting consideration, the limited economic resources of these countries are being diverted in varying degrees to the partial maintenance of their armed forces. In these cases, the end of American aid might well mean economic collapse, provided that the governments tried to keep the present force levels; but if they became weakened by attempted economies, they might invite Communist aggression. As one last complication, there is a limit to the ability of the countries effectively to absorb the assistance.

Attempts have occasionally been made to determine whether

the military or the economic aid programs of the United States are more important in Southeast Asia and whether they have a competitive relationship. Actually the two are so complementary in some of the countries that one cannot be realistically separated from the other. In fact, in a strategic Southeast Asian area near the People's Republic of China, positions of relative strength can be built by American aid only when military and economic assistance programs are treated as elements of a composite whole. Recipient governments generally press for more military aid than Washington wants to provide. They usually oppose reduction in their forces and, if the need arises, are apt to divert resources from economic purposes. On the other hand, the strengthening of the local economy will eventually enable the countries to contribute more to their national defense.

Military training is a particularly significant aspect of U.S. aid in Southeast Asia. In their own countries the Asians are taught by American Military Assistance Advisory Groups (MAAGs) or mobile teams; and instruction is also provided at institutions in the United States and Okinawa or, to a limited extent, in allied nations like Thailand and the Philippines. Although the training has emphasized military matters, the development of skills necessary for the use and maintenance of American arms and equipment has a potential, by no means fully realized, for developing badly needed technical and administrative talents. The military forces in Southeast Asia can also be profitably used with American technical aid in advancing economic development by opening new lands for settlement, building roads, bridges, and waterways, as well as providing basic education to a sizable number of young men. Training and education for leadership can be an important indirect result of the U.S. military program where the difficulties, both psychological and political, of any direct approach are obvious. Personal contacts between members of the Southeast Asian armed forces and their American counterparts, both in Asia and the United States, have already proved their value in good will.

When the over-all American program of military assistance in the area is considered, the effort is truly impressive. Of the independent countries in Southeast Asia, some kind of military assistance is or has been provided to the Philippines, the Republic of Viet-Nam, Cambodia, Laos, Thailand, Indonesia, and Burma. The Federation of Malaya is the only exception, and this new state has been aided by Britain. Defense support payments have also gone to Thailand, Laos, Cambodia, the Republic of Viet-Nam, and the Philippines. Joint United States Military Advisory Groups or MAAGs under the control of CINCPAC are maintained in Cambodia, Thailand, the Philippines, and the Republic of Viet-Nam. Laos had a Program Evaluation Office of the United States Operations Mission until April 1961; it was then converted into a regular military advisory group which was later withdrawn. In addition, there was before its integration with the Saigon MAAG in 1960 a Temporary Equipment Recovery Mission in Viet-Nam to recover American equipment supplied to France during the war in Indochina. Early in 1962 a United States Military Assistance Command, South Viet-Nam, was established and later in the year a United States Military Assistance Command, Thailand.

U.S. military aid to the countries of Southeast Asia under the Mutual Security Program in fiscal year 1959 in terms of net expenditures was officially given as $91.7 million. The Republic of Viet-Nam received the largest portion, $43.8 million, followed in order by the Philippines, $21.4 million; Thailand, $16.2 million; Laos, $6.5 million; and Cambodia, $3.8 million. In fiscal years 1950 to 1959 inclusive, U.S. obligations for military assistance came to $280.3 million for Thailand and $200.7 million for the Philippines. Since the partition of Indochina, South Viet-Nam for fiscal years 1955 through 1959 received $445.7 million, while Cambodia received $61.8 million, and Laos, $59.8 million. Annual figures continue to vary, of course, reflecting the tempo of Communist activity and the U.S. response. In fiscal 1961 military assistance was programmed to the amount of $101.4 million for South Viet-Nam, $51.9 million for Thailand, $36.0 million for the Philippines, $32.4 million for Laos, and $11.3 million for Cambodia.

At the beginning of 1959 American military and civilian personnel assigned to MAAGs in Thailand, the Philippines, the Republic of Viet-Nam, and Cambodia totaled 734 in number. Only nine of the individuals were civilians, two in Thailand and seven in the Philippines. The MAAGs in Thailand, the Republic of Viet-Nam, and the Philippines were labeled "training" while that in Cambodia was "logistical." The MAAG of 342 members in Viet-Nam was the largest (excluding the American personnel of the Temporary Equipment Recovery Mission); that in Thailand with 266 was next in size; the Philippines advisory group had 69 members; and finally came the MAAG in Cambodia, with only 57 members. In April 1961 the military advisory group in Laos was announced as consisting of 300 men and later in the year, the one in Viet-Nam was augmented from its figure of 685.

The "mix" of training, equipment, and selected forces in a Southeast Asian military aid program depends upon the needs of the individual country. For instance, during fighting in 1961, American military personnel were engaged in providing tactical advice to both Laotian and South Vietnamese units in the field. Involved in the "mix" are nearness to the possible enemy, access to outside help in any emergency, terrain, the nature of the threat, ability to make effective use of the aid, and other considerations. Conventional as well as guerrilla forces may be built up. Americans from the First Special Forces Group on Okinawa are serving in South Viet-Nam where they are active in training work. In fact, the attainment of much greater capability in guerrilla and antiguerilla warfare, "unconventional war by unconventional means," is badly needed in much of Southeast Asia.

Asian critics of American military aid are vociferous. They claim that such aid involves commitments not acceptable to a truly sovereign state, alleging that control of defense and foreign policies is being assumed by Washington with consequent neglect of local problems. Some critics assert that the acceptance of military advice affords a foreign power too much knowledge of the recipient's armed forces; others complain that the right kind of arms is not provided. Local critics also argue that opposition parties can raise charges of imperialist penetration and that national morale is undermined, leaving the recipient less able to cope with internal subversion or aggression.

Although the critics are free to express their opinions, the Southeast Asian governments are not likely to request the general termination of U.S. military assistance programs. Most of them view the strengthening of local armed forces as a factor in the failure of the international Communist movement to extend its hold in Southeast Asia, apart from inroads in Laos, since mid-1954. Moreover, the respective countries, it is clear, have scarcely been able to count on extensive military aid from other non-Communist Asian states. The American military assistance programs in the region give tangible strength and intangible credibility to collective security. Despite important budget considerations and many difficulties of execution, the United States can drastically curtail military assistance to Southeast Asia only if prepared to let the region go by default to Communist China. In the long run the American taxpayer will save money by providing adequate military assistance to the countries that can make the best use of it on the firing line.

For excellent reasons, therefore, the Department of Defense, following the recommendations of the Draper Committee in its final, composite report of August 17, 1959, has undertaken to project the planning of military aid over a five-year period. The formulation of a schedule of actions in terms of countries and areas, phased in time, has a goal of making certain that U.S. military assistance directly buttresses American national objectives. The planning of the program has also been decentralized, and commanders of unified armed forces overseas (like the Commander in Chief, Pacific) have acquired much more responsibility in the work. A Director of Military Assistance, responsible for the operation of the aid program, has been appointed in the Department of Defense, which now has to budget foreign military assistance. The International Peace and Security Act, approved by Congress in August 1961, tries to cope with the problems of military assistance in the 1960s, but constant evaluation and frequent efforts in improvement are essential in meeting the needs of a dynamic challenge.

BASES

U.S. military aid programs often serve to facilitate American access to military installations and bases in foreign countries. In Southeast Asia the United States has bases only in the Philippines, but U.S. support for the construction or modernization of military installations in other Asian countries is given partly in the expectation that American forces would be permitted to use such facilities in an emergency. The United States also owns or administers a number of islands in the Western Pacific some of which contain important bases, while a number of its Western allies have access to bases at Singapore and other strategic points in Southeast Asia. The overseas installations of the Western powers are, of course, a special target for abuse in the worldwide Communist press.

On March 16, 1947, the American bases in the Philippines were formally leased from the newly independent republic for a term of 99 years. The three principal bases (which have been retained in subsequent renegotiations) are: Clark Air Base in Pampanga, the headquarters of the 13th U.S. Air Force; the Naval Base at Subic Bay in Zambales, together with the nearby Naval Air Station at Cubi Point and the Naval Communication Facility at San Miguel; and, finally, the Naval Station at Sangley Point in Cavite, the headquarters of the U.S. Naval Force in the Philippines. All three bases are in Luzon and relatively near Manila. The United States also retains Camp John Hay, a leave and recreation center at Baguio in the Mountain Province, and a few minor installations.

In the original base agreement the American government acquired "the right to retain the use" of a much larger number of specific bases and facilities and to utilize certain others in the event it considered there was a "military necessity." The listed sites were scattered over a wide area from the Sulu Archipelago to northern Luzon. The American bases in the Philippines could be used upon call by the Security Council of the United Nations, provided the Manila and Washington governments approved. No third power could acquire bases in the archipelago without their consent.

Although the Filipino people were in favor of retaining the American military presence in the islands—the lowering of the Stars and Stripes at the Luneta on July 4, 1946, being an occasion of mixed nostalgia and jubilation—problems and incidents regarding the administration and location of the leaseholds arose to cause tension. As nationalism grew in the Asian republic and as neighboring areas acquired independence, usually without the retention of military bases or facilities by the mother country, domestic and international pressures mounted until formal negotiations between Washington and Manila on the bases agreement were undertaken. It is significant, however, that the Republic of the Philippines has never requested an end to the American military installations. If it did, the United States would probably accede, for bases that are isolated islands in a sea of local hostility lose much of their value.

When Vice President Richard M. Nixon visited the Philippines in the summer of 1956, he and President Ramón Magsaysay issued a joint statement in which, among other things, it was asserted that the United States fully recognized Philippine sovereignty over the bases and had officially taken this stand since the independence of the islands. Title claims and title papers of the bases were transferred by Washington to the Manila government. Formal negotiations between an American and a Philippine panel opened in Manila in August, but they were "recessed" in December, for agreement could not be reached on a number of questions, especially the issue of jurisdiction over military personnel of the United States for criminal offenses committed while off-duty against Filipinos in the base areas.

Discussions continued intermittently in various degrees of formality at the diplomatic level for some time; piecemeal accords were reached; and Washington took certain unilateral steps to resolve the issues. It was agreed in the projected settlement to reduce the length of the leasehold on the bases from 99 to 25 years with renewal provisions, or to terminate it earlier if both parties consented. The United States also expressed willingness to give up specified unused base areas.

Shortly before relinquishing his post as American Ambassador to the Philippines, Charles E. Bohlen signed a memorandum of agreement on October 12, 1959 with Felixberto Serrano, the Philippine foreign minister, in which an "understanding" was reached on a large number of the pending questions. The United States would consult the Philippines not only on the operational use of the base facilities in defense commitments beyond the circumstances allowed by the Manila Treaty of 1954 and the mutual defense pact of 1951, but also on the installation of sites and establishment of missiles in the leaseholds. For this, Philippine consent would be needed. Control over Olongapo, a Filipino community in Zambales, was relinquished, and certain delimitations were made in the areas of the specified bases to be kept. Substantial agreement was attained on the controversial subject of legal jurisdiction, but the final aspects of the matter would be negotiated by the next ambassador from the United States in the preparation of a treaty covering the settlement. Meanwhile, Carlos P. Garcia publicly indicated while he was president that he was willing for Washington to have missiles and atomic weapons on U.S. bases in the republic, but that congressional approval in Manila would be necessary. It is hoped that the new arrangements will lead to much closer Philippine-American cooperation on the leaseholds with greater mutuality of understanding and effort. The visits of President Eisenhower to the Philippines in 1960 and of General Douglas MacArthur in 1961 strengthened the good will between Manila and Washington. Relations cooled, however, in 1962 when Congress in Washington delayed approval of a Philippine war damage payments bill, and President Diosdado Macapagal postponed his state visit to the United States. Subsequent favorable action by Congress led to better relations.

The controversies over the American military installations in the islands pointed up some of the advantages and disadvantages for the United States in this type of overseas bases. American facilities in Luzon, however, mean more than just the security of the Philippines. They are extremely important in the forward strategy of the United States and in the projection of its influence and power in the rest of Southeast Asia. They are a symbol of Washington's determination to stand by a weak country that has confidence in America's future. The naval and tactical air forces of the United States in the Western Pacific derive part of

SOUTHEAST ASIA IN UNITED STATES POLICY

their operational strength from the logistical support afforded by the bases, which also facilitate the military exercises of SEATO and the provision of logistical aid to some of its members. In the event of local aggression in Southeast Asia the military installations would be of great value in the attempt to repel the invaders, for the concentration of equipment and a build-up of task forces are possible in the larger base areas of Luzon. These facilities clearly constitute a great asset in the military posture of the United States in the Far East, and their loss would be a factor in a possible American withdrawal eastward to the Marianas or Hawaii. But at the same time, it should be stated, the need of flexibility requires that Washington be able to carry out its essential military requirements without the installations, if necessary.

As new weapons come into their own, such as the intercontinental ballistic missile and the Polaris-missile-firing, nuclear-powered submarine, the question of the retention of American overseas bases will be more urgent. A concept of "Fortress America," with the nation's strategic retaliatory forces in the United States and under the high seas, carries the implication that allies and bases abroad are no longer necessary. Even if general war were the only consideration, the idea of "Fortress America" would imply that the United States is self-sufficient, that by itself it does not constitute too serious a target area, and that it is prepared to surrender its role of world leadership.

As the stakes are high, the determination of American security policy for the 1960s in Asian areas peripheral to the Sino-Soviet bloc has been the subject of considerable controversy in the United States. One school of thought holds that since Washington shares with Moscow thermonuclear plenty, the strategic concept of massive retaliation has lost much of its underpinning, the United States no longer has the power to honor many of its overseas commitments, and a political policy of disengagement focusing on territorial stabilization through the creation of neutral buffer states in certain peripheral areas is necessary. The opposite school maintains that massive retaliation was never a suitable deterrent to local war, that the United States can develop much more competent capabilities in brush-fire situations, and that the establishment of weak neutral buffers in traditional spatial terms ignores the dynamic, all-out nature of international communism with its doctrine of inevitable triumph through social change and its transcending of normal relations among states. A wider choice of deterrents through the development of greater conventional capabilities and the raising of the "threshold" of military response where atomic warfare would be necessary could insure that the periphery does not become the center through piecemeal erosion.

The Kennedy administration, while seeking to provide a less vulnerable and more powerful nuclear deterrent as quickly as possible, moved to strengthen conventional forces for limited and guerrilla warfare. Thus, the choice between massive retaliation and ineffective resistance or submission in peripheral areas would be broadened to include speedy, flexible, selective responses suited to the peril and conducive to credibility. This approach meant the acquisition of adequate airlift and sealift, an expansion of the Special Forces for guerrilla and antiguerrilla operations, an increase in battlefield mobility and non-nuclear fire-power, the development of stronger, highly mobile forces, the improvement in non-nuclear capabilities of fighter aircraft, an over-all expansion in military manpower with increased training and readiness, faster procurement of modern arms and equipment, and more stress on research on non-nuclear weapons.

In Southeast Asia, the problem of reducing U.S. commitments or of increasing U.S. power was not resolved in terms of one or the other. Although an American policy of relative disengagement was decided upon in Laos, all possible efforts would be made elsewhere in the region, especially in the Republic of Viet-

Nam and Thailand, to bolster the countries against Communist inroads. As military alliances *per se* cannot prevent subversion, stress was placed on social, economic, and political reform and development as major ways of countering it. Since in the 1960s Washington must be prepared and willing to face the military danger where it is greatest, namely, limited or guerrilla war in peripheral areas of the Sino-Soviet bloc, allies and bases are vital in any forward strategy.

[FIVE]

The Southeast Asia
Treaty Organization

Many of the postwar regional security pacts have occasioned a great deal of controversy, but few have been as widely criticized as SEATO—the target for repeated recriminations from the Communist bloc, from many uncommitted states, and even from various American circles. The vehemence of objections issuing from Peking and Moscow suggests more than a casual interest in the Manila Treaty; it could even be mildly suggested that this stream of Communist protests is one measure of the importance of SEATO. The uncommitted states have become less severe in their censure, however, for they have discovered that SEATO is not the rapacious imperialist monster portrayed in Communist propaganda; in fact, the increasing militancy of Peking has almost forced a number of Southeast Asian leaders at least to consider possible alternatives to neutralism. In the United States the Southeast Asia Treaty Organization has been subjected to a variety of criticisms; frequently it is alleged to be a divisive rather than a unifying factor in Asia and it is, more importantly, damned as an ineffective vehicle of U.S. policy, often being unfavorably compared to NATO; American learned journals contain scarcely an article sympathetic to SEATO. Perhaps it is time for an unagonizing reappraisal.

RATIONALE

Designed to deter overt aggression from Communist China, the Manila Treaty provides a shield for those American and related programs of assistance which may lead to the economic and social betterment of the people, to greater stability of government, and to a reduction in the potential appeal of communism in the SEATO area. The heart of SEATO is found in Article IV, paragraph 1:

Each Party recognizes that aggression by means of armed attack in the treaty area against any of the Parties or against any State or territory which the Parties by unanimous agreement may hereafter designate, would endanger its own peace and safety, and agrees that it will in that event act to meet the common danger in accordance with its constitutional processes.[1]

In an understanding accepted by the other signatories, the United States asserted that its obligations under Article IV, paragraph 1, applied only to "Communist aggression."

In an effort to cope with the urgent problem of subversion directed from outside and indirect aggression, provision was made in Article IV, paragraph 2, of the pact for immediate consultation on the steps for common defense if a party believed the political independence or territorial integrity of any member in

[1] Southeast Asia Collective Defense Treaty and Protocol between the United States of America and Other Governments Signed at Manila September 8, 1954, *Treaties and Other International Acts Series* 3170, p. 3.

the treaty area or any designated state or territory was threatened by other than armed attack or by "any fact or situation" that might menace the peace of the area. As insisted upon by Great Britain, SEATO action in any designated state or territory could only be taken at the invitation or the approval of the government concerned. The United States also agreed to the consultation formula of Article IV, paragraph 2, if aggression or armed attack other than Communist occurred.

An important feature of the Manila Treaty was the description of the "treaty area." It was defined as the "general area" of Southeast Asia and the Southwest Pacific, including all the territories of the Asian members, but excluding the Pacific area north of 21° 30' north latitude (directed at Taiwan and Hong Kong, though not by name). Although technically this definition includes only Pakistan, Thailand, the Philippines, British Malaya and Borneo, Australia, and New Zealand, a provision under Article IV, paragraph 1, allowed the signatories to add a protocol to the treaty, designating Cambodia, Laos, and the "free territory under the jurisdiction of the State of Vietnam" as areas where the provisions of the article were applicable. The only changes in the treaty area since the signing of the Southeast Asia Collective Defense Treaty on September 8, 1954, have been the removal of the Federation of Malaya through its failure to join SEATO after achieving its independence in August 1957 and the dropping of Laos as a protocol state as a result of the Geneva settlement of 1962. While Great Britain is still sovereign over the State of Singapore, the crown colonies of Sarawak and North Borneo, and the protected sultanate of Brunei, these areas remain in the SEATO territory pending the establishment of the Federation of Malaysia. Provision was made for altering the treaty area or admitting new members through unanimous decision.

The signatories of the Manila Treaty pledge themselves to strengthen their free institutions and to cooperate in those economic measures, including technical assistance, which are directed toward promoting their social well-being and economic progress. The benefits of this provision were extended by the protocol to Cambodia, Laos, and South Viet-Nam. Individually and jointly, through self-help and mutual aid, the parties promise to "maintain and develop their individual and collective capacity to resist armed attack and to prevent and counter subversive activities directed from without against their territorial integrity and political stability."[2]

The signatories to the treaty reaffirm their obligations under the Charter of the United Nations to resolve controversies by peaceful means and to avoid threats or force in international relations; measures taken under Article IV, paragraph 1, are to be reported at once to the Security Council. The treaty comes under Article 51 of the United Nations Charter, "the inherent right of individual or collective self-defense" clause, and not Article 52 concerning regional arrangements where a Soviet veto could apply to enforcement measures. The pact provides for a council to assist in its implementation and allows for the withdrawal of any party after one year's notice.

Some of the concepts found in the preamble of the Manila Treaty were reflected in the Pacific Charter; in identical language in both documents the powers declared that they upheld "the principle of equal rights and self-determination of peoples" and would "earnestly strive by every peaceful means to promote self-government and to secure the independence of all countries whose peoples desire it and are able to undertake its responsibilities."[3] In the Pacific Charter each was "prepared to continue taking effective practical measures" toward the stated objectives.

[2] Same, p. 2.
[3] Same for preamble of Manila Treaty; Pacific Charter between the United States of America and Other Governments Dated at Manila September 8, 1954, *Treaties and Other International Acts Series* 3171, p. 1.

The Southeast Asia Collective Defense Treaty embodies a number of concepts found in other instruments of American foreign policy. Inherent in Article IV, paragraph 1, is the "Monroe Doctrine" formula of involvement, as stressed by Secretary Dulles. Also present is the principle of the Vandenberg Resolution, calling for self-help and mutual aid in regional and collective security arrangements of the United States. The basic approach to subversion incorporated in 1947 in the Inter-American Treaty of Reciprocal Assistance is found in Article IV, paragraph 2. Despite differences, the fundamental design of the Manila Pact is like that of the defense treaties previously made between the United States and the Philippines, Korea, and Australia and New Zealand. As in the case of the North Atlantic Alliance, the adherence of new countries to the Southeast Asia Collective Defense Treaty would require the advice and consent of the Senate. As already noted, the Manila Treaty is, in theory, closely related to the United Nations, especially Article 51 of the Charter.

ASPECTS OF MEMBERSHIP

Is the community of interests of the signatories sufficiently strong to sustain SEATO? What does SEATO *per se* add to the community? A state will enter into an alliance only if convinced that its national interests are best served by a formal commitment. Yet to what extent are political and military interests compatible in SEATO and to what degree does the Manila Treaty further national interests? Is the distribution of responsibilities and benefits equitable and related to the actual power of the various members? Since the ability of the new states of Asia and Africa to meet obligations is often limited and subject to change, is SEATO a legalistic and doctrinaire concept without political viability? Moreover, although an alliance makes common interests more explicit and precise, it is easier in practice to identify a possible enemy than to formulate policies and programs to contain him. What has been the experience of SEATO in this respect? History records few instances where a multilateral alliance of many powers established in time of peace has actually gone to war.

The three Asian states that signed the Manila Treaty—the Philippines, Thailand, and Pakistan—considered communism a threat to their future and believed their position in world affairs would be strengthened by alignment with the United States and other Western powers. Stressing that they were assuming risks which many of their neighbors were not prepared to accept, all three hoped for increased military and economic aid from Washington.

Apart from these common considerations, Pakistan was eager to strengthen its position against India, the overwhelming problem in the foreign relations of the country since independence. And membership in SEATO might also bolster Pakistan in its dispute with the kingdom of Afghanistan over Pushtunistan. Thailand's special concern was the possibility that Indochina might fall into the hands of leaders hostile to Bangkok. Influenced by its Chinese and Vietnamese minorities, the kingdom was apprehensive lest a powerful China dominate Viet-Nam, Cambodia, and Laos and reduce the Thai to vassals. Even a militant Viet-Nam controlling the weak states of Laos and Cambodia would be a threat to Thailand. In fact, Bangkok had been pressing for an alliance with the United States previous to the conclusion of the Manila Treaty. The Philippines, already allied with the United States and closely associated with the pattern of American security in the Western Pacific, did not see in the Manila Pact any radical departure in its foreign policy. The dominating influence of President Ramón Magsaysay with his strong sympathy for the United States contributed to the willingness of Manila to join a multilateral security pact; moreover, his Liberal predecessor, President Elpidio Quirino, had long advocated a broad security arrangement in his part of the world.

All three of these Asian powers were more concerned over their own defense than that of the South and Southeast Asian area; the major unifying factor in their SEATO membership was the participation of the United States. By themselves these three states would not have made an alliance, even if they had been joined by Great Britain, France, Australia, and New Zealand; in fact, they were apprehensive lest Washington listen more to advice from Western capitals than from their own. Although the Asian members are apparently convinced that the benefits from SEATO have so far outweighed the costs, a genuine mellowing of Communist China in its posture toward Southeast Asia, a pronounced decline in American aid to the Asian states, or a failure of SEATO to act effectively in a real showdown might encourage them to withdraw from the commitment. The Laotian crisis in 1960-62 created the most strain to date in the alliance. Yet the Manila Treaty does not drastically restrict its Asian members' freedom of action. Thai recognition of Peking would be deplored by the United States, but the Manila Pact could survive it. The political maneuverability of individual SEATO members would be greater if the military tension in the Far East were relaxed.

For Australia, SEATO represented an important extension of American commitments in the "general area" of Southeast Asia and the Southwest Pacific. Since Australians look on the United States as the only Western power capable of containing Communist China, Canberra would have preferred a U.S. commitment at least as strong as the one under NATO and would be seriously concerned over any marked weakening of present American obligations. Australia would have preferred a SEATO military command, the commitment of specific forces, and the building of an infra-structure, as well as a much wider Asian membership in SEATO. Canberra welcomed Pakistan as an ally but regretted the absence of India. The strengthening of ties between Manila and Canberra through participation in SEATO was indicated in their common concern over developments in the Indonesian civil war in 1958. Should Indonesia or Java fall into the hands of the PKI, Australia's role in the defense of Malaya and other parts of peninsular Southeast Asia would be jeopardized.

Less sympathetic to the Manila Treaty than was its Commonwealth neighbor, New Zealand indicated a preference for bilateral pacts of mutual assistance rather than a multilateral alliance with only three Asian members. Yet Wellington welcomed American commitments under the Manila Treaty and was glad to have its closest friends, the United Kingdom, Australia, and the United States, as allies in the common effort to restrain Communist aggression in Southeast Asia. Prime Minister Walter Nash on occasion personally urged Nehru to join SEATO.

The United Kingdom joined SEATO largely to preserve the British presence in Southeast Asia. Although London would have preferred a treaty with a much broader Asian adherence, the British government was convinced of the need for a multilateral security arrangement in the area and saw the Manila Pact as the best attainable under the circumstances. Great Britain supported the protocol extending the mantle of protection over South Viet-Nam, Cambodia, and Laos but believed that the Geneva settlement precluded their membership. In sum, Great Britain saw SEATO as a possible deterrent to the People's Republic of China, as a shield behind which conditions favorable to political and economic stability might be created, and as a means of working with Asian nationalism.

At the time of the Manila Conference, France still hoped to preserve a major portion of its political, economic, and cultural interests in Indochina. The protocol to the Manila Treaty was viewed in Paris as a desirable barrier to Communist aggression in Viet-Nam, Laos, and Cambodia. In the SEATO countries there was some disapproval of French participation in the organization, since Paris was still too closely associated with colonialism.

It is clear that the correlation between the distribution of power and responsibility is close in SEATO, both being concentrated in the United States. In a war involving Southeast Asia Australia might well be the SEATO member next to the United States most able and willing to help outside its own territory. Yet the Philippines and Thailand by their geographical location are essential to the effectiveness of the organization; their refusal to cooperate in an emergency could be extremely serious. The United States for its part benefits from the Manila Pact to the extent that it serves to check overt Communist aggression of the Korean War type in the treaty area. Moreover, the United States' role in Southeast Asia appears less provocative to Asians when a common posture can be taken in a crisis.

At the time of the Manila Treaty negotiations, all the powers directly concerned were eager to have as wide an Asian participation as possible. India, Burma, Ceylon and Indonesia would have been welcome partners, but they chose to stay outside. In fact, India and Indonesia—and to a lesser extent Burma and Ceylon—were highly critical of the Manila Conference, accusing it of creating tensions and dividing nations. Although all four were pursuing a policy of nonalignment in world politics, the reasons for their opposition to the pact varied. India was especially concerned about Pakistan's proposed membership and feared that its rival would use the treaty to put pressure on New Delhi. Opposed to security ties with present or former colonial masters, Indonesia suspected that SEATO might be a means for the former rulers to return to power in Southeast Asia. Burma was apprehensive lest the treaty serve to bait Communist China at the expense of adjacent weak neighbors. Under Prime Minister Sir John Kotelawala, Ceylon was less hostile to SEATO but not to the point of seeking membership.

Although Cambodia, Laos, and South Viet-Nam were in favor of the protocol which extended the protection of the Manila Treaty to them, they were not invited to be signatories. A legal question arose as to whether they could be full participants under the provisions of the Geneva settlement and, as the armistice arrangements were being implemented, it was thought best not to complicate the situation. Although the Federation of Malaya might have joined SEATO upon acquiring independence, the Kuala Lumpur government hesitated to take the step because of a large Chinese minority, satisfactory defense ties with Great Britain, and a complicated internal political situation. After all, the Federation had many of the benefits of the pact through the presence of the Commonwealth Strategic Reserve on Malayan territory and through a close relationship with the United Kingdom, Australia, and New Zealand.

Despite changes of government on the part of all its Asian members, SEATO has continued in existence. *Coups d'état* have occurred in Pakistan under the inspiration of Mohammad Ayub Khan and in Thailand under Sarit Thanarat, while in the Philippines President Carlos P. Garcia and later President Diosdado Macapagal became chief executives under constitutional practice. These changes have not impaired the contractual capacity or the political viability of the Asian members. Nor is a *coup d'état* on the Iraqi pattern of 1958, basically altering the foreign policy of a participant, likely to occur.

Through the decline of its position in Southeast Asia France has lost many of its reasons for participation in SEATO. French military personnel have been withdrawn from all Indochina, except for men associated for a while with the base at Seno and those with the missions in Laos and Cambodia. Economic and cultural interests remain, but these alone would not originally have brought France into SEATO. On the other hand, General Charles de Gaulle's rise to power in 1958 has revived the global position of Paris. The French leader has urged a three-power "directorate"—France, the United States, and Great Britain—and he is aware that through SEATO Paris has a means of exerting influence in Southeast Asia. Before the Wellington meeting of the SEATO Council, De Gaulle was briefed on the organization and took an active part in instructions to the French delegation. The General believes a multilateral deterrent to Communist China is necessary and recognizes the importance of promoting economic and political progress in Southeast Asia, but he does not approve of pressuring a neutral state like Cambodia to join the organization. Although the ill will that used to exist between Thailand and France over Cambodia has largely gone, Bangkok has informally accused the French of backing the *coup* of Captain Kong Le in Vientiane and the abortive one later in 1960 against Ngo Dinh Diem in Saigon. A source of contention was removed by the French recognition of Algerian independence, for Paris had been particularly displeased when Moslem Pakistan, its ally in SEATO, showed sympathy for the Algerian rebels.

SEATO in the American Security Pattern

The Manila Treaty constitutes a link in the system of alliances supported by Washington in Asia and the Pacific. In Northeast Asia, Japan and the United States are linked by the Treaty of Mutual Cooperation and Security signed January 19, 1960; the Republic of Korea and the United States by the Treaty of Mutual Defense signed October 1, 1953; and the Republic of China and the United States by the Mutual Defense Treaty of

December 2, 1954. In the Southwest Pacific, Australia, New Zealand, and the United States are allied through the Security Treaty of September 1, 1951; and in Southeast Asia, the Philippines and the United States through the Mutual Defense Treaty of August 30, 1951. Great Britain coordinates defense planning with Australia and New Zealand, and in October 1957 signed the External Defence and Mutual Assistance Agreement with the Federation of Malaya. In the Middle East, the United States participates, though not as a formal member, in the activities of the Central Treaty Organization (CENTO), concluded as the Baghdad Pact in 1954; and on March 5, 1959, the United States signed separate Defense Agreements with Pakistan, Turkey, and Iran.

Of the members of SEATO, Pakistan, the United States, and Great Britain have the most extensive links through Asian and Pacific alliances. The United States has commitments in Northeast Asia, the Southwest Pacific, Southeast Asia, South Asia, and the Middle East; Great Britain is involved in all these areas except Northeast Asia and has additional commitments in Malaya; while Pakistan, like Great Britain, is a member of CENTO as well as SEATO. Despite the elaborate alliance system, the military forces of the Sino-Soviet bloc would have to attack in several directions to bring all the security pacts into action. It is quite possible that a local war could be fought in a number of places without involving other treaty areas. In fact, there may be co-ordinated crises in the future, arising from two or more simultaneous Communist probing attempts, designed to test where the United States will make the greater response. It is possible, however, that an armed conflict involving SEATO would spread. Viewed as a means of linking other security pacts, the Manila Treaty constitutes a deterrent across a wide geographic area to overt aggression on the part of the Communist bloc.

Political considerations are important in the absence of close ties among the various non-Communist alliances along the Sino-Soviet periphery in Asia and the Pacific. The contracting parties in one alliance may not all be willing to participate in a security pact with those in another. For instance, differing interests would presently prevent Japan and the Republics of China and Korea from becoming members of the Southeast Asia Treaty Organization. Even London, Paris, and Washington could not agree on a regional security approach to the entire Far East. Although contacts have been made between CENTO and SEATO, more permanent links are not likely. The Southeast Asia Treaty Organization will not merge into an integrated global security arrangement in the foreseeable future.

EVOLUTION OF SEATO

Although alliances may technically remain in force when the conditions that produced them cease to exist, they lose their validity when the signatories are no longer willing to implement them in a showdown. Because of the cultural, political, and economic diversity of the members of SEATO, the external pressure motivating the pact must be particularly strong to maintain an effective partnership. It is essential that the members of SEATO bear continually in mind the difference between the constant objectives of international communism in Southeast Asia and the fluctuating tactics characteristic of Communist behavior.

The pronounced danger of overt Communist aggression in Southeast Asia at the time the Manila Treaty was signed has receded only to be replaced by more indirect Communist tactics of subversion and infiltration, the encouragement of neutralism in an anti-Western context, and the careful use of propaganda, trade, and aid. Under certain conditions internal wars resulting in the possible seizure of power by local forces of "national liberation" are encouraged by the resources of the Sino-Soviet bloc. In accordance with policy expressed by the Communist parties in the Moscow Declaration of 1957 and reaffirmed the following year, local parties in Southeast Asia are trying to acquire a broader public base by cooperating with socialist and nationalist forces wherever possible and by proclaiming themselves as democratic political entities. Meanwhile, Communist rebels are seeking negotiated settlements with Southeast Asian governments, albeit still on their own terms. At the same time, it should be remembered, the militant nationalism of the People's Republic of China has served to increase apprehensions in Southeast Asia about the growing power and basic intentions of Peking. During his visit there Premier Khrushchev actually urged Indonesia not to join SEATO, a rather amazing gesture since Sukarno's island republic would probably be among the last to take such a step. Southeast Asian countries are generally becoming more cognizant of the need to cope with the Communist use of both the carrot and the stick.

SEATO has responded to the tactics of Peking and Moscow in a variety of ways. Efforts have been made to build up an organization in Bangkok more adequate to meet the needs of the alliance. Although the terms of the Manila Treaty are loosely worded, the provisions regarding structure being particularly vague, SEATO headquarters now has an organization much more elaborate than that envisioned when the Council of Foreign Ministers met for the first time in Bangkok in February 1955. Secretary of State Dulles, in fact, tried to avoid in the early stages of the pact using the word "SEATO" lest an organization like NATO be implied.

As authorized under the Manila Treaty, the SEATO Council determines the general policies of the organization. Meeting usually once a year in the capital of a member state, the Council of Foreign Ministers surveys the political situation in the treaty area in the light of the over-all international picture, reviews the work of the organization during the previous year, gives guidance for the next, and approves the budget. In the course of the survey of international developments the discussions are often quite spontaneous and frank, contributing to the broader outlook and better perspective of each participant. At the Washington meeting, May 31 to June 2, 1960, for instance, special consideration was given to the possible implications for the treaty area of the recent failure of the efforts for a summit conference in Paris. Different interpretations of world events reflect the various national interests.

The reports and recommendations of the Secretary General, the Military Advisers, and the Council Representatives are considered by the SEATO Council in its review of the year's work and in the formulation of plans for the future. Although differences have been evident on questions such as economic aid projects or policy in Laos, ways have been found to get around them. When some of the Asian members have been faced with suggesting alternatives to American aid provided them on a bilateral basis, they have not pressed their desiderata. Differences concerning the proper military posture of SEATO have been pronounced, for there is still some support for a standing force and command structure. There is also the tendency for a country to press its own international problems before the Council; for instance, at the Karachi meeting in March 1956, in the wake of Khrushchev's support of Afghanistan in its territorial dispute with Pakistan, the members of the Council supported the latter and affirmed that the treaty area extended up to the Durand Line. Approved on an annual basis, the budget was $896,860 for 1959-60, with the United States sharing 25 per cent, the United Kingdom 16 per cent, Australia and France 13.5 per cent each, and

New Zealand, Pakistan, the Philippines, and Thailand 8 per cent each.

Below the SEATO Council is the Council Representatives, a permanent body meeting normally once a month in Bangkok. Consisting of participants at the ambassadorial level, the Representatives are responsible for the over-all political guidance of the organization as well as for the control of its nonmilitary work when the SEATO Council is not meeting. Should a situation require rapid attention, a session can be called on very short notice at the request of a Council Representative or the Secretary General. Only recommendations can be made, for decision rests in the respective capitals of the SEATO members. During the height of the Laotian crisis in the summer of 1959 and again in 1960-62 the Council Representatives considered problems that necessitated urgent communications to their home governments. In 1960 they met 48 times, Laos being a major topic. Although at present the Council Representatives are diplomats who in most cases double as ambassadors to Thailand, if SEATO should develop in stature, it would probably be necessary at a certain point for the respective governments to appoint Permanent Representatives with the rank of ambassador, as is widely done in the case of NATO.

A Permanent Working Group has been established, often meeting several times a week, to discuss proposals and policy for the consideration of the Council Representatives. Consisting of a senior person on the diplomatic staff of each member of the parent body, the Group prepares working papers, often with recommendations for specific action. Much of the basic work on the diplomatic level is done by this group, which can identify subjects of disagreement at an early stage. Alternate delegates to the Permanent Working Group constitute a Budget Sub-Committee. These aspects of SEATO activity place added duties on the diplomatic missions accredited to Bangkok except for those whose governments have made other provisions. The Ministry of Foreign Affairs of Thailand handles representation from its own office since the kingdom is the host country for SEATO.

The international organization has three expert committees, the members of which are selected by the different governments. Convening periodically at SEATO headquarters and reporting to the Council Representatives are the Committee of Security Experts (CSE), the Committee on Information, Cultural, Education and Labour Activities (CICEL), and the Committee of Economic Experts (CEE). These representatives are drawn from the embassies in Bangkok, from the host country, and from the capitals of the respective members. On the whole the contribution of the three committees to SEATO has been limited, with the Committee of Security Experts making the greatest headway and the Committee of Economic Experts the least.

The Secretariat-General of the international organization has evolved from a small unit in Thailand's foreign ministry through an interim stage, consisting of a number of offices subject to the broad coordination of an Executive Secretary under the Council Representatives, and finally to the present autonomous Secretariat-General under a permanent Secretary General and his deputy. On June 28, 1956, the Thai government formally turned over to SEATO a large building on impressive Rajdamnern Avenue for use as its headquarters. Here are housed the Secretariat-General and the Military Planning Office.

On September 1, 1957, Pote Sarasin, a distinguished Thai political figure with extensive experience in diplomacy, became the first Secretary General. The leading permanent official of the organization and its spokesman, he represents it in contacts with CENTO and NATO and in visits to the SEATO countries, and he attends meetings of the Council Representatives and the Council of Foreign Ministers. The Secretary General is assisted by William Worth, an able senior public servant from Australia, who also serves as chairman of the Permanent Working Group.

The Secretariat-General seeks to advance the nonmilitary activities of SEATO through six offices: Central Services, Cultural Relations, Economic Services, Public Information, Research Services, and Security. The secretariat staff, it is significant to note, grew from six on January 1, 1956, to an authorized 108 by July 1, 1958. The staff, divided into "international" and "local" personnel depending upon the recruitment methods and the nature of the work (42 being authorized in the former class by July 1, 1958, and 66 in the latter), consists theoretically of international civil servants responsible to the Secretary General. Yet appointment on the international staff is not conducive to developing SEATO loyalties, for the individuals, nominated by the member states and not the Secretary General, are for the most part civil servants of the respective governments placed on leave without pay for a tour of duty at SEATO headquarters and still subject to recall by their own authorities. Thus the absence of a career service causes most members of the international staff to look for advancement in terms of their home governments. On the other hand, some of them are now being reappointed at SEATO headquarters and individuals can be dismissed by the Secretary General if he finds due cause. There is a definite attempt to stress Asian membership at the Secretariat General, and American personnel, for instance, is carefully limited.

The most significant change in the military organization of SEATO was the establishment of a Military Planning Office on March 1, 1957. The highest military organ is still the Military Advisers Group, which is responsible to the SEATO Council and guides all military activities of the organization. Consisting of officers at the level of chief of staff or theater commander, one nominated by each member state, the Group meets twice a year. Defense planning for SEATO is the responsibility of a

Committee of Senior Planners, one from each country, assisted by teams of "junior" planners. The final recommendations are submitted to the Military Advisers for consideration, together with proposals for SEATO military training exercises. The Chief of the Military Planning Office, who now has a Deputy Chief to assist him, is responsible to the Military Advisers Group for the functioning of his office and has liaison duties with the Secretary General.

The evolution in SEATO's structure reflects the viewpoint of the members that the aims of the Manila Treaty can be better advanced by giving them greater organizational context. At the same time there is the danger that an impressive structure can be taken for an effective organization. Here, as is clear, the attitudes of the member governments are decisive. Yet in the course of time, a real *esprit de corps* may emerge from stronger foundations.

In addition to organizational changes the objectives of the Manila Pact have been further met in the military, subversion, cultural, economic, and information fields. Here the multilateral approach has often been found preferable to the bilateral. At the Manila Conference in 1954 the United States was not in favor of the establishment of a unified military command and a standing force; it did not want an Asian NATO with joint headquarters, joint military forces, and a common strategy. As American responsibilities were world-wide and Asia contained a large number of potential trouble spots, Washington was opposed to earmarking American forces under the proposed Manila Pact for specific areas in the Far East; such a step was considered neither necessary, practical, nor desirable. Other signatories, of course, could do what they wanted. The United States, as already indicated, favored the deterrent of a mobile striking force, along with reserves strategically located, capable of hitting any aggressor at selected places and by chosen means. It was pointed out that Washington planned to keep strong air and naval units in the Western Pacific at all times, a deterrent involving the nuclear striking might of the Strategic Air Command and the Seventh Fleet and capable of protecting many as well as one. Secretary Dulles, moreover, stated in 1954 that the Manila Treaty would not require material changes in American military planning.

SEATO military activity has centered upon training exercises, defense planning, and problems of standardization. Advance preparations for a possible emergency, like operations to defend the Mekong basin in Laos or the Republic of Viet-Nam, are considered preferable to a mere *ad hoc* approach. Admiral Harry D. Felt, the American Commander in Chief, Pacific, is the U.S. member of the SEATO Military Advisers; and CINCPAC's headquarters at Pearl Harbor has become the main nexus of the growing American military participation in SEATO, especially since 1958. Moreover, the disproportionate power of the United States as compared with its allies under the Manila Pact points up the importance of CINCPAC's role. In the event of a grave emergency, Admiral Felt might assume command of SEATO forces.

In the complicated task of defense planning and related matters the SEATO Military Advisers at their first meeting in conjunction with the Council in February 1955 formulated a plan of preliminary action and determined a general course for the future. Studies were undertaken on mutual aid, communications, security, and subversion. Problems of organization were considered, intelligence surveys of certain areas begun, and priorities of action studied. In March 1958 the Military Advisers discussed a concept of defense giving basic guidance to the SEATO planners in the event of Communist aggression.

On the day-to-day working level project teams of "junior" planners in the Military Planning Office in Bangkok are engaged in specific tasks related to defense and other matters. Here are worked out agreed drafts for the detailed consideration and approval of the Senior Planners. After the plans are unanimously accepted by the members of the Military Advisers Group, they normally become a part of the plans of the various national services. SEATO officials claim excellent progress in developing military estimates and claim that defense planning is becoming more effective and realistic. The process is certain to cause interest in Communist China and may even be an element of deterrence.

The participants in military planning at international meetings do not, however, disclose their own national plans for comparable contingencies. Secrecy is maintained, for it is realized that plans can be more easily leaked by eight governments sharing the information than by one. Highly embarrassing for the organization would be a *coup d'état* in Bangkok by leaders hostile to it and their subsequent take-over of SEATO headquarters with its records and files. Although this development is unlikely, it cannot be completely ignored, the 1958 *coup* in Iraq, the headquarters of the Baghdad Pact, being a case in point. Apart from this contingency, SEATO has its own clearance and security regulations.

The combined military training exercises held under SEATO auspices are designed to improve the readiness and mobility of the armed forces of the membership. Each is given a name like "Firm Link," "Albatross," "Astra," and "Air Link," four held between February 1956 and June 1957, and may be typed as a mobility demonstration, a maritime, close air support, amphibious, harbor defense, command post, or air defense, resupply and air drop exercise. The location, of course, varies, Thailand and the South China Sea being favorite areas. Several of the exercises are major in scope involving various combinations of sea, land, and air forces from different members of SEATO while others are much more limited in objectives and participation. "Sea Lion," the fifth naval exercise, beginning April 28, 1960, was the largest up to that time with more than 60 ships from all the members, thousands of men, and over a hundred planes participating. Although there is considerable room for improvement, the exercises have made marked progress since "Firm Link," which had the characteristics of an Armed Forces Day presentation in America. The cumulative effect over the years of the military exercises will bring greater dividends in the efficiency of combined operations held in the treaty area and in SEATO readiness to meet an aggressor. At the same time the exercises, though denounced by Communist China and the Soviet bloc, serve as a physical reminder to Peking that SEATO may not bend like a reed before Mao's East Wind. The presence of observers from some Asian nonmember countries at some of the exercises is significant.

Experience in the military maneuvers has called attention to areas where it is necessary to attain nonmaterial standardization. Here the Military Advisers have assigned responsibility for logistics to Great Britain, operations and training to the United States, and staff procedures and techniques to the SEATO Military Planning Office. The difficulties of achieving progress in the nonmaterial standardization field are real, but slow gains are being made.

In the military posture of SEATO bilateral assistance programs aimed at improving individual as well as mutual self-defense are an important consideration. Australia in 1958 provided training to 69 students from other SEATO members in its service institutions, and a New Zealand training program got under way in early 1960. In 1959 service personnel from Thailand, Pakistan, the Philippines, Cambodia, Laos, and South Viet-Nam were furnished training facilities under British auspices in the United Kingdom or overseas. The French military missions in Laos and Cambodia helped in the training of local forces, while Thai, Cambodian, and Laotian officers studied at French military institutions. The Philippines has made facilities available in specialized courses for Thai, Vietnamese, and Laotian military personnel. Between the creation of SEATO and the spring of 1959 the United States enabled almost 28,000 students from the other members of the alliance to finish military training courses in its service institutions. In 1959 about 4,400 men from states in the treaty area were in service schools located in the United States or abroad.

And, clearly, American military assistance in arms and supplies on a bilateral basis to a number of SEATO members and protocol states has remained significant. It should be pointed out, however, that the bilateral military programs to strengthen individual countries would probably be maintained or undertaken with or without the existence of SEATO. Insofar as the recipients are members, the bilateral programs indirectly contribute to SEATO's posture. Thus the Secretary General in his annual reports draws attention to such efforts.

The countering of Communist subversion quite naturally occupies considerable attention at SEATO headquarters. A Special Assistant to the Secretary General with an expert staff has recently been appointed to deal with the problem. The responsibility for "exposing" and checking subversion rests with the various governments, but SEATO can be of help to them as a center for the exchange and pooling of experience. For the United States SEATO provides a forum for presenting the American interpretation of the subversion threat. Composed of individuals from the intelligence agencies and police forces of the members, the Committee of Security Experts is in a good position to carry out its work; namely, to "identify, assess and exchange information on the nature and extent of the threat of Communist subversion, internal and external, to the Treaty

Area" and, when appropriate, to "suggest possible counter-measures for the consideration of the Council Representatives and through them of other organs of SEATO."[4] The Committee's biannual surveys provide valuable insights into the complexities of internal security. In November 1957, at Baguio, SEATO held a Seminar on Countering Communist Subversion, and in February 1960, at Lahore, a second seminar stressed specific aspects of the problem and recommended countermeasures.

SEATO's Committee on Information, Cultural, Education and Labour Activities considers the nature and impact of Communist propaganda in the treaty area. Although it does not have an intelligence unit, the Research Services Office in the Secretariat-General at Bangkok collects, organizes, and analyzes material focusing on international communism and its range of activities, especially in the area covered by the treaty. The regular reports and special studies distributed to the SEATO members are generally of more assistance to the Asian governments than to most of the Western powers. Part of the material provided by the Research Services Office is used by the Public Information Office of the Secretariat-General in its statements on special subjects and in its pamphlets "exposing" the activities of the Communists. Some SEATO members assist others in training personnel in countersubversive work.

A real handicap in the attempt of SEATO to cope with infiltration and subversion is the limited Asian membership, for the Communist effort is not restricted to one country. This handicap is particularly noticeable in neighboring states such as Burma, Thailand, Cambodia, Laos, and South Viet-Nam. Since Communist inroads in Cambodia and Laos, for instance, have direct effects in Thailand and South Viet-Nam, these four countries would profit from systematic joint efforts to counter the threat.

[4] Quoted by J. A. Modelski, "The South-East Asia Treaty Organization," *The Australian Journal of Politics and History*, May 1959, p. 37.

Common membership in SEATO has encouraged cooperation among the Philippines, Thailand, and Pakistan.

SEATO is making a real attempt to expand its cultural activities. From modest beginnings a substantial program has developed, supported by the recommendations of an Ad Hoc Committee on Cultural Policy in mid-1958 and approved on a long-term basis by the SEATO Council in April 1959. A highly successful South-East Asian Round Table concerned with the impact of Western technology on traditional Asian cultures was held in Bangkok early in 1958, with the participation of Japanese and Indian scholars at a meeting under SEATO auspices being especially noteworthy. In the same year 11 research fellowships, 12 post-graduate scholarships, 30 undergraduate scholarships, 6 travelling lectureships, and three professorships were available. The emphasis in the program is properly placed on the Asian members, the three SEATO professorships, for instance, being restricted to universities in Pakistan, Thailand, and the Philippines. A Conference of Heads of Universities held under SEATO auspices in Karachi in early 1961 gave educational leaders from member and nonmember countries an opportunity to consider university questions of common interest. A SEATO cultural project in another direction involves aid to Thailand in the establishment of a Hill Tribes Museum. Although improving knowledge of respective cultures and developing awareness of common values are objectives that require many years of effort, SEATO's cultural program is basically sound and may provide an avenue for greater cooperation with nonmember Asian countries.

Besides the cultural efforts under the Manila Treaty there are numerous bilateral exchanges among the signatories outside the SEATO framework. In his annual reports issued in 1959, 1960, and 1961, for instance, the Secretary General specifically referred to the cultural programs of each of the eight member countries. It was pointed out that the protocol countries, Cambodia, Laos, and Viet-Nam, benefited from most of these programs. Thailand in 1958 offered educational assistance at the higher level to 85 students from Laos. France maintained 145 professors and teachers in Viet-Nam and Laos, and shared in providing the salaries of 200 professors and teachers in Cambodia with the Phnom Penh government. In 1959 the French budget for cultural and educational aid to these countries was about $5 million. Although these programs would have been maintained without SEATO, they tend to bolster the cultural efforts of the international organization.

The Asian members have not ceased making the criticism that they should receive far greater economic assistance than nonmembers. A combination of domestic and international considerations caused Thailand in the years 1960-62 to be particularly sensitive on this point. The Committee of Economic Experts has studied the impact of defense efforts on the economies of the member states and the various obstacles in defense production. Although the 1958 economic offensive by the Sino-Soviet bloc, especially by Peking, brought intensified SEATO consideration of the problem, a massive SEATO aid plan as a means of countering a Communist economic offensive has not been accepted in Western circles as an alternative to existing channels. Under the SEATO label Australia has allotted increasing aid in noncombat material to strengthen the military potential of the Asian members and South Viet-Nam, but this significant though modest step has not established an aid pattern among the Western powers.

Largely as a result of pressure from the Asian signatories, a SEATO Graduate School of Engineering was opened in Bangkok in September 1959. Although, apart from fees, its support comes from SEATO powers, it may be attended by properly qualified graduate students from both member and nonmember countries, with the emphasis quite naturally being placed on the training of South and Southeast Asians. The response to this opportunity on the part of Asians whose governments do not belong to the international organization will be particularly interesting to watch. Designed to increase the supply of technically trained craftsmen in Thailand, the Philippines, and Pakistan, a Skilled Labour Project under SEATO has resulted in agreements, especially on the part of the United States, to provide training assistance in certain needed fields. Australia is assisting both Thailand and Pakistan in this way, and a Military Technical Training School has been organized near Bangkok. New Zealand is providing technical training in maintenance to a number of Asians.

In April 1959 the SEATO Council approved an American proposal for a SEATO project in cholera research and asked the members to participate in the effort. As recommended by a survey mission, a systematic effort for better control and possible eradication of the dread disease has been undertaken through the establishment of research laboratories in Thailand and East Pakistan. A Conference on Cholera Research was held in Dacca in December 1960. At its meeting in May 1960 the Council decided to convert the Cholera Research Project in Thailand to a General Medical Research Project concerned with other diseases as well.

In March 1961 the Council supported a proposal for a regional agricultural research program. Two years before, at the suggestion of Thailand, it had requested the Council Representatives to consider the feasibility of establishing rural development centers in the countries of the Asian members. In May 1960 the Council noted the progress made in a Meteorological Communications Project as a result of the visit of a survey team to Thailand, the Philippines, and Pakistan, and it approved an American proposal to study the question of creating an Institute of Tropical and Sub-Tropical Agriculture. A Conference on Community Development was held in Baguio in December 1960, and the following March the SEATO Council supported a Thai proposal for a community development project in the northeast part of the kingdom. In 1960, it agreed that the Committee of Economic Experts was free to consider relevant economic problems of the member states on an advisory and technical basis, but with decisions on such subjects to be made only by the respective governments or Council Representatives.

Although economic cooperation within the SEATO framework is limited, the Secretary General in his annual report in 1959 called attention to the fact that in 1958 total aid to the Asian members of SEATO and the protocol states was estimated at more than $600 million. In his report of 1960 he set the figure at "more than $777 million" for 1959, and in the one of 1961 at about $623 million for the preceding year. He specifically referred in the reports to the bilateral aid programs of Australia, France, New Zealand, the United Kingdom, and the United States. Since the problems of poverty and underdevelopment are widespread in South and Southeast Asia, SEATO's limited Asian membership necessitates the use of channels much broader than those SEATO can provide.

The Public Information Office of the organization has the important task of winning support for the alliance and its objectives through various forms of publicity in four languages—English, Thai, Bengali, and Urdu. Employed in this work are a public relations officer and more recently a radio officer, and in October 1959 a Thai TV station in Bangkok began to carry a weekly program. SEATO publicity can be disseminated officially only through the small Public Information Office and through the channels of member governments, which represent peoples of great cultural, economic, and political diversity. Moreover, the basic climate of opinion on the whole has not been favorable, for the international organization has suffered both from the criticism of the uncommitted Asians and from the apathy of many of its own member peoples. And finally, there is the problem of how to reach large masses of Asians, especially at the village level. Despite all these obstacles, the Public Information Office is trying to make the best of the situation through an expansion and diversification of activities.

In the evolution of SEATO a significant interpretation by the United States and Thailand of obligations under Article IV was written into a joint statement issued on March 6, 1962, by Secretary of State Dean Rusk and Foreign Minister Thanat Khoman. The United States declared that its obligation under the Manila Pact to help Thailand in the event of "Communist armed attack" was "individual as well as collective." Moreover, Secretary Rusk specifically "reaffirmed" that the stated obligation was not dependent upon "prior agreement" by all the other SEATO members. As for indirect aggression, the joint statement indicated that the United States believed its SEATO commitments to Thailand and its military and economic assistance agreements with the kingdom established "an important basis" for American actions to assist the latter in coping with the matter. Included in the statement was a strong reaffirmation by the United States that the maintenance of Thai independence as well as integrity was "vital" to the American national interest and to the peace of the world. It was asserted that Washington had the "firm intention" of helping Bangkok resist Communist subversion and aggression.

The American interpretation of Article IV of the Manila Pact and the given assurances helped to remove many but not all of the Thai apprehensions about U.S. intentions and the value of SEATO which had arisen over the continuing Communist inroads in Laos. In effect, American obligations to Thailand were being placed on a basis somewhat comparable to those to the Philippines. Arms deliveries to Bangkok would also be speeded as much as possible. With different degrees of enthusiasm various other members of SEATO proceeded to interpret their obligations under the Manila Treaty as both individual and collective. Thailand believed a way had been found to bypass what it considered to be British and especially French obstructionism in SEATO.

The U.S. interpretation of the Manila Pact was given a test only a few weeks later. In early May the Pathet Lao forces deliberately broke the cease-fire in Laos, captured Muong Sing and Nam Tha in northern territory not far from Communist China, and advanced toward the Thai border on the Mekong. On May 15 after joint consideration the United States agreed to Thailand's request for the stationing of units of U.S. armed forces in the kingdom to help safeguard the territorial integrity of the country against the threat of Pathet Lao forces. Washington emphasized that the step, defensive in nature, was consistent with the Charter of the United Nations. The Secretary-General of the world organization was informed of the action. The obligations under the Manila Treaty provided the legal framework, although the "individual" rather than the "collective" interpretation of the obligations was invoked. As a result, the members that decided in the crisis to station armed forces in Thailand at the latter's request took the step under a bilateral arrangement with the Thai government. The SEATO governments meanwhile were in consultation on the situation; the Council Representatives, in fact, met on May 16 to hear American and Thai statements on what was being done to help safeguard Thai territorial integrity. They observed that "continuing consultations" were under way concerning possible action by other members. Washington, it is evident, favored a demonstration of widespread solidarity.

Great Britain, Australia, and New Zealand followed the United States in sending armed forces to Thailand. Although they were token forces—small air units from all three plus a platoon of jungle paratroopers from New Zealand—they pointed up the fact that five members of SEATO were taking concrete military measures to counter the Communist threat arising from the Laotian situation. France, as could be expected, was not willing to furnish any forces to Thailand under the circumstances; the Philippines was ultimately prepared to take the step; Pakistan was opposed to the principle of sending token troops but could be expected to help if the threat became worse. The United States, it is not surprising, provided by far the major portion of the outside forces; for a while there were 5,000 combat troops from the army, marines, and air force. Seven hundred men of the 809th Battalion of the Army Engineers had been sent to Thailand in February to help in road construction, and over 300 men were now with the Military Assistance Advisory Group. Among the combat troops the First Battle Group of the 27th (Wolfhound) Infantry of the 25th Division had already gone to Thailand in April for SEATO exercises and had stayed for subsequent joint Thai-American training. Lieutenant General James L. Richardson, Jr., an expert in guerrilla warfare, was placed at the head of a newly created United States Military Assistance Command, Thailand, under General Paul D. Harkins, who was also the commander of the United States Military Assistance Command, South Viet-Nam.

Confidence in the Manila Treaty was strengthened as a consequence of the response to Thai appeals. SEATO was viewed by a number of critics as having some teeth in it, but they still believed with reason that the real test was in the future.

SEATO and Inter-Asian Relations

Activities under the Manila Pact have demonstrated a tangible degree of cooperation among the Filipinos, Thai, and Pakistanis in the treaty area. The three Asian members are willing to associate in joint efforts partly because there are no controversies between them; their geographical separation avoids the many problems that can result from common borders. Given a broader Asian membership in SEATO, local disputes among members would probably assume greater proportions. Although the international organization has encouraged more cooperation among the Philippines, Thailand, and Pakistan than would have occurred otherwise, each is mainly concerned with problems involving its immediate neighbors, matters not effectively handled by the organization because of its restricted Asian membership. Moreover, the three Asian partners have a stronger relationship with Washington than with each other. The Philippines tends to place greater emphasis on the Mutual Defense Treaty with the United States than on SEATO; Thailand is well aware that the policy of Washington is decisive in the event of aggression against the kingdom; and Pakistan places great weight on the attitude taken by the United States.

Relations between the Asian members and nonmembers over the question of SEATO have gradually changed since the signing of the Manila Treaty in 1954. Though basically uncommitted in foreign policy, the attitudes of Indonesia, Burma, and Cambodia have fluctuated in response to both domestic and international developments. The Djakarta government of President Sukarno was extremely critical of SEATO during the height of the revolt in Sumatra and Sulawesi in 1958 but became more restrained during the mounting tension with the People's Republic of China concerning the Overseas Chinese in the archipelago. The Burmese governments of Premier U Nu tended to be more openly critical of the international organization than those led by General Ne Win. Developments in Tibet and along the Sino-Indian border have caused apprehension in Rangoon. Although

Cambodia has been very hostile to SEATO whenever Prince Norodom Sihanouk has had border flare-ups with Thailand and South Viet-Nam, the kingdom realizes its importance as a counterweight to Communist might. The Republic of Viet-Nam has remained consistently sympathetic to the Bangkok organization; in fact, President Ngo Dinh Diem has indicated a desire to join it. In Laos, different regimes have shown varying degrees of support or hostility toward SEATO. The Federation of Malaya has remained basically sympathetic to the Manila Treaty. In South Asia, India has been less critical of SEATO since its boundary dispute with Communist China assumed serious proportions.

SEATO has become less of a divisive factor among Asian states as more Asians recognize the need for its existence, given the clear-cut menace of Communist China and the inability of the countries of Southeast Asia to agree on common measures to meet the threat. In fact, if the Laotian crisis of 1960-62 had led to the dissolution of SEATO, there would have been many regrets, even if not always publicly expressed.

SEATO AND HYPOTHETICAL SITUATIONS

In the event of overt Communist armed aggression against a member state in the treaty area, Article IV, paragraph 1, of the Manila Pact would be invoked. SEATO's decision to aid the victim of aggression would have to conform to the respective constitutional processes of the signatories. It would, however, be possible for the organization to designate members to conduct the military operations. The decision to act could be taken by the Council Representatives in Bangkok upon instructions from their governments, by a specially convened meeting of the SEATO Council of Foreign Ministers, or by other means, depending on the urgency of the situation. Action taken under Article IV, paragraph 1, would be immediately reported to the United Nations Security Council.

If the armed attack were against a member state in Southeast Asia, SEATO would be the chief means for coping with the emergency. Thailand and the Philippines would not attempt through traditional diplomacy or through the machinery of the United Nations to find a substitute for SEATO, although they would undoubtedly welcome efforts on as broad a scale as possible, even if only moral, to supplement support under the Manila Pact. American aid to the Philippines would fulfill obligations under the Mutual Defense Treaty and SEATO, and to Thailand under SEATO and the further assurances of March 6, 1962. Geography, however, renders unlikely an isolated Communist attack either on the Philippine Islands defended by the superior sea and air power of the United States, or on Thailand which can be invaded by land only with the connivance of one or more neighbors.

In another hypothetical situation the Communists openly invade the two protocol states. The initial attitudes of the Republic of Viet-Nam and of Cambodia toward SEATO would differ. South Viet-Nam, which is not a member of the United Nations, would immediately invoke SEATO; but Cambodia would probably turn to the organization only as a last resort. Although military events might allow little time for decision, Cambodia would probably seek to exhaust the possibilities of the United Nations and to use the traditional methods of diplomacy, including appeals to India to intercede on its behalf. The Khmer kingdom might have a little more time for decision since a land invasion could only come through Laos, South Viet-Nam or Thailand. Either of the protocol states, it should be noted, is free to ask the aid of friendly powers.

In a third set of circumstances involving overt Communist armed aggression in Southeast Asia, this time against Burma, which is neither a member nor a protocol state of SEATO, nor subject to any special security arrangement, the only technical obligations of any signatories of the Manila Pact are those arising from common membership in the United Nations. In response to questioning, Secretary Dulles made this point clear to the Senate Committee on Foreign Relations. It would be possible for Burma to appeal for help to the SEATO powers and for them to grant it. Yet, it would be difficult for Burma to be quickly accepted as a formal member of the international organization or to receive protection as a protocol state, since each of the eight original members would have to approve in accordance with its constitutional processes. In the United States, for instance, Senate acceptance is necessary for either step. Burma would certainly appeal to the United Nations in the event of Communist attack and would also seek the active assistance of India as an interested neighbor. But in the end the United States and other members of SEATO might be the best source of help, as they could take quick action upon request without falling back upon technicalities.

If the Communists came to power in a Southeast Asian country through relatively free elections, the Bangkok organization could not intervene, for the internal affairs of a state are beyond the competence of SEATO. Usually the rising electoral strength of a local Communist party generates counterpressures to forestall its victory at the polls. Although an outside power can sometimes judiciously and discretely assist the anti-Communist forces, such foreign intervention can be a very effective Communist weapon in a highly nationalistic environment. In fact, in Southeast Asia the indigenous Communists themselves have been accused of being agents of an outside international movement.

Local Communist or pro-Communist groups have on occasion made impressive gains at the polls in three states of the region: Indonesia, Burma, and Laos. An outstanding example is Indonesia, where the PKI has become the largest vote-getter in Java and is making extensive inroads at the expense of other parties. With a claimed membership of 1.5 million in 1959 and a strength of 7.2 million in local elections in 1957, the PKI controlled through various organizations about 1.5 million workers in the leading trade union federation of the country, over 2 million peasants, some 500,000 women, 750,000 young people, and at least 200,000 former service men who fought for independence against the Dutch.

Although the party has not been officially represented in the cabinet since the independence of Indonesia in 1949, it has in general supported most of the governments since early 1952. Moreover, the PKI has an important place in the Supreme Advisory Council and National Planning Council appointed by President Sukarno under his concepts of Guided Democracy and Guided Economy. Approximately a fifth of the members of the Parliament appointed by the President in March 1960 are Communists or sympathetic to communism, a gain of about 5 per cent from the 39 PKI deputies elected to Parliament in the national elections of 1955. When the general elections scheduled for September 1959 were postponed for security reasons, it was widely believed in Indonesia that the Communists would have made further gains if the voting had been held. On the basis of its electoral strength the party hoped to join and eventually to dominate a coalition government. Although full of praise for President Sukarno himself, the PKI has opposed the restrictions on the general role of political parties in the country and has been critical of the marked influence of General Abdul Haris Nasution and the army in the nation's affairs. Rising Communist strength has produced a delicate balance among the PKI, President Sukarno, and General Nasution.

Should a Communist government gain control of a Southeast Asian country through victory at the polls, the problems confronting SEATO in the treaty area would be much more serious than those now occasioned by neutralist regimes. Yet, with the role of Tito as a precedent, it is by no means certain that a Communist government would unconditionally align itself with the Sino-Soviet bloc. Since genuine electoral victory would give such a regime more leeway than the traditional Communist takeover, the United States and other members of SEATO might find it best to adopt a cautious attitude.

Just as SEATO cannot legally intervene if the Communists should win at the polls in Southeast Asia, it cannot act against the development of militant neutralism that is abetted by the Communists and sympathetic to them. The only possible action is conventional diplomatic activity on the part of the individual states particularly concerned. In the new Asian and African countries neutralism may be firmly associated with nationalist feelings and therefore intensified by outside interference.

In Cambodia, it is argued, neutralism has often assumed militant characteristics, has been unduly encouraged by the Peking-Moscow axis, and has at times appeared to be leaning toward the Communist bloc. In guiding the policies of the kingdom, Prince Norodom Sihanouk has taken advantage of the cold war and has sought to profit from both sides. Yet it is also clear that the traditional rivalries of the Khmers with the Vietnamese and Thai have inflamed the Prince's nationalism, have aroused his suspicion of the United States as an ally both of Thailand and, in effect, of the Republic of Viet-Nam, and have made him more willing to cooperate with Communist China. The Prince is opposed to any suggestions that his country join SEATO. When he became convinced during his visit to Manila in early 1956 that the Filipinos were trying to get him to relinquish his neutralism, the trip served to weaken rather than strengthen relations between the Philippines and Cambodia.

Despite a policy of neutralism in foreign affairs, Prince Norodom Sihanouk is strongly opposed to communism in his own country. For instance, none of the members of his *Sangkum Reastr Niyum* (People's Socialist Community), which held all the 62 seats in the National Assembly as a result of the elections of March 23, 1958, was known to have Communist affiliations, although some may have had pro-Communist sympathies arising from past associations. Later, in the elections of June 10, 1962, all candidates of the *Sangkum Reastr Niyum* were returned unopposed. The Pracheachon party is a legal political front for the Communists but the membership is very small; it does not attack the Prince or the monarchy, and it strongly encourages a policy of neutralism in foreign affairs. On the other hand, since early 1956 the Chinese schools in the kingdom have been very active in promoting communism, which has made inroads among the Buddhist monks in recent years.

Cambodia's success over the long haul in pursuing a neutral policy is dependent upon a number of factors, the most important one of which is entirely outside its control. At home the government must have steady support in its posture from all significant political forces in the kingdom. If any strong pressure arises for alignment with one or another of the rival powers, the posture of neutralism is placed in jeopardy. The country should also have a national defense capability that would cause a potential enemy at least to pause before mounting an invasion. But even more important, Cambodia's policy of neutralism requires the existence of a balance of power to be successful. In a situation where one power grouping tends to offset another, a weak state may manage to steer a neutral course by adroit diplomacy. Nevertheless, the difficulties are immense, even for a country like Sweden which has more of the requirements for a successful policy on neutrality. Domestic developments inside Cambodia and the international situation in Asia may well create conditions in the future where the Khmer kingdom is no longer able to play the role of a neutral.

The concept of nonalignment in Southeast Asia raises the fundamental question as to whether a new state can enter into an alliance with a Western power or join SEATO without losing the respect of its Asian neighbors. Do the Philippines and the Federation of Malaya suffer a grave loss of prestige because of their respective ties with the United States and Great Britain? Or are the neutrals—Cambodia, Indonesia, and Burma—merely out of touch with international realities? Perhaps the example of Thailand, the only country in Southeast Asia which never lost its independence, has some bearing on the situation.

Upon achieving independence many Southeast Asian states severed their ties with the mother countries quite decisively. When independence had to be won by bloodshed, as in Viet-Nam and Indonesia, there were never any real prospects for a French Union or a Netherlands-Indonesian Union; but Malaya, despite the ending of the Emergency in July 1960, and the Philippines, despite the years since independence, still choose to maintain security ties with the former metropolitan power. The criticism in their own countries and among neighbors that they are not fully self-respecting members of the new Asia has not been sufficiently serious to cause a policy change in Kuala Lumpur or in Manila. Both governments are still convinced that the advantages of a Western alliance outweigh the disadvantages. Their conviction is shared in Bangkok where there is an absence of the emotional sensitivity so often found in countries that have recently acquired sovereignty. Thailand in SEATO is like Portugal in NATO in that it can enter into an alliance and not feel that it is weakening its traditional independence.

Although Cambodia, Burma, and Indonesia certainly reflect the widespread tendency of the newly independent states of Asia and Africa not to align themselves with foreign powers, pride in national sovereignty is not of itself sufficient to maintain neutrality over the long haul. As is clear, many Southeast Asians in the uncommitted countries near Communist China are already raising questions about policy for the future. Over the next decade, the dynamics of international communism almost certainly will reduce the possibilities of nonalignment, and alliances or security arrangements with the West will become more acceptable to Asian and African powers.

The Future of SEATO

In a consideration of SEATO's future it is necessary to distinguish between what is possible and what is desirable for the United States and to analyze the effects of each suggested course of action on Southeast Asian countries, the Communist bloc, and America with its Western allies.

Among the policies toward SEATO that Washington can adopt a number merit particular inspection. Some individuals feel that the Manila Treaty should now be abrogated and SEATO disbanded. The Communist threat, it is argued, is no longer overt aggression as in Korea but subversion as in Laos, and SEATO is not able to cope effectively with it. These critics note that the organization has failed to attract new members, that the prospects of this development are dim, and that genuine regionalism has been set back. Moreover, an alliance of Western and Asian states in Southeast Asia puts severe restrictions on flexibility and is ineffective because of the passions of Asian nationalism. According to this view, the Asians themselves must work out their own security system, if they think they need it, for without their own efforts any alliance is bound to be built on foundations of sand. SEATO, therefore, constitutes an obstacle to finding a sounder approach to international security in Southeast Asia. As for the United States, these critics argue that the best policy for its interests would be to fade into the background, though possibly expressing a willingness to help a victim of aggression if duly requested by its government. If security ties are mutually desired, the best approach at any rate is on a bilateral basis.

The disbandment of SEATO under the present conditions would be considered by its members and nonmembers alike as evidence of weakening on the part of the United States in its determination to oppose Communist aggression in Southeast Asia. Washington has put so much effort publicly and privately into its support of SEATO that a reversal in policy would cause many Southeast Asian leaders seriously to consider seeking an accommodation with Peking. Having assumed the obligations of commitment, the Asian members of SEATO would believe that they had been "let down." To prevent a serious decline of Asian faith in the United States, an arrangement of equal stature would have to replace SEATO at once. And here the valid question arises as to what could actually be done today.

The Communist world would greet the disbandment of SEATO with unrestrained enthusiasm; in Hanoi, Peking, and Moscow it would be interpreted as a step in American withdrawal from the Far East. A great propaganda victory would be achieved; even apart from other reasons, the Peking-Moscow axis would claim its unrelenting denunciation of SEATO had produced the desired results. Communist propaganda would take advantage of the misgivings in Southeast Asia, and the axis would be encouraged in efforts to weaken other American security arrangements in the Far East.

Despite certain criticisms of SEATO the Western members would not approve its present disbandment. Great Britain still has a substantial stake in the treaty area, and France under General de Gaulle is interested in the global role of the Fifth Republic. Australia and New Zealand are vitally concerned with security in neighboring Southeast Asia. All would be opposed to SEATO's abrupt end.

In terms of either practicability or results, it is neither possible nor desirable for the United States to bring about the early termination of SEATO in the present circumstances.

Another course of action might be for Washington to pursue a policy directed at the withering away of SEATO. A transition period of possibly ten years might be set for its demise. American steps could be taken on a gradual basis to soften the effects of an abrupt termination and to prepare for a possible substitute. But the objective—the abrogation of the Manila Pact and the disbandment of SEATO—would produce many of the same, though attenuated, reactions already mentioned.

If the Amercian position were openly stated, SEATO would not have to wait ten years to die; it would become a corpse the day Washington's attitude became public. The alternative, of course, would be for the United States to keep its decision a secret, but American positions on SEATO questions at various meetings would soon cause the other participants to "smell a rat." Moreover, the close ties between the United States and certain other countries like Great Britain and Australia would be impaired by American duplicity.

In practical terms, the suggested policy of letting SEATO mature like a cucumber ripening on the vine is impossible. The real question is the quick termination of the alliance. And the withering-away approach is undesirable either as a response to the Communist threat or as an indication of U.S. devotion to treaty obligations.

In marked contrast to a policy of terminating SEATO, either abruptly or gradually, would be an American course of action to strengthen it in every way possible. The conviction that a multilateral approach to security has far more utility than just a sole American effort finds its maximum application here. A supreme commander, joint headquarters, and a standing force might be instituted. Extensive economic aid under SEATO auspices might be inaugurated, and a much larger cultural program might be developed under the control of the organization. Greater multilateral emphasis might be given to SEATO's work in countering subversion, and American and allied diplomacy in Southeast Asia might put much more stress on the over-all role of SEATO.

Yet the effects of a program of maximizing the international organization might be more detrimental than beneficial. The rift between the Asian members and nonmembers could become more pronounced. Thailand and the Philippines would welcome a greater strengthening of the alliance, partly because it would place them in stronger positions. Asian countries not in SEATO would as a general rule resent the large build-up through the organization of some of their neighbors, while the inducements to join would still not be sufficiently strong to alter their present attitudes. Washington must maintain an extremely delicate balance between assistance to Asian signatories who have committed themselves and to those who choose publicly to sit on the fence. The Communists, of course, would deplore any strengthening of SEATO as evidence of American aggressive intentions in Asia, and they might try to take retaliatory measures by stirring up local trouble to divert the attention and efforts of the United States. As for the Western members of SEATO, an American policy of maximizing the organization would not be received with much enthusiasm, for they like to weigh carefully existing measures and various alternatives in the light of a developing situation. Australia, though, might be the most sympathetic to a greater strengthening of the Manila Treaty. In short, an American policy of maximizing SEATO is certainly possible, provided all the members agree, but not desirable at the present time.

A fourth course of U.S. action toward SEATO is one calling for moderate and gradual strengthening through steps not likely to arouse apprehensions among nonmember Asian states yet still significant enough to provide a growing deterrent to Communist China. Here future circumstances, such as the developing nature of the Communist threat and the emerging climate in Southeast Asia, can determine the ultimate fate of SEATO. Meanwhile the organization could have a steadying and stabilizing role in a fluid situation.

Under an American policy of moderate and gradual strengthening of SEATO, the deterrent in men and weapons would be further developed. A greater capacity for limited war in Southeast Asia will not pass unnoticed in Peking and will encourage friends of Washington. Both defense planning and military training exercises under the organization's auspices can be improved. Although more precise military commitments by the United States to its SEATO partners under the prevailing circumstances and the definitive working out of a division of roles and missions in the military field for different contingencies are not necessary at present, every possible effort must be made in Washington to have a posture of readiness and of determination to act if the need arises. Above every consideration the United States must not fall behind the Soviet Union in over-all deterrence.

On the local level the efforts of SEATO to combat subversion can be made more effective through further research and more experience. Although the Asian members of the organization should receive recognition in economic and technical assistance, SEATO should not become the vehicle of large-scale aid projects. The cultural programs can be expanded but not at the expense of neglecting nonmembers. Every attempt should be made to encourage the Asian partners in SEATO to help one another and to expand their mutual contacts. In the field of information activities there is clearly room for greater concentration and achievement.

SEATO headquarters at Bangkok could become a more effective regional center for gathering and interpreting information on security problems in Southeast Asia. Here the advantages of being on the spot and getting data firsthand are important. Policies based on the information can be formulated in the various national capitals, but real coordination can be attempted at the first instance at SEATO headquarters. There is also reason to hope that many of the organization's activities can be supported by Asian states who still do not want to join it. Observers at military exercises, participants at cultural seminars, and students in certain training programs can point the way. Thus efforts can be made that benefit Asians both members and nonmembers, that are acceptable to the Western participants, and that give the Communist states further cause to respect the independence and freedom of the countries of Southeast Asia.

Finally, if the membership of SEATO under appropriate circumstances were reduced to the states who have a primary concern in the area, the organization might be strengthened. At any rate SEATO could survive the withdrawal of France and Pakistan. An American policy of moderate and gradual strengthening of SEATO under the present circumstances is both possible and desirable. For Washington, the commitments are a calculated risk, but worth it.

[SIX]

Indirect Aggression: Challenge and Response

In the range of Communist activities in Southeast Asia the various forms of indirect aggression—infiltration, subversion, and insurgency—present extremely grave problems of internal defense to local Asian governments. Forced to cope with Communist dangers ranging from subversion of a newspaper through guerrilla warfare in the rural areas to an attempted *coup d'état* in the capital city, the governments of Southeast Asia as a whole often possess neither the political power nor the economic resources necessary to take firm measures. And lacking these capacities, they sometimes tend to equivocate, rationalize inaction, or support half-measures. The United States has determined to reinforce these hard-pressed governments, recognizing that it is much easier to take counteraction against subversion than to overthrow an established Communist regime.

Indirect aggression is also difficult to combat by means of collective security, for the evidence is often too ambiguous and the degree of provocation is frequently too low to risk the disproportionate extension of conflict implied in allied intervention—in particular, the risk of counteraction by Communist "volunteer" troops. Here SEATO faces some of its gravest problems. Whenever considering intervention in a country subjected to Communist infiltration, SEATO authorities must first investigate the situation and then decide if the danger calls for troop movements. A fast-moving crisis requires different responses, often graduated in degree of effort; but when several SEATO powers are involved, considerable difference of opinion can easily arise over interpreting evidence and determining action. Indirect aggression rarely lends itself to clear-cut legal definition, and the Communists are thereby enabled to move in the penumbra of legality. The United Nations, much larger and much more remote than SEATO, would experience still greater difficulties in actually determining the presence of indirect aggression, especially in the complicated circumstances prevailing in Southeast Asia. Finally, there is the difficult issue as to whether the attempted subversion of a government springs from purely local grievances (perhaps even well-founded grievances) or is inspired, aided, and abetted by outside Communist centers. The Western powers, singly or collectively, have no wish to find themselves intervening in some purely internal problem of a state in Southeast Asia; they have no desire to don the mantle of Metternich.

Communist indirect aggression can best be considered first by surveying its various manifestations and then by examining in some detail different countermeasures. It must be remembered that Communist violence has occurred, in differing degrees of seriousness, in every country of the region. As for the study of countermeasures, it is most revealing to focus on the Philippines, Malaya, Laos, and South Viet-Nam.

MANIFESTATIONS OF INDIRECT AGGRESSION

Countries faced with Communist subversion have to diagnose the precise dangers before trying to devise remedies. Subversion can be understood as an insidious assault from within upon the institutions of a nation, culminating on occasion in armed revolt or insurgency. If Communist inspired, subversion or insurgency is supported by international communism acting with many different weapons—psychological, economic, diplomatic, and military—as the situation dictates.

Since the Bolshevik Revolution there has been Communist exploitation of discontent in Southeast Asia. As long as the Western powers ruled most of the area, many local nationalists were susceptible to Communist support as one means of expelling the foreign masters. The Communists tried to capture the revolutionary leadership of the nationalist movement and divert it to their own ends, but their only outstanding success was with Ho Chi Minh in Viet-Nam. In almost all the area independence was won under dedicated nationalists who were not Communists, forcing the latter to develop new tactics. They could still capitalize on resentment against former imperialism if the new governments retained close economic or other ties to the former mother countries or if the metropolitan powers kept extensive economic interests. The Philippines, still containing American bases, and Indonesia, with its large Dutch investments until late 1957, presented the Communists with a number of opportunities, but on the whole the Communists could no longer pose as the vanguard of nationalism in Southeast Asia.

As the vehicle of nationalism lost much of its utility for communism, the effort to exploit economic grievances was intensified. A peasant in Pampanga in central Luzon, long exploited by his landlord and pessimistic about effective relief from his government, may listen to Communist promises. A worker in Surabaja in Java, perhaps a member of a labor union, may come to accept Communist blandishments as the best hope for him and his family. A university graduate in Rangoon, unable to find a position commensurate with his years of study and sacrifice, may hope to fulfill his ambitions through joining the Communists. A politician in Bangkok, hungry for wealth and influence, may conclude that Communist China represents the wave of the future. A mountain tribesman in Phong Saly, one of the minorities in the Kingdom of Laos, may believe his interests will be best served by cooperating with his kinsmen just across the border in Communist Viet-Nam. Impressed by the growing prestige of some relative in Canton, a Chinese journalist in Penang may dream of future advancement under a Chinese-dominated, pro-Communist Malaya. A Khmer political refugee may conclude that he can only regain his country (and his property within it) by joining the Communist movement. Intellectuals in many Southeast Asian countries, experiencing the effects of rising inflation on their low incomes, may see in the controlled economy of the People's Republic of China a method applicable to their own nations; they may also be convinced by Communist propaganda that the "imperialist" legacy still operates within their present governments. In the case of many people, of course, not just one factor but a combination causes their conversion to communism. It further seems probable that no particular cultural pattern is especially susceptible.

The exploitation of economic unrest in the underdeveloped areas creates a certain dilemma for the Communist powers. In their various aid and trade programs, the People's Republic of China and the Soviet Union claim to be reinforcing the economies of countries receiving aid. Insofar as they succeed in this official goal, it would seem that greater prosperity would tend to reduce the broad appeals of communism. Most students of totalitarianism believe that the deterioration or wrecking of a nation's economy favors Communist subversion, so here the public and the conspiratorial activities of international communism can conflict.

The Communists are well aware of the complementary value of sympathetic masses and a dedicated elite. A "hard core," carefully trained in the techniques of subversion, superbly disciplined, and fanatically devoted to the cause of communism, forms the indispensable nucleus for an eventual take-over of government. Majority support is not always necessary; if the majority is apathetic or divided, a determined minority can win power. Youth is a main target of subversion, second only to labor, for it is energetic and idealistic and holds the key to tomorrow. Burma has experienced probably the greatest penetration of a well-established national education system in the independent countries of Southeast Asia.

In the Soviet Union and China there are facilities where Communists from the area are given careful training for subversion. In efforts to infiltrate the people and to isolate and divide the opposition, the use of local Southeast Asians is of the utmost value. As citizens sharing the racial and cultural background of their fellows, they do not suffer from the handicaps facing any foreigners operating on alien soil. Speaking the local dialects and knowing the people's minds, they can easily make contacts and exploit grievances; they are also better able to conceal their links with international communism, when desirable, and to furnish intelligence. Indigenous, undeclared Communists cannot easily be stopped from infiltrating into responsible positions and quietly winning converts.

Although dedicated leadership is essential for a Communist take-over, mass support is certainly not neglected. By means of a net of "front organizations" the influence of the party can be extended far beyond its limited membership. In such organizations many individuals may not be aware that they are being used by the Communists, especially when the nominal leadership is in the hands of well-known non-Communists. The receptivity of the masses subject to subversion can be just as important as the skillfulness of Communist infiltration. If governments are unpopular or unstable and political parties fail to be effective, the Communists may seem to be the only real alternative. When matters are in the balance, mass organizations under Communist discipline may stage demonstrations, call strikes, precipitate riots, and institute sabotage, thus undermining the government and disrupting the economy. In such a "mass struggle" it is clear that certain groups have key strategic value; for instance, unions involving transport workers, dockers, or engineers, and students from the middle schools carefully organized for action. By staging successive waves of popular unrest the Communist can erode the capacity and the will of a local government to resist.

Various kinds of Communist fronts operate in Southeast Asia on both the national and international levels, often appealing to special-interest groups for specific objectives. The titles and organization of particular fronts may vary from country to country, but all attempt to reach the widest possible public by means of all the new mass media as well as old-fashioned public meetings. The fronts have been particularly active in Indonesia and Burma. Some international front organizations present a façade of popular ideals, such as peace or independence, which are widely acceptable to non-Communist opinion. In many respects these fronts are like icebergs, one-eighth above water and seven-eighths beneath. Each organization has national committees and local branches, but the pattern is not regular throughout Southeast Asia.

The World Peace Council (WPC) may be taken as a suitable example of an international front organization. The great majority of the members of the WPC are actually Communists or fellow-travelers, although only a minority of the participants are citizens of the Communist states. An Executive Bureau prepares for the meetings of the Council, held preferably in a non-Communist country and at least once a year, where appeals are launched and resolutions approved in line with Communist objectives. Both the President and the Secretary General are normally Communists or prominent fellow-travelers, as are most of the officers of the WPC. National Peace Committees in different countries nominate new members for the World Peace Council and for the Executive Bureau, but the latter is empowered to select all members from its list of nominees. Other international fronts are also represented on the Council or Bureau. In their own words the Communists seek through the WPC to maximize the "mass base of the peace movement" so that "the fighters for peace" can vigorously expose "the warmongers, the enemies of mankind."

In 1952 the WPC established a Peace Liaison Committee for Asia and the Pacific which prepared for the unofficial "Asian Conference for Relaxation of Tension" held in New Delhi in 1955, just prior to the meeting of the Bandung Conference. An Asian Solidarity Committee with subsidiary national branches came to function, and by late 1957 Africa was associated in the movement, Cairo became the center of activity, and Russian Communists assumed a more important role. In December an Afro-Asian Solidarity Conference was opened in Cairo, and an Afro-Asian People's Solidarity Council with a permanent secretariat was established. In the Far East the stress on "Asian solidarity" develops the concept that Asian countries outside the Communist fold have many common traditions with the People's Republic of China and the Soviet Union, including common opposition to "Western imperialism." The Afro-Asian Solidarity Movement is the major Communist front organization in South and Southeast Asia.

The World Federation of Trade Unions (WFTU) is now another international Communist front organization. The General Council of the WFTU includes labor representatives from Indonesia, Burma, and the Democratic Republic of Viet-Nam. An Asian Liaison Bureau of the labor front was dissolved, however, in April 1958. Cooperating with both the WFTU and the WPC are front organizations for women, youth, and students: namely, the Women's International Democratic Federation (WI DF), the World Federation of Democratic Youth (WFDY), and the International Union of Students (IUS). The WIDF, for instance, held an Asian conference in 1949 to consider the "unity of women . . . in the struggle against colonialism and for national independence, democracy and peace."[1] Other international fronts appealing to different groups are the World Federation of Teachers' Unions, the World Congress of Doctors, the International Organization of Journalists, the International Association of Democratic Lawyers, the Federation of Scientific Workers, and the International Federation of Resistance Fighters. Yet, apart from activities associated with the WFTU in Indonesia and the WPC, the impact of these different fronts in Southeast Asia is not yet pronounced.

The very titles of international front organizations illustrate the Communist penchant for words with solid propaganda value. In Southeast Asia the Communists try to associate words with positive impact—"democracy," "peace," and "social and economic well-being"—especially with the Sino-Soviet bloc while nasty words like "colonialism," "warmongering," and "capitalistic exploitation" are supposed to represent the Western powers. Party slogans also illustrate the Communist use of emotional words. As an example, the PKI in 1959 called for "struggle for an independent and democratic Indonesia" and "strengthening the international united front against colonialism and war." In

---

[1] Quoted by Jat Javangkul, "Political Subversion," *Seminar on Countering Communist Subversion* (Baguio, Philippines, 1957), p. 63.

Communist propaganda there is a striking verbal analogy between military conflict and political warfare.

It is not surprising that the pattern of infiltration and subversion in Southeast Asia reflects the legal status of the Communist party in different countries; where the party is legal, many of its operations can be carried on openly and where it is illegal, operations are entirely clandestine. If the Communists operate as a legal political party, they are eager to increase their electoral strength through appeals to nationalist sentiment and economic aspirations as well as through front organizations, obviously helpful in influencing voters. On the basis of its electoral strength the party may eventually be able to engineer membership in a "United Front" government, thus securing control over certain branches of administration. A systematic campaign is undertaken to win key cabinet posts, especially the ministry of the interior which controls the police. Eventually an attempt is made to replace cabinet officials from other parties with Communists, perhaps retaining a few subservient non-Communists for window dressing. As the Communist party comes into full control, elections are postponed until all opposition has been crushed; finally, all the apparatus of a police state is established to prevent the remnants of opposition from imitating the Communists' "evolutionary" road to power.

Where the Communist party is illegal, efforts are made to operate underground. Most of the Communist parties in Southeast Asia have gone through various phases of legality and outlawry, the latter usually because of resort to armed force against the established government. At the present time the party is technically legal only in Laos, Cambodia, Indonesia, and, of course, North Viet-Nam; and it has been outlawed in Thailand, the Federation of Malaya, the Philippines, South Viet-Nam, and Singapore. A kind of twilight zone exists in Burma where Communists in arms against the government are outlawed, while those not using armed force operate above ground. It should be noted that Lenin advocated both "legal and illegal work"; even if the party is legal in a given country, a Communist can be engaged in illegal activities as best befit the circumstances; he can use his open work as a mask for his secret activities. Where the outlawing of the Communist party drives the members underground, it is sometimes more difficult for the authorities to trace their activities. The Singapore Government White Paper of August 1957, for instance, detailed extensive Communist infiltration in the Crown Colony although the party had been outlawed since mid-1948. When outlawed the Communists can afford to conduct an all-out campaign of vituperation against their "reactionary" government; but where legal they are more apt to be selective in their criticism, perhaps censuring certain aspects of the government's domestic policy but supporting its possibly neutralist outlook in foreign affairs. In short, the Communists are thoroughly opportunistic in their attitudes toward the regimes of Southeast Asia.

Under promising circumstances the Communist parties in the region have not hesitated to resort to widespread sabotage, terrorism, and guerrilla activity—in other words, to organized violence in its many manifestations. In the terminology of the Communists a "revolutionary situation" exists whenever they believe they have a real chance to seize power. Theoretically this chance comes when subverted trade unions can bring the economy to a standstill, when the ministry of the interior and the police are subservient, and when the armed forces have been thoroughly infiltrated; but it should be stressed that these conditions are optimum. When the Communists at their Calcutta meetings in 1948 determined that there existed in Southeast Asia a "revolutionary situation," or something close to its equivalent, the prevailing conditions were basically the aftermath of the Pacific war. As the armed Communist revolts that broke out during that year in Indonesia, Burma, and Malaya failed, it could be said that the Communists misinterpreted the real situation. Yet the over-all price they exacted from the governing authorities was heavy, for the resources needed to suppress the insurrections could well have been used in economic and social development.

When armed revolts have been staged under Communist auspices in Southeast Asia, guerrilla warfare has usually been very important. For this, Mao Tse-tung's *Strategic Problems in the Anti-Japanese Guerrilla War*, written in May 1938, is an instructive guide. To achieve any real measure of success in Southeast Asia the guerrillas must utilize to a maximum the elements of surprise and mobility; they must have a knowledge of the jungle areas of operations, maintain depth, and profit from the use of favorable terrain; they must have some means of communication and an adequate intelligence network. The guerrillas themselves should be inspired with the justice of their cause, and be the military arm of a popular movement; they should receive civilian support in weapons, supplies, personnel, and intelligence. To gain their objectives, the guerrillas should restrict the development and exploitation of occupied areas in the hands of the foe, should harden the will of the civilian population to resist him, and should retard and disrupt the operations of the enemy, weaken his morale, and diminish his combat effectiveness. They should be able to exact a much heavier toll in blood and money on the part of the governing authorities than the price paid by themselves. The guerrillas may then be able to set up a permanent organizational base, enlarge it, and finally control substantial territory. At an advanced stage they may believe themselves capable of moving into positional warfare. The Viet-Minh forces, for instance, made the transition from guerrilla warfare in the jungles and swamps of Viet-Nam to the siege and capture of Dien Bien Phu.

As for the ultimate act, the use by the Communist powers of their military forces outside their territories in the classical sense of overt aggression, it seems likely that they will resort to this measure only if all other methods short of open warfare fail and if they believe a reasonable opportunity exists for a quick and inexpensive victory. And, to repeat a point, Communist China is more aggressive in Asia than the Soviet Union.

While local Communists within Southeast Asia seek to gain power one way or the other, the states of the Sino-Soviet bloc acting at the diplomatic level try to encourage those general sentiments which tend to tolerate or favor Communist policy. These attempts assume various forms such as the careful encouragement of "positive neutralism," the play on peaceful coexistence, and appeals to Asian solidarity. At the same time, efforts to inflame hostility toward the former colonial powers continue, particularly by harping on allegedly evil aftereffects of colonialism. If the rudimentary public opinion in Southeast Asia can be conditioned on international questions, popular opposition to communism may be weakened and the local Communists made stronger.

COUNTERMEASURES TO INDIRECT AGGRESSION

The most significant responses to indirect aggression have occurred in the Philippines, Malaya, Laos, and South Viet-Nam. All have faced or are facing subversion in many of its various forms; but in the Philippines and Malaya guerrillas have been largely defeated, the struggle is in full swing in South Viet-Nam, and in Laos the scales appear to have been tipped in favor of the Communists. One of the most obvious differences among the varying countermeasures taken in these countries concerns the degree of international involvement. In the Philippines the armed

Communist-led Hukbalahaps were defeated largely through national efforts; but Commonwealth forces have aided the Malayans before and after *Merdeka*, a number of international organizations have been involved in Laos, and the United States is playing an increasingly important role in counterinsurgency in South Viet-Nam.

THE PHILIPPINES

The Communist movement in its phase of an armed revolt against the Manila government reached its apogee in 1950. By the end of the previous year the Communist party of the Philippines (CPP) had an estimated active strength of 19,000; its military arm, the Hukbalahaps, 10,800; and its mass base, 54,000. Some Communists had already infiltrated into key positions in government and other influential circles. Large areas of central Luzon were dominated by the dissidents, and they were extending their influence into other parts of the islands like Iloilo in the Visayas. By 1952 the party expected to have a strength of 173,000, including the Huk fighters, and a mass base of 2.5 million; it then planned to seize power.

The fate of these plans becomes evident when it is observed that by 1962 the estimated membership of the CPP had declined to between 1,500 and 2,000, including less than 500 armed Huks, while the mass base had fallen to a possible 19,000. Apart from isolated incidents in central and southern Luzon, the People's Liberation Army (as the Huks styled themselves after 1950) no longer constitutes a military threat to the republic. Communist infiltration has been intensified, however, especially through the vehicle of Filipino nationalism. The Labor Unity Movement, the National Progress Movement, and the "Manila leftist intellectual circle" all have reflected these new efforts; and particular attention is being paid to labor unions, student groups, and government officials.

Filipino countermeasures against the Communist rebels clearly merit special attention. When Ramón Magsaysay became Secretary of National Defense in 1950, he initiated a realistic appraisal of all aspects of the Communist threat and concluded that the struggle against the foe had to be revitalized. A program of "all-out force and all-out friendship" was devised, one designed to crush the armed rebels by well-planned military force while offering a helping hand to those who renounced communism and sought integration in the national community. After Magsaysay became President of the Philippines in 1953, he led a still more determined attack upon the basic causes for popular discontent in the nation. In spite of his untimely death in 1957, Ramón Magsaysay stands out as one of the great humanitarian leaders in Southeast Asia.

For the policy of "all-out force" against the Huks the armed units of the Philippines were reorganized into battalion combat teams. Compact, self-supporting, and extremely mobile, these teams could function independently in small engagements and also join for larger operations under a united command. Eventually twenty-six of these teams came into action while specialized services were organized, including scout-rangers, dog teams, and horse cavalry. The scout-rangers, teams of an officer and seven enlisted men, were particularly effective in killing or capturing key Communist rebels. Small detachments of men were also set up in critical areas partly to stiffen communities living in the threat of Communist action and partly to preempt certain strategic terrain. Constant patrol activity served to wear down the dissidents by keeping them on the run, thus hampering their efforts to get supplies or regroup their forces. The government established a program to buy loose but serviceable arms and ammunition. Military intelligence was definitely improved, and, as confidence was restored, more civilians gave information to the authorities and withheld it from the rebels. When members of the Communist politburo working out of Manila were surprised and arrested, a serious blow was dealt dissident leadership; and in 1954 Luis Taruc, a key figure in the movement, surrendered. As part of a real effort to improve relations between the military and the people, a general overhaul of the military was undertaken, leading to improved professional efficiency as well as making many of the officers and men more effective in dealing with the public. Higher standards of discipline were imposed, morale was strengthened, and publicity was focussed on the improvements. Finally, the personnel in the armed forces was increased to 56,000.

In a complementary field of action a Civilian Advisory Committee, consisting of community leaders, was established in each province to assist in solving problems of law and order. Civilian commando units were also organized, usually led by regular service men, which maintained security in a community so that regular forces could be freed for offensive operations against the Huks. Psychological warfare was intensified in its various aspects. Monetary rewards for the capture, dead or alive, of high-ranking dissident leaders led to some being killed by their own followers. In 1960 the top remaining rebels, Dr. Jesus Lava and Castro Alejandrino, had on their heads government rewards roughly equivalent to $115,000; the figure was reduced in October when Alejandrino was surprised and captured.

As another way of weakening the dissidents, the resettlement of a number of carefully selected former Huks on army-sponsored EDCOR (Economic Development Corporation) farms has received considerable attention. The army engineers constructed the necessary installations for the settlers and their families, the navy transported them to Mindanao where the first EDCOR projects were undertaken, and other government assistance enabled them to get a new start in life. Although the amount of public land distributed was small and the number of settlers few, the program paid great dividends in publicity. The Communists, who had been stressing "land for the landless," were somewhat undercut. The army engineers, moreover, were not restricted to the EDCOR farms; they were utilized in digging artesian wells, building roads and bridges, constructing prefabricated school buildings, and assisting in other public works. Other government programs for the poverty-stricken peasants, especially in the rice granary of the nation in central Luzon, were also carried out, although the blueprints were often more impressive than the accomplishments. Resettlement projects and agricultural credit services, a Farmers' Cooperative Marketing Association and a Land Tenancy Commission to deal with agrarian disputes and tenancy problems, these and other devices were initiated or intensified in order to help the peasants. Army legal officers were even sent as field teams to assist in the solving of tenant-landlord problems.

The faith of the Filipinos in democratic institutions, weakened by the extensive frauds in the national elections of 1949, was strengthened by the success of intensive efforts to produce relatively free and honest elections in 1951 and 1953. A real attack was made by the Magsaysay administration against graft and corruption (usually styled "anomalies and irregularities" in government), while the efficiency of the public services was improved through various programs. Although the Communist party had already been declared illegal through a ruling of the Supreme Court in 1932, the Philippine Congress in the Anti-Subversion Act of 1957 specifically outlawed the organization and prescribed capital punishment for membership in it.

In the struggle against the armed revolt of the Huks, the United States gave technical and material help, but it was the Filipinos themselves who did the fighting and gained the victory.

Outside the military field, American assistance was employed along a broad front in strengthening the economy and bolstering the free institutions of the Philippines. Removal of the many ills upon which Communists thrive is a long-range process; but an energetic and able Philippine government, responding to the needs of the people, can do much to destroy the "social cancer" of the nation.

THE FEDERATION OF MALAYA

In June 1948 Communists rose in armed rebellion in the Federation of Malaya, at that time still under British rule. In its bid for power the Malayan Communist Party (MCP) sought to take advantage of the serious economic and security conditions—shortage of rice, poor housing, unemployment, inflation, and demoralization of police—still existing in the aftermath of the Pacific war. The rebellion was intended to paralyze work on the plantations and in the mines, thus denying rubber and tin supplies to the United States and destroying the dollar earning capacity of Malaya for the United Kingdom. The Communists also planned piecemeal conquest of different parts of the Federation, then consolidating these areas until they could establish the jurisdiction of a people's republic over all Malaya.

The armed rebels, later called the Malayan Races Liberation Army (MRLA), were almost entirely Chinese (and mostly immigrants at that), and only some 5 per cent of the men were Malays or Indians. The insurgents, led by Chin Peng, were inspired by both the Chinese and the Russian Communists. At its highest strength the MRLA may have included between 5,000 and 11,000 men—a formidable force for jungle operations. A Min Yuen or People's Movement, also largely composed of Chinese, operated as an undercover source to help the MRLA with recruits, intelligence, money, and supplies. While the membership of the Min Yuen may have reached somewhere between 60,000 and 100,000, most of its participants did not belong to the MCP. The Communists were not able to wreck the economy of the Federation, but they did impose a severe drain upon it. When military and civilian casualties are added together, over 11,000 were killed in the fighting; and setting aside all destruction of property, the cost of putting down the revolt is estimated at more than $500 million. Nevertheless, by 1962 the strength of the MRLA was given as less than 500, the Min Yuen may have fallen to as low as 10,000, and the membership in the MCP was estimated at 400. Since the Communist guerrillas were no longer a major security threat, the state of emergency had already been safely lifted on July 31, 1960. The MCP with Min Yuen support is now directing its major effort toward infiltrating and subverting political parties and other organizations in the Federation.

The methods used to reduce to relative impotency the armed Communist rebels in Malaya and the Philippines are worth comparison. As long as the Federation was a dependency of Great Britain, the latter had the ultimate responsibility for maintaining law and order; but after independence the United Kingdom continued its obligations, along with Australia and New Zealand, to help against the rebels. The Philippines, of course, was independent during the entire period of Communist insurrection and thus retained full responsibility.

Following the initial outbreaks in the Federation in June 1948, the British authorities declared a state of emergency throughout the country on June 18 and banned the MCP on July 23. An Emergency Regulations Ordinance, together with subsequent measures, gave the government in Kuala Lumpur extensive powers in the face of the crisis. Close cooperation was quickly established with the authorities in Singapore, and later with

Thailand when the guerrillas moved into the border area. As in the Philippines, a military effort was accelerated against the rebels in the swamps and jungles of the country. Effective adaptation to terrain, favorable to guerrilla warfare, was essential in combatting the "Communist terrorists" or "bandits." Great Britain marshalled military resources from various parts of the Commonwealth and Empire: ground, sea, and air support from the United Kingdom, Australia, and New Zealand, dayak trackers from Sarawak, units from the Fiji Infantry and the King's African Rifles, and, of course, forces from Malaya itself. Eventually an effective welding of the military, police, and civil capabilities of the government enabled it to bear heavily upon the rebels. Here the constitution of War Executive Committees at different levels was helpful.

The British considered it especially necessary to prevent the guerrillas from obtaining food supplies from villages on the edge of the jungle. Well over 500,000 Chinese squatters from whom the Min Yuen derived real support were resettled in New Villages. Through this extraordinary effort, started in 1950 as the Briggs Plan, between a fourth and a fifth of all the Chinese in the Federation (or more than a tenth of the total population) were resettled. The British were gradually able to declare more and more areas "white," or freed of the terrorists. As an indication of the improving situation, many wealthy Chinese became less willing to pay protection money to the Communists.

The effect on the rebels of Malaya's evolution to self-government and independence cannot be underestimated. Despite their propaganda, it was impossible to deny that after August 31, 1957, they were fighting the authorities of a sovereign Asian state. And another consideration should not be minimized. Previously the Malays had rallied to defend the government while the Chinese were generally passive; but under Tengku Abdul Rahman there emerged an Alliance of the United Malays National Organization with the Malayan Chinese Association, later joined by the Malayan Indian Congress, which created a real degree of cooperation between the Malays and Chinese and won an overwhelming victory at the polls in July 1955. After *Merdeka* the Alliance constituted the political foundation for the government of Tengku Abdul Rahman, the first prime minister of the state, and by winning 74 of the 104 seats in the lower house of Parliament in the election of August 19, 1959, it returned the Tengku to power.

As in the Philippines, the Communist rebels in Malaya were too far from the People's Republic of China to receive any important material assistance. A courier link has probably existed, however, and the MCP gets moral support from the Chinese Communists. At the same time, the People's Republic did not hesitate to recognize the independence of the Federation, but it is not surprising that Kuala Lumpur is still opposed to the establishment of diplomatic relations with Peking.

LAOS

Background of Subversion.

In the Kingdom of Laos subversion presented problems of greater complexity than those in the Philippines or Malaya since domestic turmoil was coupled with a direct confrontation of major powers. On the way to his inauguration in January 1961 it is significant that President-elect Kennedy discussed with President Dwight D. Eisenhower problems arising from this faraway country. North Viet-Nam and Communist China border directly upon Laos, and the frontier zones are so mountainous and so generally covered by thick jungles that the boundaries are poorly defined and hardly patrolled. Because communications facilities in the northern and eastern borderlands of Laos are nonexistent or inadequate, even with the administrative capital city of Vientiane, ideal conditions exist for infiltration and subversion. In addition to these factors, the people living in the Laotian-North Vietnamese frontier zones are tribesmen who do not think of the international boundary as a real dividing line between kinsmen living on either side. Neglected by the Lao-dominated government of the kingdom, these frontier tribes are often susceptible to Viet-Minh subversion. The Communists have thus been enabled to implement various techniques of indirect aggression at times of their choice and on a scale graduated to their own interests.

Since independence Laos has been subjected to severe Communist pressure: at home, from the Communist-dominated Pathet Lao, and from across the border, by the Democratic Republic of Viet-Nam; moreover, both these sources of pressure have been supported by Communist China and the Soviet Union. North Viet-Nam has given evidence, both before and after the Geneva settlement in 1954, that it considered Laos and Cambodia within its potential sphere of influence. In general, members of the Sino-Soviet bloc realized that if Laos fell into Communist hands, its strategic location in the heart of mainland Southeast Asia could be used to great advantage for Communist inroads into Thailand, Cambodia, and South Viet-Nam. The mere prevalence of political confusion in the kingdom, they knew, could facilitate indirect aggression; yet even without Communist pressure the Royal Government of Laos would have been continually agitated by factionalism among the non-Communist elements. The Mekong kingdom has seemed to have few of the requirements needed for a politically viable state.

Under these circumstances measures against subversion, whether on the domestic or international level, were extremely difficult to formulate and execute. A primary need was accurate information on just what was occurring at what places and at what time, but Communist propaganda can be effectively used not only to subvert the local populace but also to conceal Communist-inspired activities. If the Laotian government itself was not always able to get prompt, accurate, and reliable information, foreign governments had even more difficulties. At times authorities concerned with Laos have been forced to depend to quite an extent upon inference drawn from an emerging pattern of events.

Precise evaluation of reports of subversion presented another set of problems. As divisions within the Royal Government—civilian, military, or both—could lead to conflicting reports and competing efforts to gain international support, it was necessary for foreign governments to evaluate carefully the claims and motives both of the authorities in Vientiane and of the opposition. Genuine local grievances, not necessarily Communist-inspired, could also be the source of difficulties. As for Communist incidents, it was most desirable, if possible, to determine the real instigators of the trouble in order to estimate the immediate objectives of the indirect aggression. Ostensibly the immediate source of trouble was the Communist-dominated Pathet Lao within the kingdom, although the Democratic Republic of Viet-Nam was probably the outside instigator in many cases. The question quickly arose as to the respective roles of the People's Republic of China and of the Soviet Union, for in a rapidly changing situation it was unwise to take for granted an ironclad chain of command from the Pathet Lao to Hanoi and on to Peking and then Moscow. It is more likely that coordination among the Pathet Lao, Hanoi, and Peking usually prevailed, the support of Communist China being very important, while Moscow intervened in response to developments in the over-all global struggle.

Because crises in Laos could bear directly on the international climate, the timing of an outbreak was also significant. If the United States had possessed adequate information, it would have been much easier to exploit possible strains and frictions in the Communist bloc of nations. The long-range objective of international communism in Laos was clear—namely, to turn the kingdom into a satellite; but the immediate objectives were much less certain. They ranged from the consolidation of the Pathet Lao position in Phong Saly, Sam Neua, and Xieng Khouang, though the reconvening of the International Commission for Supervision and Control in Laos and of the Geneva Conference or its equivalent, to the formation of a coalition government in Vientiane under neutralist leadership but Communist-influenced, the possible establishment of a situation where the political party, the Neo Lao Hak Xat, could win at the polls, and even the overthrow of the Royal Government.

The proper evaluation of immediate objectives in Laos could be decisive in the determination of a response adequate to the challenge at a particular time. Actually, the Communists probably had a flexible set of immediate objectives, depending upon the success of their efforts in the light of the local and foreign response. Each crisis, in other words, may well have been an *ad hoc* situation. The level of provocation the Communists were willing to employ in Laos obviously required a counteraction on a varied and often graduated scale if success were to be achieved. And here again there was the problem of domestic politics in the kingdom. In stiffening the will and in strengthening the capacity of the Royal Government to resist, the United States tried to walk a tightrope between intervention and nonintervention in the internal affairs of the country. Actually it was not possible in the practical sense to keep out of the Laotian political caldron. Yet in the conduct of diplomacy, U.S. officials in Laos were usually more tactful than blunt.

In the cases of indirect aggression, the Royal Government was faced with a situation where the Communists deliberately made it difficult to establish in international law the existence of an armed attack. In appealing for foreign assistance, nevertheless, Vientiane had a number of possibilities open to it. The Royal Government might seek the support of the United Nations, if for no other reason than to attract world attention and marshal broad sympathy. If speed were essential, it might ask the help of friendly countries like Thailand or the United States. Up to mid-1962 Laos, as a protocol state, could invoke SEATO and thereby fulfill the important legal requirement of a formal government request. Yet this step, it was realized, should be taken on sound evidence and not as a hasty measure, for SEATO certainly would not respond to a premature and foolhardy appeal. In its policy choices the kingdom could also ask for the services of a body like the International Commission for Supervision and Control. And, of course, a combination of these and other measures was always possible.

In the summer of 1959 the subversive machinery of international communism in Laos was operating in second gear with the possibility of a shift to high. As far back as 1948 the Viet-Minh had been infiltrating Laotian villages with resident agents. On three separate occasions in 1953-54 these agents were helpful when full-scale invasions of Laos were undertaken by the regular forces of Ho Chi Minh, posing as "volunteers" aiding the "liberation" troops of the Pathet Lao. During the first invasion in April 1953 Prince Souphanouvong, leader of the Pathet Lao, set up a "resistance government" at Sam Neua, capital of the province by the same name. Sam Neua and Phong Saly, a province to the northwest, are both adjacent to the Democratic Republic of Viet-Nam, and the Geneva Conference had arranged in 1954 for the Pathet Lao forces already occupying these provinces to remain there on a temporary basis. Although the Geneva settlement required that the unity of the kingdom was to be preserved, the administration of Prince Souphanouvong refused to give practical effect to the jurisdiction of the Royal Government until a mutually acceptable agreement was reached on November 12, 1957.

During these years links between the subversive Viet-Minh and the subservient Pathet Lao were clearly shown. The Viet-Minh Communists provided a special staff near the border; they stationed a coordinating mission near the Pathet Lao headquarters in Sam Neua; and they furnished "advisers" to the various "ministries" of Prince Souphanouvong. In the military field, the Democratic Republic provided on its own soil training facilities for Pathet Lao forces, sent "advisers" to the staff of the latter, and on occasion allowed Viet-Minh troops to enter Laos for joint maneuvers. The military forces of the Pathet Lao rose from an estimated strength of less than 1,000 in 1954 to more than 6,000 in 1957. The marked increases in military equipment came from North Viet-Nam (probably from its own supplies), from mainland China, and from other Communist sources.

Even when the Pathet Lao were regrouped in Phong Saly and Sam Neua in 1954, a web of propagandists and infiltrators still remained throughout Laos. Some of the undercover agents had been carefully trained in North Viet-Nam, and they prepared arms caches, gathered intelligence, and recruited potential guerrillas. As a general rule the agents were carefully selected to work in places where they had grown up, retained friendships, and understood the local conditions. It is estimated that by the middle of 1956 more than 3,000 new recruits had been raised in Phong Saly and Sam Neua, thus releasing experienced partisans for work in other areas of the kingdom. Although subversion was attempted in every one of the ten provinces under the Royal administration, those bordering North Viet-Nam received particular attention. Provinces penetrated during the Communist invasions of 1953-54—Luang Prabang, Vientiane, Xieng Khouang, Thakhek, and Savannakhet together with the Bolovens Plateau in the south—were especially vulnerable. In addition to attempts to subvert the Lao villagers, efforts were made to subvert the ethnic minorities in the mountainous regions, particularly along the North Vietnamese frontier; some tribesmen were even encouraged to believe that the victory of the Pathet Lao would lead to a separate state for them. The Communists evidently achieved considerable success among both the Lao peasants and the ethnic minorities.

The Pathet Lao reached one of their goals in November 1957 when a coalition government under Prince Souvanna Phouma was established in Vientiane with two of their members—Prince Souphanouvong, half-brother of the prime minister, and Phoumi Vongvichit—in the cabinet. As parts of the general compromise Phong Saly and Sam Neua were subjected to Royal jurisdiction while the Neo Lao Hak Xat was recognized as a political party eligible to contest the supplementary elections for Parliament, and 1,500 Pathet Lao troops were officially integrated into the Royal Lao Army. The remainder were discharged, including 414 who were sick and disabled, but the entire 6,199 military personnel of the Pathet Lao turned over only the surprisingly limited number of 4,773 weapons. After the supplementary elections of May 4, 1958, the Royal Government informed the International Commission for Supervision and Control in Laos that the last phase of the Geneva agreements had been implemented in the kingdom.

The coalition government, however, survived scarcely a year. The success of the Neo Lao Hak Xat at the polls, coupled with continued Communist subversion, caused anti-Communist groups (especially the National Progressives and the Independents) to join forces in the Rally of the Lao People. Also, a Committee for the Defense of the National Interests was organized from among military officers, young civil servants, and businessmen. When a new cabinet was constituted on August 18, 1958, as a consequence of an enlargement of Parliament, the relative unity of the anti-Communist forces enabled Prime Minister Phoui Sananikone to leave out the two Pathet Lao representatives. The new government had a definite orientation against communism, opposing its "dangerous ideology" and seeking to prevent its "subversive dangers." Finally, on January 14, 1959, the National Assembly gave the Prime Minister special powers to reconstitute his cabinet and to govern for a year without the legislative body.

These developments were not at all to Communist liking. As it became clear that the Royal Government was seriously trying to suppress subversion, the Democratic Republic and the Pathet Lao tried to intimidate Vientiane in no unmistakable terms. On December 14, 1958, the Viet-Minh sent troops to occupy a small area along the Nam Se river in the Laotian province of Savannakhet and, in a series of notes to the Royal Government, claimed the territory. Vientiane protested to Hanoi and to the Secretary-General of the United Nations but did not try to force the Viet-Minh from the area. The Pathet Lao caused trouble through its two battalions which were officially integrated into the Laotian national army. The distribution of ranks led to controversy; and, although the Royal Government eventually yielded to the Pathet Lao demands, on May 11, 1959, the leaders of the two battalions refused to participate in the ceremony for the distribution of the ranks; instead, they ordered their forces to arm and deploy in preparation for eventualities. Three days later the Royal Lao Army gave the dissident soldiers the choice of resigning, submitting, or being considered rebels. On May 17 one battalion located in the province of Luang Prabang gave in; but the other left its camp in Xieng Khouang province the following day and escaped from encircling government forces to the North Vietnamese border, where some of its elements were reported to be fighting in the summer of 1959.

Communist China and the Soviet Union made common cause

in propaganda and diplomatic attacks upon the Laotian authorities. The Communist powers accused the Vientiane government, especially after December 1958, of flagrant violations both of the Geneva settlement and of the Royal Government-Pathet Lao agreements of 1956-57. The Laotian leaders were further criticized for their opposition to the reconvening of the international commission, alleged sympathy for SEATO, and supposed granting of American bases in the kingdom. They were charged with provoking both North Viet-Nam and Communist China, particularly the former through violations of its air space and land borders; and they were accused of cooperating with agents from South Viet-Nam and irregular Kuomintang forces. In its propaganda in June 1959 the Communist bloc was seeking to create the impression that a civil war touched off by a popular uprising had broken out inside Laos.

After fighting did begin in mid-July 1959, the diplomatic and propaganda resources of international communism were further used in support of the Pathet Lao. Hanoi, Peking, and Moscow called for the reconvening of the international commission and opposed any United Nations action or "presence" in the kingdom. A sustained attempt was made to intimidate the Royal Government and to deter the United States from intervention. Hanoi dedicated itself to the support of the Pathet Lao, styled for propaganda purposes the "patriotic movement in Laos." In fact, Radio Hanoi had for some months tripled its daily output in the Lao language. The psychological warfare of the Communist bloc, especially North Viet-Nam and Communist China, represented a very important part of its total subversive efforts in the Mekong kingdom.

The Summer Crisis of 1959

The Laotian crises in 1959 and again in 1960-62 provide an excellent opportunity to compare the countermeasures taken to indirect aggression, steps successful in the first instance and unsuccessful in the second. President Ho Chi Minh was in Moscow when a Laotian army outpost near the North Vietnamese frontier, in the province of Sam Neua, was taken on July 16 by forces under Communist control. This action initiated a series of armed attacks against units and positions of the Laotian army, especially in Sam Neua, although Phong Saly also experienced several incidents as did many other parts of the kingdom. While these military actions varied in magnitude and scope, they were basically guerrilla in character. Former members of the Pathet Lao Fighting Units, soldiers from the battalion that defected, and men from frontier minority groups appeared to constitute the main elements in the attacks. The military action reached its greatest intensity in the first half of September, particularly along the River Ma and near Sam Teu in Sam Neua, and then it degenerated into widely scattered incidents throughout the country.

In coping with the crisis, the Royal Government successfully resisted Communist and Indian efforts to reconvene the international commission. At the same time, Vientiane did not rush into involving SEATO; instead, its attempts to win foreign support were directed toward obtaining United Nations intervention and increased military aid from the United States. Yet this policy did not mean that Laos was indifferent to SEATO or, for that matter, to the sympathetic attitude of its neighbor Thailand.

On August 4 the Royal Government informed the Secretary-General of the United Nations of the crisis, simply asking him to pass on the "facts" to U.N. members. Sixteen days later, a special Laotian envoy officially invited the Secretary-General to suggest appropriate steps toward a peaceful settlement. On August 30 coordinated attacks were made at Muong Het and Xieng Kho and, becoming convinced that North Vietnamese troops had intervened, the Royal Government on September 4 formally invoked Article I, paragraph 1, and Article II, paragraph 2, of the Charter of the United Nations, requesting that "an emergency force should be dispatched at a very early date in order to halt the aggression and prevent it from spreading."[2] At the urgent request of the Secretary-General the Security Council convened on September 7 to consider the crisis in Laos. Dag Hammarskjold's basic position was that the United Nations should be prepared to help keep the peace in Laos, provided that it did not impair the arrangements made at Geneva; in consequence, he directed attention to the specific Laotian request for a United Nations emergency force.

With the support of Great Britain and France, the United States introduced a joint draft resolution calling for the Security Council to appoint a subcommittee (Argentina, Italy, Japan, and Tunisia were specifically named) to "examine the statements made before the Security Council concerning Laos, to receive further statements and documents and to conduct such inquiries as it may determine necessary," reporting back to the Council as quickly as possible.[3] The exact wording of the draft resolution is important, for the United States proposed that the Security Council undertake an inquiry rather than an investigation. The latter would be a substantive measure, thus subject to Soviet veto, but an inquiry would be a procedural step which could be approved by the vote of any seven members. During a long debate between the Soviet Union and other members of the Council over the procedural and substantive aspects of the draft resolution, the Moscow representative argued that since the resolution was substantive he could veto a prior resolution on its allegedly procedural nature. But the Security Council voted 10 to 1 that the American-British-French resolution was procedural and later proceeded to approve the measure by the same margin.

[2] Document S/4212.
[3] Document S/4214.

This Security Council decision was considered illegal by Moscow, establishing in its position a "very dangerous precedent." But the Western powers had managed to bypass a Soviet veto in order to establish a United Nations "presence" in Laos, perhaps a useful precedent for other crises. As an alternative to United Nations action in Laos, the Soviet Union indicated in a statement on September 14 that it favored a meeting "without delay" of the powers that had participated in the Geneva Conference on Indochina. The United States, Great Britain, and France rejected this Soviet suggestion in the belief that the recent action taken by the Security Council was preferable, although London and Paris were more inclined than Washington to believe that something could be worked out with Hanoi. The People's Republic of China and the Democratic Republic of Viet-Nam, of course, welcomed the Soviet proposal.

After receiving information at United Nations headquarters, the Security Council's subcommittee went to Laos on its fact-finding mission. On November 3 it reported evidence of "centralized coordination" in some of the hostile operations and of North Vietnamese provision of arms, ammunition, supplies, and help from political cadres; nevertheless, it observed that the "ensemble of information submitted to the Sub-Committee did not clearly establish whether there were crossings of the frontier by regular troops of the D.R.V.N."[4] The subcommittee noted that after September 15 a "regression" appeared to have occurred, especially in Phong Saly and Sam Neua. The report implied that the Laotian government's accusation that North Viet-Nam had committed "flagrant aggression" could not be sustained. No recommendations were made, and the Security Council did not convene to discuss the report.

Determined to keep some sort of United Nations "presence"

[4] Document S/4236, p. 31.

in Laos, Dag Hammarskjold decided on November 7 to make an independent trip to the kingdom, thereby acquiring a personal knowledge of the situation. The Soviet Union, though opposed to the visit, did not take an extremely adamant position. By traveling to Laos, Hammarskjold was further extending his conception of the office of the Secretary-General as a positive force in relaxing international tensions. Once more he was using his good offices to lessen friction and to gain the margin of time needed to stabilize an uneasy situation. After reaching Vientiane, he participated in a press statement with Premier Phoui Sanaikone; after the Laotian leader had asserted that his country would stay neutral, not becoming a "base for any foreign power bloc," the United Nations official indicated his belief that all the friends of the kingdom would rejoice at this declaration.

While still in Laos the Secretary-General summoned to Vientiane the Executive Secretary of the Economic Commission for Europe, Sakari Tuomioja, asking him to make a survey for possible U.N. economic and technical aid to the kingdom beyond the services already provided. Before Hammarskjold left Vientiane he stressed that his own evaluation of future assistance would be guided by the United Nations Charter and the "other international agreements" which provided a framework for Laotian development. The latter reference could well be to the Geneva settlement upon which the Communist bloc put so much stress.

After a month's field work, Tuomioja in a report to the Secretary-General recommended coordinated economic and social assistance to Laos by the United Nations and relevant specialized agencies. On December 17 Hammarskjold announced he had requested Roberto M. Heurtematte, Commissioner for Technical Assistance, to go at once to Laos to discuss ways of implementing the suggested recommendations with its authorities. The subsequent dispatch of a United Nations contingent to carry out the agreed program and the opening of a field office by the Technical Assistance Board further served to maintain a United Nations "presence" in the Mekong kingdom. A Swiss, Edouard Zellweger, became the personal representative of the Secretary-General in Laos. In the viewpoint of the United States, the subcommittee of the Security Council and the presence established by Hammarskjold had a "tranquilizing effect" in the crisis.

In addition to the United Nations help during the trouble with North Viet-Nam, the Kingdom of Laos achieved some success in its efforts to increase American aid. The United States was already deeply committed to the maintenance of an independent Laos through diplomatic action, through SEATO, and through its aid program which had probably saved the country from falling into Communist hands. At the beginning of the fighting in the summer of 1959 the Laotian army had 25,000 men and the village militia about 16,000, all troops being lightly equipped with arms of the Second World War or of even earlier vintage; in addition, there was a national police of some 3,000 men. Authorized American economic aid to Laos, which totaled over $190 million between fiscal years 1955 and 1959 inclusive, was utilized mainly in budgetary support for the army, police, and selected government activities, although some technical help had also been granted, especially in the fields of health, education, and agriculture. Military equipment, supplies, and other assistance were provided under the so-called "Pentalateral Agreement" of December 23, 1950 (involving Laos, Cambodia, Viet-Nam, France, and the United States). The military assistance program was administered by a Program Evaluation Office set up within the convenient framework of the United States Operations Mission which administered economic aid. The PEO supervised the provision of the arms and supplies granted the Laotian military, while a number of American technicians instructed the Laotians in the use and maintenance of the equipment. Because the French Military Mission still retained over-all responsibility for training the Laotian army, including the important assignment of tactical training, it was regrettable that cooperation among the Americans, French, and Laotians often left much to be desired. Some French considered the growing activity of the PEO an infringement in their own sphere; more than one American was critical of the French tactical training; and on occasion the Laotians wanted to terminate the French Military Mission. But matters were largely unchanged until the summer crisis of 1959 provoked a number of alterations in the aid program.

Following a formal request by the Royal Government on July 23, 1959, a request which was backed by France, the United States agreed to an emergency training program in Laos whereby American military instructors would work from six to twelve months in teams of 16 men, half French and half American. On August 26 the United States publicly approved further aid to the kingdom, asserting that the Communist threat now required "temporary emergency increases" in the army and village militia. Steps were also taken to rush arms and supplies to Vientiane, to improve the mobility of the Laotian army, and otherwise to stiffen the resistance of the country.

North Viet-Nam reacted strongly against these American steps to strengthen the armed forces of Laos. In a message to the President of the Security Council, dated September 6, Premier Pham Van Dong severely denounced the U.S. measures while calling for the United Nations to reject the "senseless request" of Vientiane for a U.N. emergency force. Referring to the summer crisis, he asserted that its "fundamental causes and the immediate reasons lie in the intervention of the Americans in Laos with the intention of transforming that country into an American military base, thus directly and seriously threatening our country."[5]

[5] Document S/4236, Annex 2, p. 2.

These allegations were supported by Communist China and by the Soviet Union.

Although the Royal Government did not invoke SEATO in the summer crisis of 1959, the Bangkok organization carefully followed developments in the Mekong kingdom. The Council Representatives considered the situation at length, and the Military Advisers reviewed it in a regular meeting held September 22-24. Different members of the alliance also sent fact-finding representatives to Laos. As previously planned, the SEATO Council convened informally in Washington on September 28 when Secretary of State Christian A. Herter presented a report on the Camp David meeting between President Eisenhower and Premier Khrushchev. Laos was given particular consideration at the session, and the eight members affirmed their determination to uphold, when necessary, their treaty commitments; meanwhile, they applauded the Security Council's "prompt action" in the crisis. Through various ways, the members of the SEATO Council worked for the maintenance of a United Nations "presence" in the Mekong kingdom. The military forces of SEATO, though kept in the background, were constantly on the alert and served as a steadying factor for Vientiane in the fast-moving developments. The over-all response of the United States, including certain military dispositions, was graduated to fit the circumstances without being provocative.

As for the Laotians themselves, the weeks of tension did not call forth a nation at arms, inspired with martial spirit against the foe; in fact, for a capital that was making headlines throughout the world Vientiane was a remarkably peaceful city. The Communist threat, although it had mounted to serious guerrilla activity, did not have the dramatic impact of a foreign invasion across a frontier. A substantial number of Laotians were simply apathetic, for the government at Vientiane had failed, for the most part, to gain the active loyalty of the people. The Royal

Government had begun to concern itself with the villages, however, notably shown in the establishment of a Bureau for Village Development in the Lao Ministry of Social Affairs and in rural development programs through Civic Action and later "Teams of Six." These efforts had not yet been successful, but some progress was being made—one factor which may have prompted Communist aggression.

The Crisis of 1960-62

The prolonged Laotian crisis that began in the summer of 1960 differed from that of the previous year both in intensity and in the seriousness of its consequences. Although there is an obvious continuity between the two crises, the tempo of Communist indirect aggression and Western response increased sharply. On August 9, 1960, a surprise *coup d'état* in Vientiane engineered by Captain Kong Le overthrew the pro-Western government of Tiao Somsanith and led to a new cabinet with neutralist Prince Souvanna Phouma as premier. Although recognized by Western, neutralist, and Communist states, the new government was not able to reconcile the contending political factions in Laos, and the subsequent political turmoil and civil war began to involve the security interests of numerous foreign powers. Within Laos, Prince Souvanna Phouma's government was supported by the forces of Captain Kong Le and by the Pathet Lao, but opposition forces began to concentrate in Savannakhet under pro-Western Brigadier General Phoumi Nosavan. On the international level, the Prince established diplomatic relations with the Soviet Union while General Nosavan looked to Thailand, led by his cousin Field Marshal Sarit Thanarat, as well as to the United States. Meanwhile the Pathet Lao, in addition to its increased influence in Vientiane, extended its penetration in Phong Saly and Sam Neua.

In the middle of December General Nosavan's troops occupied Vientiane by an act of force. Prince Souvanna Phouma having already fled to Cambodia on the ninth, a government under Prince Boun Oum, with General Nosavan as deputy premier, was established in the Laotian administrative capital. The United States, Great Britain, and France recognized the new regime in Vientiane, but the Communist powers asserted that the government of Prince Souvanna Phouma was still legal. When Pathet Lao forces advanced into the key province of Xieng Khouang, strategically linked by roads to North Viet-Nam and to Luang Prabang and Vientiane, the seat of Prince Souvanna Phouma's government was for a while established at the city of Xieng Khouang. The Pathet Lao continued the offensive until, by the late spring of 1961, they held well over the eastern half of the Buddhist kingdom.

The evidence indicates that during the entire crisis the Pathet Lao, North Viet-Nam, Communist China, and the Soviet Union worked in relative harmony, despite possible differences of interest and outlook. Taking advantage of virtually ideal conditions in Laos, the concerted forces of international communism pushed indirect aggression to a point just short of open attack. The pro-Communist forces in the kingdom achieved military positions from which they could overwhelm the pro-Western forces, unless outside powers interceded to redress the balance. Countries sympathetic to the Vientiane government had to be willing to make the apparent costs of establishing a new Communist satellite exceed the probable gains.

After the coup of August 1960, the Pathet Lao was able to draw some military strength from the supporters of Captain Kong Le and considerable political help from the neutralists of Prince Souvanna Phouma. As official representative of the Pathet Lao, Prince Souphanouvong came to have the most powerful single voice in the discussions on national unity initiated with

Prince Boun Oum and Prince Souvanna Phouma. Yet if the Pathet Lao had not been aided by the Communist powers, it is unlikely that the pro-Communists in the kingdom would have gained the upper hand. Prior to the coup of Captain Kong Le, the government of Tiao Somsanith had begun to make some headway in meeting the country's problems.

A new chapter in the crisis had opened when, at the request of Prince Souvanna Phouma, the Soviet Union began to fly in foodstuffs and fuel. After the neutralist Prince had fled to Cambodia, the Soviets undertook an extensive airlift of personnel, weapons, and matériel to the pro-Communist forces in Vientiane until, following the fall of the city, the airfield near the city of Xieng Khouang came to be a logistical center for Communist efforts. By initiating the airlift Premier Khrushchev chose to play a more direct role than ever before in the country, and his decision to intervene was probably motivated by a number of considerations. It may have been taken to forestall similar intervention by the Chinese Communists, a likely cause of a still more explosive situation in Southeast Asia. By the means of a Russian airlift, the Kremlin could largely control the tempo of the crisis and better prevent it from getting out of hand. The Soviet presence certainly proved that Moscow was not leaving the field of Southeast Asia entirely to Peking. At the same time, rivalry between Khrushchev and Mao Tse-tung over Laos should not be exaggerated. At the Geneva Conference in 1961 and 1962 Peking and Moscow operated as a team, while the Soviet airlift was certainly facilitated by Chinese cooperation. Moreover, the Kremlin's role in Laos was consistent with the Communist doctrine of supporting so-called wars of national liberation, although the Russians may be satisfied for a while with a Laos outwardly neutral but inwardly at the mercy of the Communists.

The Democratic Republic of Viet-Nam took full advantage of the opportunities offered by the Russian presence and by the local situation in Laos. Hanoi, whose role should not be minimized, sent military matériel to the Pathet Lao by overland routes, provided military technicians and advisers, and even furnished certain units of its regular armed forces. (It is estimated that 10,000 armed Vietnamese were stationed in Laos.) In addition, the day-to-day Soviet airlift originated in the territory of the Democratic Republic which served as a staging area. Communist advances in the eastern parts of Laos also facilitated Hanoi's communications with the Viet Cong, the Communist machine fighting in South Viet-Nam. Ho Chi Minh, though sensitive to relationships between Khrushchev and Mao Tse-tung, saw in their cooperation in the Laotian situation the possibilities of advancing his interests throughout the whole of Indochina.

The People's Republic of China took a less active role in the 1960-62 crisis, accepting the roles taken by Moscow and Hanoi and certainly facing a food shortage and internal difficulties at home. But Peking did contribute to the concerted Communist efforts in Laos by diplomacy and propaganda; and without the material support of Mao Tse-tung in more ways than one, the Soviet and Viet-Minh roles would have been greatly reduced in effectiveness. When it came to settling the crisis by negotiation, Peking was more rigid and more inflexible than Moscow, and it indicated willingness to send its armed forces into the kingdom if SEATO openly intervened. In fact, the Chinese Communists have recently built a road from Mengla in Yunnan to Phong Saly. Short-term benefits for the Soviet Union in Laos may still prove to be long-term gains for Communist China.

The indirect aggression of the Communist powers in Laos was sufficiently ambiguous to prevent agreement among the SEATO powers on the question of countervailing intervention. During their drives in the first part of 1961 the Pathet Lao forces kept clear both of the Mekong basin next to Thailand and of key cities like Luang Prabang, Vientiane, and Savannakhet, thus minimizing direct provocation to the United States, Thailand, and other powers. Despite their military advantages in terrain, supply, and territory held, the Communist leaders at the time presumably preferred a "peaceful" take-over through a coalition government and subsequent subversion.

The response of the Western and pro-Western powers in late 1960 and 1961 to the indirect aggression in Laos was characterized by controversy and indecision. The government of Prince Boun Oum proved itself weak, despite increased American military aid in technicians, arms, and supplies. Boun Oum's precipitate rise to power and subsequent decline pointed up the need in Washington for full agreement among U.S. government agencies in order to avoid any weakening of elements favorable to American objectives. The administration of President Kennedy, as contrasted with its predecessor, put increasing emphasis on a neutral rather than a pro-Western Laos. France had long been sympathetic to neutralist Prince Souvanna Phouma, while Great Britain had for some time been inclined toward the same viewpoint. Washington, Paris, and London clearly agreed in their opposition to a Communist Laos, but the Americans looked upon the Pathet Lao as a genuine instrument of communism while the French placed greater stress on the nationalist aspect of the organization. In the course of the crisis, these Western powers reached agreement on the need for a genuinely neutral, independent Laos. But how this ideal could be reached, given the Laotian factions and the urgencies of the cold war, was another matter. Any coalition government in Vientiane would clearly require the replacement of Prince Boun Oum as premier. Although Prince Souphanouvong might not immediately succeed him, the military strength of the Pathet Lao would remain a factor of major importance. Prince Souvanna Phouma, having already lost much of his neutralist support, could not be expected to ignore the realities of the power equation in Laos. Faced with such probabilities, it was not surprising that the regime of Prince Boun Oum came to lose courage in its future, as did the armed forces loyal to the Royal Government.

In early 1961 the Southeast Asia Treaty Organization faced its gravest test to date. A continuing U.S. military build-up in the Western Pacific and, insofar as possible and feasible, in Southeast Asia itself was already giving tangible evidence of Washington's concern. American marines, for instance, had set up facilities in Udon Thani in Thai territory south of Vientiane to service helicopters furnished to Laos, while the port of Bangkok and a number of Thai airfields were made ready for military operations. On March 23 President Kennedy's dramatic statement on Laos in a televised press conference alerted the American people, the Communist bloc, and the world at large to the explosive nature of developments in the kingdom. Considerable activity at SEATO headquarters in Bangkok was climaxed on March 27-29 with the seventh annual meeting of the Council of Foreign Ministers. Immediately at issue were a halt to the armed attacks in Laos and negotiations directed toward the establishment of an independent, genuinely neutral country.

Although the members of SEATO were divided on the question of military intervention in the Mekong state, they agreed in a communiqué issued at the end of the Council meeting that if the current attempts to end hostilities and undertake peaceful negotiations for an independent, unaligned Laos failed and the active military effort to get control of the kingdom continued, they were prepared to take action "appropriate in the circumstances" under the Manila Pact. In addition to noting with "grave concern" the sustained offensive conducted by rebel Laotian elements supplied and helped by Communist powers in violation of the Geneva settlement, the SEATO Council expressed "concern" over the attempts of an armed minority, once more backed from the outside in disregard of the Geneva accords, to overthrow the government of South Viet-Nam. The Council stated its firm determination not to "acquiesce" in such a take-over in Saigon. It indicated that SEATO should continue to follow events in Laos and Viet-Nam on a basis of constant and urgent review. The communiqué, however, did not spell out what "appropriate" action might be if the need arose in Laos.

This final communiqué of the Council of Foreign Ministers represented the maximum agreement that could be achieved under the rule of unanimity. One factor in this somewhat weak stand was the U.S. effort to avoid unnecessary provocation to Moscow. France in particular was prepared to go no further, while Great Britain, though more positive than France, was cautious and hesitant. On the other hand, Thailand was deeply aroused over the position of SEATO, for if Laos fell into Communist hands, Thailand would be wide open to subversion directed from across the Mekong River which is considered a major highway rather than a barrier. The Philippines shared with Thailand disappointment over the implementation of the Manila Treaty, while Pakistan came to question its value. New Zealand was close to Great Britain, but Australia was more sympathetic to the position taken by Thailand, the Philippines, and Pakistan. The United States, eager at the time to maintain formal unanimity and aware of the need of unity in any satisfactory diplomatic solution of the crisis, made the best of the conflict of viewpoints by adopting a cautious position. But if Washington had at that time determined upon military intervention in Laos, it is likely that Thailand, the Philippines, Pakistan, and Australia would have gone along, possibly joined by Great Britain and New Zealand.

The Laotian conflict, it should be noted, was not taken to any organ of the United Nations in early 1961 in spite of the precedent established in the latter part of 1959 when the Security Council, as well as the Secretary-General, was directly involved.

A United Nations "presence," already in the kingdom in the form of a 15-member technical mission, could not be effective under the circumstances. There was always a possibility, however, that the Security Council or the General Assembly might take up the controversy at some future point. A regional approach to the crisis was attempted when King Savang Vathana of Laos proposed in February that representatives of Burma, Cambodia, and Malaya come to his kingdom in order to denounce all foreign intervention tending to endanger the neutrality and independence of the country. This proposal never made progress, although Prince Norodom Sihanouk did become active in trying to reconcile the Laotian factions and the various foreign powers involved.

The diplomatic machinery used in 1961 by the Communists, neutrals, and anti-Communists in attempts to deal with the Laotian problem involved in the first instance the British and Russian co-chairmen of the Geneva Conference of 1954, and the International Commission for Supervision and Control in Laos (which had been adjourned *sine die* since July 19, 1958), consisting of representatives from India, Canada, and Poland. After long negotiations involving the co-chairmen and diplomats of interested powers, Great Britain and the Soviet Union on April 24 called for a cease-fire in Laos before May 12 and requested Prime Minister Nehru to convene the International Commission for Supervision and Control to verify the cease-fire in the Mekong state. Finally, they issued invitations to a 14-nation conference at Geneva, set to open May 12. The specific membership of this conference was originally suggested by Prince Norodom Sihanouk, and it included the United States, Great Britain, France, and Canada; the Soviet Union, the People's Republic of China, and Poland; India; and all the mainland states of Southeast Asia, save Malaya. The United States, long opposed to a reconvening of the International Control Commission and the holding of another Geneva conference, altered its position, although Washington insisted that a cease-fire must come into effect before the assembly met. On May 12 the International Control Commission reported that a *de facto* cease-fire existed in Laos, and four days later the International Conference for the Settlement of the Laotian Question formally began.

The Geneva Conference soon found itself involved in long, acrimonious, and complicated discussions. The main issues were the establishment of an effective, as distinguished from a *de facto*, cease-fire; the legal powers, voting procedures, and physical capabilities of the International Control Commission; and the practical application of the concepts of independence, neutrality, and national unity to the kingdom. The United States, while supporting whenever possible the government of Prince Boun Oum, called for an effective cease-fire to be constantly supervised and enforced by a reorganized, competent International Control Commission. Washington also urged the establishment of adequate international machinery to safeguard Laotian neutrality, recommended the withdrawal of all foreign military personnel from the kingdom (apart from those allowed under the Geneva settlement of 1954), and suggested the administration of a program of economic and technical assistance by an organization of neutral states from the area. For some time the outcome of the Geneva Conference was uncertain. At home American policy-makers could not ignore the impact of other grave developments. After the failure in April of rebel landings in Cuba, Congressional opposition mounted against the dispatch of U.S. troops to Laos; apart from the dangers of a Korean-type war in such a difficult area, questions were raised about the willingness of the Laotians to fight for themselves. President Kennedy, who had indicated at one time in 1961 serious intentions of intervening in Laos, pulled back.

Because the limited American response to marked Communist

inroads in the kingdom caused such widespread disillusionment and concern in many Asian countries, the Kennedy administration took a number of steps aimed at reassuring its allies and friends in Southeast Asia. In Bangkok, to take one of the most important examples, sentiment toward neutralism had become marked, and Thai officials were even considering a *rapprochement* with Moscow as a form of insurance. Shortly before the scheduled opening of the International Conference for the Settlement of the Laotian Question, Vice President Lyndon B. Johnson started on an important two weeks mission through the cities of Saigon, Manila, Taipei, Bangkok, New Delhi, and Karachi. Despite reports in Washington about the possible stationing of U.S. armed forces in South Viet-Nam and Thailand, no Asian government requested such troops during the Johnson mission, and no promises were actually given. At the same time, the possibility of a U.S. military presence was not ruled out, and prominent U.S. leaders who were opposed to armed intervention in Laos indicated their willingness to support, if need be, the defensive deployment of American troops in Thailand and South Viet-Nam. Yet, at that time, some increases in military assistance to the Thai and Vietnamese governments and further aid toward the promotion of economic development sufficed.

Despite many difficulties, the Geneva Conference on Laos was able to reach agreement by the end of 1961 on almost all the controversial issues. The major stumbling block to the completion of its work was the failure of the Laotian leaders to form a national coalition which would send a delegation to Geneva to participate in the final settlement. Prince Boun Oum, backed by General Phoumi Nosavan, was opposed to Prince Souvanna Phouma's becoming premier in a coalition government if he or his neutralist supporters held the defense and interior portfolios; Souvanna Phouma was backed by Prince Souphanouvong in his desire for the contested posts. The United States made an effort to prod

Boun Oum and Nosavan into accepting the coalition government by withholding from the Vientiane government from February through May 1962 the regular monthly installments of $3 million in financial aid.

The impasse in Laos ended in May when the Pathet Lao broke the cease-fire and overran important government territory in northern Laos, thus strengthening its control over two-thirds of the kingdom and proving further the weakness of the Boun Oum troops. Although the United States moved combat forces into Thailand, President Kennedy stated on May 15 that Washington stood for the re-establishment of the cease-fire, as well as for quick negotiations for a national union government in Laos. Yet the American troop movements carried the threat of intervention if the Pathet Lao did not restore the cease-fire. The Soviet Union criticized the U.S. step in Thailand, perhaps more for the record than for any other purpose, but it still favored a neutral and independent Laos as agreed upon by Premier Khrushchev and President Kennedy at their Vienna meeting in June 1961. The Pathet Lao forces ceased their advance and called for a resumption of negotiations.

As a consequense of the various domestic and international pressures, the rival Laotian leaders finally agreed to a coalition government of 19 ministers subsequently installed in June. Prince Souvanna Phouma was premier, holding the portfolio of defense, and one of his supporters was minister of the interior; Prince Souphanouvong and General Phoumi Nosavan held the rank of deputy premier. Each of the three main leaders had veto powers over the major actions of the others, thus reproducing in political form the triple-headed elephant on the flag of the kingdom. After the integration of the civil administrations and military personnel of the three princes, national elections would be held, leading to a new government.

The Geneva Conference on Laos which had been in recess for

five months resumed on July 2, 1962. The delegation from the coalition government of Laos was welcomed by the leaders of other delegations. Although the Communists criticized the presence of U.S. forces in Thailand, the United States, supported by the Bangkok representatives, stated that the matter was outside the competence of the conference. Shortly before it met, however, Washington had announced its intention of withdrawing a thousand marines from among the 5,000 U.S. combat forces stationed in Thailand.

The declaration on Laotian neutrality, signed at Geneva on July 23 by the powers represented at the conference (except Laos), called for each of them to undertake to respect the sovereignty, unity, territorial integrity, and neutrality of the Mekong kingdom. The signatories were to abstain from interfering directly or indirectly in its internal affairs, attaching any political conditions to aid offered the country, drawing it into any military or other arrangement incompatible with its neutrality, introducing foreign military personnel or troops into the kingdom, setting up foreign military bases in it, and using the territory of Laos for interference in the domestic affairs of another country. The Kingdom of Laos in turn pledged itself to conduct all international business along truly neutral lines. Prince Souvanna Phouma, at his installation as premier on June 22, had already disclaimed the protection of SEATO, and at Geneva the parties in the declaration agreed to respect the Laotian wish not to recognize SEATO's protection. Provision was made for joint consultation among the signatories of the Geneva agreement in the event of any threat to, or violation of, it.

Other provisions of the settlement in Laos were embodied in a protocol which specified the role and procedures of the International Control Commission of India, Canada, and Poland in overseeing the arrangement and in dealing with the withdrawal of foreign forces from Laotian soil. Within 75 days of the signing of the protocol all foreign troops, military personnel, and para-military formations were to leave the country under the observation of the inspection teams of the commission. New foreign troops, military personnel and paramilitary formations were not to be introduced; but if Laos considered it necessary, a limited number of French military instructors might remain for a limited period in order to train Laotian forces. France and Laos were to make arrangements for the transfer of the former's military installations in the kingdom to the Royal Government. No war matériel could be introduced into the Mekong state, except as the latter might decide on the importation of necessary conventional arms for national security. In its various functions the International Control Commission was required to act with the concurrence of the government of Laos. Clauses relative to the Commission's operations are not always clear, facilitating honest differences of interpretation; but W. Averell Harriman, Assistant Secretary of State for Far Eastern Affairs, pointedly noted that the Soviet Union had undertaken as a co-chairman of the Geneva Conference to assure that the Communist signatories comply with the terms of the settlement.

U.S. policy in the Kingdom of Laos reflects the grave dilemmas that have confronted Washington. Giving support to the coalition government in Vientiane is a calculated security risk for the United States, for the scales are clearly tipped in favor of international communism from both the political and military viewpoints. A Communist take-over can easily come through a *coup d'état*, through gradual tactical maneuvers, or even through a staged national election. But the chief alternatives to the U.S. policy established were very grave: either armed intervention with all its dangers of escalation or the open, quick, clear-cut assumption of power by the Communists with its immediate political and psychological consequences. A partition of the country, leaving the territory south of the seventeenth parallel and all along the Mekong in pro-Western hands, was not politically or perhaps even militarily feasible. Moreover, there is always the chance that the balance of international forces within the Communist camp and between it and the free world may continue to provide a kind of precarious neutrality for Laos. If most of peninsular Southeast Asia is to be kept out of Communist control, however, the situation clearly calls for a strong stand against Communist insurgency in South Viet-Nam and potential insurgency in Thailand. The immediate test presents itself in the Republic of Viet-Nam where the world is watching the outcome.

REPUBLIC OF VIET-NAM

Having already won remarkable success in guerrilla operations against France in the Indochina War of 1946-54, the Viet-Minh in mid-1957 began to step up the tempo of armed activities against Ngo Dinh Diem. After two years of mounting raids and assassinations in the villages, in May 1959 the Central Committee of the Communist party in North Viet-Nam called for the creation of a unified Viet-Nam through all "appropriate means." In July of the same year the party assumed responsibilities for the "liberation" of Viet-Nam south of the seventeenth parallel, and in September 1960 the Third Congress of the party approved a resolution which called in effect for the direct overthrow of South Viet-Nam's government as an "immediate task." Toward the end of January 1961 broadcasts from Radio Hanoi referred to the creation in the previous month of a "National Front for Liberation of South Vietnam," to destroy the "U.S.-Diem clique." As a tactic, the Communists later called for the establishment of a neutral regime in Saigon pending unification. The Communist party in South Viet-Nam is without question an extension of the northern party.

From a force of around 3,000 men in 1959 the regular units of the Viet Cong grew by early 1962 to some 9,000 men organized in thirty-odd battalions. At the district or provincial level, some 8,000 additional troops were believed to be active under the guidance of the Viet Cong's regular officers. The total figure rose to possibly 25,000 by the following summer. These military forces were supplemented by a large number of Vietnamese who served as village guards, propaganda or special agents, political cadres, and in other capacities of the Viet Cong apparatus. The Communists, moreover, had the active support or passive tolerance of much larger numbers of peasants and controlled a substantial part of the countryside. Political opposition in the south to President Diem also strengthened the insurgents.

The attempt to overthrow the Saigon government was clearly mounted, directed, and in part supplied from the sanctuary of the Communist north. Both Peking and Moscow backed the Viet Cong cause as a justified armed struggle of "national liberation," although the Russians were less ardent and more cautious in their support than the Chinese. The Pathet Lao inroads in eastern Laos, as already shown, greatly assisted the movement of men and supplies into South Viet-Nam; and the Vietnamese Communists have even used Cambodian territory as a sanctuary. In the spring of 1961, the Soviets began to airlift matériel to Tchepone in eastern Laos, 20 miles from the south Vietnamese border. Many key personnel of the Viet Cong had been left south of the seventeenth parallel after the evacuation of regular Viet-Minh forces in 1954-55, and other men have been kidnapped or drafted in the south. But growing numbers infiltrated from the north with some supplies and weapons either across the seventeenth parallel, or along the seacoast, or over the Ho Chi Minh trail in Laos. Although often southerners in origin, the leaders of the regular forces of the Viet Cong were almost entirely trained in the Democratic Republic. Chinese Communist military advisers in training and support functions, it should be noted, have been reported active in North Viet-Nam.

The rising tempo in guerilla raids and terrorist activity reached a stage where the future of the Saigon government was placed in doubt. In 1960 the Viet Cong succeeded in assassinating around 1,400 local officials and civilians and in kidnapping about half that number. Terrorist acts increased in 1961, and casualties mounted still further in 1962. Sabotage against transportation and communications systems, efforts to close elementary schools and stop malaria eradication, assaults on new townships—all were part of the conspiracy to weaken confidence in the Diem government. During 1961 guerrilla raids against various garrisons increased in frequency and in intensity. In September a number of attacks mounted by as many as a thousand guerrillas occurred in Kontum province.

The decision of the United States to make a major effort to prevent a Communist victory in South Viet-Nam was taken after a careful estimate of the situation and of various alternatives of action. In 1962 Vice President Johnson's visit to South Viet-Nam during May 11-13 and, especially, General Maxwell B. Taylor's visit during October 18-25 contributed to the resolution of the United States. With disengagement becoming the policy in Laos, a strong stand against Communist inroads had to be taken elsewhere in peninsular Southeast Asia or the non-Communist leaders of the area would have little actual choice but to accommodate themselves to Peking. Although a neutral Laos at the mercy of international communism could seriously impair Vietnamese and American efforts to defeat the Viet Cong, the United States was on more favorable ground in South Viet-Nam. In contrast to landlocked Laos, the Republic of Viet-Nam has a long seacoast where naval power could be more directly brought to bear; the government in Saigon under Ngo Dinh Diem was much stronger than was that in Vientiane under Prince Boun

Oum; above all, the Vietnamese armed forces in the south were more willing to fight for their country than were those of the Royal Government in Laos. A major American effort in South Viet Nam would also induce far more Congressional support than one made in the Laotian kingdom.

In order to be successful in the Republic of Viet-Nam, the United States had to approach the problems of internal defense and indirect aggression not only in military terms, but also on the political, economic, and social fronts. It was realized at the outset that the Vietnamese themselves would have to bear the brunt of the attempts to defeat the Communist guerrillas; the role of American aid would only be to reinforce the government in its efforts. In their propaganda against the "U.S.-Diem clique" the Communists have significantly sought to create the image of President Diem as a puppet of American imperialists, a theme similar to the old line of Ho Chi Minh presented as the great nationalist struggling against the French colonialists and their Vietnamese agents.

The capability of the armed forces of South Viet-Nam to cope with Viet Cong insurgency was strengthened in various ways. Lessons from success against Communist insurgency in Malaya and the Philippines were adapted to the Vietnamese environment. At the same time, the threat of a Korea-type attack from the north could not be ignored, and preparedness for this kind of war had to be maintained. The regular armed forces of the republic were increased with American aid, and the United States came to provide assistance to all the Civil Guard. By early 1963 around 12,000 Americans from the army, navy, air force, and marine corps were serving in South Viet-Nam under General Paul D. Harkins, chief of a United States Military Assistance Command. These uniformed men were not technically combat troops, but they had orders to fire back if fired upon. Some of them were involved in combat operations; for instance, men of the army's Special Forces accompanied Vietnamese soldiers into Viet Cong-infested mountains, swamps, and jungles, and marine corps and army helicopters, piloted and serviced by Americans in uniform, flew Vietnamese troops into action against Viet Cong guerrillas. A number of Americans have been killed and wounded in the course of such action. Units of the Seventh Fleet patrolled the South Vietnamese coast from Phu Quoc in the Gulf of Siam to the vicinity of the seventeenth parallel. Air force units helped in the war effort through instruction in low-level flying maneuvers. It was clear by the early months of 1962 that the United States had already passed beyond the point where it could disengage in South Viet-Nam.

The military support furnished the Saigon government officially took the form of training and matériel. The training programs covered a wide field—logistics, intelligence, communications, and the use of modern tactics in counterinsurgency and counterguerrilla warfare. Matériel suitable to the type of fighting under way was provided; modern technology was applied to counterguerrilla warfare. Improved training with adequate weapons, whether at the Self-Defense Corps, Civil Guard, or regular armed forces level, could help turn the tide.

The establishment of "strategic hamlets" in the country, basically along the pattern of the "new villages" in Malaya, represented a strategy of counterinsurgency that had military as well as economic and social implications. By concentrating people in Communist-infiltrated areas in fortified villages with radio communications to mobile defense forces that could quickly arrive by helicopter, the Saigon government could give much more protection to the peasants and far better restrict the access of the Viet Cong to supplies, food, recruits, and intelligence. With American aid, where available, the peasants would be compensated for loss of property, might develop new plots of land, and enjoy the benefits of health, education, and other facilities. They would be defended on a day-to-day basis by their own Self-Defense Corps and subjected to considerable indoctrination. "Operation Sunrise," as the first major attempt supported by the United States was called, might well be a beacon of the future. The strategic hamlets faced bitter opposition from the Communists and at least initial disapproval from those Vietnamese who disliked moving from their ancestral homes and who sometimes had to be resettled by force. In most cases, however, it is possible to fortify some established village, only uprooting the surrounding population. In its zeal for creating strategic hamlets Saigon tended to ignore the advantages of selectivity and priority in the undertaking.

Despite the difficulties of economic development in an area subject to Communist insurgency, Washington has neglected neither the importance of immediate social and economic steps nor long-term economic growth. A United States–Viet-Nam communiqué issued January 4, 1962, announced a program aimed at improving through increased American aid the standard of living of all Vietnamese. Because it is recognized that the peasants must be reached and their support won, particular emphasis is being placed on help to the villages, which have not substantially benefited from U.S. assistance in the past. In the villages economic and social programs, often short-term in nature, are being implemented by Vietnamese civilian officials. Civic Action can also be very important in this over-all effort to end peasant support for the Viet Cong. Longer-range projects in public works, education, and public health are also under way.

The question of the popular support of the Diem government constitutes an important consideration in the future of the country. The peasants must come to feel that they have a real stake in the Republic of Viet-Nam. The montagnards or mountain tribesmen who fled from the Viet Cong, who have been trained and armed under an American-supported program, and who are returning home in large numbers must not be neglected in the future. As the Communist offensive mounted, representatives of the United States urged the President to institute reforms in order to widen the base of his support in the nation. Through the medium of joint endeavor, attempts were made to cope with the problems of public administration. A Special Financial Group of fiscal and economic experts led by Dr. Eugene Staley arrived in Saigon on June 19, 1961, to formulate a financial plan for cooperation. Although President Diem announced a number of reforms, including on May 29, 1961, a cabinet reorganization, on December 8 the establishment of provincial advisory councils, and on December 29 several fiscal changes, charges of authoritarianism, rigidity, and nepotism continued. Reforms are occurring but not at a fast enough pace. Many non-Communist political opponents remain imprisoned; manipulation of the armed forces for political purposes has not been ended; freedom of speech is still curtailed. In February 1962 a plot against President Diem, symptomatic of unrest, narrowly failed. Nevertheless, the pressure which the United States put on the President for reforms has been relaxed. In the ultimate analysis such pressure can be effective only if Washington is prepared to abandon South Viet-Nam unless certain reforms are made. Despite major weaknesses, Diem's leadership was still considered the best in view; if he lost power, the succeeding regime is not likely to be Communist but, after some confusion, a military one of anti-Communist officers in Saigon.

After careful consideration the United States has officially stated that Hanoi's attempt to overthrow the Republic of Viet-Nam constitutes a "threat to the peace." Secretary of State Rusk first made a statement to this effect on November 17, 1961, and on December 8 the State Department published a document entitled *A Threat to the Peace: North Viet-Nam's Effort to Conquer South Viet-Nam*. In coping with the situation on the international level the United States is confronted with a number of alternatives. One would involve another Geneva-type conference on Viet-Nam. Here timing is very important, for the American national interest would not be served by going to the conference table until Washington could lead from strength. It might be remembered that the People's Republic of China was among the first of the Communist countries to call for such international consultations. In the immediate future, and perhaps never, it does not seem likely that the International Commission for Supervision and Control in Viet-Nam will acquire the capability to maintain peace in the country. On June 24, 1961, the Commission did take a significant decision by a two to one vote (India and Canada against Poland) that it had the right to investigate various complaints of contraventions of the Geneva armistice agreement of 1954, specifically Articles 10, 19, 24, and 27. The following June the same majority formally ruled (over a strong Polish protest) that North Viet-Nam was guilty of covert aggression and subversion against the Republic of Viet-Nam. In the same report South Viet-Nam was also criticized for some of its activities, particularly its "factual military alliance" with the United States. But, as indicated, the International Control Commission does not have the means to enforce its decisions, though the political and psychological value of its judgments should not be ignored.

The present crisis in South Viet-Nam has not been taken to the United Nations. In view of present voting procedures and membership, coupled with the ambiguity of the current threat in the Southeast Asian country, it is not likely that the world organization would be able to take effective action. Extreme difficulty, for instance, would be encountered in any present attempt to introduce a United Nations "presence." If direct, open aggression occurred, as in Korea in 1950, the issue would then be taken to the organization, if only for world moral support. SEATO has taken no concrete action to stem the Viet Cong tide in South Viet-Nam. In the event of a frontal atttack, the treaty would be invoked and probably honored by all of its members; but in the present crisis the issue seems less clear-cut to some signatories, and SEATO participation is not needed for military operations and may not be desirable for political reasons. The United States, nevertheless, welcomes various kinds of assistance to the Saigon government from countries concerned with the future of Southeast Asia. A number of countries like Australia, New Zealand and Malaya are contributing in various ways to the strengthening of South Viet-Nam in its ordeal.

What are the chances of the United States being able to prevent the fighting from spreading outside the Republic of Viet-Nam? In the first place, the present conflict is limited in objectives, area, and choice of weapons. No efforts are being made to overthrow the Hanoi regime; all the fighting is intended to preserve the republic south of the seventeenth parallel. President Kennedy, in correspondence with President Diem released on December 15, 1961, asserted that the current defense measures by the United States on behalf of South Viet-Nam would be unnecessary if the Communist leaders in North Viet-Nam halted their indirect aggression. The United States was forced into its present aid program to Saigon, it has been pointed out, only when the Viet-Minh violated the Geneva settlement of 1954. The fighting, moreover, is limited to South Viet-Nam, although some guerrilla activity north of the seventeenth parallel directed from the south should not be ruled out. Finally, the choice of arms by the United States has not led to the use of tactical atomic weapons. As long as the current concept of limited war is followed, the chances of an extension of the conflict are limited. Communist China might intervene if an adjacent neighbor is threatened, but it has no common border with South Viet-Nam; moreover, Ho Chi Minh would probably not favor

Chinese troops on his soil unless the very survival of his regime were at stake. And the Kremlin does not appear to want a Sino-American war in Southeast Asia.

At the same time a long, hard, costly struggle is in prospect to defeat the Viet Cong in South Viet-Nam. And success on the military front may well be easier than on the political, social and economic fronts. Americans with the Vietnamese armed forces are giving them not only training but also enthusiasm for their cause while the use of U.S. tactics and weapons in counter-insurgency and counterguerrilla warfare is bringing dividends. But success in building up popular support for Diem or his successor, in essential political reform, in needed social and economic measures, and in the experiment of the strategic hamlets will be necessary if short-term military gains are to be converted into long-term benefits.

IMPLICATIONS FOR THE FUTURE

The Laotian crisis of 1960-62 and the insurgency in South Viet-Nam point up the need for the Western and pro-Western powers to understand that guerrilla warfare against an ally mounted by bordering Communist countries is tantamount to direct aggression across an international boundary. In such circumstances, the United States, as the leader of the free world coalition in Southeast Asia, must be willing to face the issue squarely. As guerrilla warfare is a major characteristic of Communist wars of "national liberation," the response of the free world must not be weakened by lack of adequate interpretation. If the Sino-Soviet bloc becomes convinced that in indirect aggression it has found a vulnerable gap in the legal and political armor of the West and its friends, bolder probes and greater risks can be expected.

In the absence of an adequate international interpretation of indirect aggression, other approaches should not be ignored. For instance, the use of American-trained Vietnamese guerrillas to carry into North Viet-Nam operations like those conducted by the Viet Cong in South Viet-Nam is justifiable if the reprisals, besides countering the Communist offensive, bring home to the members of the Peking-Moscow axis their own interest in creating international barriers against indirect aggression. Although the United Nations has not been able to agree on a definition of direct aggression, a pragmatic approach to the problem has often proved effective. Indirect aggression mounted from the sanctuary of another country may have a similar history during the latter part of the twentieth century. International yardsticks already exist to point the way, but events along the Ho Chi Minh trail in Laos or north of the seventeenth parallel in the Democratic Republic of Viet-Nam may give tangible support for future steps. The problems of effective action in crisis areas where friends and foes exist, the "marchlands of mutual intervention" as one U.S. official has called them, will remain for some time to perplex American policy-makers.

SEVEN

Southeast Asian Diplomacy and U. S. Involvement

A new framework of international relations has appeared in Southeast Asia as a result of the winning of independence by most of the peoples in the area. The complex problems of foreign policy are now the responsibility of nine Southeast Asian governments, whereas before the Second World War there was but one independent nation in the region. Many of the issues of precolonial days have emerged to trouble the leaders of today, and the cold war rivalry of the great powers has further affected the interests, policies, and aspirations of the states in the area.

Among the major factors affecting American diplomacy in Southeast Asia are the relations among the governments of the region, the complex pressures exerted by members of the Communist bloc, the influence of Indian diplomacy, and the growing impact of postwar Japan. Faced with so many changing variables, the United States has difficulty in following a policy toward individual countries and toward the region as a whole that is both consistent and capable of withstanding the stresses of frequent crises. The many disputes and animosities among the countries of the area cause considerable concern in Washington. While these conflicts often arise over boundaries or minorities, they sometimes reflect personality clashes between national leaders or historic rivalries which were generally submerged during the colonial period. A dispute may focus on a particular issue, but a multiplicity of conflicting interests is usually involved.

BOUNDARY AND MINORITY CONTROVERSIES

Problems relating to boundaries and minorities are not unique to Southeast Asia, and it is almost surprising that there are not more of them in the region. In the precolonial period, concepts of territorial integrity and national sovereignty were vague, and the military power of a given ruler in effect determined the territorial extent of his state. The Western approach to sovereignty would have clearly made impossible the Chinese concept of vassals in the Nan Yang under the suzerainty of the Emperor of the Middle Kingdom. Following the establishment of Western colonial rule, the new masters made territorial agreements often defined by imperial interests without regard to the needs of the Asian inhabitants. In some instances, however, as in the Philippines and Indonesia, the consolidation of geographical areas by the colonial rulers enabled new states to emerge in their present territorial framework when Western power was withdrawn. Many of the boundaries established by the European masters were sound in conception and give promise of permanence, but the territorial confines inherited by the new states of Southeast Asia were often not to their liking. Moreover, many of these countries achieved their independence and brought inexperience into the conduct of foreign relations just at the period when Communist China was promising to emerge as the leading Asian power in the Far East.

The boundaries between Cambodia and Viet-Nam and between Cambodia and Thailand are particularly unstable. The area now known as southern Viet-Nam was once a part of the Khmer kingdom before the more powerful Annamites pushed southward to the Gulf of Siam. Cambodia still claims a substantial part of territory now in the Republic of Viet-Nam, including some islands like Phu Quoc in the Gulf of Siam, but neither Ngo Dinh Diem nor Ho Chi Minh has any intention of satisfying Khmer ambitions. As late as the Second World War, Thailand took over territory from Laos, Burma, and Malaya, as well as from Cambodia. The more recent boundary dispute between Thailand and Cambodia has been more localized than the one between Cambodia and Viet-Nam, but its intensity should not be underestimated. Though justified in stressing the past glories of Angkor, the Khmer leaders are aware that in all probability the colonial expansion of France in Indochina preserved the kingdom from partition between Thailand and Annam or extinction at the hands of one of them. While suspicious of both neighbors to the east and west, Cambodia today is more concerned over relations with the Republic of Viet-Nam than with Thailand.

Related to boundary problems are a number of other controversies, one of the most important having been that between the Netherlands and Indonesia over West New Guinea. Widely interpreted in Southeast Asia as a case of Dutch imperialism, the issue brought Djakarta the sympathy of many Asian and African governments and remained for years a source of friction not only between the Netherlands and Indonesia but also between many of the Afro-Asian and Western states. Another case that has concerned Southeast Asia and to some extent the world is the partition of Viet-Nam roughly at the seventeenth parallel. The existence of rival governments in Hanoi and Saigon has divided Southeast Asian countries on the question of recognition. None of them, except Laos, gives *de jure* recognition to the Democratic Republic of Viet-Nam despite the establishment of *de facto* relations in a number of instances, but some have granted formal recognition to the Republic of Viet-Nam. In another controversy the Paracel and Spratly Islands in the South China Sea are formally claimed by Communist China, Nationalist China, and the Republic of Viet-Nam. Occupied by the Japanese as stepping stones in their expansion southward, the islands are now largely in the hands of the South Vietnamese, who maintain they are the heirs of the French. Already subject to diplomatic claims and show-the-flag tactics, the Paracels and Spratlys could be the source of more serious trouble in the future.

In a neighboring area along the South China Sea the Philippines has for some time shown an interest in British North Borneo. In June 1962 President Macapagal formally claimed Philippine sovereignty over the territory and called for negotiations with Great Britain. Involved directly or indirectly in the controversy were not only the Philippines and the United Kingdom but also the Federation of Malaya, which expected to include North Borneo in the Federation of Malaysia, and Indonesia, which has sovereignty over all Kalimantan except British Borneo. Moreover, the alliance between the Philippines and the United Kingdom through SEATO and the participation of Malaya, Thailand, and the Philippines in the Association of Southeast Asia were impaired by the dispute. Though it was put down by British forces, the revolt in Brunei in December 1962 against the sultan revealed the conflict of various national interests. The proposal of President Macapagal the previous July for a Confederation of Malaya embracing at the beginning the

Philippines, the Federation of Malaya, Singapore, North Borneo, Sarawak, and Brunei represents a long-range rather than a short-range solution of the North Borneo controversy.

Often closely associated with the border disputes are minority problems, involving not only the Overseas Chinese and Indians, but also many other groups of Southeast Asians living in a country not their own. These peoples sometimes claim to be the subject of persecution and discrimination and appeal to their home governments for assistance. It may be that they are in a position of economic strength which both irritates the local authorities and opens golden opportunities for bribery and corruption. Or the host government may suspect them of subversive activities aimed at overthrowing the *status quo* and take repressive measures that provoke further ill will. The minorities may resist cultural assimilation which the government may try to compel. Among the possible approaches to minority problems —deportation, forced movement from one part of a country to another, international exchanges by mutual agreement, minority treaties, integration, and cultural assimilation—none has found widespread application in Southeast Asia. Rising nationalism in the area has made the problem more acute.

In recent years those minorities whose problems have contributed to international tension are usually located in the peninsular rather than in the insular parts of the area. A complex history of migration has left numerous minority groups within the present-day states. For instance, since the Annamites, Thai, and Burmans, are relative newcomers in peninsular Southeast Asia, the Viet-Nam, Thailand, and Burma of today have minority problems reflecting the history of their settlement. *Cambodia Irredenta* has many of the historical attributes of *Italia Irredenta*, and around 400,000 Cambodians live in South Viet-Nam, but the Khmer kingdom contains a similar number of Vietnamese. Thailand has an important Malay minority (around 800,000) in the southern part of the kingdom, while a very much smaller number of Thai live in northern areas of the Federation of Malaya. With *Merdeka* the latter has inherited from British rule certain minority problems affecting its relations with Thailand. The Union of Burma has made determined effort to give domestic recognition to minorities like the Shans and Karens, but dissatisfaction and unrest have contributed to instability at home and international tension. The population of Laos (estimates ranging from 1.5 million to 3 million) may include more hill peoples of different racial stock than the Lao themselves. Many of these hill peoples, it has been pointed out, live in localities adjacent to villages inhabited by tribes of similar racial origins in the Democratic Republic of Viet-Nam, a situation which was reflected in the Communist-inspired activity which shook northeast Laos in the summer of 1959.

Generally considered to be pro-Viet-Minh in their outlook and thus a source of worry to the Thai government have been some 80,000 to 100,000 Vietnamese, the great majority of whom fled from Indochina during and after the Second World War and settled in northeast Thailand across the Mekong from Laos. What to do with them has been a matter of particular concern for Thailand, North and South Viet-Nam, and the United States. In August 1959 an agreement in Rangoon between the Thai and North Vietnamese Red Cross organizations provided for the repatriation over a period of three years of those Vietnamese who wanted to go to the Democratic Republic. More than 70,000 registered for repatriation, and in January 1960 Ho Chi Minh greeted the first contingent on its arrival in Haiphong. Within two years over 27,000 went to North Viet-Nam.

In insular Southeast Asia, relations between Indonesia and the Philippines have been troubled at times by the problems created by an Indonesian minority (around 6,000) that migrated illegally into the southern Philippines and by a much smaller number of

Filipinos (a few hundred) who settled in Indonesia under similar circumstances. Although an immigration agreement was signed by the two neighbors on July 4, 1956, implementation has been difficult and friction has not been eliminated. The Moros in the southern Philippines with their Moslem religion could also become a source of trouble between Manila and Djakarta. While problems involving minorities have already troubled the relations among the countries of Southeast Asia, a potential exists for even greater international turmoil.

POLITICAL AND PERSONAL FACTORS

Personality clashes, traditional rivalries, and sharp differences on current foreign policy contribute to further misunderstanding among the states of the area. Personal relations have become a significant factor in the region's international relations with the rise to power in the newly independent countries of a number of Asian leaders, contrasting in personality and outlook but highly influential in foreign policy. The pattern of state visits made by Southeast Asian leaders to one another in the last few years is a barometer of international politics in the area. Personal diplomacy through state visits is especially associated with men like President Sukarno and Prince Norodom Sihanouk. The mutual distrust between President Ngo Dinh Diem and Prince Norodom Sihanouk or Tengku Abdul Rahman and President Sukarno and the friendship between Premier U Nu, when he was in power, and Prime Minister Nehru have been factors of importance in Asian politics. Premier Chou En-lai has not failed to impress Sihanouk in personal relations; the latter sent two of his sons to Communist China for education in 1960.

In a meeting of key political leaders of the countries in Southeast Asia, personal relationships could spell success or failure in reaching agreement. No one leader represents a country whose present strength enables him to command the respect of all his associates; nor is there a common denominator of basic interests sufficiently strong to overcome personal feelings. Historic rivalries, as already indicated, are openly reflected in contemporary Thai-Cambodian and Vietnamese-Cambodian relations; and until recent years a similar situation prevailed in Thai-Burmese contacts. An *entente* of the Malayan states of Southeast Asia, Indonesia, the Philippines, and the Federation of Malaya, has not developed, although President Sukarno and others have at times been sympathetic to the idea. Nor have the ties of Theravada Buddhism been sufficiently strong to bring about a common political outlook in Burma, Thailand, Cambodia, and Laos. Efforts by Tengku Abdul Rahman of Malaya to encourage a regional association for the expansion of cultural and economic ties among Southeast Asian states have been sympathetically received in the Philippines and Thailand but have not yet produced substantial results. Moreover, as indicated, membership in SEATO has not expanded beyond the original participants.

On the other hand, an entente has developed between the Philippines and the Republic of Viet-Nam, who face each other across the South China Sea; and at times in the past relations have been close between Thailand and landlocked Laos, especially as a result of transportation agreements. In efforts to develop the lower Mekong River, Thailand, Cambodia, Laos, and the Republic of Viet-Nam have continued to cooperate despite the serious difficulties in Cambodia's relations with its two stronger neighbors. Meetings associated with the United Nations, such as those of the Economic Commission for Asia and the Far East, and with the Colombo Plan, like those of the Consultative Committee, provide valuable forums for an exchange of ideas on common problems.

The KMT Crisis in Burma

The United States has not found it possible to remain aloof from many Southeast Asian controversies. An example of a crisis, which was not directly Communist in nature but which involved Washington, was the bitter controversy over the Chinese Nationalist or Kuomintang (KMT) forces in the Union of Burma. Rangoon's relations with its eastern neighbor, Thailand, with Nationalist China, and with the United States were all directly affected by the crisis, which was settled somewhat inconclusively in 1953.

The crisis originated when some KMT troops in sufficient number to attract attention retreated from China into the Shan State of Burma early in 1950 as the Chinese Communists had overrun Yunnan. Refusing either to agree to disarmament and internment or to leave the country, these troops eventually came to establish headquarters at Mong Hsat near the Thai-Burmese border, where an airfield was utilized to assist in the transport from the outside of arms and supplies, such as machine guns. General Li Mi, the leader of the KMT forces, was known to have flown from Mong Hsat to the island stronghold of Chiang Kai-shek. By early 1953, as a result of recruiting in the Burma-Yunnan frontier area, the Nationalist troops reached a total of possibly 12,000 and in many respects constituted the nucleus of a state within a state, defying the Rangoon authorities, administering a certain area, smuggling opium across the border to Thailand, and cooperating with some of the Karens in rebellion against the Union government.

Since they believed that the Nationalist troops could not have increased their strength if Bangkok had been strictly neutral, the Burmese were convinced that the Thai were helping the KMT forces in various ways. The eastern part of the Shan State was adversely affected when Thailand considered it necessary to close the border in early 1953, and frontier incidents arising from the military efforts of Burma to subdue the KMT forces contributed to ill will between the two Buddhist neighbors. Entering into the equation was Burmese suspicion over Thai interests in the Shans of the Union. The two governments were critical of each other both in the press at home and in the forum of the United Nations.

Burma was particularly apprehensive over the action the People's Republic of China might take in the KMT crisis. Since Chinese Nationalists had invaded Yunnan more than once from Burmese soil, Peking had excellent excuses for retaliation. For some time the Rangoon government was uncertain about the reaction of Communist China should the KMT issue be taken to the United Nations. Although the government of Mao Tse-tung openly blamed Thailand and the United States for the trouble the Nationalist forces were causing the Union of Burma, Peking exercised considerable restraint in its relations with Rangoon over the KMT troops; it wanted Burma to take adequate measures against them, but made no attempt to act itself.

In the viewpoint of the Burmese government the United States as a close friend of Thailand and Nationalist China had a real responsibility for the Kuomintang activities in the Union. It was believed that Washington could put enough pressure on the government of Chiang Kai-shek to cause Taipei to disengage from the operations under General Li Mi in Burma. Rumors were rife in Rangoon that Americans were working with the KMT dissidents and that U.S. arms and supplies were being provided them. Although the Burmese government authorities on the whole accepted the denials by high-ranking American officials both in Burma and the United States of any role in the KMT build-up, there were many in Rangoon who wondered whether the Central Intelligence Agency might be operating independently of the Department of State. Had the crisis been at its height in the spring of 1960, the credibility of the United

States in Burma might have been at a lower degree. As it was, the KMT crisis gave elements of the political opposition an opportunity to accuse the government of partiality in foreign policy. Already heavily engaged in fighting numerous other rebels, Burma's limited armed forces were diverted in part to operations against the Chinese Nationalists.

Premier U Nu believed that his government had three different alternatives in the crisis: submitting the matter to the United Nations; negotiating with Nationalist China for the withdrawal of the troops through the good offices of the United States while seeking the moral support of India in all possible ways; or trying to get a military decision through the employment of Burmese armed force. It was only after the last two alternatives had not produced the desired results that U Nu announced in an address to Parliament on March 2, 1953, that Burma would take the controversy to the world organization. Fifteen days later the Union requested the end of U.S. economic and technical aid effective on June 30, although certain projects previously begun would be allowed to continue. On March 25 Burma formally proposed that its complaint against aggression by the "Kuomintang Government of Formosa" be placed on the agenda of the seventh session of the General Assembly. The Union had concluded that Peking would not be antagonized by bringing the United Nations into the controversy, but at the same time the government did not believe it could continue to accept American economic and technical assistance without weakening its case against the KMT.

The Burmese complaint was debated in the seventh, eighth, and ninth sessions of the General Assembly, producing resolutions on April 23 and December 8, 1953, and October 27, 1954. Although in all three instances no negative votes were cast (the Republic of China abstained or did not participate), the voting did not reflect the nature of the discussion in the United Nations.

At the beginning of the debate in the First Committee on April 17, 1953, Burma attempted to prove that the Kuomintang forces were being directed and supported from Taiwan and that the Chiang Kai-shek government was thereby committing aggression against the Union. Replying on April 17 and 21, Nationalist China denied the charge of aggression as "monstrous." Taipei claimed that the Yunnan Anti-Communist National Salvation Army of General Li Mi was no longer a component of the Chinese regular army, although a varying degree of influence was exerted over the General and some of his officers. The Nationalist Chinese asserted that supplies had not officially been flown to the border region of Burma and that clearance would not be given in the future to chartered and private aircraft with that destination; and they indicated willingness to cooperate with the United Nations in the withdrawal of the troops from the Union.

Rangoon was widely supported in its position by Communist and Asian delegates while Western representatives tended to be sympathetic but more cautious, many not considering the Republic of China responsible for the trouble. Burma's neighbor Thailand believed that the forces should be disarmed and evacuated or interned but that Nationalist China should not be condemned. The General Assembly resolution of April 23 condemned the presence of the "foreign forces" in the Union and "their hostile acts" against it. It asserted that they must be disarmed and either leave Burma at once or submit to internment; it urged all states to provide no help to the troops in any way and to facilitate their peaceful evacuation upon Rangoon's request; and it recommended the continuation of negotiations through the good offices of certain United Nations members.

Both in and outside the world organization the controversy raised serious problems for American policy makers, who had been concerned about the conflict for some time. Two U.S.

ambassadors in Rangoon and two chargés d'affaires had made determined efforts to persuade the Department of State in the Truman and Eisenhower administrations to take effective steps toward removing the serious irritant in relations between the United States and the Union of Burma. When Rangoon considered taking the controversy to the Paris session of the General Assembly in 1951, U.S. officials in Burma favored the quiet use of American good offices in Taipei in an attempt to cause the withdrawal of the forces under General Li Mi. Ambassador David McK. Key was distressed over the meager results of his efforts, and later he gave up his post in Rangoon.

The mounting assertions that the United States was aiding the KMT forces (one such accusation being made in January 1952 by U Hla Aung, the Burmese envoy to Peking) were strongly denied by Secretary Acheson and later by John Sherman Cooper, an American delegate to the United Nations General Assembly, and by Henry B. Day, U.S. chargé d'affaires in Rangoon. Lincoln White, press officer of the Department of State, added his denial of the charges in March and indicated that his statement was founded upon a thorough investigation made by the Department. Nevertheless, a number of distinguished American journalists continued to write dispatches on the KMT build-up in Burma, some of them implying or stating that Americans were involved in the effort. William J. Sebald, who succeeded David McK. Key as ambassador to Burma after considerable delay, energetically took up the cause of removing a major source of friction in Burmese-American relations by urging effective measures in Taipei.

The failure of Washington to achieve any measure of success from 1951 to the spring of 1953 in reaching a solution to the controversy is attributable to a number of considerations. In the first place, it cannot be assumed that the government of Chiang Kai-shek was amenable to every suggestion from the United

States, subsequent issues involving Quemoy and Matsu providing a case in point. Yet Washington had concluded that the best settlement would come from the cooperation of the Republic of China in the disarming and evacuating of the KMT forces. The Nationalists themselves assert that in response to American appeals they agreed to forbid the clearance of all planes from Taiwan to the Burmese border area and to try to stop the collection of funds by agents of the Yunnan Anti-Communist National Salvation Army. And it is a matter of record that the Republic of China did eventually come to cooperate in the evacuation of the troops as urged by Washington.

It should also be remembered in an assessment of the U.S. role that there was an *apparent* degree of indifference for some time in high circles in the government. Nationalist Chinese sources have indicated that although the Central Intelligence Agency was originally involved in the supplying of arms and equipment to General Li Mi, it later ceased all such activities. Both in and outside official circles some Americans hoped that the potential of a second front in Yunnan against Communist China could be maintained, even though it would be limited. Others were inclined to believe that Burma was going to disintegrate as a state or fall into Communist hands and that the United States should therefore write off the country in its policy. The KMT issue in the Southeast Asian republic fortunately did not become involved in partisan politics. In summary, the United States knew of the aid going to General Li Mi from Taiwan with all its implications and may have facilitated it in an early stage, but eventually Washington made sincere though somewhat belated efforts to resolve the controversy.

These efforts, reflected in the General Assembly resolution of April 23, 1953, led to the establishment of a Joint Military Committee, consisting of Burma, the United States, Thailand, and Nationalist China, to consider ways of implementing the

United Nations recommendation. It was tentatively agreed on June 23 that the "foreign forces" would be evacuated from Burma via Thailand to Taiwan with the Joint Military Committee serving in a supervisory capacity. Since the cooperation of all three Asian states was essential if the evacuation were to succeed, the absence of good will between Rangoon and Bangkok and between Rangoon and Taipei made the work of the committee difficult. Bitter at the reluctance of the KMT forces to leave the Union, Burma withdrew from the committee on September 17, but the other three members reached an agreement in October calling for the evacuation of 2,000 men along with their dependents. Although Rangoon considered the number entirely inadequate, it agreed to grant a safety corridor to the Thai border.

The First Committee of the eighth session of the General Assembly considered the matter from October 31 to November 5 and afforded different delegates a chance to reiterate their positions in the controversy and to comment on current developments. The United States indicated that President Eisenhower was taking a personal interest in the situation. Praising Thailand for its cooperation, Washington also observed that although the Republic of China had only limited control over the troops in Burma, it intended to get as many of them as possible out of the country. Thailand threatened to assume no further responsibility in view of the questioning of its good faith in certain circles. Contacts at high levels between the United States and Burma in October and November exerted an influence on the controversy. It is reliably reported that Premier U Nu sent a personal letter to President Eisenhower in October, and the following month, during his Far Eastern tour, Vice President Richard M. Nixon visited Rangoon where he was briefed on the crisis by U.S. embassy officials. He was concerned that a satisfactory solution be found as quickly as possible, the controversy still being such

a major cause of misunderstanding in Burmese-American relations.

Evacuation of the KMT forces by way of Thailand began on
November 7, 1953, and involved an American airlift to Taiwan.
When debate in the First Committee of the General Assembly
was resumed from November 27 to December 4, Burma stressed
the limited number of troops being evacuated and the few
weapons being given up, while Thailand noted that there was
too much of a disposition to expect Washington and Bangkok
to carry the evacuation burden. In its resolution of December 8
the General Assembly, among other things, noted the beginning
of the "limited evacuation," indicated "*concern*" over the surrender of few arms, and urged that efforts be continued for the
evacuation or the internment of the "foreign forces" and the
"surrender of all arms." Although the repatriation of the 2,000
men and their dependents was completed by the end of the year,
Rangoon was convinced that some 10,000 KMT troops remained.

In 1954 an offensive launched by the Burmese armed forces
led to the capture of the Mong Hsat airfield on March 24. The
Joint Military Committee supervised further evacuation of KMT
troops, and when the operations ended on September 1, a total
of almost 7,000 "foreign forces" and their dependents had been
moved from Burma to Taiwan. Meanwhile, on May 30 General
Li Mi announced the end of his command, and Taipei had disclaimed all responsibility for the troops refusing repatriation,
estimated at the time to number 3,000 or more and to be
equipped with a significant quantity of weapons. Burmese military operations continued against them, and in early 1955 some
of the Chinese were forced to flee to Laos and Thailand.

Despite the fact that the backbone of the KMT military effort
had been broken, the controversy was still a potential source of
international trouble. When it flared again in early 1961 as a

result of Burmese military operations against the dissidents and evidence of continued support by airlift from Taiwan, feeling ran high once more in Rangoon against Washington, Taipei, and Bangkok. Following energetic diplomatic action by the United States, in March and April some 4,000 Chinese irregulars and their dependents were airlifted by Chinese Nationalist transports to Taiwan from Thailand, where they had been driven by Burmese forces. Some stragglers remained in Burma and Thailand, but the greatest concentration was reported in Laos.

CAMBODIAN CRISES WITH THAILAND AND THE REPUBLIC OF VIET-NAM

Although the KMT controversy in Burma received world-wide review, a number of other disputes need only a match to light the fuse. For instance, a given crisis in Cambodian relations with Thailand or South Viet-Nam, or with both at the same time, may vary in details, but a pattern has been well established in past developments and is unlikely to change in the near future. Unfortunately, the struggle between the United States and Communist China to win support in Southeast Asia has so occupied American public attention that general interest in these non-Communist controversies has been much limited. Nevertheless, since these disputes are sometimes emotional and highly explosive they have to be considered by American policymakers, often on a day-to-day basis.

In the case under consideration, mounting tension between Cambodia and South Viet-Nam and between Cambodia and Thailand led to a series of closely related incidents between June 1958 and February 1959 that gave promise of serious long-range consequences in Southeast Asia. An incursion of South Vietnamese troops into eastern Cambodia was followed by a flare-up of the Thai-Cambodian dispute over the ownership of Preah Vihear, and then by a succession of plots, abetted by certain South Vietnamese and Thai, to overthrow the regime of Prince Norodom Sihanouk.

Regular troops of the armed forces of the Republic of Viet-Nam began an invasion of Cambodian territory on June 18, 1958, pushing several kilometers into the province of Stung Treng. In reality, they picked up a border marker, placed it near the limit of penetration, mined the area, and withdrew within two days to South Viet-Nam. Saigon asserted its forces had not invaded Cambodian soil, for the territory was Vietnamese. In many respects a no man's land, the border is not well defined and has for some time been a subject of incidents. Moreover, the Saigon government claimed that Khmer armed units had previously attacked Vietnamese civil guards who were seeking to prevent the flight of some political prisoners to Cambodia after their escape from a detention post. In fact, both sides have engaged in operations in pursuit of dissident groups across the border. Irregulars, like remnants of the Hoa Hao sect defeated by Ngo Dinh Diem, have been active in the area, and combined military operations have not been possible because of Khmer opposition. Cambodia, furthermore, has allowed prominent refugees from South Viet-Nam, foes of Diem, to live in the kingdom but claims that they are not permitted to engage in political activity against the Saigon government.

In retaliation for the Vietnamese incursion, Phnom Penh ordered several battalions of its army to the troubled area. As propaganda attacks by both countries against each other mounted, memories of past border incidents as well as recriminations over treatment of minorities were revived. Neither side could forget disputes over boundary claims, over the distribution of assets which had been held in common under the former French rule, over trade and payments, and over the rank of official representation. A further emotional factor contributing to the tension was the complete lack of confidence between Norodom Sihanouk and Ngo Dinh Diem, the former being dubious about the long-range future of the Republic of Viet-Nam and the latter thinking that Sihanouk was opening Cambodia to communism.

Although Cambodian leaders were critical of the United States for not restraining its Vietnamese friends and suspected that Washington hoped to use the dispute to put pressure on the Khmers to join SEATO, the Phnom Penh government asked Washington on June 25 to use its good offices as a friend to both Asian countries to stop the Vietnamese "annexationist maneuvers." In another step the International Commission for Supervision and Control in Cambodia was requested to investigate the scene of trouble. A general invitation was also issued by the highest Phnom Penh authorities to friendly foreign powers to send representatives to the kingdom and see for themselves what was happening, and an appeal was dispatched to the parliaments of the world to exert pressure on Saigon. Prince Norodom Sihanouk suggested informal talks with President Ngo Dinh Diem, but an inflammatory editorial in Saigon against the Cambodian leader prevented an early meeting of the two officials.

Meanwhile, tensions had been increasing in the border dispute between Thailand and Cambodia over Preah Vihear, the site of an old Khmer temple, now in ruins, occupied by Thailand but claimed by Cambodia. Cambodia's recognition of the People's Republic of China in July 1958 had been critically received in Bangkok, where the action was interpreted as a step which might open its eastern neighbor to further Communist inroads. In early August, Thailand declared a state of emergency along the border on the grounds of its apprehension over Communist infiltration by Chinese living in Cambodia. Growing press and radio attacks on both sides reflected the antagonism between Prince Norodom

Sihanouk and Field Marshal Sarit Thanarat. Nevertheless, as a result of Sihanouk's visit to Bangkok in July, negotiations began on August 18 between the Cambodian and Thai governments on boundary issues, communications, customs, and related matters. The discussions were broken off in early September since neither party was willing to make a mutually acceptable agreement. On the day Cambodia's delegation left Bangkok a hostile demonstration occurred in front of its embassy there.

After further border difficulties, including the Khmer arrest of a number of Thai accused of trying to steal paddy in Cambodian territory, Phnom Penh on November 24 moved to suspend diplomatic relations with Thailand, which, in turn, quickly stopped communications and trade, closed the border, and sent armed reinforcements to the area. Cambodia asserted that Thai artillery fired across the boundary on November 26, and a Thai vessel was detained at Poulo Way four days later. When Bangkok claimed that Cambodia was kidnapping Thai citizens and Phnom Penh railed against Thailand for taking Cambodians into custody, the release of arrested nationals by both sides became an immediate issue. The Khmer government informed the Secretary-General of the United Nations of the crisis, and the Bangkok authorities agreed that the use of his good offices would be helpful in the dispute. Should the two countries fail to agree on the legal ownership of Preah Vihear, Cambodia assumed the position that the issue should go to the International Court of Justice, while Thailand after careful deliberation concluded that the Court should decide whether it had jurisdiction in the case. In the midst of the controversy the officially inspired *Réalités Cambodgiennes* observed that neither the East nor the West would permit Thailand to invade Cambodia in force, for the equilibrium of Southeast Asia would be upset and world peace would be endangered.

As in the case of Viet-Nam, Cambodian officials were suspicious of the role of the United States since the Washington and Bangkok governments were formally allied in SEATO. Phnom Penh had recently recognized Communist China, and Sihanouk had agreed to more economic aid from the People's Republic during a visit to Peking a few weeks later. Washington had made clear its regret over the Khmer recognition of mainland China. Phnom Penh believed that the United States could restrain Thailand in its policy toward Cambodia if the effort were really made.

In August 1958 tension was reduced between South Viet-Nam and Cambodia by a visit of Ngo Dinh Nhu, brother of President Diem, to the Khmer capital, although a return visit by Sihanouk to Saigon was still delayed. In January 1959, a special representative of the Secretary-General of the United Nations, Baron Johan Beck-Friis, was making progress through his good offices in persuading Thailand and Cambodia to resume diplomatic relations, but no quick solution of the Preah Vihear question was in sight.[1] Then the early part of the year, the Phnom Penh government announced two related plots against Sihanouk, allegedly instigated by Sam Sary and Son Ngoc Thanh in January and by Dap Chhuon in February. This further complication of Cambodia's relations with its stronger neighbors again caused frayed tempers in Saigon, Bangkok, and Phnom Penh and stirred further Khmer suspicions about American policy. Cambodian officials suspected that dissidents in the kingdom were receiving arms and money as well as clandestine radio support from neighbors, especially South Viet-Nam, and that rebels living outside the country, particularly in Thailand, were being assisted in various ways with foreign aid. Spying, smuggling, and intrigue became so well known that the Khmer government was warned of plots by more than one diplomatic mission in Phnom Penh;

[1] In June 1962 the International Court of Justice by a vote of 9 to 3 ruled that Preah Vihear was on Cambodia territory.

indeed, friendly governments competed with each other in warning the Khmer authorities of the plotting.

In January Thailand's name was associated with the alleged effort by Sam Sary and Son Ngoc Thanh to overthrow the Khmer government through scheming to organize a nucleus of dissident Cambodians abroad assisted by "certain foreigners." During the next month Cambodian troops loyal to Prince Norodom Sihanouk took over control of Siemreap province in the western part of the kingdom and deposed the governor, Dap Chhuon, who was accused of leading a plot with Sam Sary and Son Ngoc Thanh but fled before he could be arrested. He died while attempting to reach the Thai border but not before evidence left behind of Vietnamese complicity had been disclosed.

In the controversies involving Phnom Penh, Saigon, and Bangkok, it is often difficult for foreign diplomats to learn exactly what is happening and where responsibility should be placed, especially right after an incident has occurred. During the plotting against Sihanouk early in 1959, the French, Soviet and Chinese Communist embassies informed the Khmer government of certain intrigues, but the American mission did not take comparable action though it was aware of the plots. Cambodian officials were critical of the United States, though the latter honestly disclaimed all part in the plotting.

The People's Republic of China and the Communist bloc have definitely profited from the crises between Phnom Penh and Saigon and between Phnom Penh and Bangkok. Obviously influenced by relations with his neighbors, Norodom Sihanouk moved from a visit to Peking in February 1956 to a trade and payments agreement with Communist China the following April, an accord on economic aid in June, a visit to Moscow in July and the acceptance of a hospital as a gift from the U.S.S.R.

In May 1957 there was a trade and payments agreement with the Soviet Union, followed by further aid from Moscow and various accords with a number of other Communist states. Those events culminated in Cambodia's recognition of Peking in July 1958, the subsequent exchange of ambassadors, and the acceptance of increased economic aid from the People's Republic. Mutual pledges of greater diplomatic, cultural, and economic cooperation were exchanged during Chou's visit to Cambodia in May 1960, and toward the end of the year a treaty of friendship was signed.

Since Communist China has also expressed willingness to give military assistance, it seems clear that relations between Cambodia and its neighbors to the east and west must be normalized as soon as possible if external Communist inroads in the country are to be checked. Because of its military weakness, the Khmer kingdom is in no position to defend itself for long against an outright attack from either Thailand or the Republic of Viet-Nam, nor could it launch a successful invasion in the territory of these neighbors. While the Cambodian armed forces, a nucleus of around 30,000 men equipped by the United States, are at best able to keep internal order, much larger numbers of men are being armed and trained in Thailand and the Republic of Viet-Nam with American military assistance.

Possible American Policies in Non-Communist Southeast Asian Disputes

The KMT crisis in Burma and the Khmer crises with the Thai, and South Vietnamese highlight the complex policy decisions required in Washington. With its objective of promoting friendly relations among the non-Communist states of Southeast Asia and reducing the points of friction wherever possible, the United States can choose among a number of possible courses of action. Theoretically, Washington could follow a *laissez faire* policy, doing nothing about the disputes, letting each argument run its course, and accepting developments as they occur without any effort to influence them. In the controversial case of the repatriation of Vietnamese in Thailand to the Democratic Republic, for instance, Bangkok and Saigon had differences of opinion while the United States was torn between its opposition to raising Communist prestige by the voluntary return of the refugees or settlers and its support for the principle of freedom of choice, so important in the negotiations leading to the Korean armistice. By following a policy of noninvolvement, Washington might neither make enemies nor open itself to charges of favoritism. Such a policy might help to remove distrust of American intentions in Phnom Penh; moreover, many French officials in the kingdom, who are critical of the United States and suspect it of trying to replace the French "presence," would welcome a passive American role. It is even possible that both Thailand and the Republic of Viet-Nam would favor a U.S. policy of noninvolvement in their difficulties with Cambodia, for they might feel less inhibited.

The situation, however, is far more complex than just the problem of Thai-Cambodian and South Vietnamese-Cambodian relations. Phnom Penh, it must be remembered, can call upon Communist China for assistance in an extreme emergency, and Hanoi can always help if circumstances would seem to advance Communist interests. Moreover, as long as the armed forces of Thailand, South Viet-Nam and Cambodia are supported with American military aid and the economies of all three countries are bolstered by U.S. economic assistance, Washington has a very practical stake in their mutual relations. Should armed conflict break out, the U.S.-equipped and -supplied forces of Cambodia would be fighting the U.S.-equipped and -supplied forces of Thailand or Viet-Nam, or both. And at present all three states have American military assistance advisory groups.

Open hostilities between Cambodia and one or more of its stronger neighbors could have disastrous effects, even if Communist China and North Viet-Nam refrained from intervening. Any weakening of a non-Communist state in Southeast Asia is an invitation to greater Communist activity within the country and even to possible future overt aggression if geography or circumstance permits. Apart from this consideration, the hopes for responsible international conduct on the part of the non-Communist states of Southeast Asia would suffer a severe setback if hostilities broke out between any of them. Regional cooperation, limited as it is at present, would be retarded, and the cooperative effort to develop the lower Mekong might be one of the first casualties. SEATO would certainly be weakened. All in all, the United States is too directly involved in Southeast Asia to pursue a truly passive policy in the relations among the governments of the area.

An opposite course of action, at least theoretically possible, would be for Washington to intervene in all the controversies of the region on the grounds that any dispute potentially involves American interests. The United States obviously has a lever through its ability to grant or withhold military or economic aid to a given country at a particular time, and over a period of years the forces of a state can be strengthened to the extent that a neighbor may become apprehensive about their possible use. After all, military units developed for initial resistance to Communist overt aggression can also be used in regional quarrels. Indeed, it can be argued that the United States bears a certain degree of indirect responsibility should armed forces built up with American aid in one Asian country be used in aggression against a neighbor. At least, Washington may have a moral obligation to exert pressure for moderation in controversies that threaten to be serious.

Nevertheless, the United States would find itself in a difficult position if it had to pass on the merits of each dispute and take an open part in its settlement. The controversies are often highly complicated, accurate information is not always available or is frequently difficult to acquire, and the issues of right or wrong are debatable. Washington could easily place itself in a position where it was regularly intervening in a series of crises. It might make enemies of all and friends of none, and drive Cambodia, for instance, into the welcoming arms of Mao Tse-tung. Moreover, the United States would be constantly charged in the Afro-Asian world with intervening in the problems of Asian states. Although Washington clearly has responsibilities in the relations of Southeast Asian countries, a policy of active intervention in all their disputes would not advance American interests.

A third course of action open to the United States would be to advocate the settling of controversies among the non-Communist states of the region through international organizations or bodies. Here the United Nations might play an important role as an intermediary in handling a dispute. Washington would be relieved of the difficulties of a unilateral role, with all its potentialities for trouble; and the consideration of controversies in an open U.N. forum might also have a dampening effect on the provocation of new incidents.

Nevertheless, the submission of Southeast Asian disputes to the world organization does not necessarily mean that the best solution, or even a mutually acceptable one, will be found. Voting in the Security Council or the General Assembly often reflects considerations of world politics far removed from the immediate issue at stake. For example, a controversy between Cambodia and Thailand, if submitted either to the Security Council with its privilege of a veto or to the General Assembly with its requirement of a two-thirds majority, could easily lead to a clash based on cold war politics. Furthermore, the need for speedy action in a fast-developing situation might not be met. At any rate, if the United States did not abstain, it would have to vote on the issues, quite possibly committing itself to a definite stand for or against a given government. In the event of a stalemate in the United Nations, the presentation of both sides in open debate could easily result in heightening the ill feeling.

The good offices of the Secretary-General of the world organization or his representative provide a means that in certain situations may be used to advantage, a case in point being the resumption of Thai-Cambodian diplomatic relations in 1959. Yet here the personal stature of the Secretary-General can be more important than the office itself, and the attitude that he chooses to take in a controversy can be a factor of major significance. The stationing of a United Nations "presence" of some sort in a troubled area can also be a factor conducive toward stabilizing a situation. But it is clear that authorizing and stationing a United Nations "presence" in a given country involves legal and procedural considerations of great complexity. During the Indochinese hostilities Thailand ran into a Soviet veto on June 18, 1954, when it sought approval of a draft resolution in the Security Council providing for direct United Nations observation in the kingdom under the Peace Observation Commission. On the other hand, in a procedural step taken during the Laotian crisis in 1959 the Security Council appointed a subcommittee over the attempted veto of the Soviet Union to study the situation. The effective use of the world organization's machinery in settling disputes in Southeast Asia depends to a major extent upon the nature of the controversy.

The best course of action for the United States in dealing with controversies among the non-Communist Southeast Asian countries is to pursue in the respective capitals a policy of adroit diplomacy—quiet, unpublicized, skillful diplomacy. Subject always to impartiality or to relevant treaty obligations, careful advice can be given when sought and good offices or other facilities provided when appropriate. This approach clearly does not involve complete withdrawal or complete involvement when a dispute arises. Nor does it mean recommending the participation of the United Nations or another international body in every argument. Each crisis can be considered to a large extent on an *ad hoc* basis, with the level of intensity determining the American response.

In personal contacts with leaders like Ngo Dinh Diem, Norodom Sihanouk, Sarit Thanarat, and with other officials, American diplomats can quietly urge the cessation of plotting, the peaceful settlement of disputes by the countries themselves, and the adoption of a good-neighbor policy. A summit meeting of Southeast Asian leaders obviously should not be initiated by the United States, but encouragement should be given if it promises not to impede the development of a common attitude against Communist expansion. Official and unofficial visits can be encouraged among Southeast Asians at different levels; in fact, closer ties between lower echelons can be important for better understanding. Filipino humanitarian activities in South Viet-Nam, for instance, have brought dividends in the promotion of good relations. In some cases diplomats from other Asian countries, who, like their American colleagues, favor conciliation of differences, can help in advancing common objectives.

In the cultivation of friendly ties among Southeast Asian states, a premium is placed on the American ambassador's ability as a diplomat. Not only must he himself seek, often in personal relationships, to implement basic American objectives in a given country, but he must also try, usually on an informal basis, to promote cooperation among neighbors who may be mutually antagonistic. Hence Thailand must be convinced that Washington values its membership in SEATO; neutral Cambodia must be assured that the United States supports its nonalignment and does not seek defense ties unless mutually desired; the Republic of Viet-Nam must be certain that Washington stands behind its posture toward North Viet-Nam. Although local governments should be told of verified plots if the information contributes to stability, no attempt should be made to seek favor by contesting with other embassies as to who has the best and most timely intelligence.

Lasting solutions to most of the problems in the relations among Southeast Asian states will not be found immediately. The prospect, perhaps optimistically stated, is for gradual improvement in the contacts among the countries—improvement punctuated with occasional flare-ups, but looking toward the establishment of responsible international behavior. In their tasks American diplomats in the area must be well informed, flexible in approach to crises, respected by the key leaders of the host country, and able to keep their sense of humor and perspective.

[EIGHT]

The Economic Dynamics of Stability

Changing economic conditions in Southeast Asia are largely responsible for many of the problems related to political stability in the area. Society is in transition, and the forces of reconstruction appear to be presently at a disadvantage against the forces of disintegration. Over the next decade the cumulative effects of Western and Communist economic activities and programs are certain to have much greater influence on stability and security than hitherto experienced.

Basic economic conditions in Southeast Asia cannot be rapidly changed within the political context likely to prevail in the area. Although Southeast Asia as a whole could sustain many more than its present population of some 216 million, population pressure will continue in certain parts of the region like Java, the Red River delta, and central Luzon. Experience has proved that plans for transferring people from the crowded part of a country to a less settled area (e.g., from Java to the outer islands or from central Luzon to Mindanao) are difficult to implement; economic, sociological and political considerations often combine to create an impasse. These demographic problems should also be considered in a broader perspective: it is probable that today's world population of over three billion will be more than doubled by the end of this century with most of this expansion occurring among peoples presently living at the subsistence level. Southeast Asia is bound to be affected both through population growth on its own soil and on that of its neighbors.

The population problem for the region becomes more complex when it is noted that a speedy increase in food production throughout the area does not seem likely. Over 70 per cent of all production in Southeast Asia is agricultural, but potential yields are far greater, even in the light of the limited data available on physical resources. Although better methods of cultivation could increase productivity, greater capital formation is needed for fundamental changes. In the 1950s agricultural output in Southeast Asia as a whole kept pace with population increase, but the present high rate of population growth, around 2.0 per cent each year, will probably rise even higher. The trend to greater urbanization is also certain to require more food from the countryside, and here it should be stressed that problems of distribution already cause difficulties. For some time Southeast Asia will continue to be divided into areas with a food surplus, like Thailand and Burma, and those with a food deficit, like Indonesia and Malaya.

In the field of health and sanitation the average life expectancy of some 35 years points up the need for great improvement. Disease thrives among the poverty-stricken, and health and sanitation conditions must be made better if human resources are to be utilized for a higher standard of living. Some evidence of improvement is found, however, in the high birth rate and in the falling death rate. A malaria-eradication program is already having remarkable success, offering real promise for other accomplishments in the future.

If Southeast Asia is to break through the poverty barrier, substantial *per capita* increases in income are essential, and in many respects there is a race between progress and increasing population. The present *per capita* income in Southeast Asia is estimated to average less than $100 a year; in contrast, the figure for each American is said to be $2,100 a year. As the annual rate of increase in terms of net domestic product has remained low throughout Southeast Asia, economic development is retarded. There is obviously a widespread lack of savings available for domestic investment, another situation aggravated by population increase. A gradual expansion in the output of farm and factory workers is certainly needed, and the nations must somehow save more than they have in the past. Yet the societies of the region have neither found the exact formula nor achieved the momentum necessary for an economic "take-off." Meanwhile the large disparity in living standards between the advanced and the underdeveloped countries is increasing.

In many capitals of Southeast Asia industrialization is almost a magic word—signifying modernization at home and prestige in the family of nations. At least one country, the Philippines, now has many but not all of the technical requirements for a take-off. The leaders of the region clearly want industrialization, even by socialist means if necessary. They see in modern technology the physical possibility of rapid progress; they are comparing with keen interest the economic programs in India and Communist China; and they want foreign aid in financial support and technical assistance, often preferring the multilateral to the bilateral approach.

But the road to industrialization and economic development is not easy; among other things, it requires substantial capital investment and a reservoir of technical, entrepreneurial, and managerial skills. Development planning can easily lack realism, as some Southeast Asian governments have learned, for the process of industrialization is complex and hard to implement. In a region where nine-tenths of the people are still peasants and fishermen living in a basically subsistence economy, the foundations for industrialization are weak. Furthermore, being divided ethnically, socially and economically, the people cannot readily change their plural society into an integrated and assimilated whole. During the colonial period, only recently concluded in most of the area, the small middle class consisted largely of Chinese and Indians; above them were the European officials and businessmen and below them the indigenous population, chiefly peasants and fishermen. Independence has brought the end of the rule of Western officials, the advent to power of indigenous leaders, a marked decline in some countries in the important role of Western businessmen, and a real effort of most new governments to regulate and minimize the activities of the Chinese and Indian middle class. The "vestiges" of imperialism are often a convenient scapegoat for the new leaders. Sukarno, for instance, looked upon Dutch shipping, banking, and investments as remnants of the colonial era, yet the subsequent liquidation of these interests contributed to economic dislocation in Indonesia. Since the achievement of independence has not yet basically altered the economic status of the bulk of the indigenous population, a plural society in transition offers many targets for information and aid programs from the outside.

Modern technology is considered by Southeast Asian leaders the vehicle of making a quick transition from the centuries of underdevelopment to the atomic age. But here the need for a reservoir of skill is essential. Despite definite improvement, educational facilities in Southeast Asia are still limited; merely to raise the literacy rate, not to mention advanced training in technical know-how, presents real challenges to the authorities. In public services, the task of making government a going concern, even with a minimum of efficiency, is formidable. Nevertheless, although eager to have foreign technical assistance, the leaders do not desire to be in a permanently dependent situation; they want their own people in the foreseeable future to make the skilled contributions to the development of the economy. It is, therefore, ironic that the present capacity of the countries to absorb their secondary school and even college graduates is definitely limited in many fields. When it is also noted that educated and semi-educated Southeast Asians tend to concentrate in the cities, contributing to the economic and political imbalance between urban and rural populations, the importance of providing through development more vocational outlets for an expanding school population is evident. Other social effects of industrialization are certain to be profound, especially among the growing class of wage earners and the expanding urban population.

Despite all the difficulties already encountered in their limited experience, the leaders of Southeast Asia hold fast to their goal of industrialization. A steel mill has sometimes become as much a symbol of national independence as the traditional insignia of state. When pledged to achieve industrialization by the quickest route, some local leaders see in socialism with its centralized planning and state activity a short cut to their goal, but they do not generally favor the methods used by the Chinese Communists. Yet if the major efforts in India should fail, the People's Republic of China would be certain to achieve much more success in its attempt to portray itself as a model for Asian development.

Agrarian unrest in certain parts of Southeast Asia will probably remain serious, but it should not be unduly stressed for the area as a whole. Low productivity, it should be emphasized, requires for its remedy technical know-how and extensive capital investments: better irrigation, flood control, experimental farms, fertilizer and seeds, pest control, and land redemption or development schemes. Reforms in marketing, credit, and land ownership also enter into the equation, while community development programs, as shown in the Philippines, can be important in rural improvement.

Perhaps agriculture provides a more realistic basis for development in the near future than any plans for quick industrialization. Even where factories are built, the home market may not be large enough to absorb production, basic services like transport or power may be inadequate, and skilled labor may not be available. Among Southeast Asian leaders, political considerations are usually more significant than strict economics, and visible industrial programs toward meeting immediate needs have real political impact. As important elements of the masses, especially in the cities, become convinced that poverty can be licked, mounting pressures are exerted on governments; yet, as economic development grows, expectations tend to increase, and unless the needs are reasonably met, marked instability can result. In contrast to efforts for quick industrialization, a more rational approach toward development in much of the area would concentrate on immediate requirements, perhaps in the improvement of agriculture, transportation, and power facilities. After a sound basis for general expansion is laid, a realistic program of limited industrialization leading toward balanced economic growth could then be expedited. But when all is said and done, economic viability is an elusive goal in the complex world of today.

The Communist Bloc Economic Offensive

In programs of trade and aid the Communist bloc has made substantial inroads in Southeast Asia. As the single representative of the bloc in the region, the Democratic Republic of Viet-Nam gets substantial aid, but Indonesia, Burma, and Cambodia have also been recipients of considerable economic and technical assistance. Indeed, Indonesia has received such substantial amounts of both economic and military aid that it might be classed, in terms of recipients of Soviet assistance, with North Viet-Nam. Laos has constituted a special case, for the Soviet Union from late 1960 gave extensive military assistance to the Pathet Lao and neutralists, and after the Geneva settlement of 1962, the Soviet Union and other Communist states provided economic aid to the coalition government of Prince Souvanna Phouma. Even the absence of diplomatic relations, in the case of the Federation of Malaya, has not prevented commerce with Communist states; and a SEATO member like Thailand was being wooed in late 1960, in 1961, and again in 1962 by a Soviet offer of economic aid. Trade penetration, it should not be forgotten, has on occasion been an effective Communist weapon and has a great potential, especially for upsetting local markets. The economic offensive of the Sino-Soviet bloc offers no grounds whatsoever for Western complacency.

In its aid programs the Peking-Moscow axis is moved by a number of considerations. The establishment of a Communist "presence," beyond merely diplomatic representation, is facilitated (a Chinese Communist economic mission even preceded an embassy in Cambodia). Concentration can be placed on certain "target" areas where dividends are likely to be the highest; Indonesia has received the largest amount of Sino-Soviet aid among the non-Communist countries of Southeast Asia because of its strategic location, its receptivity, and its potential importance to the bloc. Economic assistance can serve to bolster local groups that are Communist or sympathetic to communism; it can even facilitate the efforts of subversive agents. Although technicians sent abroad are primarily concerned with the application of their skills, some can be intelligence agents using the assistance program as a front. The trade and aid offensive of the Peking-Moscow axis can also lead to the economic dependence of certain underdeveloped countries upon the Soviet bloc. When Burma was shipping a substantial portion of its rice to Communist states, especially in 1956, the Union found itself becoming economically tied to them. For good reasons, though without success at the time, the Pathet Lao in early 1957 sought to force the Royal Government to accept economic and technical aid from Communist China as a condition for a political truce in the kingdom.

The primary motivation behind the Sino-Soviet trade and aid offensive is political. In 1955 Nikita Khrushchev frankly asserted to a group of American Congressmen: "We value trade least for economic reasons and most for political purposes."[1] Both Moscow and Peking gain in international prestige by venturing into the economic and technical assistance field. The countries selected are usually uncommitted in the cold war, and the anti-Western overtones of neutralism are encouraged as an indirect means to *rapprochement* with the Peking-Moscow axis. Indonesia is urged to liquidate foreign economic interests in the archipelago; Asian-African states in general are encouraged to nationalize foreign assets on their soil. A sustained effort is being made to loosen all the Western ties of Burma, Cambodia, and Indonesia and to cultivate good will toward the Sino-Soviet bloc. When neutral countries are not satisfied with some of the terms of Western trade and aid, the Communist nations seek to capitalize on grievances. Propaganda from Moscow and Peking stresses that "capitalist imperialist monopolies" can only survive by controlling "colonial economies" (that is, by preventing in-

---

[1] *The Sino-Soviet Economic Offensive in the Less Developed Countries,* Department of State Publication 6632 (Washington: GPO, 1958), p. 6.

dustrialization in the underdeveloped countries) and urges the newly independent states not to "pawn" their resources to foreigners when making long-range plans for economic development. The American aid program, in other words, is portrayed as a cunning, streamlined conspiracy designed to perpetuate imperialism in a new guise. Through all available channels the two leading Communist powers point to their own struggles in the transition from backwardness to modernization, seeking to inculcate a community of interest with the states of Asia and Africa. Rapid industrialization is encouraged, often at the expense of a balanced economy, as one of the ways of creating rapport between the rulers of the people's democracies and many new Asian and African leaders.

The members of the Communist bloc who participate in this economic offensive have varying interests for their activity. The East European satellites in their desire for markets for manufactured goods and sources of raw materials are more economically motivated than the Soviet Union and Communist China, which appear less interested in orthodox criteria of trade. Peking is certainly more concerned over prestige in the international community than the already established Soviet Union. It is probable that no comprehensive master plan exists for the trade and aid offensive of the Sino-Soviet bloc in the underdeveloped areas; yet in Indonesia, Cambodia, and Burma the international Communist economic effort, especially if it is intensified, must require some degree of coordination. At present the "national bourgeoisie," not the weak industrial proletariat, is the class target which the Soviets seek to win; but as industrialization proceeds with Communist assistance, a strong working class will come into being, thus creating a possible base for a Communist take-over. On the other hand, some Communist leaders may seek through the trade and aid programs to encourage hopes, create frustrations, and capitalize on disillusionment. It is likely that international communism is quite pragmatic, utilizing time and circumstance in a given country on an *ad hoc* basis.

The Sino-Soviet bloc seeks to make its aid program attractive to the recipient countries. In contrast to the careful U.S. procedures, economic justification is not needed for a project; government reforms are not required before its implementation; accounting checks are not made; and speed in negotiations and execution is stressed. By these gestures the recipient is led to believe that no "strings" are attached to the aid. The Communist aid program gives the recipient a wide choice in the selection of projects; payment for goods and services is possible in surplus crops, other local products, and convertible currency; low interest rates are charged (typically 2.5 per cent) and the period of the repayments is favorable; finally, "package" deals contain items that are especially appealing. The assistance is carefully timed, highly publicized, generally well administered, and calculated to have a visible impact. The quick paving of the streets of a capital city may make a greater impression among the masses and certain of the elite than the slow construction of a dam. Aid through bloc aviation agreements, though economically not justified in many instances, may bring dividends to the Communists in certain Asian and African capitals. Receptivity for bloc aid is growing even among close friends of the United States who want to be less dependent upon Washington. At the same time it is obvious that Communist economic assistance would not be forthcoming if political objectives were not being forwarded (Yugoslavia on occasion has experienced a "postponement" of credits); and eventual dependence upon the Sino-Soviet bloc could be used for pressure and blackmail.

Most of the assistance from the Communist grouping consists of intermediate and long-term credits for the purchase of goods and services from Communist states. The Soviet Union is generally opposed to grants, but Communist China has made them to a number of countries like Cambodia. As the credits are not always or necessarily drawn upon at once, they are often utilized over a number of years with related agreements on repayments as individual projects are undertaken. Technical assistance by the Communist bloc is integrated with the trade and aid effort and does not constitute a separate program. Training, usually at the expense of the recipient nations, is provided in the Communist countries, who also send technicians to the recipients. When repayment is considered, the over-all cost of the assistance provided to the underdeveloped nations is low.

The Communist economic offensive got under way in 1954, although it was June 1956 when the People's Republic of China made its first grant of economic aid. By the end of 1959 agreements had been concluded with 19 states involving a total of $3.2 billion in grants and credits of which $2.5 billion was for economic assistance. By the middle of 1962 total bloc aid in grants and credits rose to over $7.2 billion distributed among 29 countries, comprising $4.9 billion for economic assistance and almost $2.4 billion for military aid. Aid from Communist China has constituted merely 6 per cent of this total amount, ranking far below the U.S.S.R.'s share of 78 per cent and even after the 13 per cent contributed by the European satellites.

In the first five years of the offensive, between July 1, 1954, and June 30, 1959, Cambodia received $34 million in Communist bloc economic assistance, Burma $17 million, and Indonesia $239 million (in addition to $163 million in military aid). During his visit to Indonesia in February 1960, Khrushchev further agreed to provide a credit of $250 million for economic and technical assistance; and in January 1961 he approved Djakarta's request for the purchase of substantial additional military equipment, especially for the air force and navy. In 1962 total bloc credits to Indonesia mounted to more than $1.5 billion. Early in the previous year the People's Republic of China gave Burma a long-term credit of over $80 million for economic and technical help. Cambodia's aid from the bloc rose to around $65 million by the middle of 1962. It is not surprising that the number of Communist technicians employed in economic programs has also shown an over-all increase. In the last six months of 1959, for instance, the Sino-Soviet bloc had 175 economic technicians in Cambodia, 75 in Indonesia, and 65 in Burma; and in the first six months of 1962 the respective figures were 170, 410, and 60.

The patterns of Communist aid to Burma, Cambodia, and Indonesia present variations. Burma faced a serious economic problem in 1954 as a result of a decline in the markets for its rice and an accumulation of stocks. Dependent largely upon rice exports for its foreign exchange and eager to maintain its development, the government felt it necessary to turn to the Communist bloc. Soviet "gift" projects such as a technological institute, a hotel, and a hospital were accepted, but Burma asserted they would be matched by return "gifts" of rice or other products. In 1956 Peking agreed to a credit of $4.2 million for a textile mill. But Burma's big step in aid from Communist China came with the economic assistance agreement of 1961. As a result of this agreement, Communist technicians are expected to be increasingly active in the Buddhist country.

During part of the last decade Burma experienced on occasion overpricing, delivery of damaged goods, and some long delays in the bloc's trade and aid program. The Communists even re-shipped some Burmese rice to Ceylon and Indonesia, causing Burma to lose foreign exchange it might have acquired through direct sales. When the market for rice improved in the non-Communist world, Rangoon sought successfully to reduce its barter trade with the Sino-Soviet bloc. Moscow then took a number of steps to improve trade relations with Burma, but opposed grant aid to the country, favored at the time by Prime Minister Ne Win. Disappointment arose over the progress of

Soviet construction projects; the hotel in Rangoon, for instance, was not well designed for the tropics. Yet when Premier Khrushchev visited Rangoon in early 1960, he agreed with Ne Win to advance scientific and cultural exchange. Through its latest aid effort Peking has obviously capitalized on the settlement of the Sino-Burmese boundary dispute, and Communist China's imports from Burma significantly rocketed to $49.2 million during the first nine months of 1961 as compared to only $6.4 million for all of 1960.

In Cambodia Communist China has also been more active than the Soviet Union in aid programs. An agreement between Peking and Phnom Penh signed on June 21, 1956, provided for grants to the equivalent of $22.4 million largely for the building of cement, plywood, paper, and textile factories, and Chinese technicians had a prominent role in implementing these projects. Further Chinese help extended in 1958, including provision for financing a small iron and steel works, brought total aid to $28 million; and in 1960 the figure rose to $49 million. A national radio station has also been installed in the kingdom as a Chinese gift. Peking furnishes goods which are sold in Cambodia, creating a kind of counterpart fund for aid, and the program is reported to have been relatively successful. The Soviet Union has provided limited assistance to Phnom Penh in the form of a 500-bed hospital under a $6 million grant, but in late 1960 during Sihanouk's visit to Moscow plans were made for further aid. In addition, a Czech credit has been extended for various purposes. Apart from Chinese imports under the aid program, trade between Cambodia and the bloc, despite a number of agreements, has remained small.

Both Moscow and the East European satellites as well as, to a far less extent, Peking have been active in economic assistance to Indonesia. The expansion in the economic relations of the island republic with the bloc did not really get under way until after 1953. In these early years East Germany provided a credit of

$8.6 million for the building of an integrated sugar refinery and Czechoslovakia $1.6 million for a tire and rubber goods factory as part of an expanding program. Eventually in early 1958 the Indonesian Parliament approved the acceptance of a development credit of $100 million from the Soviet Union. As the trouble between the Djakarta government and the rebels in Sumatra and Sulawesi made conditions acute, Chinese Communist credit in rice and textiles valued at $11.2 million was accepted. Further assistance from Peking in the form of textile equipment worth $12 million (part of a $30 million credit) was negotiated in June 1959, but implementation problems arose; in 1961, however, Peking did agree to furnish textile plants. It should be remembered that Indonesian seizure of Dutch interests toward the end of 1957 created economic dislocations which afforded opportunities for Communist economic intervention. In the two years immediately following the expropriations Poland, for instance, contracted under a credit arrangement to provide ships and build four shipyards valued at $41 million. In a gesture of good will, the Soviet Union even agreed in 1959 to construct a stadium and auxiliary sports centers for the 1962 Asian Games, the credit amounting to $12.5 million. But the milestone in the Communist aid program was Khrushchev's pledge in February 1960 of a credit of $250 million. With the expansion of the different projects and with mounting military assistance, opportunities for bloc technicians in Indonesia have markedly increased, and more Indonesians are being trained in various Communist countries.

Trade between Indonesia and the Communist world has greatly increased since 1953, but it is still a minor part of the islands' total trade. In 1958 Indonesia's trade with the Communist bloc amounted to only some 9 per cent of total imports and less than 8 per cent of total exports. Djakarta has also found that some shipments of rubber, tin, and other products involved in barter agreements with Communist states have at times been resold in traditional Indonesian markets. Nevertheless, long-term agreements are diverting an increasing percentage of Indonesian exports to the Soviet Union.

The extensive series of trade pacts which Communist states have made with Indonesia, Burma, and to a lesser extent with Cambodia offer further evidence of the Moscow-Peking trade offensive in Southeast Asia. As of June 30, 1961, it was estimated that Indonesia had ten trade (or trade and payments) agreements in force with members of the bloc; Burma, nine trade agreements; and Cambodia, six agreements involving both trade and payments. Having gained momentum since 1953, the Communist trade expansion is closely bound with economic aid and technical assistance programs in a concerted effort to gain political influence. Besides the formal trade agreements, the Communist bloc dispatches trade missions, participates in fairs and exhibitions, and intrudes propaganda into its expanding commerce. Although the trade of the Sino-Soviet bloc with the underdeveloped countries represents only a small proportion of all Communist trade, the bloc's total trade turnover with the underdeveloped areas increased 295 per cent in seven years—from $860 million in 1954 to $3.4 billion in 1960. This remarkable rate of growth far exceeded the increase of bloc trade with the industrialized parts of the non-Communist world. At first the People's Republic of China had chiefly exported food products and raw materials but, when domestic conditions permitted, it began to send abroad manufactured goods like cotton textiles, chemicals, or cement (and even steel products). The Eastern European satellites have stressed exports of machinery and other capital goods, but the Soviet Union has sent abroad raw materials (sugar, wheat, lumber, and petroleum) as well as manufactured commodities (cement, cotton textiles, petroleum products, rolled steel, and machinery).

The Communist bloc is certain to increase its economic potential and, therefore, its capacity to offer greater programs of aid and technical assistance. Despite the Soviet Union's own needs for capital and its economic obligations to certain other states in the bloc, it will be better able in the years ahead to furnish assistance to underdeveloped countries. Led by East Germany and Czechoslovakia, the European satellites will be capable of continuing, if not increasing, contributions in industrial machinery and equipment. Even Communist China, notwithstanding all domestic difficulties, has not reduced its exports to the underdeveloped countries or curtailed its aid programs. In the years ahead its capacity for a single-handed economic offensive in Southeast Asia should not be underestimated.

U.S. ECONOMIC AID PROGRAMS

American economic assistance to the countries of Southeast Asia antedates the Sino-Soviet bloc offensive by several years. Even without the growing Communist challenge, it should be stressed, Washington would have maintained substantial economic programs to assist Asian countries devastated by war or facing the problems of independence. The basic objective of American economic aid in the less developed countries, like those of Southeast Asia, is to help as many of them as possible in the shortest feasible time to develop their economies so that they can reach the stage of self-sustained growth. American assistance is extended on a broad front in the hope that the people of a country may profit by it and have a stake in their nation's future. The wide gap between the extremes of the rich and the poor would be narrowed. Governments would be directly encouraged to promote social justice and progress by necessary improvements in fields like public administration, housing, health and sanitation, taxation, and agrarian reform. Under this broad objective U.S.

economic aid in Southeast Asia has a potential for shaping the contours of a transitional society.

Obviously the recipient government and the United States must be in basic agreement on common objectives, for failure in this respect would reduce to a minimum or prevent efforts to generate a local momentum toward self-sustained growth. Such agreement is also conducive to compromise on priorities in country-wide planning. Furthermore, the need to aim toward independence of American aid, not perpetual dependence upon it, is essential. No true Southeast Asian nationalist wants to be a permanent dependent of an outside power, regardless of a continuation of immediate and visible returns. Nor does the American policy-maker or taxpayer desire to perpetuate the cost of foreign aid.

Under this basic concept of U.S. economic assistance two highly significant by-products emerge, often being themselves considered the main objectives. The first by-product, the prevention of the expansion of communism in Southeast Asia, is clearly a matter of great importance. American stress on this aspect is perhaps more significant in terms of congressional appropriations and public support at home than in some countries of Southeast Asia that certainly need to be bolstered against the inroads of communism but whose outlook on world politics keeps them from being openly anti-Communist.

The trade and aid offensive of the Sino-Soviet bloc in Southeast Asia has clearly added a new dimension to the rationale of the U.S. economic assistance programs. The Communists have introduced projects intended to win the attention and sympathy of Asians, raising questions of Western countermoves. In the long run the United States will probably achieve sound and permanent political dividends by economic programs that would make good sense even if the Peking-Moscow axis were not seeking to make economic inroads. Moreover, if Washington has an adequate and effective program in a country like India, Soviet aid may even contribute to the net benefit of the populace.

Another by-product of the basic rationale in American aid to Southeast Asia is the clear-cut desire to increase political stability by means of reinforcing economic growth. The assumption is made that a higher standard of living will reduce sources of discontent and encourage stable conditions. At the same time a firmer base can be provided for responsible political and economic relations among the Southeast Asian countries, for if they can balance conflicting domestic pressures without totalitarian methods, they are more apt to be good neighbors within their region and even within the world community. Although the underdeveloped nations themselves have to make by far the greater effort in the planning and use of their human and material resources, American assistance can on occasion furnish just the margin required for steady improvement. When a particular project is completed, it is obviously up to the Asians themselves to make the best use of their new assets. For instance, the Thai-American Friendship Highway and the Cambodian-American Friendship Highway, built with U.S. aid, must prove their peacetime value in terms of actual use by the local peoples.

But in some respects economic assistance is not conducive to stability. Expectations can well exceed practical fulfillment; foreign aid can serve to uproot many long-established foundations of traditional society; it can even be used to further corruption; and, finally, in the event of a Communist take-over, any new assets can be used by the new regime. Social structures in transition always present problems of adjustment for various groups both inside and outside the governing class. Yet, despite inevitable dislocations, the facing of the inevitable in a rational, responsible, and democratic way is for many countries the only real alternative to a Communist revolution. Governments in Southeast Asia must respond to changing conditions, for political rigidity can result in accumulated tensions that seek an illegitimate outlet. Maintaining a modicum of stability in a society suffering the pains of economic development is difficult but by no means impossible.

The achievement of a breakthrough where self-sustained economic growth may be possible in the foreseeable future has become a priority in American aid to a number of Asian countries, particularly India. In selecting countries for a concentrated effort, Washington had to be convinced at the outset that they could advance American interests in Asia. If humanitarian considerations alone were involved, all areas of free Asia could almost equally qualify for the attempted breakthrough. At the same time American officials have been speculating about a "reverse domino effect" upon communism if "islands of development" emerge, capable and willing to give substantial help to less developed neighbors. First, however, the selected recipients must have the determination and the discipline to pull their peoples up by the bootstraps. Political decisions involving some sacrifices of immediate satisfactions for the sake of long-range achievements are essential, but it is not easy for a generation faced with the urgent requirements of today to plan and work for a better life for the next or even the third generation.

Economic development in India requires what has been called an adequate "social overhead and infrastructure." Adequate leadership is essential, and the response to leadership among the people must be fairly sympathetic; a national purpose must be articulated; and the institutions of the state must be sound yet flexible. The Indian government, moreover, must be willing to pursue policies in trade, taxation, and investment that will not obstruct American efforts to help the development program. If American stated goals correspond broadly to those of key Indian groups and if American criteria and inducements are used judiciously, the Indian government can look upon the U.S. role as cooperation rather than intervention. "Institution building," the improvement of some existing institutions and the establishment of others, may be remarkably advanced by a free exchange of ideas and experience. Many skills—technical, professional, and executive—must certainly be acquired to achieve the desired Indian goals, and America can lend and teach some of these skills. But the process of nation-wide uplift in broad economic and social advancement will take many years. Americans who tend to aim for and to expect rapid and momentous results are apt to be disappointed.

Early in 1961 the Kennedy administration launched a "Decade of Development" as a major aspect of U.S. foreign policy. Profiting from the experience of the 1950s and anticipating the needs of the 1960s, the formulators of this program gave a new look to an old problem. While the final plans were evolutionary rather than revolutionary, certain important new emphases emerged. The Decade of Development called for assistance planned and financed on a long-term basis, a foreign aid administration reorganized at home and abroad, and more correlated help by other industrial nations. Along with necessities and responsibilities, opportunities for the United States were stressed. In addition to its traditional objectives, military assistance would, whenever possible, contribute to civil works and economic development. The aid program attempted to reduce planning in terms of single projects and to maximize over-all country planning with a system of priorities. The transfer of economic aid from a year-to-year basis (often associated with short-term objectives) to a long-range basis would better enable Washington and the political leaders of recipient nations to plan and execute programs of general economic development. Since underdeveloped economies vary from primitive conditions to the near breakthrough stage, it was emphasized that each country would have to be considered as an individual case. Mass education was stressed as one of the keys to economic growth in a democratic framework.

Under the former Mutual Security Program (MSP) economic assistance in Southeast Asia had been provided under six categories: defense support, special assistance, technical cooperation, Development Loan Fund (DLF), contingency fund, and a group of miscellaneous programs. Defense support was closely related to military assistance, for the countries receiving it had military aid agreements with the United States; it sought to help them maintain their relatively sizable military establishments without jeopardizing their economic or political stability. The defense posture of the Philippines, Thailand, the Republic of Viet-Nam, Cambodia (and even Laos for a while) was strengthened by the economic aid under defense support.

Special assistance, like that projected for Burma in fiscal year 1961, called for providing economic aid to given countries which needed it to help preserve their freedom and stability. These nations did not receive military assistance from the United States.

Technical cooperation (Point IV in President Truman's inaugural address of 1949) provided for help in the expansion of technical capacity. Indonesia was among the many states that benefited from the effort. Along with Thailand, Viet-Nam, and the Philippines, Indonesia also cooperated with the United States under the Mutual Security Program in certain training operations on its soil for participants from other underdeveloped areas.

The Development Loan Fund, established in 1957, sought to provide loans that could not be made from the International Bank for Reconstruction and Development, private investment, or other similar sources. For instance, DLF aid went into road construction in the Federation of Malaya. As a safeguard against unexpected situations the contingency fund proved valuable; it was used in the Laotian crisis of 1959 when Communist-inspired guerrilla activity became pronounced. Other programs under the MSP economic classification included items like aid for malaria control or for atomic research equipment in the Atoms for Peace effort. Outside the Mutual Security Program the Export-Import Bank extended loans to some Southeast Asian countries, and surplus farm goods under the Agricultural Trade Development and Assistance Program (U.S. Public Law 480) were provided in connection with American economic aid. Beginning chiefly as an attempt to dispose of domestic surpluses, Public Law 480 became a valuable instrument of foreign economic policy.

For fiscal year 1959 total U.S. economic aid to the countries of Southeast Asia in terms of obligations was officially given as $546.9 million. The Republic of Viet-Nam received the largest amount, $206.9 million, followed by $148.9 million for the Philippines, and then Thailand and Indonesia with $58.9 million and $53.6 million, respectively. Laos, Cambodia, and Malaya were relatively close to one another (the exact figures being $25.4 million, $24.6 million, and $20.2 million), and Burma was far down the list with $8.4 million. The figures for fiscal year 1961, officially cited in 1962, showed a substantial drop to $353.9 million. After this cut was distributed among the countries of the region, Viet-Nam's share dropped to $150.5 million and aid to the Philippines, Indonesia, and Thailand was almost halved to $87.0, $33.0, and $25.4 million, respectively. With $32.7 million Laos received a little more than in 1959 and Cambodia with $24.3 million remained at almost the same level. Finally, aid to Malaya shrank to $0.4 million and to Burma, to $0.6 million.

In terms of total economic assistance, over a period of years, Viet-Nam after the partition of Indochina received in aid obligations between fiscal years 1955 and 1959 inclusive $1,216.5 million, and the Philippines between 1946 and 1959 $1,177.9 million. The latter figure includes $634.6 million for Philippines Rehabilitation and the former $0.1 million in 1954 for aid to Voluntary Relief Agencies. Between fiscal 1951 and 1959 Indonesia received

$373 million, Thailand $240.5 million, and Burma $96.4 million. Officially included in the aid obligations to Indonesia were an Export-Import Bank loan of $100 million in 1950, a loan of $63.6 million to buy U.S. surplus property in 1947, and assistance to the amount of $4.1 million in 1946 in civilian supplies. (The figure for Thailand also included a loan of $6.2 million to buy U.S. surplus property in 1946, and for Burma a similar loan of $5 million in 1947.) Between fiscal 1955 and 1959 Laos received in obligations $190.8 million, Cambodia $173.4 million, and the Federation of Malaya $21.5 million. The total for Malaya was made up of $20 million from the Development Loan Fund in fiscal 1959 and only $1.5 million between 1955 and 1959 just to Voluntary Relief Agencies. The sum total of U.S. obligations for economic aid to the Southeast Asian countries for the periods defined was officially given in 1960 as $3,490 million.

By way of contrast it is estimated that in the single fiscal year 1959 Americans spent $30.4 billion buying and operating automobiles and $3 billion on television and radio. In that same year an aid program of $3.4 billion would amount to only 0.74 per cent of the gross national product and 4.3 per cent of the federal budget. As a final note, in that year 88 cents of every military assistance dollar was spent in the United States.

Under the Act for International Development which Congress approved at the end of August 1961, reflecting the President's message of March 22 on foreign assistance, the categories relevant to long-term social and economic development are Development Loans, Development Grants, and Development Research. The loans are the chief focus of the effort, being largely for capital projects and repayable in U.S. dollars at little or no interest over periods extending up to 50 years. The grants are chiefly for developing human resources through education and technical assistance, but in some cases they are for communications, roads, and harbors. The research funds are designed to find techniques and tools leading to better use of the aid money, thus giving decision-makers a wider range of choice. The category of Supporting Assistance is centered on meeting strategic and political needs, such as assisting countries in the support of their military defense effort, helping them to keep U.S. military bases, preventing them from experiencing economic conditions that would endanger American political interests, and preventing them from becoming dependent solely on economic aid from the Sino-Soviet bloc. Supporting Assistance is widely used for financing commodity imports in a selected number of nations. The Contingency Fund category is to meet unexpected developments and emergencies, whereas the International Organizations category is to assist ten programs under the United Nations, three under regional organizations, and one under an *ad hoc* grouping.

The Decade of Development approach further stressed another vehicle of American aid, Food-for-Peace, with its program of distribution overseas of surplus American agricultural commodities; and it also supported investment surveys and broader guarantees to encourage U.S. private investments abroad. The Peace Corps of American volunteers, serving in developing areas in various capacities at the request of the host governments, soon proved itself a valuable human element in the Decade of Development. Organized as an agency in the Department of State, the Peace Corps has a director with the rank of an Assistant Secretary. In Southeast Asia Peace Corps volunteers are already serving in the Philippines, Indonesia, Thailand, Malaya, North Borneo, and Sarawak.

A significant aspect of the foreign aid program in President Kennedy's initial plans was the long-term funding of development loans by means of borrowing authority for the U.S. Treasury over a period of five years. On May 26, 1961, the President requested Congress to authorize him to borrow $900 million in fiscal year 1962 and $1.6 billion in each of the next four years.

Additional aid would be authorized from repayments, around $300 million per annum for five years, from previous foreign loans. The rest of the program would be subject to the usual yearly appropriation process. Congress insisted on annual appropriations for development loans but approved of long-term authorization. The total request of the President for foreign aid for fiscal year 1962 was $4,475.5 million, of which economic assistance was $2,590.5 million and military assistance $1,885 million. As could be expected, Congress reduced the figure in both the authorization and the appropriation process. The budget of the economic aid program reflected the greater emphasis on loans as compared with grants, and on development purposes as compared with nondevelopment ones. Grants would be made available beyond the conclusion of a given fiscal year. Under the requested Food-for-Peace legislation, sales for local currencies to the amount of $7.5 billion for five years (ending December 31, 1966) and grants (chiefly for relief) to the extent of $1.5 billion for the same period would be authorized.

Experience has shown that it is always difficult and often misleading to separate American aid programs into fixed categories. In fact, U.S. aid programs should probably be viewed in their totality from the perspective of American national objectives. As already stressed, military assistance and supporting assistance are particularly related, and aid in strictly economic development enhances the ultimate military posture of a state by building up its power potential. The exact "mix" of U.S. economic and military assistance varies from country to country. Local circumstances necessitate various combinations, and emergencies create needs for prompt and special attention. Important in the "mix" is the position taken by the government in the cold war; Indonesia presents a different pattern from the Philippines or, again, Burma from Thailand. The basically *ad hoc* pattern of American assistance to the different countries of Southeast Asia has occasioned criticisms that the general program in the region is lacking any over-all plan.

Various domestic pressures in both the donor and recipient countries affect the strategy and even the tactics of foreign aid. In the controversial matter of population control, for example, the administrations of President Eisenhower and President Kennedy have affirmed that a foreign government must formulate its own policy and work out its own methods. Although unchecked population expansion threatens to cancel out advances in economic development, both Republican and Democratic administrations have steered clear of the moral and political questions that would arise if the United States openly encouraged birth control in the developing countries.

The task of administering economic aid, now taken over by the Agency for International Development (AID), has been a continuous U.S. responsibility for more than twenty years. The present assistance effort was preceded by the lend-lease program, the United Nations Relief and Rehabilitation Administration as well as Government and Relief in Occupied Areas, and the Marshall Plan which constituted in the words of Charles E. Bohlen "the first coherent measure of economic recovery."[2] Along with the different tasks in the postwar years the administration structure has changed, and even the names of the controlling agencies have been altered to reflect different emphases. Under the latest act an attempt was made through the organization of a new agency to centralize planning, provide unity of direction, and clarify responsibility. Besides taking over the former functions of the International Cooperation Administration, AID is now responsible for the Development Loan Fund, the Food-for-Peace program (in its relations with foreign countries), and the local currency lending of the Export-Import Bank. AID is an

[2] Charles E. Bohlen, "Economic Assistance in United States Foreign Policy," The Department of State Bulletin, March 28, 1960, p. 497.

agency within the Department of State; its chief (called Administrator) is an Under Secretary of State, reporting to the Secretary of State and the President. Along with three staffs in the Administrator's office in Washington are three program offices and four management staff offices, as well as the four regional bureaus—one each for the Far East, Near East and South Asia, Africa and Europe, and Latin America. These regional bureaus under four regional assistant administrators have the chief responsibility for making and implementing U.S. programs in their respective areas. Although operational responsibility for the programs of military assistance provided under the International Peace and Security Act remains with the Department of Defense, the Secretary of State gives over-all direction and supervision.

Personnel in these increased aid efforts has been expanded until it is not surprising to find that overseas Foreign Service employees are closely matched in number by AID employees and those Americans under contract for foreign assistance. In many capitals the embassy staff is well outnumbered by AID personnel. A "little America" or an extensive U.S. presence in the capital of a small state has raised real problems in relations between Washington and the local host. (Laos was once a case in point.) But in view of the scope of U.S. aid programs in some countries, it is often difficult to reduce the number of Americans needed on the spot. Criticisms of U.S. officials in Southeast Asia were dramatized in *The Ugly American*, a book that stressed certain weaknesses rather than many strengths of the overseas employees of the United States.

The various aid missions in Southeast Asia have to function within the framework of the American official community. The director of the local mission has operational responsibility, but he reports to the ambassador. He is a member of the country team along with the ranking officer or official of the military advisory group, the information service, or any other major unit, and the team operates under the ambassador's chairmanship. If its members are cooperative, the country team functions well, but it breaks down if various individuals disagree and readily appeal without hesitation to their superiors in Washington for support. In such a case controversies may have to be ironed out not at the local level but in Washington. President Kennedy has taken steps to strengthen the over-all role of the U.S. ambassador. All these considerations are important, for in today's diplomacy of modernization the contacts between states of vastly differing technology and power present many more problems than those associated with the classical diplomacy of the old European state system.

The future of American economic and technical aid to the countries of Southeast Asia is linked with the broad problems of development in many other areas of Asia and Africa. Yet the multifarious threat of Communist China to Southeast Asia will give an impetus to U.S. aid programs not generally found in countries geographically remote from the Peking-Moscow bloc, even though all the developing states share in varying degrees the pressures arising from the growing needs and demands of their peoples. Under the circumstances, the termination of American economic aid to Southeast Asia is not at all likely in the foreseeable future. The situation calls for a sustained program over many years backed by an assured budget, administered with effective machinery, and guided by a sound concept of what has been called "overseasmanship." It is also necessary to keep constantly in mind the correlation of the over-all U.S. government effort with the programs of sympathetic governments, of private foundations, and of international organizations. A successful long-range effort, of course, cannot be dissociated over the years from a certain reorientation on the part of Congress and of the American people. But if the effort is successful, the development of Southeast Asia can contribute to the economic prosperity of the United States, produce a local economy better able to support military needs, help immunize against communism, and serve to advance democratic institutions.

MULTILATERAL ECONOMIC AID

One of the most significant characteristics of recent years is cooperation between several industrial nations in order to assist in the economic development of "backward" countries. Besides offering their own bilateral aid programs, a number of industrialized powers like the United States, France, Great Britain, and the Federal Republic of Germany also participate in a variety of multilateral programs. The decline of empire has removed some of the old incentives which prompted colonial powers to develop their overseas possessions, but there is a growing realization that in a shrinking world the welfare of mankind is indivisible. Both political and humanitarian considerations motivate the Western supporters of bilateral or multilateral foreign aid. Assistance can be used toward advancing the common interests of a group of states, and it can also contribute to the establishment of a world order beneficial to all. In fact, many Western officials would maintain that national interests and world order are now two sides of the same coin.

The advantages for the United States of multilateral economic aid are considerable. Western European nations and Japan, all fully recovered from the Second World War, are in a position to make substantial contributions in a multilateral attempt to aid the newly independent countries of Asia and Africa, thus reinforcing American efforts. Recipient states are far less sensitive to criticism offered by experts employed by an international organization than to the remonstrances of a single outside country, especially one of the world powers. Multilateral programs can be carried out in some political climates where bilateral efforts are very much suspect. Where the United States plays a major role in UN aid efforts it is well protected through weighted voting and other safeguards against any unsound use of financial resources.

Under certain conditions the multilateral approach to assistance can be less expensive as well as more efficient, a fact not always remembered. American experts cost more than those from many other countries, and a multilateral program can draw upon technicians more suited to a modest budget and often available in large numbers. When consideration is made of other donors as well as the efforts of the recipient in a multilateral approach, for every dollar of its own the United States may see at times as many as seven others added.

The fundamental fact is that the economic challenge of the day requires a new perspective in international cooperation. Bilateral aid certainly has its place, but the problems of economic development over a large area transcend the horizons of any two governments. Cooperation among the donors of the free world is essential, as is mutuality between them and the developing countries; for without such common endeavors the Sino-Soviet bloc will use political schism to further its own penetration. Established cooperation through the United Nations or other multilateral organs already points the way to future progress. The use of economics as an instrument of international policy in the free world is bound to be increasingly important. Eugene R. Black, former head of the International Bank for Reconstruction and Development, has already shown in the Indus River settlement the potential of "development diplomats."

Under the auspices of the United Nations a number of specific institutions have emerged which are helpful to cooperative efforts in economic aid. The International Bank for Reconstruction and Development (IBRD) has proved its worth, and its capital has been doubled; so have the International Monetary Fund (IMF), whose resources have been greatly increased, and the International Finance Corporation (IFC), an affiliate of the International Bank. To these lending institutions has been added the International Development Association (IDA), closely affiliated with the IBRD, with initial resources of $750 million. The United Nations Expanded Program of Technical Assistance, the Special Fund authorized in 1958, and the Operational, Executive and Administrative Personnel program or OPEX (begun in the same year under the regular budget) are also pulling their weight.

Outside the United Nations the Development Assistance Group of ten capital-exporting countries constituted a consultative forum devoted to discussing the most effective capital flow for economic growth. With the Organization for Economic Cooperation and Development (OECD) succeeding the Organization for European Economic Cooperation (OEEC), the work of the Development Assistance Group can take place in a new framework. In another direction consortia have been formed to provide aid to India and Pakistan in their economic development plans. Finally, the much-publicized Colombo Plan began as an international effort outside the United Nations to help the countries of South and Southeast Asia raise their living standards through aid in economic development and technical assistance. Organized in 1950 by a number of British Commonwealth members and dependencies, the Colombo Plan eventually included as "donors" Australia, New Zealand, Canada, Great Britain, the United States, and Japan while aid was received by India, Pakistan, Nepal, Ceylon, Burma, Thailand, Malaya, Singapore, the Philippines, North Borneo, Sarawak, Indonesia, Bhutan, South Korea, Cambodia, Laos, and South Viet-Nam. It was estimated that up to June 1959 the six "donor" countries had contributed the equivalent of more than $6 billion, although it should not be overlooked that the United States alone had provided about $5,660 million. Actually the word "donor" is relative, for many recipients of Colombo Plan aid also contribute some assistance, especially in the field of training; indeed, by 1960 there were few recipients that had not rendered help to one or more fellow participants. In the strict sense, assistance under the Colombo Plan is provided on a bilateral basis, but yearly conferences of all members through the Consultative Committee afford important forums for comparison and evaluation of the various programs. The frankness of these discussions enables all members to acquire more insight into the common economic and social problems of South and Southeast Asia.

Unfortunately regional cooperation as exemplified by the Colombo Plan is limited. Political considerations even restrict progress in the economic field where there is possibly the greatest single potential for regionalism. At the Simla Conference of certain Asian states, held to discuss the value of some kind of an institution like the Organization for European Economic Cooperation, it was significantly concluded on May 13, 1955, that an "intermediary regional organization" would not be advantageous. From its headquarters in Bangkok the United Nations Economic Commission for Asia and the Far East has been considering the many similar economic problems of Asian countries, but it has not yet succeeded in developing any substantial regional consciousness. Participation by the Soviet Union in ECAFE has further reduced the possibilities of cooperation among all the members. Yet the United States by its various economic activities in Southern Asia is making some contributions to regional understanding. Between fiscal years 1956 and 1959 inclusive the Asian Economic Development Fund committed $85.1 million. In 1956 a survey was arranged under American auspices for a possible regional telecommunications network for Thailand, South Viet-Nam, and Laos. Washington encouraged the establishment in 1961 of an Asian Productivity Organization to exchange on a broad regional basis technical information. The United States, Thailand, and South Viet-Nam have participated in a joint maritime research program in the South China Sea and Gulf of Siam. The Indus Basin project, involving substantial American aid to India and Pakistan, exemplified three important aspects of the U.S. assistance effort—self-help, regional cooperation, and contributions from other industrialized countries.

A significant step in economic regionalism in peninsular Southeast Asia is the multilateral attempt to develop the lower Mekong basin. At its thirteenth session in March 1957, ECAFE officially endorsed the suggestions of Thailand, Cambodia, Laos, and the Republic of Viet-Nam that the preliminary studies undertaken by its secretariat be jointly continued with the four riparian countries. In October these governments convened a Committee for Co-ordination of Investigations of the Lower Mekong Basin whose main functions were to "promote, co-ordinate, supervise and control the planning and investigation of water resources development projects in the lower Mekong basin."[3] The Committee includes one member from each state vested with plenipotentiary authority, and decisions are made unanimously. In March 1959 Dr. C. Hart Schaaf, who combined distinguished U.N. service with extensive experience in Southeast Asia, was appointed by Secretary-General Dag Hammarskjold as Executive Agent of the Co-ordination Committee. The Advisory Board consists of Indian, French, Australian, and American representatives.

Although the lower Mekong basin had been the subject of a number of studies, two appearing from ECAFE in 1952 and 1957 and one from ICA in 1956, it was the January 1958 report

[3] Statute, Committee for Co-ordination of Investigations of the Lower Mekong Basin (unpublished).

of the United Nations Survey Mission, headed by Lieutenant General Raymond A. Wheeler, that produced the greatest impact. Based on a three-month survey of the river, the report recommended a program of systematic, multipurpose investigations over a five-year period at an estimated expenditure of some $9.2 million. Within a month the Co-ordination Committee had adopted this program.

A rich variety of assistance in the Mekong scheme has come from the United Nations and its specialized agencies, from individual countries, private sources, and from the riparian states themselves. Concrete aid has been forthcoming from the United States, France, the Netherlands, Iran, Israel, the Republic of China, Italy, the Federal Republic of Germany, Pakistan, India, the Philippines, Japan, Canada, Australia, New Zealand, and Great Britain. For its part, the American contribution now totals $4.7 million. By late 1961 Cambodia, Laos, Viet-Nam, and Thailand had pledged $1,670,340, mostly in local funds for the undertaking. The Ford Foundation has financed the Gilbert White Mission on economic aspects of Mekong development. As of January 1, 1962, the scheme had total resources of over $14 million. The U.N. Technical Assistance Board acting with the Bureau of Technical Assistance Operations, the Food and Agriculture Organization, the World Meteorological Organization, and the Special Fund have all helped the project. Cooperation has also developed with the World Health Organization, UNESCO, IBRD, the International Labor Organization, and the International Atomic Energy Agency. As might be expected, the Executive Agent and the Co-ordination Committee work closely with the Executive Secretary and secretariat of ECAFE.

After the complex investigations of the lower Mekong basin are completed, the execution of projects relating to hydroelectric power, navigation, and transportation; flood control, irrigation, and drainage; agriculture, forestry, and fisheries, and min-eral resources will be time consuming and expensive. The lower basin of the Mekong is some 1,500 miles long and embraces approximately 230,000 square miles. The 17 million inhabitants of the area are under four different sovereignties and vary in ethnic, religious, and linguistic composition as well as political outlook. If full advantage is taken of the new resources that will come as a result of river development, the living standards of the area will have to be markedly improved and realistic goals must be shaped in the light of present and future capacities of the riparian states. With these considerations in mind, steps have been taken toward the early development of four major tributaries, one in each country. Political differences among neighbors must also be settled or minimized in a successful program; and so far, it should be stressed, the Co-ordination Committee has continued to meet despite serious disputes between Cambodia and its neighbors to the east and west and grave unrest in Laos. Perhaps the most significant aspect of the development scheme to date is the widespread cooperation inside and outside Southeast Asia that it has occasioned. The "Mekong Spirit" may be a signpost for the future.

Although American participation in multilateral aid programs has many advantages, Congress and the taxpayers must be convinced that the interests of the United States are not sacrificed. Domestic politics can easily affect American participation in multilateral programs, perhaps to a greater extent than in bilateral operations. Political leaders do not want to see the United States committed to development projects which may get beyond its own ability to influence or perhaps even control. But if a long-range national objective is the promotion of a stable world order, the multilateral approach to American assistance is likely to bring dividends in terms of both the national interest and the world community.

Other Economic Problems

About five per cent of U.S. exports go to Southeast Asia and approximately five per cent of American imports come from the area. Around a fourth of the trade of Southeast Asia is with the United States and another fourth with Europe; as has been noted, trade is limited among the countries of the region except in a few items like rice. The expansion of commerce under favorable conditions is mutually profitable, although at the present time a Western attitude of "trade, not aid" presents an alternative in absolute terms that is undesirable. Current surpluses of certain primary commodities in the area and the future challenge of certain competitive manufactured products in the world market must be reckoned with in considerations of commerce. Washington is faced, and will continued to be faced, with important decisions involving domestic interests in trade with the developing countries.

International differences of opinion can easily arise from U.S. policies toward trade and aid in Southeast Asia. In May 1960 the United States agreed under its Food-for-Peace program to provide India for rupees with a reserve of American surplus rice and wheat worth $1,276 million, market value, over a four-year period. The apprehension of Thailand over the possible effects of this agreement on its rice sales abroad led to the resignation of Thanat Khoman, the Thai foreign minister. He quickly reconsidered, but the impasse in relations between Bangkok and Washington over the subject remained. The development of a strong demand during the year for Thai rice and arrangements to sell almost all the exportable crop by mid-July reduced, at least temporarily, the friction.

Many countries in Southeast Asia depend heavily for their foreign exchange upon a few items of export. Malaya earns almost 46 per cent of its foreign exchange from rubber exports and 8 per cent from tin; Indonesia gets almost 35 per cent from rubber and 12 per cent from tin. Fluctuations in the prices of rubber and tin are, therefore, a most serious problem for such countries. For example, in 1951 rubber was selling as high as 88 cents a pound, but in the next two years the price dropped precipitately to 20 cents. The world price of rubber rose again to about 36 cents in 1954, and then another sharp drop occurred in 1957; a recovery followed, but well into 1959 the price was a little above 30 cents a pound. Tin also has fluctuated in price, even more noticeably than rubber, and international marketing arrangements for tin, while useful, have obviously not yet solved the problem.

Since the United States is a large importer of tin and rubber, it is blamed to quite some extent for the hardships caused by price decline. Sales of tin and rubber from surpluses in the large American stockpiles, though done in consultation with key producing countries and calculated not to depress the market, have aroused apprehension and resentment. The European Economic Community has also caused concern in Southeast Asia, for the governments are not certain how their countries will be affected over the long run. Because the United States is trying to facilitate a partnership between the industrialized nations of the West and the developing countries of Asia, Africa, and Latin America, it is significant that Washington is moving toward a far more active role in international commodity agreements and other arrangements aimed at price and market stabilization.

Private investment in Southeast Asia from outside the region is another important factor in international economic relations. During the colonial period it was largely responsible for the development of certain aspects of the economy, particularly plantations and mines. Since V-J Day and the emergence of the independent states, however, the private investor has been more reluctant to put money into the area. Apart from internal disorder in many of the countries, the complexities of working with local bureaucracies (often suspicious of all "foreign capitalists") coupled with frequently high rates of taxation, dangers of expropriation without adequate compensation, and the problems of remitting profits or repatriating capital tend to remind investors of other countries considered better risks. In 1958, new direct investments by American citizens and companies, excluding reinvested earnings of subsidiaries, amounted to $398 million in Canada, $312 million in Latin America, $173 million in Europe, and only $143 million in all the rest of the world.

Yet American and other private capital, along with the provision of technical and managerial talents, can make a real contribution far beyond the present scale to the developing areas of Southeast Asia. And in some of the countries emergent political conditions and attitudes indicate a better environment for the foreign private investor. In 1959 Thailand and Malaya, for instance, made specific efforts to attract a greater amount of private capital. Washington is also trying through various ways to encourage private investment in the developing areas. Agreements having investment incentive clauses are being negotiated; investment surveys are being emphasized; more trade missions are going abroad; an investment guaranty program has provisions favorable to American private investors. In fiscal 1961 the MSP gave increased emphasis to support for the private economic sector of countries receiving American aid. Local institutions, like development banks and investment promotion organizations, are being created or strengthened to assist foreign as well as local private investment.

The United States has moved a long way from the days of "dollar diplomacy," sometimes supported by an American gunboat; the protection of commercial interests is still important, but better ways have been devised. That the United States is not neglecting its own interests is illustrated in the 1959 requirement that the procurement policy of the DLF should give primary emphasis to American goods and services in financing the foreign exchange costs in development projects. Subsequent steps taken in 1960 included the reduction of overseas procurements by ICA and of purchases of military equipment abroad by the Defense Department. Other cases in point, which antedate the crisis arising from the large dollar outflow, are provisions related to the protection of American shipping, the stockpiling of certain strategic materials, and the disposal of surplus agricultural products.

Obviously the economic problems of Southeast Asia will long challenge the policy-makers in Washington. Conditions in the area, the threat posed by Sino-Soviet economic inroads, the issues associated with American aid, whether on the bilateral or multilateral basis, and the traditional problems related to normal trade, commodity prices, and private investment, all call for constant study and evaluation. However much a truism, it bears repeating that policy must be flexible to meet change while resolutely promoting the objective of laying the economic foundation for stability and security in ways mutually beneficial to the States of Southeast Asia and the West.

NINE

The United States and Southeast Asian Leadership

In the complex politics of Southeast Asia the United States is deeply concerned with many of the problems of local leadership. Apart from the obvious domestic dangers of inadequate leadership, the international consequences of political instability are frequently grave. While the new Asian leaders are committed to developing national unity, any basic consensus is often a remote ideal in the fledgling countries. The inconstancies of leadership in a transition area like Southeast Asia cannot be ignored by the United States and other interested nations.

Authoritarian regimes have long been customary in the region. Whether the old era of Asian potentates is considered, or the interval of Western colonial rule, or even to a considerable degree the period of independence after the Second World War, there is no mistaking the influence of authoritarianism. In the annals of Burma, for instance, there is a continuous authoritarian tradition through the kings, later the British governors, and then the administrations of General Ne Win. Ngo Dinh Diem in Saigon and Ho Chi Minh in Hanoi both continue in many respects the authoritarian line stretching back through the French governors-general of Indochina to the Annamite emperors. In parts of pre-colonial Southeast Asia, especially the islands now known as the Philippines and Indonesia, local chiefs or sultans never acquired the widespread and sustained dominion of the kings of Burma or emperors of Annam. In the Philippines numerous caciques were paramount in various localities until the colonial period, but they were gradually brought under the centralized and authoritarian regime of the Spanish and early American governors-general, whose tradition of strong rule continued under some of the Filipino presidents of the Commonwealth and the Republic. As for Thailand, the autocratic powers of the kings before the forced granting of the constitution of 1932 were, apart from interludes, transmitted direct to a military oligarchy.

In spite of the heritage of the past, efforts to achieve constitutional democracy in all the newly independent countries of Southeast Asia (save for the totalitarian state in North Viet-Nam) were made. They reflected a system of values based primarily upon the model of the former metropolitan powers on their home soil and specifically rejecting traditional Asian concepts of authoritarian rule. The forms of Western democracy were generally adopted: written constitutions, widespread suffrage and elections, political parties and national parliaments, and cabinet or presidential governments. If formal structure rather than political dynamics were the basis for evaluation, the fledglings of Southeast Asia often represent ideal models of constitutional democracy.

But it soon became evident that a new trend toward authoritarianism was developing in the region. Disillusionment was setting in as a result of great expectations and limited fulfillment.

The countries were not stabilized by large middle classes so often central to the development of democratic institutions. The new governments, inspired with the winning of independence, had made too many plans and promises beyond their actual capacity to transform blueprints into reality. In most of the countries lack of adequate preparation for the functioning of constitutional democracy was also a basic cause of disillusionment. This type of government is perhaps the most difficult kind in the world to transplant, and the key concept of the "loyal opposition" was found very hard to apply in practical terms; after all, even with many decades of experience some Western powers still have their own periods of aberration. Moreover, constitutional democracy had somehow to be adjusted to the cultural environment of Asia before it could succeed. Although local nationalist leaders placed great stress on inculcating their Asian heritage in the political institutions of independence, they did not know how to combine this heritage with Western constitutional democracy. In seeking a synthesis, Ngo Dinh Diem, for instance, accepts both the Confucian concept of "government by virtue" and the Western ideal of "government by law."

Experience has demonstrated that while a period of tutelage is essential in the process of developing democratic institutions, this tutelage can come either before independence as a deliberate policy of the metropolitan powers or after independence in a period of strong indigenous leadership. Constitutional democracy has best functioned up to the present time in the Republic of the Philippines and the Federation of Malaya. In the former, the United States began to prepare the country for self-government relatively only a few years after acquisition; and the Commonwealth interval was a formal period of tutelage preceding the proclamation of independence on the Fourth of July, 1946. In the Federation of Malaya, the process of preparation by the British was much more speedy but it proved effective. On the other hand, in Indonesia, where parliamentary democracy has presently failed, the Dutch gave the people no real tutelage for self-government, and the break was preceded by violence and bloodshed.

Attempts by the new governments to make constitutional democracy work in Southeast Asia coincided with great domestic and international tension. The destruction and dislocation occasioned by the Japanese occupation were followed by the relatively rapid grant of independence and the immediate task of making government a going concern. The growing demands of the people compared with the limited resources of the authorities, the agitation of local Communists—all helped to produce an environment not conducive to the transplanting of democracy. On top of these domestic pressures developments in the cold war strained the Southeast Asian governments by raising dangers of new intrusions, by bringing serious divisions among them in outlook, and by requiring grave decisions in foreign policy. Perhaps it is surprising that constitutional democracy has functioned as well as it has in Southeast Asia.

The creation of political stability in the region may or may not be associated with democratic institutions. Here stability involves cohesive leadership sufficiently strong to preserve the integrity of the state and to make possible orderly development. A common assumption is that in the process of raising the standard of living political stability in a democratic framework is produced or at least facilitated. Although an expanding economy in terms of an increase in per capita income better enables a government to meet the needs and demands of the people and thus to provide the economic underpinning of democratic institutions, the leadership of the state in the process need not necessarily be inclined toward democracy. In fact, an authoritarian regime has certain advantages in pulling a nation up by the bootstraps through complete control and regulation of the economic system and political processes. The economic transformation of the Soviet Union in a generation despite the destruction caused by the German invasion is a case in point. At the same time human values like the rights of the individual and the consent of the governed through democratic processes are ruthlessly sacrificed.

Even though a rising standard of living may not lead to democratic institutions, struggling democracies are seriously threatened or set back in a deteriorating economic situation. The Great Depression, for example, paved the way for the collapse of the Weimar Republic and the rise of Hitler, although Germany was industrialized and had a high standard of living. In Southeast Asia, where even normal fluctuations in the price of key exports affect the economy of many countries, another world depression would probably lead to consequences that would set back for many years the progress already made in building democratic institutions. The rising middle class would be hard hit, a point of increasing significance as its numbers grow. The governments of the Philippines and Malaya, to be specific, would be blamed by the public for the economic decline and might resort to totalitarian methods to stay in power, if only in an effort to prevent a Communist take-over. In Indonesia deteriorating economic conditions as a result of the inability of the government since *Merdeka* to cope adequately with grave problems have already contributed to the current collapse of parliamentary democracy. In the Republic of Viet-Nam, where the government is directly menaced by the Communist threat from the north and by growing subversive activity within its territory, a continued decline in the economy could pave the way for a Communist take-over unless greater assistance efforts by the United States were forthcoming. Although democratic processes are in abeyance in Thailand, a failure because of a depression to find outlets for its rice (or to get the equivalent returns in outside aid) could produce the conditions needed by the Communists for success.

For an expanding economy, whether or not within a frame-work of democratic institutions, adequate national leadership with the willingness and capacity to act according to needs of the situation is clearly a *sine qua non*. And, adequate leadership is just as important in the development of democratic institutions. The three variables—a rising standard of living, political stability with sound leadership, and the growth of democratic institutions—are, of course, subject to changes in degree of emphasis and significance from country to country in Southeast Asia. Although leadership strong enough to sustain economic growth can ordinarily maintain political stability, the importance of democratic institutions should not be minimized. On balance, it can be stated that in the long run democratic processes are most apt to provide political stability, because the expression of dissatisfaction and the programs to cope with it through democratic means constitute a greater stabilizing factor than do repression and the possibility of revolution. Widely needed still are viable political institutions that will enable power to be held and transferred by the consent of a workable majority.

Before they withdrew, the Americans and the British bequeathed to the emerging ruling elements of the new states in the Philippines, Malaya, and Burma a deeper belief in democracy than did the Dutch and French upon leaving Indonesia and the states of Indochina. Indeed, it can be argued that the paternalism of Paris and The Hague toward their possessions in Southeast Asia was in turn assumed to quite an extent by the new leaders toward their own peoples.

The complicated process of producing stability in a democratic framework has been evaluated too much in terms of absolutes. If the postwar constitutions of the new states have not worked well in practice, if adherence to forms rather than to substance has prevailed, if political parties have served to create village schisms rather than to provide legitimate outlets for public expression, there is a tendency to judge the entire democratic experiment a failure. But learning is a process of gaining self-reliance by experience, of making mistakes and trying not to repeat them, of moving from one stage to the next until the goal is reached. Even if the early postwar experiment in democratic processes in many Southeast Asian countries has failed to live up to initial expectations, much has been gained through the very experience. In some cases attempts can now be made on a graduated, evolutionary basis with self-imposed steps of tutelage. Dr. Sun Yat-sen in his *Chien quo ta kang* foresaw phases in Chinese political development; he did not expect the achievement of all his goals in the first phase. Most of the new states of Southeast Asia sought perfection immediately upon achieving independence; now with second thoughts they are moving more gradually toward their goals. "Guided democracy," to use an expression of Sukarno, and "basic democracies," to employ one of Mohammad Ayub Khan, may be justified if they lead in the end to full popular participation in government among the masses in the cities and countryside. And here, of course, is the danger that vested interests can come forward from the right or even from the left, which seek to forestall or prevent such evolution. Various devices can be tried such as differential representation with the number of elected members in parliament increasing and the number of appointed ones decreasing as democratic institutions take root. At the same time it is still necessary to guard against mistaking the structure of government at a given period for political realities. Thailand's experience in differential representation in parliament is a case in point.

THE ELITES

Independence brought to the helm of state the small nationalist elites who were flourishing in the concluding phase of the colonial era. Although the nationalist politicians managed in most cases to achieve independence without bloodshed, they were looked upon by the people as revolutionary heroes, for they considered it necessary to use pressure techniques conducive to revolutionary fervor. As could be expected, the expression, intensity, and timing of the pressure greatly varied from country to country, much depending upon the initial and subsequent response of the metropolitan power.

The dominant Filipino nationalist elite, for instance, campaigned vigorously for independence in a political framework that permitted it. Indeed, it is significant that the Tydings-McDuffie Act of 1934 antedated by many years the formal independence commitment of other colonial powers to their possessions in Southeast Asia. On the other hand, the Malayan nationalist elite was the last to achieve *Merdeka*, but this was due much more to the slow development of nationalism in the Federation than to the hesitancy of the British. In Burma the nationalist elite achieved its goal in 1948 because, in part, of an earlier change in British government from a Conservative to a Labour ministry; in Cambodia, because of French involvement in a shooting war concentrated for the most part in the Vietnamese section of Indochina. Although subject to qualifications, the most clear-cut example of a nationalist elite achieving *Merdeka* in the orthodox concept of revolution against the Western colonial power is found in Indonesia where the "police actions" and other repressive measures of the Dutch were resisted by the local nationalists. Sukarno eloquently has noted: "We fought the Dutch with pointed bamboo stakes."

Whether or not the goal was achieved by bloodshed, the efforts of the Southeast Asian countries to win membership in the family of nations were a unifying factor among the nationalist elites. Differences among leaders in a given country could be temporarily submerged and patched up in the common effort—

thus, Burmese like Nu, Ba Swe, and Kyaw Nyein and Indonesians like Sukarno, Hatta, and Sjahrir could work together. In fact, some leaders like Norodom Sihanouk of Cambodia were galvanized into greater zeal for independence by apprehensions lest other members of the local political elite gain advantage by agitating even more ardently for it. In the case of Laos most of the nationalist elite was at one time sharing exile in Bangkok where political leaders of various persuasions found a common denominator in calling for independence from the French.

The nationalist politicians of Southeast Asia were largely educated in Western schools, either abroad or in their own countries. Their various concepts of nationalism, democracy, socialism, and communism were generally provided through Western channels. In seeking to establish constitutional democracy in Southeast Asia, the nationalist elites generally looked for precepts to the metropolitan governments of the Western powers, which many Asians had observed first-hand in travel and residence abroad. They usually considered the colonial administrations in their own countries as repressive and reactionary; although indirect rule, as practised by Britain in the greater part of Malaya through the various sultanates, sometimes provided the means for emerging nationalist politicians to give modern application to old forms. Direct colonial rule, on the other hand, presented the rising nationalist elite with a challenge to combine effectively traditional Asian values with a modern, Westernized government. Toward the indigenous aristocratic elite, usually associated with the colonial regime, the nationalist politicians frequently showed considerable hostility, particularly in Indonesia, although Malaya appears to be an exception.

As a result of their education the nationalist leaders of Southeast Asia strongly reflect the cultural impact of the modern West, notwithstanding their efforts to honor their ancient Asian heritage; their facility in the language of the former colonial power is a case in point. Some of them may still feel almost more at home in an European environment, although they recognize that too high a degree of Westernization reduces their effectiveness in Asia. Having generally broken with the indigenous aristocracy and having severed political (though not cultural) ties with the West, the nationalist elites find themselves in the process of adjustment. Such acculturation brings many complex, psychological problems for the leaders and for the people of a loosely structured society.

Most of the nationalist politicians in power have sought to maintain the standards of living set in high governing circles in the West or in erstwhile colonial circles in Asia. The residencies of the former governors-general, for instance, are now often inhabited by nationalist leaders who preserve in many respects the pomp and circumstance associated with the viceregal tradition. The new nationalist leaders have often found the cost of maintaining the dignity of their offices excessively high; at the same time great opportunities for graft and corruption have been opened, especially to those who license trade or control the state revenues, and the free press in Southeast Asia often resounds with charges and countercharges of betrayal of the public trust. In the Philippines, for example, considerable space in the newspapers is devoted to the alleged venality of officials (usually of the party opposed by the particular paper!). Graft and corruption are indeed common in Southeast Asia, but partisan accounts of this universal problem are often exaggerated.

Although the nationalist politicians were most influential in the achievement of independence and in the early history of the state, the Asian bureaucracies of administrators, technicians, and educators should not be neglected. At the time of independence such people already constituted an elite in some countries; they were neither conspicuous in the headlines nor responsible for great decisions, but they were essential in the effort to make government a going concern. The size, training, and experience of the various corps of administrators varied from country to country, depending upon the policies of the colonial powers and the length of transition to independence. The Americans in the Philippines had trained a local civil service and entrusted it with increasing duties over a period of many years. The British in Burma and Malaya also developed a career service of indigenous administrators, although the political atmosphere was different and the actual goal of independence was more remote than in the Philippines. But the French and the Dutch did not make comparable efforts in their possessions; and when independence came to Indonesia and the states of Indochina, there were grave shortages of qualified administrative personnel. In some cases European administrators have remained in Southeast Asia at the request of the new governments, while the process of training local civil servants was speeded in the hope that they could soon replace the foreigners.

Where the colonial powers developed Asian military forces, they did it for strictly imperial reasons; they were obviously not concerned with shaping Burmese or Vietnamese national units. Foreigners dominated the officer corps while the professional soldiers were generally trained and equipped along Western lines. The Philippines constituted an exception in the over-all pattern, for the transition period of the Commonwealth was used to develop the future armed units of the republic. On the other hand, the Burmese military as a national force came into being only as a consequence of the Second World War. Although local indigenous troops in some cases fought their Western masters, no military leaders of great stature emerged in the transition to independence. Moreover, in the early years after *Merdeka*, the officer corps of the military did not constitute an influential elite, despite considerable success in suppressing Communist-led insurrections.

Relationships among these three elites of nationalist politicians, administrators, and the military are influenced by the sequence in which each emerged into public life, as well as by the role each assumes or seeks in the body politic. If the three elites appeared at about the same time, the chances of cooperation among them are greater than if they became influential in succeeding periods; for rising into authority may mean partially displacing another group, thus increasing possibilities of distrust and friction. Each Southeast Asian country has its own pattern; in Burma the administrators well preceded the politicians and the soldiers, but in the Philippines there was closer correlation. Although other elites, centered around such interests as religion, labor, and business, enter into the over-all pattern in Southeast Asia, they have not yet assumed the widespread significance of the nationalist politicians, the administrators in the broad sense, or the officer corps of the military.

Now that the winning of independence for most of the area has receded into history, how have the nationalist politicians fared in facing the problems of statehood? The qualifications essential for revolutionary leadership against the colonial powers were in many respects not those needed for the intricate task of political reconstruction and economic development. The new government leaders were sincere in their efforts to help the masses, but they often did not really know how to go about it. Some of them were not able—emotionally or intellectually—to make the arduous transition from revolutionary patriotism to responsible administration. And sometimes the passions engendered by the struggle for independence made them unwilling to seek or to take competent advice from the outside. Once *Merdeka* was realized, there was a widespread conviction that the worst was over and that reconstruction would somehow be accomplished. An attempt could always be made to perpetuate the spirit of the revolution in order to direct attention from domestic problems. In the search for distinct national ideologies, the leaders made little permanent progress. Concepts like *Pantja Sila* and *Pyidawtha* in Indonesia and Burma never took deep root, and in the Philippines, no real efforts was even made to formulate and inculcate a national ideology.

In some parts of Southeast Asia political parties were among the first of the Western-imported institutions to fail. Actually they were never developed to a degree of cohesion or effectiveness comparable to parties in the United States or Great Britain; they rarely had real grass roots among the masses. Loyalty to a key person or clique rather than attention to great issues or specific programs was characteristic, for the personality cult in its various manifestations is a real political phenomenon in Southeast Asia. A certain religious, nationalist, or economic focus might be associated with a particular party, but the latter never became a really effective way of expressing the different interests of the people. Rather, the political party system represented the different interests of various leaders or factions of the nationalist elite. Status, the key to power and influence in governing circles, was won and held in most instances in terms of personal relationships. Party platforms were drawn up, campaigns were conducted, and oratory reached a zenith before an election; yet it often became evident when parliament met that public discussion was to final decision as far apart as A from Z in the alphabet. Parties in power were often accused of using the taxpayers' money for campaigns or other ways of perpetuating their position.

In the Philippines, where the party system has been given the longest opportunity to develop, a pattern is emerging which begins when one large political party wins overwhelming control of the Congress along with the presidency. This majority party then starts to lose its effectiveness through schisms among its

SOUTHEAST ASIA IN UNITED STATES POLICY

leaders, causing many to join the main opposition party which, in turn, grows strong enough to achieve an overwhelming electoral victory. (Filipino politicians sometimes seem to shift from one party alignment to another like partners in an old-fashioned square dance.) In contrast, Indonesia witnessed the rise of many political parties—especially the Communist (PKI), the Nationalist (PNI), Masjumi, and Muslim Teachers (NU)—with a consequent instability of cabinets and an eventual decline in party influence. Both of the Vietnamese republics, as well as Cambodia, are in effect one-party states. Although Burma was governed for several years after independence by a coalition of parties and groupings called the Anti-Fascist People's Freedom League, friction among its main leaders has led to its division. The Federation of Malaya still has a coalition of key parties under the Alliance, but even here the forces of disintegration are not absent. In contrast, the Communist party when allowed to operate above ground tries to take full advantage of the weaknesses of its rivals. Usually well-organized, disciplined, and financed, it seeks to profit from the lack of unity and occasional corruption of other parties, while making a real effort to win over the masses.

Like the nationalist politicians, the elite of the administrators has undergone many changes in the years since independence. Standards of efficiency widely declined, in part because departing Western officials and advisers often failed to leave behind them a sufficiently trained corps of Asians, and in part because the bureaucracies became clogged with a plethora of new officials, often semi-educated and ill-prepared for their jobs. Many patriots of the revolution sought government employment, and they were soon joined by growing numbers of poorly trained graduates from the expanding schools. The old colonial bureaucrats managed in some instances to hold their own and even become stronger, but time told against them. Besides, they had sometimes become too Europeanized, causing difficulty in get-ting along with their new anticolonial masters.

Along with these developments, the functions of government have greatly increased, providing many real opportunities for the competent administrator, technician, and educator. Public responsibility is expanding in fields like health and sanitation, transportation and communication, elementary, secondary, and higher education, not to mention state-owned or -operated busi-ness enterprises. As the concept of the welfare state takes deeper roots, the role of the administrator will be even greater. It is hoped that young intellectuals in larger number will find em-ployment, acquire stature, and contribute to modernization. A youthful specialized elite of professionally trained managers and technicians, many of whom have acquired their skills abroad, is already moving into positions of influence both inside and out-side government. Patriotic, disciplined, and modernized, this elite is coming of age when the control of the state is in Asian hands.

It was not until the late 1950s that the officer corps of the mili-tary began to play an important role in the politics of a large part of Southeast Asia. In Indonesia Lieutenant General Abdul Haris Nasution became one of the most powerful representatives of authority in a country suffering from instability and disorder. In Burma General Ne Win twice became prime minister in an effort to put a stop to threatened political chaos, and under his premiership the officer corps has been even more active in the affairs of government than in Indonesia. In Laos the Committee for the Defense of the National Interests, which rose for a while to a key position in the kingdom, was largely under military domination. Of course, the military regime of Field Marshal Sarit Thanarat is indicative of the type of government that has con-trolled Thailand in most of the years since 1932, but this mili-tary oligarchy became still more absolute with the Field Marshal's *coup* in October 1958. When faced with dissident violence, Prince Norodom Sihanouk of Cambodia found the Royal Khmer Army dependable in putting down Dap Chhuon's rising in February 1959; and Ngo Dinh Diem discovered that most of his armed forces stood fast against an attempted military *coup* in November 1960. Although the Philippine and Malayan armed forces have been largely successful in ending Communist revolts, the military of the two countries have not shown any real marks of political initiative.

The rise to influence and, in some cases, to power of military leaders in Southeast Asia is the result of a number of factors: particularly, the decline of political parties, the frequent failures of civilian leadership to cope with urgent problems of reconstruction and development, and the inefficiency of many administrators. When measured against these kinds of failings, the military in Southeast Asia appear to possess many of the attributes needed for insuring stability. The officer corps in general is dedicated to the nation, disciplined to duty, and eager to get things done. The enforcement of discipline is often conducive to national cohesion, for it weakens ties to a particular faction or locality. The military are anti-Communist in outlook; many of the members have fought armed Communist rebels, and others are still fighting them. The officer corps, whose members are often well chosen, possesses attributes of leadership not widely found in Southeast Asia outside the military profession. These men are also a modernizing influence, being reasonably well trained in the complex techniques of organizing and maintaining a modern army, and an increasingly large number have studied abroad. If given the opportunity, it is clear that they have the ability to acquire a still wider variety of technical skills in management, administration, and other fields. Officers and men alike can become one of the most advanced segments of society, combining defense and development. When they leave the service, the education and skills acquired can continue to be put to good use.

By stepping into the gap created by the weakening or failure of the other elites, the military have been providing in some cases the tutelage needed to produce conditions of political stability. If these officers do not succeed or if the civilians who come after them fail, the road may well be paved for an eventual Communist take-over. The current political elite in Southeast Asia has not abandoned the goal of constitutional democratic government, and it is hoped that the military interventions into politics may help create the habitual respect for authority and law which underlies free institutions. It is still premature to conclude that democracy has failed in Southeast Asia.

At the same time the value and effectiveness of the officer corps should not be overestimated. Some of the officers are corrupt, and factionalism is frequently common, even extending to the ranks below. There is still a widespread absence of needed technical skills, and most of the men lack the statesmanlike vision necessary for the great problems of economic development. They often need to work in harness with civilian administrators, despite the frequent weaknesses of the latter. The military, moreover, usually prefer action to persuasion, and freedom can be sacrificed if liberal ends are used to justify authoritarian means. There is always the danger that a military oligarchy will seek to perpetuate itself and thus create more of the problems it claimed to remedy.

The leadership of the countries in Southeast Asia will probably continue in the foreseeable future to present a variegated pattern —the military predominant in Thailand and probably in Burma, a delicate balance of the politician and the military in Indonesia, and a political elite dominant in the Philippines and Malaya.

A general depression or Communist victory could obviously change the picture, but alternate elites of sufficient potential do not appear to be developing very rapidly.

THE POPULAR BASE

With nine-tenths of the people living in a subsistence economy as peasants or fishermen, the outlook of the vast majority of Southeast Asians is still largely restricted to their own villages. For these people national government in their capital is far away. Widespread illiteracy and limited communications, joined to a real degree of economic self-sufficiency, contribute to the isolation of the villages. It is not surprising that representative institutions of government have been generally weak, for members of parliament have, for the most part, neither consulted with these constituents nor considered themselves responsible to them. What government the peasants have experienced above the village level has largely been from bureaucratic hands. Loyalty to the known village cannot easily be extended to the unknown nation, and the process has been complicated when different ethnic, linguistic, or cultural groups have been included within the boundaries of a state. The peasants rarely associate the national government or its Westernized leaders with themselves. It is noticeable that no significant peasant parties exist in the region. At the same time the nationalist political elites have widely permitted the peasants to retain and consume more of their production than the colonial authorities, a possible precaution against difficulties.

Yet it is tempting to underestimate the political role of the peasant. In the past he showed himself capable of being aroused by the movement for independence; now he appears at the polls when elections are held, he urges his children to go to school in order to prepare themselves for a better life, and he is beginning to realize that his age-old poverty is no longer inevitable. The impact of the "revolution of rising expectations," more noticeable in a ruling elite, quite naturally varies among the peasants within a country, but the general outlook of the peasants is certain to undergo a greater and faster change in the years ahead. The expansion of communications and transportation, the zeal for mass schooling, the development of mass media, and the effective use of propaganda techniques—all will extend the experience and the imagination of villagers.

But it is in the cities of Southeast Asia where the pace of change is now more marked. The rise of urban power is outdistancing the decline of the landed gentry, a situation capable of bringing grave political disequilibrium unless the gap is successfully bridged. In the cities are concentrated many of the facilities enabling change, including television in Manila and Bangkok. Above all, the urban areas have greatly increased in population, and since the war municipal services under the new regimes have been often unable to cope with the expansion. Because living conditions in terms of food, clothing, and shelter are generally severe, unrest has been generated. The usual presence of Chinese and Indian shopkeepers and moneylenders has also usually served to accentuate differences. As a result of the limited industrialization already accomplished, an emerging urban proletariat is beginning to apply pressure through labor unions now capable of increasing unrest and creating new tensions.

Yet possibly still more important is the plight of many young people who, having completed their limited education, increasingly flock to the big cities to get a white-collar job. Many of them have been disappointed in their quest, and they contribute to the unemployment which is already widespread in the urban centers of Southeast Asia. Even if the young people have secured a position in the swelling government service, rising inflation has cut real income for all those dependent on fixed salaries. If they have come to consider manual work beneath their dignity and station, they are loath to return to their villages; removed from the immemorial patterns of village life and cut off from traditional family ties, they appear to be victims of a society in transition. Nevertheless, they are showing increasing determination not to acquiesce in the situation, and they have come to expect more of the government than the peasants. Many have developed a more realistic conception of public service and a broader outlook on their place in the state; many think in terms of the country as a whole, well beyond village horizons.

As the urban areas of Southeast Asia once provided the locale of the nationalist elite who won independence, they are now providing the locale of many dissatisfied, partially educated youths whose political influence can be more significant in the foreseeable future than that of the peasants. Along with the growing proletariat in the cities, these young people could be successfully used by irresponsible forces from the left or from the right, unless serious government efforts are taken on their behalf. Once more a sustained program of social and economic development, of modernization, can provide opportunities for widespread useful employment in both the cities and the countryside.

U.S. POLICY TOWARD LEADERSHIP IN SPECIFIC CIRCUMSTANCES

The United States has to be realistic in dealing with the leaders of Southeast Asia. Public opinion on most specific issues in the various states is hard to determine, and public support cannot be easily mobilized on most subjects. In each country where Washington has official contacts problems arise almost daily to perplex the policy-maker, and circumstances often call for the determination of a specific American policy to meet a particular need.

In Southeast Asia the United States has had the greatest opportunity to influence political development in the Philippines. Not only was this true during the colonial period but also in the early years of independence. U.S. political institutions were considered the model, and American citizens could express ideas on the democratic processes of government without being suspected of interference. In this Philippine attitude U.S. economic and military aid after the last World War was not the deciding factor. Yet many Filipinos are the first to admit that a "show window of democracy" did not come into being in the island republic, although many Americans would claim that the Filipinos have developed democratic institutions as well as could be expected under the prevailing circumstances. The case of the Philippines indicates how very difficult it is for one country to implant in another directly or indirectly its own experience in political processes. And a stage is now rapidly approaching in the island republic, if it has not already arrived, where, for instance, attendance in an American-run school for the study of practical politics in the framework of democracy would be a political liability in the future careers of the students.

The election of Ramón Magsaysay to the presidency of the Philippines in November 1953 represents the ultimate limits of American policy in a national election in Southeast Asia. At the outset it should be asserted that the political career of Magsaysay was not a creation of the United States. This claim, made in different circles on both sides of the Pacific, fails to take into full account the complex political situation in the Philippines. Under conditions of peace and prosperity Magsaysay might never have emerged to prominence and, in fact, might well be alive today. But the turmoil occasioned by the Huk rebellion coupled with economic distress produced a situation where a man with Magsaysay's personal magnetism and mass appeal, anti-Communist outlook, and genuine interest in the people could come to the forefront.

What the United States did in the rise of Ramón Magsaysay was to publicize him, which was perhaps not necessary, and to press for free elections, pressure which was probably needed. Visiting American journalists wrote articles favorable to Magsaysay when he was Secretary of National Defense and when he was running for the presidency. At the same time publicity largely adverse to President Elpidio Quirino appeared in the American press. As close ties were maintained with the former colonial power, its press reaction was highly publicized in the newly independent country where elections were intensely contested and freedom of the press prevailed. The National Movement for Free Elections (NAMFREL) was an organization, theoretically non-partisan but essentially sympathetic to Magsaysay, which was supported to quite an extent in its activities by American government funds. U.S. officials publicly asserted they were not taking sides, but they openly called for free and honest elections. Since President Quirino won office in the national election of 1949 that was characterized by widespread instances of fraud and terrorism, a call for free elections could not but reflect on him. Senator José P. Laurel, a staunch defender of Magsaysay during the campaign of 1953, also vaguely called for American help in the preservation of Philippine democracy. Moreover, on election day, November 10, officers of the Joint United States Military Advisory Group were seen near some of the polling places, obviously showing their interest in free balloting. During and after the campaign President Quirino himself publicly charged the United States with intervention.

Although Washington is not responsible for the victory of Magsaysay or for the relatively free, honest, and peaceful balloting on election day, the evidence indicates that it influenced the outcome. However, the cards were not overplayed; if they had been, Magsaysay would have become in the public mind a puppet of the United States and would have lost his appeal. It is doubtful if Washington will ever again have a similar opportunity in Philippine elections or, for that matter, take like steps, limited as they were, to affect the results. The real significance of the national election in 1953 is that a long-entrenched administration could be overthrown by democratic processes.

In Indonesia the greatest test of American policy toward leadership came during the Padang Revolt in 1958, especially when it was uncertain whether or not the insurrectionists would succeed or fail. Washington was faced with a situation involving the main elements of leadership and power at the time in Indonesia—President Sukarno, General Nasution, the insurgents in parts of Sumatra and Sulawesi under a number of able leaders, and D. N. Aidit of the Indonesian Communist party (PKI).

Dynamic, eloquent, personable, Sukarno was the very symbol of Indonesian nationalism. Although he still was the most influential leader in his country and had great mass appeal, he was declining in public stature. Bung Karno had long been able to balance off various other leaders and groups; in 1958, for instance, Nasution and Aidit, having both pledged their support of him, represented the most important elements in the equation. But with the open rebellion in parts of Sumatra and Sulawesi and with the marked decline of political parties, the President's efforts to maintain equilibrium had become more restricted in the available number of variables. Moreover, in seeking to advance his concept of "guided democracy," first announced in February 1957, he had assumed more powers himself. He had broken with Mohammad Hatta, for many years his able vice president. Sukarno was still convinced he could manipulate and control the political leaders and forces of Indonesia. But despite the presence of a number of able civilians like Dr. Djuanda, he was failing to give the nation the type of dedicated and sustained leadership necessary for economic rehabilitation and development. In a foreign policy styled "independent and active" Sukarno had promoted the establishment of diplomatic ties with the Sino-Soviet bloc and his country's acceptance of military and economic aid from various of its members.

General Nasution had emerged as the most influential military figure in the country. Young, energetic and competent, Nasution had had a varied military career of success and adversity. Although the General acquired particular distinction by his role in crushing the Madiun Revolt of the Communists in 1948 and was a target of attack by Aidit and the PKI since his rise to power and influence, he was perhaps as much non-Communist as anti-Communist and always a devout Moslem and a true nationalist. The armed services of the nation, it should be stressed, were not monolithic; they had rivalries among and within themselves; units had at times been mutinous. Decisions were hard to make and execute; discipline was often lax and corruption not absent; certain groups were infiltrated by the PKI. The army was widely considered more favorably inclined to the Western powers, the air force to the Communist bloc, and the navy somewhat in between. General Nasution, although the most powerful single officer, may not have had the actual control or the will essential to assure a successful take-over and continuance in power; he had on occasion failed to take advantage of a possible opportunity to supplant Sukarno. Meanwhile the military had vastly increased its role in government as a result, among other things, of the state of danger decree in the islands.

The leaders of the Revolutionary Government of the Republic of Indonesia (PRRI) numbered among the most capable of the country: Sjafruddin Prawiranegara, Sumitro Djojohadikusumo, and Mohammad Natsir as civilians and Colonel Maludin Simbolon, Colonel Kawilarang, Lieutenant Colonel Ahmad Hussein, Colonel John F. Warouw, and Lieutenant Colonel Ventje

Sumual from the military. Frustrated over the failure of reform efforts within the government, concerned over the treatment of the outer islands by the central authorities, and opposed to what was considered a pro-Communist orientation in Djakarta, they took up armed revolt. Indonesia certainly had need for men of their character, but the basic problem was how to give them an opportunity to make an effective contribution. Into eclipse with them had gone the Masjumi party, many leaders like Natsir being openly or covertly associated with the revolt.

As for the Communists, the youthful leader, D. N. Aidit, had been skillfully guiding the PKI, despite differences of opinion within its leadership. A dedicated Communist who had visited both Moscow and Peking, he tended at the time to lean more toward the U.S.S.R. than to the People's Republic of China, considering the former a more valid model for take-over in Indonesia. Others in the party shared contrary viewpoints and were more influenced by Peking. Particularly since 1953 the PKI had pursued the tactics of a "national front," while increasing its membership and expanding its various supporting organizations on an extensive scale. Although highly vocal in praise and flattery of Sukarno, Aidit had criticized certain aspects of the President's program and firmly opposed the growing role of the military with its curbing of Communist activities. The party itself had acquired greater respectability, a strong voice in the Supreme Council established by Sukarno, and much better opportunities for infiltration and propaganda. Indeed, President Sukarno, General Nasution and many political leaders in Indonesia had become concerned lest the PKI should grow so strong it could take over the government through the ballot or by a *coup d'état*.

When the PRRI (based on areas in central and northern Sumatra and northern Sulawesi) was proclaimed on February 15, 1958, it appeared that the Padang Revolt had a good chance to make headway and force a compromise upon, or perhaps supplant, the Djakarta government. But its ineptitude both in military operations and in civil government and the surprising determination of the national authorities coupled with the response of the armed forces reduced the PRRI to guerrilla warfare in the short period between March and June.

The United States followed carefully the struggle for Indonesian leadership during the critical months of the revolt. The importance of the island republic to the American position in the Western Pacific was discussed in high circles, the navy, for instance, being particularly concerned. With its naval power Washington could "quarantine" Indonesia, a factor of great importance, of course, in the shipment of arms from the outside. Indonesia's strategic location between the Pacific and Indian Oceans and linking peninsular Southeast Asia and Australia, its important human and material resources, and its potential as the strongest power in all Southeast Asia provided many reasons why the United States did not want the country to fall into the hands of the Communists.

American allies and friends were also concerned. The Philippines, already apprehensive over the inroads of the PKI in its southern neighbor as well as being sensitive to events in nearby Sulawesi, and Nationalist China, strongly opposed to Communist expansion, were sympathetic to Indonesian developments that might strengthen opposition to communism. The Federation of Malaya, recently independent, and Singapore, still a British dependency, were eager to have a non-Communist Indonesia next door. Warfare involving neighboring Sumatra was certain to raise serious international problems for authorities in Kuala Lumpur and Singapore. Australia, responsive to events in the Near North, did not favor the rise of any forces inclined toward the Sino-Soviet bloc. And the Netherlands, still holding West

New Guinea, was opposed to any strengthening of the hostile Djakarta regime.

Although agents of the PRRI operated in neighboring Singapore, Malaya, the Philippines, and Taiwan, the insurgents did not make a big effort upon their revolt to get foreign help. Yet many of them thought in the early months they had the sympathy of the United States in their struggle. Despite their anti-Communist outlook, the leaders called for an "independent" foreign policy and wanted to buy weapons as their resources permitted. It is significant that they sought direct Western aid only when it was too late. Even so, Djakarta officials were convinced of American duplicity in providing arms to the rebels; in particular they believed that two U.S. allies, the Philippines and the Republic of China, were helping the PRRI in material measures short of open intervention, including the use of staging areas and the provision of weapons and supplies. When a rebel bomber piloted by an American, Allan L. Pope, was shot down by government forces over Ambon on May 18, feeling was intense in Djakarta against the United States, and the low point in American-Indonesian relations was reached. Djakarta officials had been unsuccessful in various efforts to get U.S. arms for several months before the outbreak of the revolt. The Communist bloc, however, had responded to the request for weapons and, when the fighting began, proceeded to throw its support behind the Sukarno government. Overt American aid for the rebels could have precipitated an effort by the Communists to take comparable steps on behalf of the central authorities. Looming over the horizon was the possibility of a Communist Java in a divided archipelago.

In the complicated situation occasioned by the Padang Revolt, Washington was uncertain what to do, some officials favoring one course of action and others another. It is argued that at an early stage the United States could have intervened to alter the outcome. Or a revision of American policy on the West Irian issue might possibly have produced moderation in Djakarta and helped bring about a negotiated settlement with the Padang authorities. In its regular session at Manila, held March 11-13, 1958, the SEATO Council of Foreign Ministers did not consider Indonesia as a formal topic, but the rebellion was the subject of much informal discussion. Possibly ANZUS provided a better forum for consideration of the controversy. Djakarta officials were quick to accuse SEATO of complicity in the revolt, accusations loudly supported by the PKI and the Peking-Moscow axis.

Regardless of the concern and discussion in Western and pro-Western circles, events moved so fast in Indonesia that the time for effective help to the PRRI quickly passed. The United States soon altered its policy by stressing positive support for the Djakarta government. Substantial material aid, announced in July, August and at later dates, was forthcoming. (In one arrangement U.S. small arms were flown to the island republic in August.) Thus, with the military decline of the PRRI, apart from guerrilla warfare, Washington clearly decided it was best to provide assistance to President Sukarno but at the same time to build up non-Communist and anti-Communist forces, especially those represented by General Nasution and certain other leaders. Ambassador Howard P. Jones, succeeding John M. Allison, who relinquished his embassy post during the crisis because of dissatisfaction with U.S. policy in the island republic, came to personify the new course of action.

In Indonesia's future the key men of the PRRI, though discredited and defeated, cannot be overlooked, if only because of their rare qualities of leadership. According to some observers, an ideal succession to Sukarno would be a cabinet headed by Mohammad Hatta and supported by General Nasution, with a policy of opposing strongly the PKI while bringing the best men of the PRRI back into government participation. In searching for elements of stability upon which to base policy in Indonesia the United States has to be flexible, judicious, and—above all—tactful.

Thai leadership has raised special problems for Washington. American security interests are deeply involved in a country where different factions of a military oligarchy occasionally contest for power, and *coups d'état* are not infrequent. The policies of successive Thai governments and of the United States in its relations with them must be founded on a common outlook in foreign affairs if the security links between Bangkok and Washington are to survive.

Since 1950 when Thailand cast its lot with the United States, formal ties of alliance not coming until 1954, the kingdom has had several governments under different prime ministers: Field Marshal Pibulsonggram (April 1948-September 1957), Pote Sarasin (September 1957-December 1957), General Thanom Kittikachon (January 1958-October 1958), and Field Marshal Sarit Thanarat who assumed the office in February 1959. Two men have been most influential in Thai politics during the period, Field Marshal Pibulsonggram and Field Marshal Sarit Thanarat. Clearly the manipulation of military forces and the problems of succession have been of prime concern in the political processes of the kingdom. At present two prominent former prime ministers, Pridi Phanomyong and Field Marshal Pibulsonggram, are in exile, while two members of the current cabinet, General Thanom Kittikachon, Deputy Prime Minister and Minister of Defense, and General Praphat Charusathien, Minister of the Interior, are mentioned as successors to Field Marshal Sarit. And yet, paradoxically, in the Thai system of government there is stability within a framework of instability, for the *coups* in Bangkok bring new personalities to the helm without causing widespread bloodshed or deeply affecting the people. As a result of the *coup* of October 20, 1958, for instance, the constitution of 1932 was abrogated and the National Assembly was dissolved, but General Thanom, the previous premier, became deputy premier in the cabinet of Field Marshal Sarit that was appointed in February 1959. Sarit, in fact, has been the source of power since the *coup* overthrowing Pibulsonggram in September 1957. Although elections have been held at times, democracy is obviously not firmly embedded in the Thai political system. Nevertheless, factors conducive to stability are the monarchy, Buddhism, and the civil service, as well as underpopulation, widespread peasant ownership of land, and an abundance of rice.

With Thailand as its only SEATO ally in peninsular Southeast Asia, the United States, realizing the kingdom's strategic importance and appreciating its anti-Communist posture, is eager to remain on good terms with the successive governments in Bangkok. In its own national interest Thailand wants to preserve its security ties with Washington as long as they are beneficial. But Bangkok must be frequently reassured that vis-à-vis Communist China the United States is not a declining power in the Far East, that Thai participation in SEATO can bring benefits, and that Washington will give special consideration to an ally as compared to a neutral.

American relationships with Thai leaders since 1950 indicate that a democratic regime in the kingdom is not a prerequisite for an *entente* or even an alliance between the two countries. Basic Thai stability in an anti-Communist framework was and is a primary consideration. In the circumstances the United States must take care to avoid tying itself too closely to one political leader in Bangkok, as happened in the case of Field Marshal Pibulsonggram. And although Washington believes in the separation of military and civilian powers at home, it is not quite in a position to recommend a similar policy for the Thai.

As the kingdom may soon face increased Communist pressure along its exposed Laotian boundary, Thai and American efforts to counter the incipient threat call for maximum cooperation. Here is a case where Communist incipient and potential insurgency can be checked if energetic and timely measures are taken. It is important that any foreign forces stationed in rural Thailand in defense of the country establish sound relations with the peasantry, for friction might cause the local peasants to look upon the forces defending them almost as a foreign occupation. The Thai program with American assistance aimed at developing the poverty-stricken northeast, thus blocking a road of Communist penetration, must be thoroughly implemented. Almost a third of the kingdom's population, people usually closer to the language and customs of the Lao, is found in this depressed area bordering Laos and Cambodia. The expenditure of around $300 million over a five-year period can bring dividends in peasant support for the government. In the years ahead, the mutuality of interests between Bangkok and Washington will certainly face even greater tests.

Problems of leadership for the United States in Cambodia focus squarely on Prince Norodom Sihanouk. Whether as king, chief of state, premier, or private citizen, Sihanouk dominates the Khmer scene. Emotional, dynamic, and astute, he is popular with the people, and his leadership is accepted by almost all the politicians. Son Ngoc Thanh, perhaps his only real rival, has operated above ground and below ground in vain attempts to supplant the Prince. Other men like Sam Sary, once high in government councils, have plotted in vain to overthrow "Monseigneur," the title given him in the French press. The army has maintained its loyalty, as Dap Chhuon found out in 1959; and the Cambodian Communists have now learned it is best not to attack Sihanouk and the institution of the monarchy. Probably there is only one Cambodian who at times exerts very much influence over him, his mother, Queen Monivong Kossamak, wife of the late King Norodom Suramarit. In the event of the sudden death of the Prince, a real vacuum in Khmer leadership would occur. Although there is always the chance of a *coup* in Phnom Penh, the likelihood at the present time is remote.

Norodom Sihanouk decides questions of foreign policy with very few domestic restrictions on his will. Determined to pursue a course of neutrality toward both sides in the cold war and even toward the other uncommitted states, he maintains a delicate balance (with occasional aberrations) between the Sino-Soviet bloc and the Western alignment. Yet his immediate concern, as has been stressed, is South Viet-Nam and Thailand, countries he considers hostile in their attitudes toward Cambodia.

Against this background U.S. relations with the Khmer kingdom have fluctuated greatly since its independence in late 1953. Illustrative of the problems posed for Washington was Sihanouk's extension of *de jure* recognition to the People's Republic of China in July 1958, along with announced plans for the exchange of ambassadors. Although Peking already had an economic mission in the kingdom, formal recognition had wide implications: both Bangkok and Saigon were directly concerned, the diplomatic struggle between Peking and Taipei was intensified, and to some extent this simple diplomatic action stirred the cold war at the global level.

The United States believed that the closing of the Chinese Nationalist consulate in Cambodia along with the establishment of a Chinese Communist embassy would increase the incidence of infiltration and subversion. The 350,000 Chinese in the kingdom would now look much more to Peking than to Taipei for inspiration; the 400,000 Vietnamese would be subjected to greater Communist pressure, especially by the Viet-Minh; and the Khmers themselves would be exposed to much more Communist propaganda. Although Sihanouk has minimized the dangers of subversion in his country, many American apprehensions about the internal effects of Cambodia's recognition of Peking are being realized. Outside the Khmer kingdom, the Prince's step was bitterly resented in the bordering states of South Viet-Nam and Thailand, and it was naturally condemned in Taipei. The recognition was used in the cold war as proof of Cambodia's understanding of the future stature of Communist China and the Sino-Soviet bloc; Taipei received one more check, Peking took another step forward in global prestige.

Nevertheless, what could the United States really do about the matter? On July 24 Lincoln White, the press officer of the Department of State, commented: "While we, of course, do not question the right of the sovereign Government of Cambodia to take any steps which it considers to be in the national interests of its people, we regard this action as regrettable."[1] Ambassador Carl W. Strom was recalled to Washington to report on the meaning of Cambodia's action, and American officials gave thought to the future of U.S. economic and military assistance to the kingdom. Certainly Washington did not want to render aid to a country that would fall into Communist hands; but if the chances were good that Cambodia would still be able to maintain its independence and neutrality, the United States would want to help it in the effort. Furthermore, the army, heavily supported by the United States, was considered friendly to Americans, and the cessation of military aid would affect its outlook. It was realized that Sihanouk, who was anti-Communist at home, did not want his country a member of the Sino-Soviet bloc. Moreover, his recognition of Communist China was in the framework of his relations with Saigon and Bangkok; it was precipitated by a serious border incident with South Viet-Nam. There is little reason to doubt the Prince's statement that he would prefer a

[1] *The New York Times*, July 25, 1958.

Communist Cambodia to one dominated by his neighbors to the east and west.

Under the circumstances the United States continued its economic and military aid program to the Khmer kingdom as the soundest course of action. In view of the border crises the cessation of assistance could have driven Sihanouk into the arms of Peking. During his visit to Communist China from August 14 to 27, 1958, the Prince was received with the highest honors and subjected to the greatest flattery, but he made no agreement for the acceptance of arms from Mao Tse-tung. Characteristic of Sihanouk's policy of neutralism was his subsequent visit to the United States. As he had preceded his visit to Communist China with conferences in Rangoon with Premier U Nu and in New Delhi with Premier Nehru, so he went to New York to represent Cambodia at the General Assembly of the United Nations before he met President Eisenhower at the White House. In the course of his visit to Washington he also met Secretary of State Dulles and other high-ranking officials; and before returning to Phnom Penh, Sihanouk visited a number of American cities, made several speeches, and received a favorable reception. Back in Asia he indicated that the friendship of his kingdom with the United States was steadily improving and that Americans better understood Cambodia's neutrality. Thus Washington made the best of the delicate situation precipitated by the Prince's recognition of Peking. But there was no inclination to believe that the pattern of Cambodian-American relations would change as long as Sihanouk was at the helm of state in the Khmer kingdom.

In the Republic of Viet-Nam American policy toward leadership has obviously centered on Ngo Dinh Diem. At the conclusion of the Geneva Conference on Indochina in 1954 the prospects for an independent South Viet-Nam seemed slight, and Ngo Dinh Diem must receive much of the credit for confounding the predictions. Faced with apparently insurmountable obstacles in almost every direction, Diem proved that he was neither a puppet of France nor dependent on the "French presence." In July 1954 he became premier of the State of Viet-Nam headed by the last Emperor of Annam, Bao Dai; in October 1955 he replaced the latter as chief of state; and in October 1956 he became president of the Republic of Viet-Nam. In this period he used force or threats of force to reduce to impotence the Binh Xuyen (an organization of armed gangsters who controlled the police and vice of Saigon) and the irregular armies of the Hoa Hao and Cao Dai religious sects. Beginning with successful defiance of Bao Dai's military and civilian sympathizers, he went on to compete with Ho Chi Minh as a nationalist leader in Viet-Nam, building a southern anti-Communist state to challenge the Viet-Minh in the north. Ngo Dinh Diem refused to carry out the provisions of the Geneva settlement of 1954 which called for consultations between North and South Viet-Nam on national elections as a prelude to national unification. He stated publicly his conviction that such elections could not be free in North Viet-Nam and, therefore, should not be held. The Communist world was highly critical of this viewpoint, but the United States and a number of other countries supported Diem. In fact, the sympathy and backing of Washington in the mid-1950s were probably indispensable to the political survival of the Vietnamese leader. At the same time he indicated that he was no American puppet, for he accepted some advice and some he rejected.

Beyond the shadow of a doubt the President is still the dominant figure in his republic, and some great part of this dominance is due to his honesty, industry, and high sense of vocation. Determined to use authoritarian methods when necessary, he is respected rather than loved by his fellow countrymen. As a Roman Catholic, he represents a minority religion. The President permits hardly any political opposition and delegates rel:

tively little authority save to his brothers and certain other relatives. While a power vacuum would certainly occur in South Viet-Nam if Diem should suddenly cease to be the center of government, he is not grooming any obvious successor. He has shown considerable survival capacity, but the attempted military *coups* in Saigon in November 1960 and February 1962 leave no grounds for complacency. His methods have been the source of much controversy in both Viet-Nam and the United States. Serious internal problems will continue to confront the Vietnamese leader; for some time, it is clear, Communist insurgency will present the greatest challenge. The question is often raised whether his regime commands sufficient internal support to combat the Communist threat effectively. If he can provide adequate leadership to his troubled country in the years ahead, he will be a major contributor to the success of the mounting U.S. effort to help preserve the independence of the Republic of Viet-Nam.

Future U.S. Policy Toward Leadership

First of all, the United States must always be concerned with identifying elements of stability in Southeast Asia. With due allowance for time and circumstance, these elements must be at least broadly consistent with American values. Future conditions will increasingly require that the leaders or elites supported by the United States be willing and able to cope with the problems of modernization arising from the growing needs and demands of the people. Here the United States can assist by helping to train the managers and technicians needed, broadening the horizons of the military in its expanding duties, and giving more attention to programs affecting the youth of the nations; it can promote projects that may serve to bridge the gap between different groups undergoing modernization at varying rates, and try to keep within bounds programs affecting political, social and economic development so as to minimize the forces of disequilibrium. Within its margin of influence Washington can help the new states better define the range of policies open to them.

The achievement of national unity, a key to effective leadership in the countries of Southeast Asia, is an essential goal which the United States should encourage in all possible ways. Although a real degree of national unity can be achieved in terms of specifics, the sentiment of nationalism is apt to be negative and xenophobic rather than positive and patriotic if irredentism bedevils territorial unification or if a neighbor commits or threatens aggression. The average citizen in the village or even the city also finds it difficult to extend loyalty from a popular figure to the abstract concept of the state. For him the symbols of the flag or the national anthem cannot yet be substituted for the living reality of a long-established leader. Indeed, conditions conducive to rightist or leftist authoritarianism can arise if the populace is bewildered by a swift succession of leaders.

Since the creation of national unity is closely related to communications, the United States can assist here by various means acceptable to the leadership and the people. Even if the ruling national elite is cohesive and progressive, it still needs to reach down to the masses to be really effective. The revolution in communications is increasing the diffusion of new ideas, while the improvement in transportation is speeding the mobility of the people.

As the ruling elite becomes increasingly able to communicate with the masses, the question of how it will use its new contacts assumes growing importance. This involves the effective channeling of the political dynamics of a country. The elite in power, moreover, can better cope with problems if the values held by the people are adequately articulated. In the process of reconciling long-established mores with the requirements of modernization, the countries of Southeast Asia can be helped if the United States can exemplify the articulation of political values reflecting the aspirations and ideals of free men and if it uses its moral and physical power to maintain freedom of choice in the developing countries. In its greater stress on the principle of self-determination, the United States can find more common ground with the newly independent peoples. The values they ultimately choose will greatly affect their role in the international community and the balance of the future.

In general, Washington must not base policy upon the expectation that the countries of Southeast Asia can or will transform into living reality the principles of constitutional democracy without considerably more experience and without more favorable conditions. The age of tutelage must be accepted in much of the region. While the ruling elite must have the requisite strength, the power base must be widened to cope effectively with change. In terms of personalities, men like Sukarno who represent charismatic, highly emotional leadership will probably present more difficulties for U.S. policy than those like Tengku Abdul Rahman who are pragmatic in their approach to solving problems, for it is easier to negotiate on a day-to-day basis with Asians who may approach issues in somewhat the same way.

Over the long run representative government is a key aspect of political viability. Through this means legitimate channels can be established for the orderly articulation and expression of aspirations, viewpoints, and values which arise with the emergence of new interest groups or other forces in the body politic. The basis for participation in government is broader and more dynamic, while the ruling elite may be better able to deal with the loyal opposition. Representative government serves as a means for developing new leaders and tends to place restraints on the executive, the bureaucracy, and the military. Accountability and responsibility are necessary for political viability.

There is more to the popular participation in government than the holding of elections. Americans sometimes tend to judge democracy largely in terms of voting for candidates who seek office. In the developing countries political participation at the local level in such activities as community development has a great potential in arousing widespread interest and establishing a popular stake in the future. By such means Communist attempts to capture the people at the grass roots are weakened or frustrated. Through various programs the United States can encourage political participation in different activities which serve to strengthen the popular foundations of government.

Regardless of the type of government, the United States must continue to recognize that foreign policy for many years will remain chiefly in the hands of a few persons in the capital cities. The people in Southeast Asia have little concern about, or knowledge of, international relations. A few issues where public opinion is marshalled on nationalist grounds or the existence of local attitudes toward foreigners across a boundary or toward minorities like the Chinese affecting individual livelihood are the only significant qualifications. Because popular interest in most international problems cannot be sustained, the formulators of foreign policy will have for some time an especially wide latitude in the decision-making process. The Southeast Asian leaders will usually be more concerned with domestic issues than with foreign; they will tend to react on a day-to-day basis to international problems facing them; they will be very sensitive to any outside pressure. Sometimes their public statements and personal convictions will differ. Yet the professional diplomats of the area, many starting with little training, are rapidly acquiring experience not only through the passing of time but also through the expanding functions of diplomacy on the bilateral and multilateral levels.

Although a real degree of influence on governments is inescapable in countries engaged in modernization where the United States has extensive interests and programs, Washington must not acquire a reputation of openly intervening in the domestic affairs of the states in Southeast Asia. Influence under the "New Diplomacy" must be tactfully exerted.

In many countries Washington will remain in a position to strengthen (or to weaken) the sources of government support. The reorganization of police, necessary fiscal reforms, required alterations in long-established administrative procedures, all are cases in point. By assisting business, the military, or the bureaucracy, the United States may be strengthening the government and at the same time may be building up multiple sources of potential power and leadership. In the countryside, aiding land reform will help the peasant but may well alienate the landlord; the latter may be an anti-Communist bulwark today, but the former may be a source of real power tomorrow. If the regime Washington aids is popular, both governments profit; but U.S. assistance to an unpopular regime can be easily interpreted as an effort to keep it in power, and anti-American feeling can rise. In seeking popular support, the choice of projects and personnel, the handling of the program and the related publicity are naturally important. The United States must seek through its policy and aid in Southeast Asia to support elements of stability generally favorable to the West both in and outside any current government.

Just as Washington should not as a general rule tie itself too closely to one man or one administration, save possibly in the face of an extremely grave Communist threat, the United States must try to retain some links with the non-Communist "outs." This attempt is very difficult, for the government in power in

Southeast Asia does not usually welcome foreign contacts with the opposition. It is even more difficult when all opposition has gone underground. The succession to leadership in such an instance may be all the more important for the American policymaker. Yet even where a country is badly divided between contesting factions, Washington may be able to encourage generally desired programs like education.

The U.S. effort in Southeast Asia should be broad and flexible so that if one aspect of it fails with a particular government in power, other aspects will succeed. Or if a new regime dislikes certain parts of the American program, other parts can continue or new ones be added. Here indeed is a prime reason why the United States should seek to develop contacts with as many segments of society as possible and find common interests with them.

Change being the order of the day in Southeast Asia, effective American use of it is a key to successful policy. In this connection a doctrine of political development supported by the West for the new states of Asia and Africa would fill a real need. A doctrine that could capture the imagination and win the inspiration of the newly independent peoples, one that could present a rationale for their political being and rise above local national prejudices, would serve the parties. It would also counter the *mystique* of communism. A doctrine of political development should be operational in terms of the present as well as flexible to cope with the institutions promised by scientific man.

TEN

Cohesion Of The West: Difficulties and Adjustments

In spite of the rapid collapse of the European empires in South-east Asia, many Western states still have important strategic and economic links to the region. In these continuing or new rela-tions the United States occupies a position of some importance; for America's world-wide interests, in association with its vast economic and military capability, force Washington to concern itself actively in almost all important global developments. In addition to the United States, the Western powers presently involved in Southeast Asia are Great Britain, Australia, New Zealand, and, to a lesser extent, France and the Netherlands. The interests and policies of each of these countries vary in the region, not always coinciding with those of the United States, but on a large number of the issues there is substantial agreement. As the main proof of this common concern Washington is for-mally allied with all these powers, save the Netherlands. In many respects the Netherlands, with its concern for West New Guinea, has constituted a case by itself. Nevertheless, this concern was interwoven in the interests and policies of all the Western powers, especially the Commonwealth of Australia.

THE UNITED KINGDOM

Although Great Britain's power and influence in Southeast Asia have substantially declined, London still has extensive interests in the region. Within the area the external defense and foreign affairs of the State of Singapore have been in British hands, while the United Kingdom's responsibilities in Hong Kong influence London's policies in the region. North Borneo, Sarawak, and Brunei are currently dependencies, and the Federation of Malaya continues to be a member of the Commonwealth of Nations, although the Federation of Malaysia, as planned, will end British colonial rule in the region. Southeast Asia is an important link between India, Pakistan, and Ceylon in the Indian Ocean and Australia and New Zealand in the Southwest Pacific, while trade and investments, transportation and communications add to the sum total of British interests in the area.

On the whole, the British record in Southeast Asia is one of achievement. Following upon the Second World War the immediate problems of the United Kingdom were relief and rehabilitation, and the restoration of orderly government in dependent areas. It was also necessary to cope with rising nationalism in a way that would bring independence through peaceful, constitutional means.

In cooperation with Australia and New Zealand, the military effort of Great Britain has centered on Malaya and Singapore, an important strategic area for all three of them. At the military service level London, Canberra, and Wellington have for some years coordinated defense planning in what has been called the ANZAM region; namely, Malaya, Singapore, British Borneo, Australia, New Zealand, and the adjacent seas, with a definite focus on Malaya and Singapore. In 1955 the three powers agreed upon the creation of a Commonwealth Strategic Reserve with armed contingents from each to be based in Malaya and Singapore. Although the Reserve was engaged in fighting the Communist guerrillas in the Federation, it also had broader Commonwealth defense obligations.

The impending independence of the Federation of Malaya, a date set for August 31, 1957, raised questions relating to its role as a sovereign state of the Commonwealth in defense arrangements. An Agreement on External Defence and Mutual Assistance between London and Kuala Lumpur (Australia and New Zealand becoming associated with the relevant parts) provided for the continued stationing in the Federation of such British land, sea, and air forces, including a Commonwealth Strategic Reserve, as Kuala Lumpur required to assist in the external defense of the new state and in the carrying out of "Commonwealth and international obligations." The forces would, of course, continue to be utilized as long as needed in the fighting against the Communist rebels. Arrangements were made about the necessary base facilities for the British, as well as for the training of the Malayan military.

Under the defense agreement the Federation pledged itself to cooperate and take the action it considered necessary in the event of an armed attack on the British dependencies of Singapore, North Borneo, Brunei, Sarawak, and Hong Kong, or on the United Kingdom's units in them or in the Federation of Malaya. Great Britain promised to take comparable action if Malaya or its forces were the subject of similar aggression. Provision was made for consultation if the threat of such an attack arose against the forces and areas listed, or against the peace of the Far East. Significantly, an article provided that in the event of a threat to the peace or an outbreak of hostilities outside the areas specified Great Britain would have to secure the Federation's agreement before its forces could start active operations involving bases in Malaya's territory. If London desired, it could withdraw its armed units, but their return would depend upon Kuala Lumpur. Moreover, the British agreed in the pact to consult the Malayans "when major changes in the character or deployment of the forces . . . are contemplated."[1] Under the provisions of the defense arrangement it is clear that the Federation could not be used as a SEATO base of operations unless the terms of the Anglo-Malayan alliance itself were applicable or unless Kuala Lumpur decided in the situation to grant approval. On the other hand, the British maintained their base facilities in Singapore and were free to use them as the occasion demanded.

Phoenix Park, Singapore, has sometimes been called "the little Whitehall of the Far East." Here is located the Office of the Commissioner-General for the United Kingdom in Southeast Asia which has coordinating and advisory functions for British policy from Afghanistan to Japan, including also Australia and New Zealand. Malcolm MacDonald and Sir Robert Scott served successively as Commissioners-General since the inception of the Office in 1948, and now the post is held by Lord Selkirk who also doubles as United Kingdom Commissioner for Singapore, an enlargement of the functions of his predecessor. He continues the duties of being Permanent United Kingdom Delegate to the Southeast Asia Treaty Organization. The senior representative in Singapore of the Foreign and Colonial Offices, Lord Selkirk is a noncareer official in contrast to Sir Robert Scott, but the Deputy Commissioner-General for Southeast Asia is a British Foreign Service career officer. The Commissioner-General and

[1] Agreement on External Defence and Mutual Assistance, United Kingdom and Federation of Malaya, *United Nations Treaty Series*, 1958, v. 285, no. 4149, p. 64.

his Deputy have a number of assistants, usually specializing on one or more countries. The Office itself has a Joint Intelligence Bureau, a component called "Security Intelligence Far East," a Regional Information Office, and advisers on police activities, civil aviation, labor, shipping, and regional education.

Notwithstanding the diversity of the countries and problems, the United Kingdom has obviously considered the Office of the Commissioner-General an asset. Yet the dual role now performed by Lord Selkirk has in some circles been looked upon as a downgrading of the Office, although the Prime Minister prevented the altering of the title from Commissioner-General to Commissioner. U.S. officials in Singapore for their part have found Phoenix Park valuable for Anglo-American liaison in various activities of common interest.

Despite its change of status from a Crown Colony to a State, Singapore remains an area of strategic value both to the United Kingdom and to its allies in Southeast Asia. The base facilities are important in the calculations of ANZAM, the Commonwealth Strategic Reserve, the Anglo-Malayan defense alliance, and SEATO. Although the possibility of developing the island of Labuan, now a part of North Borneo, as an alternative base has been considered, the project would be expensive and the ultimate value debatable. There is, however, a division of opinion concerning the long-range importance of Singapore as a base complex.

The Crown Colony of Singapore was established and separated from the mainland in 1946 at the time of the establishment of the Malayan Union, which preceded the Federation of Malaya of 1948 and included the same territory: the former Federated Malay States, the Unfederated Malay States, and the British Settlements of Penang and Malacca. Although the British government officially indicated in 1946 that it was not its policy "to preclude or prejudice" the fusion of the island and the mainland at a later period, the "form and timing" of the association were a matter which the two should work out themselves. There has been considerable practical cooperation between Singapore and the Federation, both before and since the latter's independence; in fact, Great Britain has followed a policy based upon the defense of Malaya as a whole. While the government of Singapore, whether under Chief Ministers David Marshall and Lim Yew Hock or under Prime Minister Lee Kuan Yew, has called for a merger, the Federation under Prime Minister Tengku Abdul Rahman has long opposed it. The addition of the large population of Singapore, just over 1.6 million, of whom far more than two-thirds are Chinese, would result in a numerical preponderance of the Chinese over the Malays. The economic superiority of the Chinese in both Singapore and the Federation and the predominately leftist sympathies on the island would add to the problems of Kuala Lumpur. In 1961 and 1962, however, steps were under way which were planned to lead by the end of August 1963 to a Federation of Malaysia to include Singapore, the Federation of Malaya, Sarawak, North Borneo, and Brunei. The British government approved, though some officials preferred an earlier union of British Borneo. Prime Minister Tengku Abdul Rahman supported a "Greater Malaysia" as a means of solving the problem of a merger of Singapore with the Federation, while Prime Minister Lee Kuan Yew saw it as an answer to many of Singapore's problems.

Several years earlier, in 1957, agreement had been reached at a constitutional conference in London between representatives of the Crown Colony and Great Britain for the establishment of the State of Singapore which would have self-government internally, with the United Kingdom in charge of external defense and foreign relations. In the proposed state Great Britain would retain a complex of base installations; subject to British approval, Singapore would handle commercial and cultural relations with third parties. In regard to the complicated topic of internal security, which had been the basic reason for the collapse of previous constitutional negotiations in 1956, it was agreed that Singapore would take the responsibility while London would retain a vital interest. An Internal Security Council would be created consisting of seven members: three from Singapore; three from the United Kingdom, including the commissioner; and the seventh from the Federation of Malaya, subject to its approval, which could be terminated on a six months' notice. If the government of the State of Singapore did not honor a decision within the competence of the Council, its chairman, who was the United Kingdom's commissioner, would advise the head of state in Singapore, the Yang di-Pertuan Negara, on what to do; and under certain conditions Britain could suspend the constitution.

Elections for the 51 seats in the Legislative Assembly were held on May 30, 1959, the People's Action party (PAP) winning 43; the Singapore People's Alliance of Lim Yew Hock, 4; the United Malays National Organization, 3; and an independent, 1. Under a greatly enlarged suffrage 90 per cent of the voters went to the polls. The moderate faction of the militant PAP provided the basis of the government, whose members were sworn into office June 5, with Lee Kuan Yew as the first prime minister. Believing in "democratic socialism," the youthful leader of Singapore, a Cambridge-educated lawyer, made real progress together with his ministers in establishing law and order, in running an honest administration, and in making the new constitution a going concern. Lee sought to find jobs for the large numbers of unemployed, to develop among the Chinese loyalty for Singapore as their homeland, and to reduce the appeals of communism. Especially aware of the youth problem, since almost 60 per cent of the rapidly growing population was below 21 years old, he instituted the "work brigade" for unemployed young Singaporeans who had finished their schooling. Although Lee Kuan

Yew was disappointed in the amount of foreign investment and the rate of economic development in Singapore, in the light of the over-all needs, he was well aware of the continued importance of the island as an entrepôt.

An underground party since they were declared illegal in mid-1948, the Communists appear to be held in restraint, though their strength has not been reduced. In the struggle against Communist control of the PAP, Lee achieved a measure of success, but infiltration tactics by Communists and their sympathizers continue to be directed toward Chinese middle schools, labor unions, and, of course, political parties. Although the Prime Minister believed that a government must be able to rule effectively, he did not favor a totalitarian solution, and by the summer of 1961 his majority in Parliament had dwindled to only one. The success of his efforts for a merger with the Federation, with Singapore having local autonomy in fields like education and labor, became a major consideration in the future of his government.

In the event of a crisis between the British and Singaporean authorities, a strike could be threatened by the 40,000 local civilian workers at the big base complex, who are largely Chinese and are influenced by the PAP. The British, on the other hand, have the ability to cut off the food supply of the island, and in a very short period the effects of such an action would be severe. If Singapore were independent, like all its neighbors except British Borneo, it would probably seek to pursue a neutralist policy. The importance of the island as an entrepôt would be somewhat balanced by the attitude of the Chinese, who remain proud of their culture and who are glad to see Peking once more have a strong voice in world councils. On the other hand, a definite pro-Western posture is foreseen when the Federation of Malaysia materializes. Plans have been made to extend the current Anglo-Malayan defense agreement to cover the area subject to the new government and to allow the United Kingdom to keep the base facilities at Singapore and to use them both for the defense of Malaysia and the Commonwealth and for the maintenance of peace in Southeast Asia. Communists and pro-Communists in Singapore, Sarawak, and Brunei were among those actively opposed to the planned federation.

The record of Anglo-American cooperation in Southeast Asia is on the whole very good, in spite of occasional disagreements on organizing security in the area, such as those during the Indochina War and during the Geneva Conference of 1954. Contrary to the opinion of some British officers, Washington has not generally advocated the limiting of military discussions on Southeast Asian security to Britain, Australia, New Zealand, and the United States, for, in the judgment of many Americans, leaving out the Asians would raise considerable difficulties. Nor does Washington wish to commit forces to SEATO on a long-term basis, although some British officers have been willing to take such a step. Nevertheless, Americans and British cooperate in large measure to advance the objectives of the Manila Pact, while the aid programs of London and Washington in the area reflect the common goals. Occasional suspicions in American circles about ANZAM have disappeared. for it has not detracted from ANZUS or SEATO. The United States does not interfere in the affairs of Singapore, and relations between American and British officials on the island are cordial. On the mainland Washington recognizes the United Kingdom as the most influential foreign power and has real admiration for the way the London and Kuala Lumpur governments have handled subversion. On the basis of their own experience the British have urged considerable flexibility in approaching the challenge of indirect aggression, Laos being a case in point.

The greatest divergence in Anglo-American policy in the Far East is the United Kingdom's recognition of the People's Republic of China in contrast to the United States' opposition to establishing relations with Peking. Despite a growing concern in Parliament, however, the London government supported an American formula which involved putting in abeyance in the U.N. General Assembly the seating of representatives from Peking in place of those from Taiwan. This "moratorium" formula was replaced in September 1961 when New Zealand with Anglo-American support called for putting the problem of Chinese representation on the agenda of the sixteenth General Assembly. London agreed the subject of representation was "important" in the voting on December 15 but supported a Soviet resolution calling for the removal of Taipei's representatives and their replacement by Peking's. Obviously the strong American support for the Chiang Kai-shek regime on Taiwan does not meet with a sympathetic response in Great Britain; yet London and Washington have come to a mutual understanding of each other's position on the two Chinas; each derives even a certain advantage from the posture of the other. Fortunately, in Southeast Asia the Western split on China policy has not had severe ramifications.

AUSTRALIA

The interests of the Commonwealth of Australia have come to be extensive in Southeast Asia. Japanese expansion to the very gateways of the continent, including a direct though minor attack in 1942, brought home to the people of Australia its geographical proximity to Asia. Moreover, the decline of the American, British, French, and Dutch colonial empires in Southeast Asia left a number of weak Asian states whose sympathy to Australia in a crisis could not be taken for granted. Instability in the neighboring islands of Indonesia created real apprehension in Canberra. Australians noted that Great Britain, mother of the Commonwealth of Nations, had declined in power, while China, long divided and weak, had taken the place of Japan as the rising threat to the Near North. Though a country whose power potential would eventually place it in a much stronger position in world councils, Australia was not able in the mid-twentieth century to make a large contribution to security in Southeast Asia. Yet, in the years ahead it might easily become the most important Western rear base for the region, a major arsenal of democracy, and a location for medium and long-range missiles—a series of developments that Communist China would like to prevent.

Canberra's main interest in the Near North is security. Australia has no territorial possessions in the area, but it controls eastern New Guinea bordering on western New Guinea (now transferred to Indonesia). Trade between the Commonwealth and different countries of Southeast Asia is increasing, and the possibility of Britain's eventual entry into the European Economic Community has strengthened Canberra's interest in a common market involving certain states of the Far East and Southwest Pacific. Australian investments in Southeast Asia are limited, but they too have a potential of expansion. As for political consideration, Australia wants the countries of the region as good neighbors; clashes among them and domestic upheaval weaken the area as a whole and raise problems in foreign policy for Canberra.

Diplomatic missions have been established in Rangoon, Bangkok, Vientiane, Phnom Penh, Saigon, Kuala Lumpur, Manila, and Djakarta. Although Australia is aware that it might serve as an intermediary between the states of the Near North and the big Western powers, the fact remains that the country is Western by political ties, tradition, and population. Moreover, the so-called "White Australia" restrictions on Asian immigration are widely considered as discriminatory in Southeast Asia. Yet the large number of Asians studying in the country under the Colombo Plan and other auspices is having a moderating effect.

The course of the Pacific war revealed that the United States was the Western power most able to help Australia, and today America ranks next only to Great Britain in popular interest. After the war Canberra was eager to make an alliance with Washington in a regional framework, but the United States hesitated for some time. On January 21, 1944, Australia and New Zealand had signed a pact at Canberra calling for the establishment in the Southwest and South Pacific of a "regional zone of defense," based on the two dominions and extending through the islands located north and northeast of Australia and on to Western Samoa and the Cook Islands. A formal alliance between Australia and the United States with New Zealand as the other partner came on September 1, 1951, with the signing of the security treaty, widely known as ANZUS. Both Canberra and Wellington were still apprehensive about the future of Japanese militarism and saw in the prospective Japanese peace treaty, ardently supported by Washington, the opportunity for concluding an American alliance. Influenced by the rise to power of the Chinese Communists, the outbreak of the Korean War, and the need for a Japanese peace treaty, the United States came to favor broader commitments in Pacific security. In the circumstances Australia and New Zealand were pleased with ANZUS and accepted the peace treaty with Japan, while the United States extended its formal commitments in the Pacific.

The tripartite security pact provided that an armed attack on any of the signatories in the Pacific area would be considered dangerous to all of them; should such an attack occur, they would take action to meet the common peril within the framework of their constitutional processes. The area of armed attack was given as the metropolitan territory of the signatories and the Pacific islands subject to their jurisdiction, along with their public vessels, aircraft, or armed forces in the Pacific. Another article provided for consultation in the event one of them believed that a threat existed to the independence, territorial integrity, or security of any of them in the Pacific area. The treaty was indefinite in duration, and it provided for a Pacific Council composed of the members' foreign ministers or their deputies so organized that it could meet at any time. The first session of the ANZUS Council was held in Hawaii where it was announced on August 7, 1952, that the organization necessary to implement the pact had been created and annual meetings of the Council would be held.

The absence of the United Kingdom as a signatory reflected the policy of the United States to restrict its commitments in the Far East. For Australia and New Zealand, the situation was different; as members of the Commonwealth, they looked to Great Britain as the key link in the world association. And it would be difficult for them to stay neutral, for instance, in a Chinese attack on Hong Kong. If the United Kingdom had been a signer of the security pact, the United States would probably have assumed commitments for the British in Hong Kong and Southeast Asia. The participation of Great Britain might also have brought to the forefront the question of France's membership and its possessions at the time in Indochina. And the Philippines was also interested in the pact, an aspect of concern in Washington. Not without reason, the ANZUS Treaty was described as a step "pending the development of a more comprehensive system of regional security in the Pacific Area," as stated in the preamble and in Article VIII.[2]

By membership in SEATO Australia further expanded its responsibilities in Southeast Asia. The Manila Treaty received bipartisan support in the Commonwealth and public opinion has appeared favorable. Canberra's ability to make an increasing con-

[2] Security Treaty between the United States of America, Australia, and New Zealand signed at San Francisco September 1, 1951, *Treaties and Other International Acts Series* 2493, p. 5 and p.6.

tribution to SEATO and to security in Southeast Asia is founded upon the growing industrial base of the country. The Pacific war and the Indochina conflict have prompted Australian military planners to shift their traditional focus on the Middle East to Southeast Asia. In addition to its contribution to the Commonwealth Strategic Reserve in Singapore and Malaya—one reinforced infantry battalion, three air squadrons of different types, and a few vessels—Australia has organized a mobile brigade prepared for tropical combat, has acquired Hercules troop carrier planes, and has established an air supply route from Australia to the Philippines, British Borneo, and Malaya. As already noted, token forces along with those from New Zealand and Great Britain were stationed in Thailand in the spring of 1962. Fully aware of the dangers of indirect aggression, Canberra has called for greater efforts in the antisubversion field, and the government has been eager to train on its own soil security personnel from Asian countries.

In some respects Australia is able to serve as a diplomatic buffer in SEATO between the weak Southeast Asian members and the Western "Big Three." In SEATO disputes Australia can at times exert a moderating influence, and outside the Manila Pact the ties between Canberra and Kuala Lumpur are particularly strong. Even the possibility of an Indian-Australian *entente* cannot be entirely ruled out. The Commonwealth is clearly one of the influential representatives of the West in Southeast Asia.

A sharp dispute arose in the Australian House of Representatives when the Canberra government officially announced on April 1, 1955, that in time of peace it intended to station Australian troops in Singapore and the Federation of Malaya. Although the Liberal-Country party coalition of Prime Minister Robert Gordon Menzies won by a vote of 55 to 41, the opposition Labour party accused the government of supporting colonialism in Malaya and expressed opposition to military service outside Australia in peacetime. After attending the conference of Commonwealth Prime Ministers in London earlier in the year, Menzies had visited Washington in March where he discussed with President Eisenhower security in Southeast Asia, including the stationing of Australian forces in the area. On April 20 the Prime Minister told his House of Representatives of an "agreed statement": the United States considered the defense of Southeast Asia of "very great importance"; Malaya with Singapore was termed "an integral part" of the area; the tactical use of armed forces would necessarily be worked out at the service level, but the American government considered "effective coöperation" of this kind to be "implicit in the Manila Pact."[3]

Australia played a highly important role in the origin and growth of the "Colombo Plan for Coöperative Economic Development in South and South-East Asia." The undertaking originated as the Spender Plan, which was proposed by the Australian Minister for External Affairs, Percy C. Spender, at a conference of foreign ministers of the Commonwealth nations at Colombo in January 1950. Canberra now contributes each year about 0.1 per cent of its national income to the Plan, while in the area of technical assistance, the 2,000th student under the Plan arrived in Australia in 1957, and many experts from the Commonwealth have been sent to Asian countries.

Founded upon a heritage of good will and basic common objectives, Australian-American relations represent in most respects an ideal pattern of international behavior. Differences are usually minor and can often be settled in private, and little anti-Americanism is evident in the Commonwealth. In 1962, however, Australia became concerned over the American support for Britain's entry into the European Economic Community with its adverse effects on the Commonwealth preference system. Despite con-

[3] Text of Agreed Statement, *Current Notes on International Affairs*, April 1955, pp. 289-90.

siderable pressure at times to do so, Canberra still does not recognize the People's Republic of China, although Peking has been able to contract for substantial grain deliveries from Australia as well as from Canada. The previous American moratorium formula for not seating Chinese Communist representatives in the General Assembly of the United Nations was consistently supported by Canberra. In the voting on December 15, 1961, the Australians considered the subject of representation "important" and opposed the Soviet resolution favoring Peking. Any change in U.S. policy on recognition would be quickly reflected in Australia. Although Canberra would not want to be drawn into a Pacific war over the Formosa Strait, in the crisis of 1958 it supported Washington's position that force should not be used to settle territorial disputes. If the United States had not taken a strong position in the crisis, the Australians believed that the Chinese Communists would have been encouraged to probe more vigorously at the free world position in the Far East. On October 1 of that same year the ANZUS Council at a meeting in Washington significantly agreed that any threat or use of force was a "serious menace to the peace of the area" and deeply concerned the three members.

The governments in Canberra and in Wellington have both been eager to keep ANZUS from becoming obsolete and have desired to continue regular meetings of the Council and of the Military Representatives. In some respects the ANZUS group can function on a more intimate basis than the larger SEATO: certain problems can be discussed that would not even fit into the framework of the Manila Treaty. As proof that Washington also recognizes the value of the tripartite pact, the U.S. Commander in Chief, Pacific, represents the United States at both the meetings of the ANZUS Military Representatives and the SEATO Military Advisers. For a while there was some feeling in Canberra and Wellington that Washington had lost a degree of interest in ANZUS, but they interpreted the successful meeting of the Council in Canberra on May 8-9, 1962, and the delay in holding the regular SEATO Council session as an upgrading of ANZUS in the United States.

Both in and out of SEATO, Australia can exert a moderating influence when issues such as China policy threaten to disrupt Anglo-American relations in the Pacific and Far East. Yet Canberra's policy commitments do not give it a wide range of maneuverability, and its positions can often be anticipated well in advance of any attempted move.

NEW ZEALAND

Although New Zealand is much more distant from Southeast Asia than is Australia, the Dominion, like its larger Commonwealth neighbor, has come to realize the strategic importance of the region to its future. As an earnest of this awareness New Zealand contributes an infantry battalion, a light cruiser, and an aircraft transport and a light bomber squadron to the Commonwealth Strategic Reserve in Singapore and Malaya. The fact that Southeast Asia has replaced the Middle East in New Zealand's overseas military planning is better understood in government circles than among the population at large, one reason being the many veterans who fought in the latter area. Nevertheless, the Japanese conquest of Southeast Asia in the Second World War brought home to New Zealanders, isolated though their country is in the expanse of the South Pacific, the dangers of hostile forces in the strategic region to the northwest. And the imperialism of Communist China in Southeast Asia gives Wellington no grounds for comfort. Moreover, New Zealand does not want to see itself open to Asian migration, although relations with the growing minority of indigenous Maoris rest on fairly solid foun-

COHESION OF THE WEST: DIFFICULTIES AND ADJUSTMENTS

dations. In fact, Maoris are well represented in Wellington's contribution to the Commonwealth Strategic Reserve. It is clearly in the country's interest to promote collective security in Southeast Asia through SEATO, which has bipartisan support and general acceptance. At the same time the Dominion is eager to encourage the well-being of the people of the area and to have friendly relations with their governments.

In July 1955 Wellington established the Office of the Commissioner for New Zealand in Southeast Asia with Singapore as the headquarters. The Commission had diplomatic and consular functions, promoted trade, and was concerned with Colombo Plan negotiations and to some extent with the work of SEATO. The Commissioner himself represented New Zealand at SEATO in Bangkok and became ambassador to Thailand. When Wellington later decided not to retain the position of the Commissioner for New Zealand in Southeast Asia, a high commissioner was sent to Kuala Lumpur, a commissioner to Singapore, and the ambassador to Thailand (or chargé d'affaires) became the SEATO Council Representative.

The Dominion's foreign policy in Southeast Asia is greatly influenced by the positions of the United Kingdom, Australia, and the United States. Without the Commonwealth and American ties, New Zealand would not have its present role in the region. Great Britain is still the most influential power in the external relations of the Dominion, and through London, Wellington is linked with many other members of the Commonwealth. Fully aware of Great Britain's sensitivity, especially under Prime Minister Churchill, about the membership of ANZUS, New Zealand was glad to have the mother country in SEATO.

Ties between Australia and New Zealand have grown since the common experience of the Second World War, the Australian-New Zealand agreement of 1944 at Canberra, the beginning of cooperation in ANZAM, and the formation of the Commonwealth Strategic Reserve in Malaya. Both countries, it should be added, are active in the work of the Colombo Plan. Yet there are differences between Wellington and Canberra; some New Zealanders are critical or scornful of Australians, many of whom tend to ignore their neighbors to the east. The criticism is like that within a family, however, and no divorce of interests is at all probable.

Today New Zealand looks to the United States for its security; no longer can Great Britain, which once ruled the seas, afford the Dominion protection in time of crisis. ANZUS and SEATO provide the multilateral framework of U.S. pledges to defend New Zealand. In both organizations cooperation is marked, although the much larger membership and more critical current problems of SEATO afford greater opportunity for differences to emerge. Wellington has generally not been a go-between in SEATO for the Asian members and the "Big Three"; because of close ties with Great Britain, such a role may not be possible. Outside SEATO, New Zealand's relations with the Federation of Malaya are conducive to a high degree of rapport. Wellington decided in 1955 to station peacetime forces in the country and, after its independence, agreed to become associated with the Anglo-Malayan defense agreement through the Commonwealth Strategic Reserve. Yet, even so, the Dominion does not deliberately seek to influence the Malayan state in foreign affairs.

In China policy New Zealand refuses to recognize the People's Republic and supported for many years the American moratorium formula on the question of its seating in the U.N. General Assembly. In the sixteenth General Assembly in 1961 it voted the same as did Australia. At the same time there is real pressure for the recognition of Peking. During the Formosa Strait crisis of 1958 the Dominion opposed the use of force by Communist China but did not wish to become involved in a war over the controversy. In spite of some criticism of the United States in New Zealand, the relations between Wellington and Washington are cordial, and New Zealanders have not forgotten the arrival of U.S. forces in the Second World War when their country was practically defenseless. The Dominion, moreover, would like to expand exports to the United States, especially if traditional markets in the United Kingdom are going to be drastically reduced or lost through eventual British participation in the European Economic Community.

FRANCE

The interests of France in Southeast Asia have markedly declined since the end of the Indochina War in 1954. Although Paris once had an important empire in Indochina, which was sometimes called the French "balcony on the Pacific," the independence of Viet-Nam, whether viewed from Hanoi or Saigon, and of Cambodia and Laos has ended French territorial interests. In the South China Sea, to be sure, France claims the Spratly Islands; yet the Republic of Viet-Nam, the Philippines, and both Communist and Nationalist China all dispute the claim. In the SEATO treaty area the only territory actually remaining under the tricolor consists of some Pacific islands like New Caledonia, which is southeast of New Guinea and northeast of Australia. Although France maintained a base for some time at Seno near Savannakhet in Laos, as allowed by the Geneva settlement of 1954, Paris did not take advantage of the right to maintain another in the Mekong valley. In a move showing its feeling against the French the Laotian government of Premier Boun Oum took over a small section of the base at Seno in February 1961. As has been noted, French military missions are maintained in Cambodia and Laos, and French advisers have been active in various Laotian ministries. All things considered, French political influence today is strongest in Cambodia, declining in Laos, weak in South Viet-Nam, and extinguished in North Viet-Nam.

The remaining interests of Paris in Indochina are cultural and economic. The French language is still widely used; Roman Catholicism has deep roots in Viet-Nam; and French educational institutions are active in Cambodia, Laos, and South Viet-Nam. Cultural missions function in Saigon, Phnom Penh, and Vientiane, and France attracts a good number of students from the area. Even in the Democratic Republic of Viet-Nam the French cultural impact has not entirely vanished, whereas in Cambodia it has remained very strong.

As for economic matters, French trade with Indochina has declined since the end of the colonial period; no longer is the commerce of the area channeled largely to or from France and its associates. French investments have also declined; they are practically ended in North Viet-Nam, although they are still flourishing in Cambodia. Despite the changes in French economic interests, Paris still has a sizable stake in the area as a whole, and French economic and technical aid continues in South Viet-Nam, Cambodia, and Laos. Although France has not participated in the Colombo Plan, it is active in ECAFE; and in 1947 France had signed an agreement with Australia, New Zealand, the Netherlands, Great Britain and the United States setting up a South Pacific Commission designed to promote the economic progress and social well-being of the people living in the non-self-governing territories of the South Pacific administered by the signatories.

General Jean de Lattre de Tassigny, High Commissioner and Commander in Chief in Indochina in 1950-51, had advocated a security pact for Southeast Asia, for he believed the loss of Tonkin to the Communists would lead to the fall of Indochina and then of all Southeast Asia. Some of his concepts lived on after his death in January 1952. A year later, as the Indochina War mounted in intensity, France joined with the United States, Australia, New Zealand and Great Britain in a Five-Power Staff Agency to further military coordination in Southeast Asia. With the signing of the Manila Pact, however, the United States was not prepared to continue the Five-Power Staff Agency.

Franco-American relations in Southeast Asia have not been so cordial as those between Great Britain and America. Although the United States provided substantial military and economic aid to France and the Associated States of Indochina in the latter stages of the Indochina War and gave careful consideration to military intervention during the crucial battle of Dien Bien Phu, many Frenchmen resented the influential role of Americans in South Viet-Nam and Laos after the Geneva settlement in July 1954. Nor did France's more prominent position in Cambodia (compared to the other two states) prevent hard feeling between some Frenchmen and Americans in the Khmer kingdom. In fact, Washington has often been blamed for the political, economic, and cultural decline of France in Indochina today. While Franco-American differences in Indochina are reflected in SEATO, the leadership of General Charles de Gaulle has brought considerable agreement between Washington and Paris on a number of SEATO questions. Both powers cooperated at least to some degree in the Laotian crises of 1959 and 1960-62. Paris maintains that its policy in Indochina reflects the experience of many years of close contact and is based on the principle of sound realism.

France, like the United States, does not recognize the People's Republic of China, whose role in the Indochina War and posture toward Algeria have antagonized Paris, although in June 1961 a government-sponsored agency sold barley valued at around $10 million to Peking. Paris supported the previous American moratorium formula on Chinese representation in the U. N. General

Assembly, and voted with the United States, Australia, and New Zealand on December 15, 1961. President de Gaulle is well aware of the growing importance of Communist China in global affairs and of the problems it presents to the world.

THE NETHERLANDS

Following the achievement of independence by Indonesia, Dutch interests in Southeast Asia came to focus on the territory which was called Netherlands New Guinea by The Hague, West Irian by Djakarta, and West New Guinea in United Nations circles. Even before the Dutch decided to leave the area, their large economic stake in Indonesia had largely vanished, for the controversy over West New Guinea was a major factor in leading the Djakarta regime to seek the liquidation of the remaining Dutch economic interests. This policy was greatly intensified after November 1957, when the General Assembly of the United Nations failed to adopt a resolution on West New Guinea which was supported by Djakarta. The economic and cultural break between Djakarta and The Hague has been much more clear-cut than that between France and Indochina.

The international activities of the Netherlands in Southeast Asia have included participation in ECAFE and the South Pacific Commission but not in the Colombo Plan. In 1962 the withdrawal of the Dutch from West New Guinea led to their leaving the South Pacific Commission. Although the Netherlands was interested in becoming a signer of the Manila Pact in 1954, there was strong opposition from some other powers who did not want to make commitments to the Dutch possession of West New Guinea or to emphasize the issue of colonialism in Asia. Events have shown that SEATO would have been seriously compromised by the Netherlands' participation and could not have gained its present acceptability in a large part of Southeast Asia. Yet, on occasion the Dutch brought aspects of the Indonesian question to NATO, and at a summit meeting on December 19, 1957, the Council viewed "with concern" developments in the island republic.

The West New Guinea controversy was much more than a dispute between Djakarta and The Hague: it involved Australia directly and the other members of SEATO to varying degrees; it aroused widespread interest in the Afro-Asian world, being generally considered an example of Western colonialism; and it received global attention by its appearance on the agenda of the United Nations General Assembly.

The background of the dispute was complex. In 1949 at the Round Table Conference which led to the transfer of sovereignty from the Netherlands to Indonesia, agreement could not be reached on the political status of West New Guinea. It was decided to keep the *status quo* with the proviso that within one year after the transfer of sovereignty the question of the status of the area be determined through direct negotiations. Efforts for a solution failed for many years. Since the territory was generally considered *Indonesia Irredenta* in the island republic, nationalistic sentiment was inflamed, but the Netherlands did not want to bow to Indonesian pressure, having already yielded all the rest of the previously Dutch Pacific islands.

Though large in area (about 161,000 square miles), West New Guinea has an estimated population of only 700,000 people who are not mainly of Indonesian race or culture, but are Papuans like those of eastern New Guinea. Beyond the coastal fringe areas, the primitive culture of the indigenous population has been hardly changed. There are resources of oil and gold in West Irian, but the real extent of these and other possible assets is unknown. An important landing strip and terminal for jet passenger planes has been constructed at Biak.

The Dutch maintained that they had a sound legal case; in fact, they proceeded to make Netherlands New Guinea a part of the kingdom by amending their constitution in 1952. Although limited economic interests such as those in petroleum, as well as matters of prestige and concern for Christian missionaries and the small number of Eurasians in the area, have been factors in the position of the Netherlands, The Hague stressed that it had an obligation to the indigeneous people who should be prepared for the exercise of self-determination just as soon as possible. In September 1961 the Dutch indicated to the General Assembly of the United Nations that they were willing to relinquish sovereignty over the contested area, to place it under the jurisdiction of the world organization pending self-determination by the Papuans, and to continue to help the people. The sixteenth General Assembly, however, failed to pass any resolutions on the subject.

The Indonesians likewise claimed sound grounds in their case for West Irian; it was a part of the former Dutch empire in the East Indies. They argued that the transfer of sovereignty did not, could not, and should not exclude any portion of the Netherlands East Indies. Some of the leaders in Djakarta publicly stated that West Irian under the Dutch could be used as a springboard against the republic.

Djakarta took the controversy to the General Assembly at the ninth, tenth, eleventh and twelfth sessions. Although the subject was thoroughly debated, Indonesia failed to get the two-thirds majority needed for any draft resolution it supported, except during the tenth session when there was no objection to one hoping that the negotiations foreseen in an Indonesian-Dutch statement of December 7, 1955, would be fruitful. On November 29, 1957, the draft resolution, which in effect simply called for the resumption of discussions between The Hague and Djakarta with the possible assistance of the Secretary-General of the

United Nations, failed to pass by a vote of 41 in favor, 29 opposed, and 11 abstaining. The Western powers were divided, with Australia, New Zealand, Great Britain and France supporting the Netherlands and the United States abstaining. The Soviet bloc strongly defended Indonesia on the grounds that the issue was colonialism as well as the cold war and charged that West Irian was being prepared as a SEATO base. Almost all the Afro-Asian states backed Indonesia in the controversy.

Canberra was especially active in defense of the Dutch position both inside and outside the United Nations. Although Australia had championed the cause of Indonesian independence, it preferred a friendly Netherlands to an uncertain Indonesia in possession of West New Guinea. Basic to the Australian posture was the realization of the importance of New Guinea in the defense of the continent, as was so well brought out in the Pacific war. The northeastern section of the island is a part of the Australian Trust Territory of New Guinea under the United Nations, whereas the southeastern section, Papua, is a possession of the Crown. Together they constitute the administrative union of the Territory of Papua and New Guinea. In a statement on November 6, 1957, before the General Assembly vote of November 29, Canberra and The Hague called for greater cooperation in a number of matters relating to the entire island. Such an effort, it was indicated, would contribute to the advancement of the indigenous people of New Guinea. The following October the first conference between the Dutch and Australians on administrative cooperation in the area was held in Canberra.

The Padang Revolt in 1958 with all its implications was watched with considerable interest in Australia. After it failed, both Canberra and The Hague were concerned lest weapons which the United States and Great Britain had then decided to sell to Djakarta be used by Indonesia for aggressive purposes toward Netherlands New Guinea. Canberra observed, however, that the Indonesian government had given assurances that it would not use force to get West Irian.

Noting that Indonesia's military potential had been strengthened and calling attention to "aggressive elements" in the island republic, the Dutch decided in the spring of 1960 to send reinforcements—jet fighter aircraft, some light antiaircraft artillery, a reinforced infantry battalion, and an aircraft carrier, the *Karel Doorman*—to Netherlands New Guinea. It was also planned to establish a corps of Papuan volunteers who would begin training in 1961. Even with the Dutch reinforcements the total military personnel at the time would probably be not more than three or four thousand men, largely associated with the navy; but Djakarta accused The Hague of "playing with fire," and some officials believed that NATO should restrain its Dutch member. On May 6 the diplomatic mission of the Netherlands in the Indonesian capital was stormed by angry students; tensions between the two governments increased as a result of the mutual recriminations; all trade came to a halt; and Indonesia severed diplomatic relations on August 17. The following November the Dutch announced plans to strengthen further the defenses of Netherlands New Guinea, while the Soviets continued to assist the Indonesians in a military build-up.

Australia did not find membership in SEATO helpful in the West New Guinea dispute. The three Asian members almost always voted for Indonesia in the General Assembly, the Philippines alone showing some hesitancy toward Djakarta's cause. Although New Zealand, Great Britain, and France backed Australia's stand, the general attitude of the United States in the United Nations did not please Canberra; and, given the division among SEATO members, Australia outlined its position on West New Guinea to its colleagues but went no further. Both Australia and Great Britain are aware of unofficial viewpoints in Djakarta that a greater Indonesia should include British Borneo, Portuguese Timor, and eastern as well as western New Guinea. If eastern New Guinea were attacked, Article IV, paragraph 1, of the Manila Treaty would be applicable, although under the pact Washington has formally restricted its pledge to circumstances of "Communist aggression."

In 1959 Australian policy toward the West New Guinea controversy became a subject of some speculation when Indonesia's Foreign Minister Subandrio during a February visit to Canberra issued a communiqué with the Australian Minister for External Affairs, R. G. Casey, which stated that Australia would not oppose any Indonesian-Netherlands agreement "by peaceful processes," but, pending such an accord, it would continue to recognize the sovereignty of the Dutch over the area. During his visit Subandrio stated that Indonesia would not use force to solve the controversy, for if it should, Djakarta would have to face the United States and Britain as well as the Netherlands and Australia. Prime Minister Menzies himself visited Indonesia in December and received President Sukarno's personal assurances that Djakarta would not use force in the dispute.

The Subandrio-Casey communiqué of February 1959 was inspired by Australia's effort for better relations with Indonesia and did not represent a retreat from support of the Dutch, although it was so viewed by some Australians. In the past Prime Minister Menzies has considered the possibility of an independent, united New Guinea, and neither The Hague nor Canberra has wanted to prejudice the eventual self-determination of the Papuans. After the departure of the Dutch, Australia would certainly have preferred a united, independent New Guinea, possibly as a member of the British Commonwealth of Nations, to Indonesian control, but the former possibility disappeared in 1962. Some comfort was provided in the final communiqué of the ANZUS Council on May 9 which reaffirmed the "obligations of mutual assistance" in the case of armed attack on Australian New Guinea.

Washington was plainly faced with a dilemma in determining its policy on West New Guinea. The Netherlands was an ally under the North Atlantic Treaty, yet Americans were genuinely opposed to colonialism and sympathetic to Asian nationalism. Moreover, the United States had played an active part in the emergence of Indonesia as a sovereign country; it was a member of the Committee of Good Offices and its successor, the United Nations Commission for Indonesia, both created by the Security Council. Neither the Dutch nor the Indonesians were satisfied with the American role. The Dutch were critical both of what they considered to be unjustified U.S. intervention and of Washington's refusal to sell them weapons for use in Indonesia after the first police action. Although the Indonesians were less critical than the Dutch, they considered U.S. support for Indonesian nationalism to be insufficient. Later the Netherlands was further incensed when the United States, alone among the members of the South Pacific Commission, declined to be represented at the opening of the first partially elected Legislature Council of Netherlands New Guinea on April 5, 1961. Throughout the history of the West New Guinea controversy there were divided counsels in Washington concerning the attitude that the United States should assume in the General Assembly of the United Nations. Abstention in the past obviously pleased neither Indonesia nor the Netherlands.

After the Kennedy administration took over in 1961 the dispute was thoroughly reviewed in government circles. In December armed infiltrators from Indonesia initiated a systematic effort by sea and air to establish themselves in West Irian, and the Dutch continued to build up their defending forces to a total of between 8,000 and 10,000 men. Meanwhile Moscow was augmenting the military capability of Indonesia by an extensive program of military assistance and was urging Sukarno to take West Irian by force. It became increasingly evident that open warfare might drive Djakarta into the arms of Moscow, while a peaceful solution to the controversy might encourage a more independent Indonesian posture. The impasse on West New Guinea in the sixteenth U.N. General Assembly, the Dutch moves toward government by Papuans in the dependency, and the Indian seizure of Goa in late 1961 further contributed to the possibility of an open Indonesian attack in 1962.

Having decided that the circumstances required a positive effort on the part of the United States, the Kennedy administration made persistent, quiet, and judicious attempts for many months to get the Dutch and Indonesians together. It became known that the United States favored turning West New Guinea over to Indonesian administration with the exercise at some time of self-determination by the Papuans. Considerable doubt, however, existed about the validity of self-determination in the foreseeable future, given the primitive status of the Papuans. Moreover, there were those who did not believe that Indonesia would allow a genuine plebiscite even with United Nations participation. The American approach capitalized on the Dutch desire to disengage without loss of face in West New Guinea.

With the support of U Thant, then Acting Secretary-General of the United Nations, preliminary, closed talks between the Dutch and Indonesians were held on March 20-23, 1962. Present at the negotiations as an intermediary at U Thant's suggestion was Ellsworth Bunker, a former U.S. ambassador, who worked in liaison with the Department of State although he was technically a private citizen. Blaming the Dutch, the Indonesians refused to continue the talks, but the United States did not relax its efforts, and in May Bunker's proposals for negotiations between the contestants were made public. Supported by the United States and praised by U Thant, they called for the replacement over a two-year period of Dutch administrators by United Nations personnel who would be followed by Indonesian officials. When the administration of West New Guinea had been transferred to Indonesia, the Papuans would be given an "opportunity to exercise freedom of choice" with the assistance of the United Nations, but the exact timing would be subject to negotiation. Following the signing of the agreement by Djakarta and The Hague, the two powers would resume diplomatic relations. The Bunker proposals were eventually accepted in principle by both contestants, the Indonesians being in favor of them whereas the Dutch were critical of U.S. policy. But as President Kennedy aptly observed at a press conference, the United States was ready "to have everybody mad, if it makes some progress."

Washington welcomed the formal agreement on West New Guinea signed by the Netherlands and Indonesia on August 15, 1962. In accordance with carefully prepared plans the General Assembly of the United Nations approved on September 21 a resolution enabling the world organization to participate in carrying out the settlement. A United Nations Temporary Executive Authority under the Secretary-General, with a United Nations Administrator and a Pakistani military force of some 1,400 men, was established, and the world body assumed West New Guinea's administration on October 1. The schedule called for the transfer of the administration to Indonesia as quickly as possible after May 1, 1963, and for the exercise of self-determination, with the advice, assistance, and participation of a United Nations Representative and his staff, to be completed before the end of 1969.

As a whole, the general unity of the Western powers in Southeast Asia—the United States, the United Kingdom, France, Australia, New Zealand, and even the Netherlands—is pronounced. Although there have been certain differences on issues, such as those involving China or West New Guinea, the controversies have generally been conducted with restraint and with mutual respect. The close security, economic, and other ties between many of the Western powers and many Southeast Asian states represent an important bridge between the East and the West. It would be unfortunate if the Western countries, now that the colonial empires are largely gone, should withdraw from Southeast Asia. Greater understanding and sympathy are needed in the future, not just from those Western powers who have security arrangements or close political ties in the area, but also from the others who share a common intent in a stable world order.

[ELEVEN]

Counterweight Potential of India and Japan

In the developing distribution of power in Asia, relations among China, India, and Japan promise to be increasingly important in the coming decade. The growing influence of Peking, New Delhi, and Tokyo has already modified the polarization of power between the United States and the Soviet Union that dominated world politics after the Second World War. Such prominent positions in world politics have scarcely been a matter of choice for the rising Asian powers. Even if China, India, and Japan had sought, singly or in unison, to remain aloof from the prevailing world struggle, they would still find themselves unavoidably involved in the international politics of Washington and Moscow.

There are great differences between the power potentials of Peking, New Delhi, and Tokyo. By almost any criterion of power China clearly ranks higher than India, and Japan is in third place. Neither India nor Japan, acting alone, is likely to become an effective counterweight to China, but acting together they could have an important role in creating a stable pattern of power among Asian states. In any realistic consideration of future relations among Peking, New Delhi, and Tokyo, political determination must be considered along with the material elements of power. This critical factor involves great imponderables like the future pattern of alliances and the future leadership of China, India, and Japan, when men like Mao Tse-tung and Nehru are gone from the scene. At present Tokyo and New Delhi are in the early stages of discovering and understanding each other, though contacts are expanding and projects involving economic and technical cooperation are increasing. Between them lies the great and threatening power of Communist China, and the Himalayan crisis may be accelerating their discovery of mutual interests.

The United States in its Asian policy can assist in the strengthening of both India and Japan and can also encourage them in greater cooperation in the Far East. At the same time it has to be careful lest it weaken some of its own interests in the process. Southeast Asia is a critical area where relations among New Delhi, Tokyo, and Washington provide real opportunities for cooperation. It affords a testing ground for the development of an Asian counterweight to Peking.

IMPORTANCE OF SOUTHEAST ASIA TO INDIA

The influence of India in Southeast Asia is, among Asian states, surpassed only by that of Communist China. India's location and size, population and natural resources, and basic (if limited) industrialization are factors of power contributing to its influence on neighboring areas; moreover, since independence in 1947 Prime Minister Nehru has spoken for India in words that have commanded the attention of the world. India's total impact has recently declined in Southeast Asia, however, as a result of growing nationalism within the newly independent countries of the area and changing relations between New Delhi and Peking. The former's acquisition of Goa by armed force, though widely viewed as an act against colonialism, also caused some misgivings.

For a number of reasons Southeast Asia is a region of considerable importance to Indian policy-makers. The region's coasts and islands command the eastern sea approaches to the subcontinent. Burma has a land boundary with India, but the terrain is rugged and difficult; communications between the two neighbors are much easier by water. Japan's attempted invasion of India during the Pacific war proved the difficulties of military operations along the western frontier of Burma and suggests the advantages of sea-borne invasion mounted from Southeast Asia. As most of India's trade is also carried across the ocean that borders three sides of the country, the command of the seas in friendly hands is of vital importance to New Delhi, but the drastic decline of British sea power in the Indian Ocean has created a vacuum that has not yet been filled. A strong navy at the disposal of a great power, based, say, on Singapore, could have profound influence on India. In long-range strategy the Peking-Moscow axis may possibly seek to dominate the Indian Ocean; China might aim for the eastern approach at Singapore as the Soviet Union seeks the western approach at Suez. It should be noted that the United States has already considered maintaining an American fleet in the Indian Ocean area.

But the importance of Southeast Asia to New Delhi extends far beyond considerations of strategy. The Indian government has a deep interest in the politics of the region, for it is convinced that the best way to destroy the appeals of communism is through the improvement of the economic and social conditions of the common man. Moreover, sizable Indian minorities exist in Burma and Malaya while smaller concentrations are found throughout what has sometimes been called "Further India." In contrast to Peking's general policy, New Delhi does not approve of the principle of dual citizenship. Overseas Indians are advised to choose between retaining the citizenship of their native country or acquiring that of the state where they are now living. Although opposed to discriminatory practices in Southeast Asia, New Delhi has exercised considerable restraint in its relations over the subject with local governments; and in foreign policy it has not sought to use the Overseas Indians, either openly or covertly, to advance its national objectives. India values the neighboring region in part as a testing ground for its concepts of foreign policy; for instance, the *Panch Shila* (the Five Principles of Peaceful Coexistence) have been given an opportunity to flourish or perish. The support that India frequently receives from some of the countries of the area strengthens New Delhi's position in the United Nations and in world affairs.

Southeast Asia is also important to India as a market for some of its products, especially textiles, and as a source for some of its imports, especially rice. Patterns of trade established when India, Burma, and Malaya were all parts of the British Empire are still important, though modified by international and domestic developments. Presumably the further industrialization of India and a rise in the purchasing power of Southeast Asia could lead to closer and mutually advantageous economic ties.

It would be unrealistic not to note the other side of the coin, namely, the importance of India to Southeast Asia. Long before the Europeans arrived the Hindu civilization had permeated much of the area; even today its influence is strong in most of peninsular Southeast Asia west of Viet-Nam, as well as in Bali. The present ties between Cambodia and India are based in part upon mutual awareness of a common cultural heritage. To many Southeast Asians in influential places India presents a favorable contrast to Communist China, even though they realize the latter has far greater physical power. They are aware that the disappearance of New Delhi as a center of non-Communist influence in Asia might make it impossible for their own countries to remain outside the Communist bloc. A Peking-New Delhi axis (not to mention any links to Moscow) might well generate irresistible pressures against Southeast Asia. But India has been and remains a stabilizing factor in the region, a contribution of considerable importance to an area where the elements of instability are so pronounced. By not intervening in local controversies and by advocating the peaceful resolution of differences, New Delhi has thrown its diplomatic influence on the side of moderation. India has certainly not ignored its national interests, especially those close to home, and its nonalignment policy has not been appreciated in many capitals; yet few Southeast Asians consider New Delhi a current troublemaker or a potential aggressor.

INDIAN OBJECTIVES AND POLICY IN SOUTHEAST ASIA

In its general national objectives, India wants the countries of Southeast Asia to be independent, peaceful, and prosperous. In consequence, New Delhi opposes colonialism in the region, whether from the East or the West, favors nonalignment as conducive to peace, and considers economic and social development essential for the well-being of the people. In proportion to the full realization of these aims, India believes that communism would fail in all its efforts, that the "area of peace" in the world would be expanded, and that New Delhi's own position would be immeasurably strengthened.

The implementation of Indian objectives in Southeast Asia has been marked by the vigorous use of all possible channels of diplomacy. New Delhi is represented in every capital of the area, including a consul general in Hanoi. Prime Minister Nehru has traveled extensively in the region and has received many distinguished guests from the region in his own capital; as a result, he has personal contacts of long standing with many local figures. (Nehru's departure from the political scene could easily reduce India's prestige in the region, at least until a new leader of stature came to the forefront.) Bilateral discussions involving many of New Delhi's leaders and diplomats have been supplemented through various kinds of multilateral diplomacy; meetings of the prime ministers of the Colombo Powers, for instance, found India taking a prominent part. Because India provides the chairmen of the international supervisory commissions in Viet-Nam, Cambodia, and Laos, it has been in a key position in Indochina. As a leader of the Afro-Asian bloc of the United Nations, New Delhi has influenced many votes in the General Assembly and in the Security, Trusteeship, and Economic and Social Councils. Membership in the Commonwealth of Nations has periodically brought together the prime ministers of several countries deeply concerned with the future of Southeast Asia. Conferences associated with the Colombo Plan or with different activities of the United Nations usually find Indian representatives active in the discussions.

Despite all the vicissitudes of Asian politics, the *Panch Shila* have not been relegated to the background, and these principles still guide New Delhi's policy toward Southeast Asia. Under prevailing circumstances many Indians consider the Five Principles of Peaceful Coexistence the best guarantee against aggression and subversion in the area. When the *Panch Shila* were adopted by Prime Minister Nehru and Premier Chou En-lai in 1954, India hoped a moral barrier of such strength had been erected that no power, not even gigantic Communist China, would want to bring upon its shoulders the universal opprobrium that would result from violation. The weak countries of Southeast Asia, incapable in any case of holding back Chinese armies, could now put their faith in the *Panch Shila* and devote their limited resources to economic development instead of expending them on military build-ups. If the states of Southeast Asia would thus keep aloof from the cold war, they would offer the great powers no pretext for interference and would also help to relax world tensions. Communist China, for its part, would receive the reassurance of independent and friendly neighbors to the south, neighbors barring themselves to Western military penetration. Freed from apprehension of China's intentions in the Himalayas and in Southeast Asia, New Delhi could make greater headway in its own programs of economic and social development.

In three particular areas of Southeast Asia—Burma, Indonesia, and Indochina—India has at times been very influential. Its relations with the Philippines and Thailand have tended to be correct but routine, and with the Federation of Malaya more cordial but still limited. Toward Burma, however, India under Nehru has shown a particular desire for close ties, reinforced by historical, economic, and security considerations. Although there are certain sources of ill will between New Delhi and Rangoon—problems arising from the Indian minority in Burma, boundary questions involving the Nagas, and disagreement at times over the export price of rice—these issues have not been allowed to damage the friendship between the countries. Nehru's personal ties to U Nu have not been duplicated in his relationships with other Burmese premiers, U Ba Swe and Ne Win, but common interests have still prevailed.

India has given Burma diplomatic, economic, and even on occasion military support. When the question of remnants of Kuomintang forces in Burma was argued in the U.N. General Assembly, India staunchly championed its neighbor's cause. In discussions with Communist China over Southeast Asian problems Nehru has indicated his sympathy for Burma. New Delhi made a generous settlement on the debt owed by Rangoon when Burma became separate from the Indian Empire in 1937; it also made possible financial help to the Union and provided technical assistance. At one critical time when the government of Premier U Nu was fighting for its life against the insurgents, the prompt supply of Indian arms was important in keeping the regime in power.

The border agreement reached by Premiers Ne Win and Chou En-lai in Peking on January 28, 1960, had important implications for India. When Chou En-lai visited Burma in April, it is not surprising that he was well received. On October 1 a treaty was signed in Peking establishing the newly defined border. Under its terms Burma yielded to the People's Republic the three villages of Hpimaw, Gawlum, and Kangfang in the Kachin State, as well as the Panghung-Panglao district in the Wa State, but in return it received sovereignty over the Namwan Assigned Tract. Through this arrangement Peking, which has asserted that the McMahon Line with India is invalid, has in effect accepted the McMahon Line (with some modification) insofar as it pertains to Burma. The border agreement, which established a joint committee for the delimitation of the boundary, was accompanied by a nonaggression treaty between Peking and Rangoon. Burmese leaders believe their success in boundary negotiations with China was tactically due to the difficulties in relations between ، Peking and New Delhi.

India made an important contribution to the emergence of Indonesia as a member of the family of nations. But long before then some of the leading nationalists of both countries had known each other, among them Nehru and Hatta, and at the Asian Relations Conference in New Delhi in the spring of 1947 Nehru made a special effort to have Sjahrir present. When the

Dutch undertook their first and second police actions against the Indonesians, New Delhi strongly supported its island friends both within and outside the United Nations, and in January 1949 it played host to an international conference on the Indonesian question.

Since the achievement of *Merdeka* the ties between New Delhi and Djakarta have been reasonably close though in recent years they have tended to be considerably less intimate. Irritants have arisen over the Asian Games, and problems have developed in the wake of the Sino-Indian conflict. Both countries have followed a foreign policy of nonalignment, and their positions in the United Nations have been similar on most cold war, colonial, and economic questions. In addition, India gave Indonesia staunch support in its claim to West New Guinea. The two Asian republics have made several arrangements for military cooperation: in 1956 an agreement provided for Indonesian air force officers to be trained in India and for equipment to be sold, loaned, or exchanged; a similar accord for naval cooperation was reached in 1958; and in 1960, a third provided for cooperation between the two armies. The small Indian minority—about 40,000 in 1952—does not impair the ties between New Delhi and Djakarta. Friendship, cultural, and trade agreements have helped relations, while state visits have widened personal contacts. Moreover, both countries in 1959 and 1960 shared another common experience—serious difficulties with the People's Republic of China.

As a result of the Geneva Conference on Indochina, India became deeply involved in the future of Cambodia, Laos, and Viet-Nam. New Delhi had viewed with serious concern the warfare in the area, especially as it increased in intensity and in international complications. Sympathetic to Asian nationalism and interpreting the conflict (at least in its early stages) as a just struggle against French imperialism, India was favorably disposed toward Ho Chi Minh, although withholding diplomatic recognition from his government. But as the Viet-Minh leader appeared more obviously as a Communist, New Delhi came to see the Indochina War in a broader perspective.

Although India was not a formal participant at the Geneva Conference in 1954, V. K. Krishna Menon was active in behind-the-scene negotiations. Nehru approved of the Geneva agreements, and the Colombo Powers, who had previously indicated deep concern over the fighting in Indochina and had offered suggestions about a resolution of the conflict, threw their moral support behind the settlement. New Delhi earnestly hoped that the Geneva arrangements would bring an end to hostilities so destructive in nature and so dangerous for world peace. It was also in favor of the widespread international recognition of Cambodia and Laos as independent countries.

After the Geneva Conference India had to face squarely the problems of a partitioned Viet-Nam, a divided Laos, and a Cambodia where questions of national integration were serious. India had a delicate but crucial role to play as chairman of the international commissions for supervision and control in the three countries, for one member, Poland, was a signer of the Warsaw Pact, and the other, Canada, a signatory to the North Atlantic Treaty. Not only must New Delhi strive to achieve the objectives of the Geneva settlement in Indochina itself, but it must also cope with the pressures of the cold war at the highest level. Moreover, the three commissions were very much limited in their authority; they could only investigate, supervise, and recommend; the execution of their decisions depended upon the authorities in Hanoi, Saigon, Vientiane, and Phnom Penh.

Yet, despite the international complexities, India believed that the best hopes for the future of peace in Indochina depended upon the full implementation of the Geneva agreements. It favored early elections in Viet-Nam to unify the country; it

wanted the International Commission to reconvene in Laos in
1959 as a result of the resurgence of hostilities between the Royal
Government and the Pathet Lao; and it has supported Cambodia's desire to keep the international body in the country. In trying to maintain a balance between Warsaw and Ottawa, New
Delhi caused Canada to emphasize Western interests, if only to
keep its Indian Commonwealth partner further removed from
the Communist posture.

India's relations with the individual governments in Indochina
have varied since the Geneva settlement. Although sympathetic
to Cambodia's neutral attitude toward the cold war, New Delhi
has sought to keep out of the quarrels between Phnom Penh and
Bangkok, Saigon, and Hanoi; and when India has become involved in Cambodian-South Vietnamese and Cambodian-North
Vietnamese difficulties as a member of the international commissions, it has decided the issues on an *ad hoc* basis. The clash between New Delhi and Vientiane in 1959 on the activation of the
International Commission in Laos reflected a complicated situation. Backed by Ottawa, London, and Washington, the Royal
Laotian government successfully took the position that, since it
had fulfilled its obligations under the Geneva settlement, the International Commission had lost its basis for existence. The
Pathet Lao, supported by Warsaw, Hanoi, Peking, and Moscow,
condemned Vientiane's stand and called for the reconvening of
the body. India agreed with the Pathet Lao position on this issue; yet despite these and other difficulties, the government of
Laos is aware of India's support for the political independence
and integrity of the kingdom.

New Delhi has also become prominent in the relations between
North and South Viet-Nam. The International Commission has
lost many of its original responsibilities which arose immediately
from the Indochina War and its members are not currently involved in problems relating to national elections, but the body

helps to prevent open aggression in the country. India has moved more into a position of equating Hanoi and Saigon; President Ngo Dinh Diem has risen in stature in New Delhi while President Ho Chi Minh has just about held his own. Indian relations with South Viet-Nam have had their difficult moments but they have tended to improve over the years. On the other hand, a continuation of discord between Peking and New Delhi could cause ill will between India and the Democratic Republic of Viet-Nam.

INDIA AND PAKISTAN

Relations between India and Pakistan directly affect Southeast Asia. If these two rivals in the vast subcontinent once ruled as the Indian Empire of Great Britain, could agree and cooperate instead of dissipating their strength against each other, they might together make a great contribution toward a better future for Southeast Asia. Strong bonds exist between the Indian and Pakistani military and civil services; yet in varying degrees of intensity old differences have contributed to the schism in foreign policy between New Delhi and Rawalpindi, especially sovereignty over Kashmir, the allocation of canal waters of the Indus River system, trade questions, refugees and their property, boundary demarcation, and financial problems arising from partition. India maintains cordial relations with Afghanistan, whereas there is enmity between Kabul and Rawalpindi. Pakistan's membership in SEATO and CENTO has stood in marked contrast to India's policy of nonalignment; Rawalpindi has formal allies in Southeast Asia, whereas New Delhi has only friends.

Although some of the problems in the relations between India and Pakistan have already reached or are reaching solution, it will take time and effort to find a compromise on Kashmir and to reduce the ill will and suspicion in both countries, especially among the leaders and the refugees. In late 1962, however, Indian and Pakistani officials began discussions on the Kashmir question, which were urged by the United States and Great Britain as a consequence of the Chinese Communist military offensive against India in the Sino-Indian border territory. It was believed in Washington and London that sustained American and British military aid to New Delhi would be greatly dissipated if India and Pakistan could not settle their differences and, in due course, undertake the joint defense of the subcontinent. Rawalpindi, which had been receiving U.S. military assistance since 1954, was greatly aroused over the American and British military aid being rushed to India, for it feared that the arms would be used at some future time against Pakistan. Pressure mounted in favor of withdrawal from SEATO and CENTO and in support of a neutralist posture. Within this context, the government of President Mohammad Ayub Khan significantly agreed to delimit the boundary with Communist China along the Pakistani-held territory in Kashmir next to Sinkiang. At the same time Pakistan believed that the advantages of a pro-Western alignment outweighed the disadvantages. Both India and Pakistan are aware that, as officially stated, Washington is strongly opposed to any aggression supported by arms from the U.S. military aid program and would, upon request, help the victim.

Despite the serious difficulties between India and Pakistan, there is little competition between them for leadership in Southeast Asia. Indeed, any attempt to become the leader of the region would boomerang, for no state in the area wants to be a satellite of New Delhi or Rawalpindi. Because of the greater influence of the western part of the country in its politics, Pakistan has tended to look more toward the Middle East than to Southeast Asia. In the event of a global war Rawalpindi believes that Moscow, working in cooperation with Afghanistan, would be the real threat to South Asia, while Peking would be largely occupied in Southeast Asia. In the latter area Burma is the only state with which Pakistan has a common boundary; relations between the two governments, though occasionally marred by border incidents and the refugee problem in the Arakan territory, are correct. With respect to possible ties, the common denominator of the Islamic religion has not been sufficiently strong to produce an *entente* among Pakistan, Indonesia, and the Federation of Malaya. In brief, any American effort to exert influence in Southeast Asia through Rawalpindi is not likely to be successful.

INDIA AND COMMUNIST CHINA

Of far greater impact on Southeast Asia than Indo-Pakistani problems are India's relations with the People's Republic of China. The states of the area have experienced this influence under two widely contrasting situations: the first when New Delhi and Peking were both stressing the principles of peaceful coexistence in their foreign policy, and the other when the two large Asian powers were in serious conflict over a number of important questions. It is ironic that Tibet was the subject of the agreement in April 1954 between India and Communist China that embodied the Five Principles, yet only five years later it became the occasion for a serious deterioration in relations.

During the earlier period of considerable rapport between India and China, Peking found many of New Delhi's policies to be favorable, including India's recognition of the People's Republic of China in December 1949, its advocacy of seating Peking in the United Nations, its critical posture toward the Chiang Kai-shek regime on Taiwan, its refusal to attend the Japanese peace conference at San Francisco, its conciliatory position during most of the Korean and Indochina wars, and its critical attitude toward

SEATO. Moreover, Peking gained a degree of respectability in the Asian-African uncommitted world partly through New Delhi's sympathy, which was reflected in its diplomacy abroad. The Bandung Conference in April 1955, representing the full bloom of peaceful coexistence, created an impression of Sino-Indian cooperation as one of the living realities of the new Asia. Yet India's security interests along its frontiers with China and Pakistan are paramount considerations for Nehru. His Himalaya policy toward Nepal, Sikkim, and Bhutan has been influenced by his attitude toward developments in Tibet and by his reaction to the posture of Communist China. Although there is a parallel between the traditional Caribbean policy of the United States and New Delhi's security stand in the Himalaya area, the great threat for India is nextdoor, not separated by an expanse of water.

The Tibetan revolt against Communist China in March 1959, the overthrow of the local Communist government in Kerala the following July, and the shedding of Indian blood in the Sino-Indian border incidents later in the year produced a crisis in the relations between Peking and New Delhi. The atmosphere of *Panch Shila* dissolved when the security interests of India were at stake. After the armed forces of China had moved into Tibet in 1950, India had recognized that suzerainty over the country resided with the People's Republic; efforts were also made in New Delhi and Peking to resolve difficulties arising from traditional Indian interests in the area. But the Tibetan rebellion in early 1959, followed by the flight of the Dalai Lama from Lhasa to sanctuary in India, aroused deep feelings of animosity on both sides of the Himalayas. New Delhi resented Chinese suggestions of Indian complicity in the revolt, and Peking was incensed by India's severe criticism of the suppression of the insurgents. Even though the Dalai Lama was not allowed to establish a government in exile in India, his very presence served to focus attention on the plight of the Tibetans. In Southeast Asia, widespread criticism of Peking's policy toward Lhasa was reinforced by the common ties of Buddhism. The Federation of Malaya co-sponsored with Ireland a resolution adopted by the United Nations General Assembly on October 21, 1959, calling for "respect for the fundamental human rights" of Tibetans.

Domestic developments within India contributed to the *détente* between New Delhi and Peking. As a result of political factionalism in an election in 1957, the Communists in the state of Kerala were able to form a government even though they had won only 35 per cent of the popular vote, independents they supported accounting for another 5 per cent. In July 1959 President Rajendra Prasad of India dismissed the Communist regime of Chief Minister E. M. S. Namboodiripad on charges of misrule, and New Delhi established an interim government to restore law and order, a step which was widely interpreted abroad as a policy of firmness toward Indian Communists. When elections were next held in February 1960, the Communists and the independents they backed increased their popular vote to 43 per cent, though they lost heavily in the number of Assembly seats. A non-Communist cabinet was established by a coalition of three opposition parties (the Congress party, the Moslem League, and the People's Socialists) who together had acquired 94 Assembly seats and 53 per cent of the popular vote.

The overwhelming reason, however, for the crisis in relations between India and the People's Republic of China was the long-smoldering but now open controversy over the boundary between the two nations. Border clashes causing the loss of Indian lives at Longju in August 1959 in the North-East Frontier Agency and at Hot Springs in October in the Ladakh district of Kashmir were accompanied by an exchange of bitter notes between Peking and New Delhi. Although the Chinese had long been publishing maps showing their boundaries well within territory claimed by the Indians, a so-called case of "cartographic aggression," the People's Republic decided to claim officially about 51,000 square miles along portions of the 2,500-mile border with India. Condemning it as a product of British aggression, Peking specifically rejected the McMahon Line in the northeast, a line which was considered by New Delhi as the official boundary, made firm by treaty, right, usage, and geography. Moreover, China had constructed a road across the Aksai Chin plateau of eastern Ladakh as a part of the Tibet-Sinkiang Highway. India, for its part, stressed its determination to defend Bhutan, Sikkim, and Nepal against aggression, and watched with concern Chinese border disputes and difficulties involving the three Himalaya areas. Nehru came to condemn Communist China bitterly as an imperialist, aggressive power, determined to acquire Indian territory and to sow dissension among Asian neighbors. He made it clear that his country would fight, if necessary, to resist aggression. Here he had the support of public opinion and all political parties except the Communists, who equivocated. A conference in New Delhi between Chou En-lai and Nehru in April 1960 failed to resolve the differences, the latter informing parliament that he had been confronted with a "hard rock" of views. On June 3, 1962, the Sino-Indian accord of 1954 on Tibet expired.

The following October Peking began a successful military offensive in the border areas of India in the Ladakh district of Kashmir and in the North-East Frontier Agency. Communist China was motivated by a number of considerations. It wanted to be able to dominate strategically the Himalayas, to apply strong pressure on India, and to influence much more than in the past Nepal, Bhutan, and Sikkim. Undoubtedly strategic considerations were more significant in Ladakh than in the North-East Frontier Agency where the tactical requirement of sealing the border to stop operations by Tibetan dissidents was a matter of concern. Peking was also eager to humiliate and isolate New Delhi in the Afro-Asian world, to show it as unworthy of leadership, and to inculcate the image of the "New China" as a great power whose viewpoints counted in world councils. It sought to discredit Prime Minister Nehru and convince the Communist states that he was, after all, a pro-Western bourgeois leader. By using force Peking wanted to create conditions where India would have to negotiate at a great disadvantage. Peking's limited military objectives at the time were shown not only in its failure to choose certain options like an invasion of the Chumbi Valley, but also in its dramatic announcement on November 21 of a unilateral cease-fire and of the intention to withdraw beginning December 1 a distance of 12.43 miles behind the lines of actual control as of November 7, 1959.

Neither the short- nor the long-range effects of the Chinese offensive should be underestimated. Indian nationalism reached a high pitch of intensity, and the country rallied behind the government in resistance to the Chinese attack; even the Indian Communist party found it necessary to support the government. With the weakness of India's defense revealed as its army retreated before the invaders, New Delhi, still clinging officially to nonalignment, sought military aid in arms and supplies, especially from the United States and Great Britain. In 1960 Washington had sold India some surplus C-119 Flying Boxcars, reportedly at a reduced price, to help in supplying military personnel stationed in remote mountainous areas of the North-East Frontier Agency and Ladakh. But beginning November 3, 1962, U.S. emergency defense assistance was airlifted to India; American C-130 turbojet cargo planes with U.S. personnel were soon made available for New Delhi's war effort. The British also came unhesitatingly to the military aid of the Indians. Embarrassed by Communist China's offensive against India, the Soviet Union reluctantly endorsed Peking's position in the controversy but subsequently agreed, as previously arranged, to deliver some MIG-21 jet fighters to India. New Delhi had already bought and received some transport planes and other aircraft from the Soviet Union.

The neutral nations of Asia and Africa failed to rally to any real extent behind India in its hour of crisis. Among the neutrals, Indonesia, Burma, Cambodia, the United Arab Republic, Ghana, and Ceylon met in Colombo in an effort to find some solution mutually acceptable to Peking and New Delhi. As for the pro-Western states in Southeast Asia, the Philippines and Thailand were sympathetic to India though they tended to believe that Nehru was paying the price of nonalignment; the Federation of Malaya showed considerable sympathy for its Commonwealth partner.

The probable continuance of the boundary controversy is a matter of real significance in the future of world politics. Washington and Moscow believe the dispute should be quickly settled by peaceful means. Each prefers India uncommitted rather than aligned with the other, and each is buttressing its policy with substantial economic and technical aid. Although the United States realizes that a formal alliance with India might lead to closer Sino-Soviet cooperation in the subcontinent, Washington officially supports New Delhi in its position regarding the boundary in the North-East Frontier Agency. And here the United States encounters a similarity in the viewpoints of Peking and Taipei on the justice of the Chinese claim.

The Sino-Indian dispute has already dealt a serious if not fatal blow to New Delhi's efforts to be a bridge between the People's Republic and non-Communist Asia. The countries of Southeast Asia can no longer look to India as having a moderating influence on Peking. The Five Principles of Peaceful Coexistence upon which Nehru had relied in relations with China have been weakened, perhaps to the point of extinction. India's posture as the great mediator ceases to be valid when bloodshed occurs along its boundary with the leading contestant for power and stature. It would be difficult to think of New Delhi under current conditions as being able to really help end a future war of the Korean or Indochina type.

Yet the long-range prospects may indicate a different posture. If India can substantially augment its defense potential not only through the expansion of its armed forces with extensive American and British aid, but also through successful economic development with considerable foreign assistance, and if a *rapprochement* can be reached with Pakistan, New Delhi will be much better able to cope with the long-range threat of the Chinese Communists. At any rate, it is unlikely that India's nonalignment will ever again be the same as it was prior to Peking's attack in October 1962. On the other hand, it is improbable that New Delhi will seek membership in SEATO despite a fuller comprehension of the objectives of the Manila Treaty. Actually, the choice in India's foreign policy is not limited to participation in a military alliance or to blind faith in the Five Principles of Peaceful Coexistence. In the long run the recent experience New Delhi has had with the People's Republic means a better understanding both in and outside government circles of the dynamics of Chinese communism, a real appreciation of Western efforts to cope with it, and, as a result, a foreign policy still committed to nonalignment but much more sympathetic to the West than to the East.

INDIA AND THE UNITED STATES IN SOUTHEAST ASIA

Differences between Washington and New Delhi relating to Southeast Asia have in the past focused to a large extent on the China question, but recently India's more critical attitude toward Communist China and its more friendly posture toward the

United States have reduced the distance between the two governments. Neither New Delhi nor Washington is likely to alter its stand on the recognition of the People's Republic, on its seating in the United Nations, or on the role of the Republic of China on Taiwan. But as far back as December 1959 the visit of President Eisenhower to India drew attention to the broad areas of agreement between the two countries and dramatized the mutual understanding of each other's different viewpoints.

The United States is faced with the question of whether or not to support, and if so, to what extent, India's role in Southeast Asia in the hope that New Delhi can best advance American objectives in the region. A policy in which India is the mainstay in Washington's efforts in the area would certainly have widespread implications. In the first place the United States might find it desirable to alter some of its viewpoints on the China question. This modification would not mean the abandonment of the Nationalists on Taiwan, but it might imply a "two Chinas" policy. The basic American premise that Communist China is deterred in Southeast Asia only by the threat of superior power would certainly be tested, for India does not currently have the military capability to make its viewpoints respected in the region. The United States would still have to be prepared to move in a critical situation. Furthermore, New Delhi would not want at present to make any advance military commitments for joint action. As for the moral strength India has purported to represent, Peking has already given ample evidence of how much value it places on that element.

American alignment with India in Southeast Asia could have real repercussions in Rawalpindi, which has long questioned U.S. aid to countries who do not assume a common responsibility to act against possible aggression. Apprehension was aroused in Rawalpindi by the incident of the U-2 flight from Peshawar over Soviet territory in May 1960, which led to a threat of retaliation from Moscow if such operations were allowed to continue from Pakistani territory. The Pakistanis are also sensitive to American criticism of U.S. military assistance to their country. Widely considered to be sympathetic to India, the administration of President Kennedy gave a particularly warm reception to President Ayub Khan in Washington in July 1961 in an effort to remove Pakistani apprehensions.

America's attitude toward India's role in Southeast Asia should not ignore the interests of Japan. Both New Delhi and Tokyo have economic interests in the area, and are in competition for markets for manufactured goods. As Japan grows in international stature, its political influence will expand in the area and will have a greater impact on India. If Washington draws closer to New Delhi at the expense of Tokyo in Southeast Asia, relations between Japan and America could suffer.

Both Great Britain and the Soviet Union would observe with great interest a close alignment of American-Indian views in the region. Neither the United Kingdom nor the Commonwealth members, Australia and New Zealand, would want any Indian-American alignment to weaken the basic security obligations of Washington in the area. The Soviet Union, being eager to maintain ties with India and at the same time keep its alliance with Communist China, would not favor an American-Indian alignment if this imperiled its own relationship with New Delhi or interests in Southeast Asia. Nevertheless Moscow might secretly not disapprove of a development in Indian-American relations that might have the effect of putting a brake on Peking in the area.

In Southeast Asia itself the consequences of close cooperation in policy between Washington and New Delhi would vary from country to country and would depend on the exact form of the cooperation. Whether allied with the United States or unaligned, every country would resent any appearance of a New Delhi-

Washington axis trying to dominate its internal affairs. And Communist China would do all in its power to stir up any latent suspicions. There is a real possibility that an American-Indian alignment focusing on India's role in the area would create as much division in foreign policy among the local states as exists today.

Although close political or military cooperation between Washington and New Delhi in Southeast Asia does not appear feasible at the present time, American sympathy for India in its difficulties with Communist China can serve to strengthen the position of both governments in Southeast Asia. Any improvement in relations between Rawalpindi and New Delhi through U.S. efforts can enhance their influence in promoting common objectives of peace and stability in the region. Japanese-Indian cooperation with American support can be furthered in Southeast Asia despite the obstacles of the future. Possibly more Anglo-American-Indian collaboration can be brought to bear in the area. Finally, developments within Southeast Asia beyond the control of outside powers—an election, a sudden death—might lead to closer Indian-American ties. Although neither New Delhi nor Washington can control most events in the area, they should be prepared to turn them to advantage wherever and whenever feasible.

In the ultimate analysis, the possibility that India may stand with the United States against aggression and subversion in Southeast Asia depends in large measure upon the prospects for India itself. The success or failure of the economic breakthrough attempt, and India's long-term ability to withstand Chinese Communist pressure along the northern boundary will in large part determine New Delhi's future. Another great intangible is the succession to leadership when Nehru is no longer the dominant figure, and here the range of predictions of India's future varies from political fragmentation into a number of rival states (some dominated by communism) to a great power rank along with Communist China. But whatever the future holds for the 454 million Indians will greatly affect the peoples of Southeast Asia and the policy of the United States in the area.

JAPANESE INTERESTS AND POLICY IN SOUTHEAST ASIA

Policy-makers in Tokyo have long shown interest in the Nan Yo or Southern Seas. Japan became one of the leading architects of the area through its role during the Pacific war. The acquisition of Formosa in 1895, the achievement of great power status through the Russo-Japanese War, the rise in its naval might in the Western Pacific, and the growing image of Japan in the Nan Yo as a country that exemplified "Asia for the Asians" created conditions favoring the expansion of Japanese influence in Southeast Asia. The conflicts of policy in Europe upon the emergence of Hitler's Third Reich and the rise of the militarists to domination in Tokyo greatly helped Japan to expound its New Order in Greater East Asia and to make its military bid for the conquest of the Nan Yo.

If, in the months before Pearl Harbor, Tokyo had properly evaluated the ultimate chances of Hitler and had remained neutral in the European conflict, there is a real possibility that the ranking powers of the postwar world would have been the United States, the Soviet Union and Japan. Tokyo's pre-eminent position would have presented an entirely different pattern of international relationships in the Western Pacific and Eastern Asia. In the ultimate analysis, it was the vacuum created by the extinction of Japanese power in the Far East that led to the dimensions of today's crisis.

Within a relatively short period after going to war with the United States in December 1941, Japan was able to overrun

Southeast Asia, the first time in history when all the region came under the rule of one power. A blow was dealt to the Western colonial nations—the United States, Great Britain, the Netherlands and France, which had previously agreed to Japanese inroads in Indochina—from which they would never fully recover. The real question in Southeast Asia after the Second World War was not the return to the *status quo ante bellum* but the adjustment of the metropolitan powers to the rising Asian nationalism. In retrospect Japan was a great catalyst, especially in Indonesia and Indochina. If Tokyo had won the war, the puppet states it created in the Philippines and Burma would have functioned within the Co-Prosperity Sphere of Greater East Asia; but with the imminence of defeat, Japan encouraged the independence of Indonesia, Annam, Cambodia and Luang Prabang.

Nippon's formal surrender in Tokyo Bay on September 2, 1945, marked the beginning of a new phase in its relations with Southeast Asia. The military hegemony was destroyed, probably never to be revived; the Japanese minorities living in certain areas were soon to be repatriated; Japanese assets in the region had to be salvaged or liquidated. But Tokyo first had to rehabilitate itself in the international community before it could face as an independent state the new Southeast Asia it had helped to shape by war.

At present Japan's interests in the region are predominantly economic. The survival of Nippon is related to foreign trade, for maintaining the stream of its manufactured exports is essential to pay for necessary imports of food and raw materials. Perhaps no country of similar industrial stature is so meagerly endowed with key raw materials; in fact, over 80 per cent of its industrial raw materials together with some 15 per cent of its foodstuffs have to be imported. Japan possesses only 6 of 33 metallic minerals used in industry, and it must import the bulk of its iron ore, a third of its coking coal, more than 90 per cent of its petroleum, and all its rubber, cotton, wool and bauxite. Imports and exports must be increased if Japan is to maintain what it considers an essential rate of economic growth. The recent achievement of self-sufficiency in rice production is a notable development, but the country believes it must find even more markets, be more competitive, and devote more production to exports, while continuing to fight trade discrimination and support trade liberalization. The ultimate foreign policy of Japan, the only industrialized nation of the Far East, and now the fourth biggest industrial complex on the earth, will probably be largely determined by economic considerations.

In South and Southeast Asia Tokyo has placed considerable emphasis in its trade promotion program. Over a fourth of Japan's exports (28 per cent in 1955) go to the vast area stretching from Pakistan to Indonesia in contrast to less than 20 per cent in 1934-36. In terms of imports, over one-fifth (21 per cent in 1955) come from the area, as compared with less than one-sixth in 1934-36: But despite increasing percentages, South and Southeast Asia have scarcely compensated for the startling reduction in Japanese exports to China, Korea and Formosa from about 45 per cent in the mid-1930s to 5 per cent in 1955 and the reduction in imports during the same periods from around 30 per cent to some 7 per cent. In partial compensation, Japanese exports to the United States did increase from 16 per cent in 1934-36 to 22 per cent in 1955, and imports from 25 per cent to 31 per cent during the same year. But in marked contrast the United States in 1955 exchanged only 3.8 per cent of its imports and 4.7 per cent of its exports with Japan, these ratios of trade being actually lower than the prewar percentages.

These trade statistics underline the political complexities in American economic policy toward Japan as it affects Communist China and Southeast Asia. In many respects Tokyo and Washington have similar objectives in Southeast Asia. Japan wants the region to have a much more important place in its economic future, believing that relations on a mutually profitable basis can be greatly strengthened, and it realizes that maintaining the independence of the states in the area free from Communist domination is an essential prerequisite. In opposing colonialism in its various manifestations the Japanese seek to identify themselves with the prevailing sentiment of the Afro-Asian world; as fellow Asians, they are trying to develop close cultural relations with the peoples of Southeast Asia. Tokyo is not presently prepared to enter into a multilateral security agreement such as SEATO; yet, by maintaining defense ties with the United States, it can contribute indirectly to the security of the region.

If strategically-located Japan fell under Communist domination, the entire position of the non-Communist world along the vast arc from Northeast to South Asia would be gravely imperiled. In weak countries resistance to communism would be greatly lessened and the forces of accommodation immeasurably strengthened. The American position along the island ladder off Asia's eastern shores would be seriously impaired. Should the industrial facilities and skills of the Japanese ever be added to the economy of the People's Republic of China and the industrial might of the Soviet Union, the weight of the resulting economic axis in the Far East would have incalculable consequences for the free world. Japan is perhaps the greatest bulwark of free world strength in non-Communist Asia. Furthermore, as an example of phenomenal postwar recovery within a democratic framework, Japan serves to a certain extent as an ideological counterweight to Communist China in Asia. If the Japanese rejected democracy in favor of authoritarianism, the ideological repercussions would extend far beyond the shores of the island empire.

Tokyo has tried to implement its objectives in Southeast Asia through a variety of ways. Diplomatic missions have now been established in Manila, Djakarta, Kuala Lumpur, Saigon, Phnom

Penh, Vientiane, Bangkok and Rangoon. Nobusuke Kishi, while he was prime minister, and other high-ranking officials have traveled extensively in Southeast Asia, and many of its leaders have made visits to Tokyo, including President Sukarno, President Carlos P. Garcia, Premier U Nu and Prince Norodom Sihanouk. As a participant at the Bandung Conference, Tokyo tried to strengthen its position in the uncommitted world. Japan is a member of the Afro-Asian bloc in the United Nations and a donor country in the Colombo Plan.

Although Japan faces many hindrances in its policy of economic diplomacy in Southeast Asia, those arising from the Pacific war are gradually disappearing. When the Japanese forces invaded the Nan Yo they were greeted, or at least tolerated, by many of the inhabitants; but "Asia for the Asiatics" soon came to mean Asia for the Japanese, and Tokyo threw away many of the opportunities open in 1941. Atrocities led to hatred of Japan; widespread destruction, especially in the liberation of certain Southeast Asian areas toward the end of the war, was attributed to the Japanese aggressor. Yet the pattern of ill will toward Tokyo was not uniform in the region. Perhaps the bitterness was greatest in the Philippines, where Japanese atrocities and wartime destruction were pronounced, and the war also left a heritage of ill will in Indonesia and Burma. On the other hand, in Indochina and especially in Thailand (a technical ally of Tokyo in the conflict) anti-Japanese sentiment, though noticeable, was not strong.

Time has tended to efface the sharpness of personal memories, and Japanese diplomacy has contributed to the healing process in part because Tokyo has not attempted to avoid responsibility or conceal regret for the misery it caused in Southeast Asia. (This attitude was well exemplified by the Nipponese representatives at the Bandung Conference.) Although anti-Japanese sentiment is still latent in the Philippines and to a lesser extent in

Indonesia, it no longer constitutes a severe handicap to the conduct of international relations.

A change is also occurring in the Southeast Asia attitude toward Japan's future rule in the Far East. Having experienced the effects of its military conquest, the people feared the emergence of a powerful and militant Japan. Prior to signing the Japanese peace treaty at San Francisco the Philippines as well as Australia and New Zealand insisted on security pacts with the United States. There was a widespread conviction in Southeast Asia that the United States was advocating a peace settlement that was too lenient in view of Tokyo's past record and too conducive toward the re-establishment of Japanese power. As it became clear that the Nipponese were not hastening to build up their armed forces and were not trying to re-establish their military position even in Northeast Asia, apprehensions over Tokyo's future as an armed power lessened. The growing might of an aggressive Communist China overshadowed concern about Japan; and Peking's efforts to encourage apprehension in Southeast Asia over Nipponese intentions have not been marked with success. Nevertheless, Tokyo's economic diplomacy in the region, even if not supported by military might, is generally received with considerable reserve.

The problem of reparations for some time constituted a serious obstacle to the accomplishment of Japanese objectives in Southeast Asia. Agreements, slow to be forthcoming, have now been made, but their implementation has often raised difficulties. On the other hand, Nippon's payments in goods and services have been linked with economic development, and agreements for Japanese government or private loans have accompanied the reparations accords. The complementary relationship between industrialized Japan and underdeveloped Southeast Asia is underscored in the settlements, with Tokyo emphasizing reparations as a means of economic cooperation for mutual advantage.

The deadlock in negotiations with Southeast Asian claimants was not broken until Japan signed a peace treaty and reparations agreement with Burma on November 5, 1954. Then came a reparations agreement with the Philippines, signed on May 9, 1956, followed by a peace treaty and reparations accord with Indonesia on January 20, 1958. The Republic of Viet-Nam was the last to reach a reparations agreement with Japan on May 13, 1959. The government of Ho Chi Minh for its part refused to recognize the accord as binding on Viet-Nam. Laos and Cambodia waived reparations claims, but the former signed an agreement for economic and technical cooperation with Japan on October 15, 1958, and the latter on March 2, 1959.

Under these reparations agreements (excluding the accords on economic cooperation), Japan has pledged itself to pay a total sum equivalent to $1,012,080,000. For a while the annual average amounted to $75,000,000, corresponding in 1958 to 2.6 per cent of Nipponese exports, or 0.3 per cent of the national income. Tokyo also agreed in the negotiations to provide in long-term loans and investments the equivalent of at least $716,600,000. As a result of the stress in Southeast Asia on industrialization and economic development, Japanese reparations are largely in capital goods. Even before the reparations agreements were reached, the prewar markets for textiles in the region were declining and capital goods were in rising demand. It is believed in Tokyo that after the reparation settlements have been fulfilled, Japanese capital goods will continue to find important markets in an expanding Southeast Asia.

Although technical assistance is an aspect of Nipponese programs in the region, whether under reparations settlements, the Colombo Plan, United Nations sponsorship, or other auspices, its potential has not yet been realized. With the greatest reservoir of technological skill in the Far East the Japanese claim they are in a special position to make substantial contributions to technical aid and training programs in Southeast Asia. They stress that Nippon is no longer a military power, that they are fellow Asians, and that they have the skilled labor available for immediate use. Tokyo would like to expand its programs in the region not only because they contribute to the economic and social development of the less developed peoples, but also because the programs can help in expediting the production of raw materials needed in Japan, provide outlets for the employment of Nipponese technicians, and contribute through expert advice to industrialization and thus, in the longer run, to greater markets for Japanese goods. There was set up in 1956 a Technical Cooperation Company with capital from 37 private Nipponese firms.

Many Southeast Asians, on the other hand, have still been reluctant to encourage the presence of any large number of Japanese experts. The Philippine government, for instance, welcomed Nipponese technicians engaged in salvage operations of ships sunk in the last war but made provisions to regulate personal contacts between Filipinos and visiting Japanese lest incidents should occur. Burma has been much more receptive to Nipponese experts who have become prominent in the implementation of the reparations settlement. Training programs for Southeast Asians in Japan have made unnecessary the presence of Nipponese in certain activities in the region. In time, the hostility to Japanese technicians will recede, and already there is marked improvement throughout the area as a whole.

Although progress in developing Nipponese trade in South and Southeast Asia is slow but steady, the import and export statistics have not reflected the optimism once widely prevalent in Tokyo. Japan is facing stiff competition in capital goods exports from the United Kingdom, the United States, and the Federal Republic of Germany, and in textiles from India and at times from Communist China. Some of the raw materials Tokyo wanted are either now insufficiently available or more expensive than in dollar areas. Nippon lacks the advantage of membership in any trading area or currency bloc. Western grants, credits, and loans have helped to channel trade between former colonies and metropolitan powers. If used as a chief alternative to normal trade, reparation payments can interfere in developing ordinary commerce between Japan and a recipient country. Moreover, a large number of controls exist in Southeast Asia, such as tariffs to protect local industries, quotas on certain items, inability to convert currency, and other restrictions. The administration of these controls has often been ineffective, causing serious impediments to trade and leading at times to charges of favoritism and corruption. Above all, the purchasing power of Southeast Asia is low. Development programs cannot bring overnight changes while often their effectiveness is weakened by population increases and domestic inflation.

Japan has for some time been interested in furthering economic development in the region through extensive cooperation with the United States. Prime Minister Kishi, an exponent of this approach, proposed to President Eisenhower during a visit to Washington in June 1957 the establishment of a Southeast Asia development fund, with the United States providing the greater part of the capital and with Japan contributing technological skill and equipment, all in the interests of an integrated program. The Southeast Asian countries have not widely welcomed the proposal, and the United States had declined to throw its weight behind it. In 1960 the Nipponese cabinet approved the establishment of an official agency to handle a loan fund equivalent to $14 million for development projects in Southeast Asia.

Despite the poor reception given Kishi's development plan in Washington, Japanese-American cooperation in the region has occurred along a number of lines. Nationals from South and Southeast Asian countries have received technical training in Nippon financed by the International Cooperation Administration and the Tokyo government. Japan has also served as a source of supplies and equipment bought by ICA in its offshore procurement program for use in Southeast Asian countries. The Orissa project wherein Nippon and the United States are cooperating with India in the development of an iron ore deposit points up other possibilities in Asia. And, of course, Japan and the United States participate jointly in the International Bank for Reconstruction and Development, the United Nations Expanded Program of Technical Assistance and the Special Fund, the Economic Commission for Asia and the Far East, the Colombo Plan, and the International Development Association. Nippon was also a participant in the Development Assistance Group and is now in its successor, the Development Assistance Committee.

Japanese private investment in Southeast Asia is increasing, but at a relatively slow pace. Examples are found in projects in Indonesia, Malaya, Singapore, Burma, Cambodia, and the Philippines. Joint enterprises involving Japanese private capital stand out, with loans as well as contracts for technical assistance being significant. It has been suggested that Japanese private investors are unduly hesitant and cautious about their prospects in Southeast Asia.

Japan and Communist China

In any consideration of American policy toward Japan as it affects Southeast Asia the question of relations between Nippon and Communist China must occupy a prominent position. In contrast to a long-standing dislike of Russia, Tokyo feels basically close to China for historical and cultural reasons as well as geographic and economic considerations. Many Japanese believe that a substantial increase in trade with the People's Republic is both desirable and possible. Recalling the extensive trade between the two countries before the last war when China (including Manchuria) was their best customer and a major source of iron ore and coking coal, these Japanese are disappointed in the relatively slow development of economic relations with South and Southeast Asia. The removal of political barriers against Peking would, they claim, lead to a resumption of full-scale trade, beneficial to both parties. In marked contrast to these hopes, in 1955 the entire Sino-Soviet bloc received only 1.8 per cent of Japan's exports, while Japan drew about 3.0 per cent of its imports from Communist countries. Strategic considerations have restricted the trade, and in 1958 Peking halted its slim commerce in a vain effort to influence the domestic politics of Japan. Previously trade delegations had been exchanged and unofficial agreements had been made between trading and fishing interests in the two countries. Trade and contacts were resumed on a modest scale in the fall of 1960, and they have tended to increase since then.

Yet even if economics and politics were not wedded in Sino-Japanese relations, the People's Republic today is not the Nationalist China and Japanese-dominated Manchukuo of the 1930s. It is doubtful if Communist China, given its industrialization program and its agricultural difficulties, can provide Japan with any substantial part of its required imports. Nor does China offer a large market for Japanese consumer products or probably even for capital goods. Problems of exchange are important, but political considerations are more significant. When all is said and done, Peking is willing to trade only on political and economic terms which Japan finds difficult to accept. Moreover, the outlook for extensive Japanese-Russian trade is not basically promising.

Japan's recognition of the Republic of China on Taiwan, its maintenance of the embargo on strategic exports to the Communist bloc, and its ties with the United States restrict the scope of relations with Communist China. Although Tokyo has sought to develop trade and stimulate cultural relations with both Taipei and Peking, the limits of its policies have in effect been set by American policy toward the China question. If the present relations did not exist between Washington and Tokyo, Japan (particularly under a Socialist government) might well recognize the People's Republic, seek closer ties with both Peking and Moscow, and try to pursue a neutral policy in world affairs. Even the conservative Japanese Prime Minister, Hayato Ikeda, asserted in July 1960 that normal relations with mainland China were "advisable" and economic and cultural ties desirable, provided that Japan was respected and not fooled by the Communists. Yet in cold reality it appears unlikely that the Communist bloc will replace South and Southeast Asia in Tokyo's economic future.

CURRENT JAPANESE-AMERICAN RELATIONS

American relations with Nippon, presently based on strong economic and security ties, are subject to a complex pattern of change. For many years Japan had large deficits in commercial trade with the United States; during the period 1946-56 the total trade deficit amounted to $6.0 billion, but various types of American aid and expenditures and subsequent special procurement outlays arising out of the war in Korea amounted to $6.2 billion over the same period. Aware that large procurement expenditures could not be expected to continue, Japan sought to reduce its dollar trade gap by locating nondollar sources of imports and by expanding and diversifying exports to the United States. As a customer for American exports, Japan is now second only to Canada; indeed, for several agricultural commodities Nippon is first. This position, however, cannot be retained without a high level of Japanese exports to America. As the United States has become the most important trading partner of Japan, American import policy—subject as it is to marked domestic pressure from the textile, clothing, and other industries—is a real key to the future of relations between Washington and Tokyo. If Japan's markets in the United States are greatly restricted or seriously imperiled, where will it turn?

As for matters of security, U.S. policy toward Nippon has greatly changed in the years since V-J Day. Desiring to make Japan a neutral "Switzerland of the Pacific," General Douglas MacArthur encouraged constitutional provisions where war was renounced as a sovereign right of the state and armed forces would not be maintained. Although Japan retains the inherent right of self-defense, the development of an army, navy, and air force in the traditional sense has raised serious political and constitutional problems. The Socialists have opposed rearmament, and a two-thirds majority of both houses of the Diet is needed to amend the constitution.

After the Chinese Communist expelled the Nationalists from the mainland and then intervened in Korea, the United States realized the need for a Japan that would be both friendly and strong. In 1951 the Japanese peace treaty ended the U.S. military occupation. The related security pact between Japan and the United States was intended to protect the former from Communist aggression; but as Nippon's Self-Defense Forces expanded (partly with American aid provided under a mutual defense assistance agreement of 1954), as the nation's economy improved, and as the country rose in diplomatic stature, a growing need for a new distribution of responsibility for defense became apparent. The United States had already announced in June 1957 that it would withdraw all American ground combat forces, leaving chiefly air and naval units. When Douglas MacArthur, 2nd, nephew of the General, assumed his post as ambassador to Japan, his chief task was to negotiate a new security pact.

After discussions in Tokyo over a period of fifteen months, a treaty of mutual cooperation and security between the two countries was signed in Washington on January 19, 1960, replacing upon entry into force the previous security treaty. In the new pact each signatory recognized, under Article V, that "an armed attack against either Party in the territories under the administration of Japan" would endanger "its own peace and safety" and each "would act to meet the common danger in accordance with its constitutional provisions and processes."[1] The parties would consult at the request of either whenever it believed that Far Eastern or Japanese security was threatened, as well as on matters relating to the treaty's implementation. Tokyo granted the United States the use of areas and facilities for land, sea, and air forces in order to contribute to Japan's security and the preservation of peace and security in the Far East. Subject to constitutional provisions, both signatories would preserve and develop their capabilities, through means of self-help and mutual assistance, to resist armed aggression. The status of the armed forces of the United States in Nippon and the use of the areas and facilities by the former were spelled out in separate provisions in an agreement accompanying the treaty.

In the treaty arrangement categories providing for prior consultation between the two parties were significantly defined as "major changes in the deployment into Japan of U.S. armed forces, major changes in their equipment, and the use of facilities and areas in Japan as bases for military combat operations to be undertaken from Japan other than those conducted under Ar-

---

[1] Treaty of Mutual Cooperation and Security between the United States of America and Japan Signed at Washington January 19, 1960, with Agreed Minute and Exchange of Notes, *Treaties and Other International Acts Series*, 4509, p. 3.

ticle V [Treaty of Mutual Cooperation and Security]."[2] It was stated in a joint communiqué issued on January 19 that President Eisenhower assured Prime Minister Kishi that "the United States Government has no intention of acting in a manner contrary to the wishes of the Japanese Government with respect to the matters involving prior consultation under the treaty."[3] The actual duration of the pact is ten years at the end of which either party may terminate it upon a year's notice. Under an exchange of notes a United States-Japan Security Consultative Committee was established.

It is clear that Tokyo is primarily concerned with the joint defense of its own territory and wants to escape military involvement in Southeast Asia or elsewhere insofar as humanly possible. In May 1962 apprehension was expressed when U.S. air force units were sent from Japanese bases to Thailand. Japan, moreover, has never forgotten the destruction of Hiroshima and Nagasaki and is eager to avoid the dangers of becoming an atomic battlefront in any future war. Concern exists that an American military presence will lead to an attack or retaliation in a conflict where Tokyo has no direct interests.

The security treaty was strongly criticized in Communist China and the Soviet Union, which desire a neutral Japan as a preliminary step to a Communist Japan. Moscow went so far as to repudiate a promise made to Tokyo in October 1956, upon the re-establishment of diplomatic relations, to restore Shikotan and the Habomai Islands at the conclusion of a Soviet-Japanese peace treaty. After the U-2 episode of May 1960 the Kremlin asserted that it would strike U.S. bases in Nippon with nuclear

[2] Same, p. 15.
[3] Joint Communiqué, January 19, 1960, *The Department of State Bulletin*, February 8, 1960, p. 180.

arms if the facilities were utilized in espionage flights over the U.S.S.R. or other operations against it. Nevertheless, the American bases tend to restrain the Peking-Moscow axis from taking forceful action against Japan. The Tokyo government has remained determined to keep the security ties with the United States while trying to establish a *modus vivendi* of some sort with the Soviet Union and Communist China.

Japanese ratification of the security pact was accomplished under disturbing conditions that raised a number of serious questions about the future relations between Tokyo and Washington. Mob violence in protest against its approval was so pronounced in Tokyo that the Kishi government reached the conclusion it could not guarantee the safety of President Eisenhower during his projected June trip. The cancellation clearly fulfilled one of the demands of the agitators. In the House of Representatives the Socialists strongly opposed the Liberal-Democrats on the issue of ratification. Although the latter had the necessary votes to approve it, the step was unexpectedly taken in the early hours of May 20 after the Socialist deputies had been ejected by the police for creating a disturbance. Left-wing elements among students, labor, and intellectuals—aided and abetted by Japanese Communists and reportedly financed by Peking and Moscow—were vociferous in their condemnation of the treaty, taking advantage of a complexity of attitudes—neutralism, pacifism, anti-Americanism, and pro-communism. Fanatical mobs of enraged students repeatedly demonstrated against the approval of the pact, while strikes and work stoppages were called in an effort to prevent ratification. Zengakuren, a national student federation that was radical though faction-ridden, spearheaded the demonstrations and Sohyo, a big labor federation of 3.5 million members, was active in the organized campaign of threat and intimidation. A press generally hostile to the treaty added to the furor. Nevertheless, Prime Minister Kishi stood firm, refused to resign or dissolve the House of Representatives, and the pact was automatically approved under Japanese parliamentary procedure on June 19. Kishi subsequently gave up his office, being called by some a "casualty of the cold war." The Liberal-Democratic party selected as his successor Hayato Ikeda, a champion of close ties between Washington and Tokyo.

The riots over ratification raised doubts about the political stability of Japan and the future of democracy in the country. If a small minority, well organized and fanatically motivated, could threaten the constitutional authority of a democratically chosen government representing the majority of the electorate, and if the public remained generally indifferent to the pressure, Japan stood in danger of falling into the hands either of the extreme left or, in an effort to forestall it, of the extreme right. The crisis brought this potential threat out into the open, though it may serve in the long run to rally the forces of democracy.

The effective implementation of the new security treaty over the years, of course, depends upon the genuine cooperation of the Japanese authorities. Although the demonstrations against the approval of the pact were not staged near the American installations, the eight major air bases and the big naval stations at Sasebo and Yokosuka could lose their value in a hostile environment. The loss of these facilities would be a severe blow to the United States in the Western Pacific; the Seventh Fleet, for instance, would have to fall back for major services to Pearl Harbor in Hawaii or the U.S. Pacific coast. Rearward positions in the Bonins and Marianas could only partially compensate for those in Japan. Okinawa would remain under U.S. administration, but during President Eisenhower's visit to the island in June demonstrations by left-wing youth groups pointed up the agitation for the return of the Ryukyus to Japanese administration.

FUTURE U.S. POLICY TOWARD NIPPON IN SOUTHEAST ASIA

Against this complicated background must be considered the future course of the United States toward Japan's role in Southeast Asia. Washington might, for instance, choose to center its policy on Nippon as the best way of advancing American interests in the region. Anti-Japanese sentiment is subsiding in the area; controversial issues like reparations have been or are being settled; Japan does not constitute a military threat to the region. Though sentiment for neutralism is strong in Japan, the country is still an ally of the United States and its government has long been interested in securing U.S. cooperation in its economic plans for Southeast Asia.

An American-Japanese entente in the region would have widespread implications. Although hard to visualize at present, there is a long-range possibility that Japan might develop an interest in expanding and joining SEATO or participating in some other arrangement. If Japanese-American cooperation in Southeast Asia is pushed, Tokyo may eventually be willing to accept mutual security obligations in the area. It is still doubtful whether over the long haul Japan will restrict its alliance policy to a bilateral approach and to the geographical limits of the present security treaty with the United States. Moreover, Washington might consider Japan's participation in a multilateral pact for the security of the Far East more advantageous than just a bilateral arrangement of expanded geographical scope. There is a comparable example in Europe. The Federal Republic of Germany has become an ally of the United States in the framework of NATO, a security arrangement that has the psychological advantages of multilateral participation. Nevertheless, Germany is aware that the most important aspect of the alliance for itself is the security relationship with the United States. Japan is certain to pursue a cautious policy in expanding its defense ties to countries in the

Western Pacific or Southeast Asia, but Washington must watch carefully the course of events and be prepared to capitalize on any favorable trends or developments.

If American policy in Southeast Asia were focused on Japan's future in the area, the United States would be tying itself to the vicissitudes of Nipponese politics. Should the Socialists eventually overthrow the Liberal-Democratic party, a neutralist orientation may dominate Tokyo's outlook. Washington might find itself in a position without alternatives and obliged to make the best of a bad situation. It is axiomatic in foreign policy that a nation should not commit itself to a course of action whereby it may lose its influence over a situation and find itself drawn into a chain of circumstances unfavorable to its own interests. In the July crisis of 1914 Germany was placed in such a predicament; so was Italy when Mussolini became identified with Nazi Germany before and during the Second World War. Spain under Generalissimo Francisco Franco avoided that predicament.

In contrast to various relatively remote defense possibilities, Japanese proposals for close economic cooperation with the United States in Southeast Asia have already required decision in Washington. While clearly wishing to enhance the economic future of Nippon, the United States must consider its own commercial interests in Japan as well as in South and Southeast Asia. Neither the United States nor Japan is, in any case, in a position to dictate the economic policies of the region; other trading countries—notably Great Britain, West Germany, India, and Communist China—also enter into the economic equation. Since the United States has already suffered from being associated in the viewpoint of many Southeast Asians with European colonial powers, Washington wants to keep clear of any remaining anti-Japanese feeling in the area. International communism would also be quick to label joint American-Japanese economic policy in the region as streamlined twentieth-century imperialism. In view of the various factors involved, the United States will gain more from cooperating with Japan in Southeast Asia in specific economic projects involving trade and financial arrangements, possibly on a multilateral basis, than in a comprehensive bilateral partnership for the development of the area.

The effect on Communist China and the Soviet Union of American-Japanese collaboration in Southeast Asia would depend upon a number of political and economic variables. If the relative power position of Japan were strengthened, the Communist bloc's influence in the Far East would be proportionately reduced. The aid programs of Moscow and Peking in the region might be less effective if faced with large-scale, imaginative, Japanese-American projects, and American support might bolster Japan's efforts to meet Chinese trade competition. Under current circumstances, the position of Nationalist China in Southeast Asia might also be strengthened through the collaboration of Washington and Tokyo.

On the other hand, the effects on Communist China and the Soviet Union of a Japanese-American entente in the region would be limited. It is obvious that such an entente could not by itself restore Nippon to the status of a great power. Moreover, as long as the Peking-Moscow axis continues, it is certain that Japan's strength in Asia, even if growing measurably and augmented by American support, is at a disadvantage. The Soviet Union, of course, is directly affected by Japan's military and economic posture in Northeast Asia, while Communist China is concerned over Nippon's position there and in Southeast Asia as well. In economic policy if Communist China embarks on a sustained program of dumping goods and pre-emptive purchasing in Southeast Asia, it can seriously disrupt existing trade patterns, including those of Japan. As for foreign aid, an extensive Japanese-American economic effort in the region would probably not cause Peking and Moscow to cease their assistance programs;

if anything, they would be tempted to make greater efforts.

The importance the Communist world attaches to Nippon is found in the suggestion once made by Premier Khrushchev that the Sino-Soviet and American-Japanese alliances be replaced by an Asian security pact of the interested powers, and in the sustained efforts over the years of both Moscow and Peking to isolate Japan from the United States. Stalin once reportedly told a visiting American that Russia with Japan would be invincible. Any and all efforts by the United States to strengthen Nippon will be opposed and countered, as far as possible, by the Peking-Moscow axis.

New Delhi would not look with favor on extensive economic cooperation between Tokyo and Washington in Southeast Asia lest its own trade with the region suffer. Indeed, New Delhi can scarcely be expected to welcome Japanese influence anywhere in the area if it occurs at Indian expense. On the other hand, the impact of Communist China menaces the future of both countries in Southeast Asia. It is not surprising that Peking's attack on India in late 1962 was criticized in Tokyo, which showed its disapproval by willingness to give nonmilitary aid to New Delhi. The United States does not want to weaken its relations with India by unduly encouraging Japanese economic expansion in Southeast Asia.

With their political, economic, and strategic interests in the region, Australia and the United Kingdom would dislike seeing their position impaired in any way by an American-Japanese entente in the area. If the United States ever put a greater stress on ties with Japan than with Australia under SEATO and ANZUS and Great Britain under NATO, it would be bitterly resented in Canberra and London. British and Australian commercial interests in Southeast Asia could also be adversely affected by marked Japanese economic inroads.

Finally, Nipponese-American collaboration could easily

weaken the position of the United States in the countries of the region. If the nations of Southeast Asia observed extensive support by the United States behind Japan's efforts, they might conclude the two countries were seeking to establish a kind of economic condominium over the region. Although such a conclusion would not be true, acceptance of this notion among influential Southeast Asians could drastically affect international relations. In its policy toward Japan's economic aspirations in Southeast Asia, the United States has to be aware of, and responsive to, the sensitivities of the governments of the area; after all, these governments have the final responsibility for their own countries.

A delicate international balance evidently exists in Tokyo's economic diplomacy in Southeast Asia. Any intended support of the United States for its Japanese ally must be balanced against other American commitments. In a complex pattern any American step, whether political or economic, is likely to have widespread ramifications. Under these circumstances the United States is pursuing the wisest policy toward Japan's activities in Southeast Asia—encouragement short of extensive collaboration.

Toward an Asian Counterweight

The interests of New Delhi and Tokyo, as well as Washington, require the establishment of an Asian counterweight to Peking. Southeast Asia would clearly profit from any such concerted efforts insofar as they tend to develop an Asian equilibrium. For its part, the United States can cautiously, patiently, and quietly encourage this course of action. Communist China itself may prove to be a catalyst of this policy by arousing more concern and stimulating greater cooperation among many of its neighbors. The countries of Southeast Asia may become receptive to

—even eager for—joint Indian and Japanese efforts to limit the expansion of China.

A formal alliance between New Delhi and Tokyo would not be necessary. An Asian *entente cordiale*, with the United States in the background, is probably preferable to any direct alliance between India and Japan or multilateral guarantees among these two powers and Washington. The current obstacles in both Tokyo and New Delhi to effective cooperation in Southeast Asia may appear today to be insurmountable. Yet during the Second World War who could have predicted the radically new international alignments among the victors and the vanquished which took place only a few years after V-J Day? When threats to basic national interests are fully identified, any nation seeks friends in the face of common peril.

[TWELVE]

U. S. Policy for the Future

Although the historical record can provide perspective for the future, recent events in Southeast Asia have occurred at such a rapid pace that it is difficult to evaluate them and to anticipate future changes. Within a generation almost every country in Southeast Asia has passed from Western colonial rule through Japan's New Order in Greater East Asia to independence; now the independent countries are threatened by the thrust of Communist China. No one can accurately foresee what the political map of Southeast Asia will be a generation hence. For the United States events in the region demand constant study and evaluation —both to minimize adverse developments and to take advantage of favorable opportunities.

FUTURE CONDITIONS AND U.S. OBJECTIVES

In the coming decade the most important international concern of most (and perhaps all) Southeast Asian states will be the rising

[404]

power and mounting threat of Communist China. When the People's Republic begins to build a stockpile of nuclear weapons, this menace to the region will increase; but even outside the military field, the political and economic influence of Communist China is bound to expand. The over-all strategic importance of Southeast Asia, moreover, is likely to increase rather than decrease in the years ahead. For the foreseeable future the United States must hold fast as the strongest single bulwark against Communist Chinese ambition to dominate Southeast Asia. The countries of the region, though becoming more apprehensive about Peking's intentions, will tend to bend like reeds in the face of Communist pressure *unless they have a reasonable alternative.* With the anti-Western feelings associated with the colonial era inexorably receding into the background and with the gradual rise of a new generation of Asian leaders, many of the governments of the area will become more sympathetic to the United States. This new attitude does not necessarily mean that they will all soon rush into a multilateral security pact with Washington; but better understanding can encourage a wider and more meaningful range of contacts between Southeast Asia and the West, including greater flexibility in defense arrangements.

In the coming decade the Southeast Asian states will also become increasingly aware of the power of Japan and India and of their potential as counterweights to the might of Peking. The three giants of the new Asia—Communist China, Japan, and India—may develop a power balance of their own, but interactions within such an Asian system would still be strongly influenced by the global pattern of forces led by the United States and the Soviet Union. Toward the end of the twentieth century, however, great changes may occur in the distribution of world power and in the composition of international alignments.

Although the countries of Southeast Asia will develop more contacts with the world at large in the next decade, it cannot be expected that they will rapidly achieve mutual understanding among themselves. Among the many states of the region it will take years to destroy rivalries or end disputes often reaching far back into history; and it will require some time before the countries will seriously work for an effective regional organization. Regionalism is something that cannot be forced upon the participants; the feeling of common interest must grow from within. But these considerations do not bar increasing cooperation among several states on specific matters and growing awareness of the common problems of the region.

As a consequence of widespread pressures for economic development and social progress measured against the limited capital and technical resources of Southeast Asia, the governments of the area will continue to welcome outside aid. Economic and technical help will be sought from almost all sources, and the question of accepting assistance from the Sino-Soviet bloc in the coming decade will raise even more serious problems than in the past. Although economic and social progress in a democratic framework will be generally preferred, local leadership will continue to be a critical and largely unpredictable element in the equation.

As the decade unfolds, what should be the U.S. objectives in Southeast Asia? In an evolving situation, what kinds of change should Washington seek to encourage or to inhibit? In realistic and positive terms, American national interests will be best served by the maintenance of the political independence and territorial integrity of the states of Southeast Asia, cooperating with one another as good neighbors, under stable governments adequately responsive to the needs of the people. As the Asian peasants and city-dwellers achieve a greater stake in the future of their nations through economic growth, if properly managed, they will also acquire firmer determination to defend their countries against subversion and aggression. The United States should do all that it can to encourage this evolution. Given the militant nature of the Communist threat, military defense against direct and indirect aggression must be a fundamental U.S. objective in Southeast Asia, for without security all other goals collapse like a row of dominoes when the first is pushed over. Yet, as the states of the area gain in internal strength and external posture, the maintenance of security should become less of an American holding operation, and more of an Asian undertaking expressed in broader patterns of cooperation. In encouraging stability Washington should recognize the dynamics of change, support democratic processes, and seek the assistance of friendly outside powers. Although the Minuteman is a better symbol than the Redcoat in Southeast Asia, the United States in its goal of encouraging stability must associate itself with processes of orderly transition.

Possible Security Policies

In the light of U.S. objectives in Southeast Asia during the next decade, it may prove useful to examine a number of security models. The established SEATO arrangements must by no means be neglected, for in the foreseeable future it appears that the Manila Treaty will be maintained in force. At present there are few signs that SEATO will be greatly strengthened or broadly expanded in scope. Nevertheless, this consideration does not obviate a study of alternatives; and new international circumstances, of course, may lead to other approaches.

The North Atlantic Treaty Organization presents one of the possible models for security in Southeast Asia. If the Manila Treaty were amended to incorporate the principle that an attack on one signatory is tantamount to an attack on all, commitments to defensive military action would be more precise and SEATO would have more "teeth" in it. Extending the NATO analogy to problems of organization suggests that a joint military force under joint headquarters with one supreme commander might be instituted in Southeast Asia; specific allied forces, committed to the defense of the region, might be permanently stationed in strategic areas on the mainland as well as on the islands. But officials in Washington have no desire to raise once more the difficult constitutional issues, concerning the relation between the executive and the legislative branches, which would accompany any extension of the NATO defense commitments to SEATO. The elaborate defense structure of NATO is not considered feasible in Southeast Asia where not one of the SEATO allies has a common boundary with another and where the distribution of power is extremely disparate. Under the circumstances, building a Southeast Asia Treaty Organization after the pattern of the North Atlantic Treaty Organization appears to be neither attainable nor desirable.

A system of bilateral defense treaties covering much of Southeast Asia has been suggested whereby the United States and each other signatory would come to each other's defense in the event of armed attack in a specific area. The so-called Monroe Doctrine formula that such aggression would endanger the peace and safety of both parties and therefore each would act to meet the common danger according to its constitutional processes could be incorporated. One model for consideration might be the Mutual Defense Treaty between the United States and the Philippines signed in 1951, and another the Treaty of Mutual Cooperation and Security between the United States and Japan signed in 1960. Bilateral treaties unquestionably have their uses, especially when a power wants to limit its commitments and when rivalries are rife in a region, but the nature of the Communist threat in Asia calls for more than a piecemeal effort. Joint planning to meet emergencies is important, and combined military exercises help to reinforce the deterrent. The military commitment of the member states of SEATO located in the treaty area is at present the broadest multilateral example in Asia and the Pacific of full reciprocity with respect to territory. The establishment of an extensive system of bilateral security pacts in Southeast Asia comparable in scope is not presently possible; furthermore, such a diversified system would not meet the real requirements of the time.

The precedent established by the Locarno Pact has on occasion been mentioned as a possible solution to the defense problem of the region. At Locarno in 1925 Great Britain, Italy, France, Belgium, and Germany signed a treaty whereby the parties severally and collectively guaranteed the existing boundaries of Germany with France and Belgium. Any aggressor in this region would theoretically face the armed forces of the other four powers, and the indentification of the aggressor was to be made by the Council of the League of Nations, except in case of "flagrant violation." Berlin signed arbitration conventions with Paris and Brussels, and arbitration treaties with Warsaw and Prague, and both the latter also joined with Paris in mutual assistance treaties in case of German aggression. (It should be remembered, however, that Germany was unwilling to guarantee its 1925 eastern boundaries as definitive while Great Britain and Italy accepted no obligations on that front.) Associated with the Locarno Pact, as the complex settlement came to be called, was Germany's entrance into the League of Nations in 1926, and for a few years the "Locarno spirit" of cooperation prevailed in many European capitals.

At the Geneva Conference on Indochina in 1954 Foreign Secretary Eden had considered a "reciprocal international guarantee" among all members of the conference to buttress the settlement, along with a collective defense treaty among the non-Communist states. On June 23 he mentioned in the House of

Commons that the "reciprocal arrangement" on Indochina might be like Locarno. The reaction in Washington was prompt and highly critical, Congress registering real concern. Might not a Locarno-type arrangement for Indochina involve signing a treaty with Peking and seating Communist China in the United Nations? Would not the Communist possession of territory in the area be guaranteed? The Communists also proved hostile to the Locarno guarantee approach unless it was made "collective," meaning unless they retained a veto on its implementation, and there is every reason to believe that the Colombo Powers would not have guaranteed an Indochina settlement. On June 29 President Eisenhower and Prime Minister Churchill asserted in a joint communiqué that they would not participate in any arrangement confirming or lengthening the "unwilling subordination" of previously sovereign countries. Washington is still opposed to any guarantee of Communist North Viet-Nam and still reluctant to sign a security treaty or any other pact with Peking.

The Monroe Doctrine has sometimes been suggested as fundamentally adaptable for U.S. policy in Southeast Asia. In order to clarify U.S. interests in the region President Kennedy might make a unilateral American statement echoing the words that President Monroe used in a message to Congress on December 2, 1823: "But with the Governments who have declared their independence and maintained it, and whose independence we have, on great consideration and on just principles, acknowledged, we could not view any interposition for the purpose of oppressing them, or controlling in any other manner their destiny, by any European [or Asian] power in any other light than as the manifestation of an unfriendly disposition toward the United States."[1]

[1] James Monroe, Seventh Annual Message, December 2, 1823, *A Compilation of the Messages and Papers of the Presidents,* James D. Richardson, compiler, v. 2 (Washington: Bureau of National Literature and Art, 1903), p. 218.

Such an interposition, as it could be pointed out in the terms of the original statement, would be "dangerous to our peace and safety." Yet when five of the newly independent Latin American states had wanted to make alliances with the United States or to obtain promises of its assistance in the event of European intervention, Washington refused to go beyond its unilateral warning to European states, including Russia, which were looking at the New World with a hungry eye.

The Monroe Doctrine formula has the asset of never having been constitutionally challenged as changing the relationship in power between the chief executive and the Congress. Yet, with or without the formal approval of Congress, it is doubtful if the President of the United States would want to proclaim a unilateral Monroe Doctrine for Southeast Asia. In the first place, the highly nationalistic states of the area would resent such a unilateral American step unless they specifically requested it, which is unlikely at present. Despite the disparity in power, the multilateral approach to security in the area is much more suitable for relations among sovereign states. In fact, the principles of the original Monroe Doctrine are reflected in the multilateral approach of the American republics to security in the Act of Chapultepec of 1945 and the Inter-American Treaty of Reciprocal Assistance of 1947.

An American Doctrine, resembling the U.S. public law now applicable to the Middle East, has been suggested as a model for policy in Southeast Asia. At the request of President Eisenhower on January 5, 1957, a joint resolution was passed by Congress asserting that the United States is willing to employ its armed forces to help any state or grouping of states in the Middle East asking for "assistance against armed aggression from any country controlled by international communism."[2] The President would

[2] *Public Law* 85-7, 85th Congress, 1st sess. H.J. Res. 117 (March 9, 1957).

determine the necessity for any action, and the use of the forces would conform to the U.S. Constitution and treaty obligations. In the same resolution the role of American economic and military aid to the Middle East was also stressed, and certain financial provisions were approved. Under this Eisenhower Doctrine the United States clearly does not make advance commitments to a specific course of action, and the President has considerable power of discretion in deciding what particular measure to take in the face of a crisis. Such an American Doctrine extended to Southeast Asia would not meet adequately the problems of subversion, nor would it cope with crises that are non-Communist in origin; in addition, it might discourage a multilateral, regional approach to security. In spite of the possible advantages of placing the United States more in the background and of stressing the role of the Southeast Asian states in defense, under current conditions an American Doctrine on the Middle East model does not seem likely or desirable for the area.

Washington might also make greater efforts to support regionalism in Southeast Asia. Despite the current obstacles, a political association in a regional framework might ultimately come into existence. The benefits of U.S. attention to the common problems of a given region may possibly outweigh any losses due to dispersion of effort. Tengku Abdul Rahman in his call for the creation of a Southeast Asia Co-operative Group or an Association of Southeast Asia (ASA) has directed attention to the needs of the area. When the Philippines, Thailand, and Malaya joined in 1961 to inaugurate ASA in Bangkok they sought to advance social and economic progress in their part of the world. At the same time, other countries like Burma preferred to develop bilateral ties as cautious steps toward future regionalism.

From many modest beginnings the foundations for real political cooperation in Southeast Asia may be laid in the course of time. The Nordic Council where representatives of the parliaments and governments of Norway, Sweden, Denmark, Finland, and Iceland discuss matters of common concern has been mentioned as a model. At a later stage something like the Organization of American States (OAS) might come into existence. Committed to cooperative social, economic, and cultural development, to solving disputes within the American community by pacific means, and to common action in the event of aggression, the OAS has a current membership of all but one of the twenty-one republics of the Western Hemisphere; it functions through a structure that has gradually evolved to suit the special needs of the inter-American community. Such a regional political association in Southeast Asia, if it functioned effectively, might be able to deal with many problems such as those which have embroiled outside powers in Laos over the last decade.

Washington, of course, cannot by itself create regionalism either on a formal or an informal basis in Southeast Asia. The initiative, it has been frequently repeated, must come from the nations themselves. In the final analysis effective regionalism is based upon positive nationalism and reflects a high degree of political maturity. The small powers of Southeast Asia will require some time before they can effectively cope with serious problems on a regional basis, and in this period the United States will have many opportunities through its various programs systematically to assist in the development of regionalism.

As a national policy in Southeast Asia, Washington might deliberately encourage through diplomacy the development of genuine neutralism. In a cold war context the United States might conclude that genuine neutralism in the region was preferable to alliances which might not stand the test of a crisis. Neutralism, it has been noted, is often used by newly independent Southeast Asian countries as an assertion of national independence and as a means of trying to balance one outside power against another. By actively associating itself with neutralism in the region the United States would currently be identifying itself with one of the important attitudes there. In fact, Washington has moved from a position of criticism to one of tolerance and then of understanding. Yet, if the uncommitted countries of Southeast Asia are more inclined, as time passes, to choose security through collective measures, backed directly or indirectly by the United States, Washington should by all means encourage the effort. In other words, American support for genuine neutralism is valid only under a given set of conditions; it should not be considered a permanent policy in view of the developing situation in Southeast Asia and the Communist stress on neutralism as a temporary phase and on local wars of "national liberation."

The circumstances, furthermore, call for Washington to maintain by all feasible means those alliances which are mutually advantageous. If the United States puts increased emphasis on the importance of neutralism, it will tend to weaken ties with some of its allies, unless definite measures are taken to reassure them. And yet, can any common ground be found in American policy toward allies and toward neutrals? The United States has relations with more than 50 uncommitted nations and alliances with more than 40 others. Although the dilemma in policy is serious, it offers some opportunities for constructive effort. If the issue in world affairs is posed between Communist coercion and free choice for both allies and neutrals, if commitments to the United Nations receive greater emphasis, and if the principle of self-determination is given more attention, the differences between allies and neutrals may be reduced and more common interests developed. Nevertheless, it should be emphasized, the United States needs both the support of its allies and the good will of the neutrals.

A possible security approach for at least a part of Southeast Asia, especially along common borders with Communist China, is neutralization. Burma and Laos come immediately to mind while North and South Viet-Nam as well as Cambodia have sometimes been mentioned. In the latter grouping the Democratic Republic alone has a common border with China, but the unification of Viet-Nam would change the situation.

As a condition intended to bar a state of war, neutralization may be guaranteed, limited, permanent or voluntary, or it may have the contrary qualifications. Unless provisions of demilitarization or other limitations are included, a neutralized state can arm as it so desires. "Perpetual neutrality," an expression frequently used, has come to mean neutralization with no limitation on time. Switzerland is commonly given as an example of a neutralized state, the European powers having agreed on November 20, 1815, to acknowledge the "perpetual neutrality" of the country and to guarantee the integrity and inviolability of its territory. As far back as the Peace of Westphalia in 1648 the independence and neutrality of Switzerland had been recognized. Nevertheless, the Swiss took care to arm themselves, a factor contributing to the maintaining of their neutrality in the last two world wars. Switzerland became a member of the League of Nations but today is almost unique among states in not being a member of the United Nations. Another model is Austria, whose parliament on October 26, 1955, adopted a constitutional law declaring the "perpetual neutrality" of the nation of its "own free will." Austria would maintain forces for national defense but would not make any military pact or allow foreign bases on its soil. Vienna has obtained the recognition of its "perpetual neutrality" from the United States, the Soviet Union, France, and Great Britain. Unlike Switzerland, Austria is a member of the United Nations.

The neutralization of Burma, Laos, Viet-Nam, and Cambodia as a group might take the form of a guarantee by a number of powers like the People's Republic of China, the Soviet Union, the United States, and Great Britain. Or, a reciprocal guarantee of the neutralization of the area might be given by the partners of the Peking-Moscow axis and the signatories of the Manila Treaty. In a speech to the U.N. General Assembly in September 1960, Prince Norodom Sihanouk specifically suggested the neutralization of Cambodia and Laos with international guarantees of their territorial integrity and unity by Washington, London, Paris, Bangkok, and Saigon and by Moscow, Peking, and Hanoi. An Austrian-type neutrality for Laos received support from the United States and the Soviet Union, but implementation proved hard. At the Vienna meeting of President Kennedy and Premier Khrushchev both approved of a neutral Laos along the general lines of Burma or Cambodia.

The belt of states in Southeast Asia subject to neutralization might have limited armed forces or be demilitarized, but the countries would not be permitted to maintain foreign bases or foreign forces on their soil. While they could remain members of, or might be eligible for membership in, the United Nations, they would not be able to make alliances. Because of the Communist threat of indirect aggression, effective neutralization would have to extend beyond the classical concept of neutrality in international law or of nonalignment. Some type of international guardianship assuring, under national sovereignty, freedom of choice within a country would be essential. In this respect, neutralization is not a negative concept placing prohibitions on a state but a positive one allowing it to keep its integrity and to develop according to its own traditions and aspirations. International machinery whose effectiveness is not crippled by a Communist veto would be necessary.

The prospects for effective neutralization in Southeast Asia are dim since the Communists are not prepared to give real substance to the concept. Both Viet-Nams are revisionist in outlook, and Cambodia has territorial claims against its neighbor to the east. Significantly Cambodia failed after the conclusion of the

Geneva Conference on Laos in 1962 in its efforts to convene a similar assembly to make a comparable arrangement for its own neutrality. The Communist countries favored the proposal, but the United States and others opposed it. President Kennedy informed Prince Sihanouk that he believed "official letters" of assurance were preferable.

The British Commonwealth of Nations has been suggested as a possible model for international relations in Southeast Asia. In this association security aspects are to a large extent minimized; many members are not linked by military commitments to others, though in some cases a formal security pact is scarcely needed. Apart from the few remaining dependencies, the Commonwealth is a loose association of independent countries from every inhabited continent but one, acknowledging important common interests despite a wide divergence of outlook. The members owe allegiance to the Crown or recognize the Queen as Head of the Commonwealth. The periodic meetings of prime ministers provide valuable opportunities for an exchange of viewpoints and sometimes for a meeting of minds on problems of mutual interest. Several Commonwealth members are adjacent to Southeast Asia: to the west and northwest of the area, India, Pakistan, and Ceylon; to the south and southeast, Australia and New Zealand; and in the very heart of the region, the Federation of Malaya. The Union of Burma chose not to remain within the association. Although it is highly improbable that the countries of Southeast Asia as a whole will become members of the Commonwealth of Nations, it provides an example of international cooperation beyond the normal relationships of states. The security problems of Southeast Asia, however, require a clearer focus than that provided in a loose association like the Commonwealth of Nations.

American reliance upon the United Nations as the principal means of preserving the peace in Southeast Asia has sometimes been suggested. Here the effectiveness of the world organization depends upon the circumstances of the aggression. Where a powerful invader has decided at all costs to conquer some neighbor, the United Nations is faced with the problem of rapidly organizing forces able to counter aggression. But the great powers' veto in the Security Council coupled with the changed membership of the General Assembly render much more difficult a repetition of the United Nations action in Korea. The international organization must depend upon its members for military support, as it currently has no permanent peacekeeping forces of its own or even adequate "stand-by arrangements" for use in world crises as they develop. Under these circumstances, effective action might well be held up or even be not forthcoming.

On the other hand, in a situation where the aggressor has limited objectives or limited forces, there is a real opportunity for the United Nations to take effective action. Yet this opportunity, it should be stressed, arises more from the attitudes and capabilities of the contestants than from any strength of the world organization. Military units from a number of members can be sent under the auspices of the international body, like the United Nations Emergency Force in the Middle East, to police an area during or immediately after the withdrawal of hostile forces, but subject to agreement between the parties to the controversy. Besides offering important facilities for supervising a truce, the world organization can provide the face-saving formulas so often vital to the resumption of peaceful relations among sovereign states. Through multilateral intervention under the United Nations a breakthrough in the traditional concept of nonintervention may eventually be achieved.

When asked to cope with indirect aggression, the world organization may be able to help stabilize the situation. A United Nations presence on an *ad hoc* interim basis introduced directly by the Secretary-General or through a fact-finding board authorized by the Security Council or the General Assembly may be effective. A U.N. presence can also take a number of permanent forms such as the stationing of a representative of the Secretary-General or even a technical assistance mission under some prominent head. Moreover, a premium can sometimes be found in the "quiet diplomacy" or, under certain circumstances, the "preventive diplomacy" of the Secretary-General. Hence the attacks of the U.S.S.R. on Dag Hammarskjold, its championship of "tripartism," and its assertion that there are no neutral men, only neutral nations, were a grave challenge to all non-Communist countries. The development of the operational capacity of the United Nations in the field, supported by the United States, is an index to the future influence of the world organization.

It is clear that in its policy in Southeast Asia Washington cannot look upon the United Nations as the sole instrument of keeping the peace. In the event of open aggression by Communist China in the region, the world organization would not be nearly as effective as in the Korean War. Yet in a less serious situation, like the one arising in Laos in the summer of 1959, the introduction of a U.N. presence in some form could have a stabilizing effect. Under certain circumstances the world body can exert considerable moral pressure.

Some of the various models for security in Southeast Asia are not exclusive of others. Desirable combinations are theoretically possible and might well be attainable, providing a means of meeting the manifold challenge of new conditions arising from an area in flux. The instrumentalities of the United States may also vary, depending on the nature of the model, simple or complex, selected for security. A treaty, a policy speech by the chief executive, a presidential declaration to Congress with or without its subsequent formal approval, a diplomatic note of prime importance to one or more states, or a weighty communication to the United Nations—all these and others are available. Diplomacy at the summit has possibilities, but they should not be exaggerated. And in the application of security arrangements a wide variety of courses is open to the policy-maker, including brinkmanship, a form of risk-taking that sometimes removes the perils of a war of miscalculation.

GUIDELINES FOR POLICY

In the coming decade the United States should have a dynamic policy in Southeast Asia that extends beyond the widely accepted boundaries of the area, that is graduated in approach to fit the changing international climate inside and outside the region, that is shifting from a short-range American holding operation to a long-range Asian position of strength, and that is able resources and instrumentalities. At the same time the United States must be prepared to take risks and to be the object of criticism. Solid achievements should serve as guides charting future courses of action.

It is essential that U.S. decision-makers understand the conditions confronting them in Asia, and that they be aware of what the United States can and cannot accomplish in Southeast Asia. Projecting the future in terms of probabilities can be helpful, but here human limitations are pronounced. Indicators of coming Communist actions—the direction and intensity of propaganda, VIP visits, military moves, and the interplay of various factors —must be carefully watched.

Future relations between the United States and Communist China will greatly influence, perhaps even dominate, the course of American policy in Southeast Asia. Questions of U.S. recognition of the People's Republic of China and of its seating in the United Nations arouse considerable interest in the United States but, placed in broad perspective, these issues are only tactical aspects of the over-all problem of American policy in Asia. If Washington recognizes Peking on the latter's terms, the primary Communist objective of acquiring Taiwan would in effect be achieved, Peking would be strengthened in Southeast Asia (especially among the Overseas Chinese), and the United States would be weakened as a great power in the Far East and in the world. The appetite of Communist China would only be whetted for further gains at the expense of its neighbors and the Western powers. At the other extreme, an all-out offensive by the United States aimed at overthrowing the Peking regime, possibly restoring the Nationalists to power on the mainland, is not desirable when the total costs of achievement are realistically weighed against the possible advantages. A third world war, of course, introduces different considerations.

The current U.S. policy of seeking to quarantine Communist China in almost every way short of military measures is still widely supported in the United States but continues to be criticized in many circles abroad. Peking is achieving a real measure of success in breaking through the barriers of diplomatic isolation, while the special trade restrictions instigated by the United States have been largely relinquished abroad, save for those that refer to the entire Communist bloc. It is also neither possible nor desirable to ignore Communist China in any worldwide program for controlling armaments, whether atomic or conventional; apart from the weapons of the People's Republic itself, there is also the possibility of Soviet stockpiles and facilities on Chinese territory if the occasion demanded it. Many of the problems of Asia, especially the divided nations of Viet-Nam and Korea, may eventually require negotiations with Peking if any long-range solutions are to be achieved. The United States has already participated in international gatherings with the People's Republic and as a result of the difficulties over the Quemoy and Matsu islands, channels for direct discussion at the ambassadorial level have existed since 1955. It is now sometimes argued from a *theoretical* standpoint that increased formal contacts by Communist China in the world community, both inside and outside the United Nations, would have a slow but perceptible influence on its outlook. The present American policy, it is furthermore contended, is a divisive element among the friends and allies of Washington.

A U.S. policy based upon the recognition of two Chinas has been suggested, but whether it could ever be translated into reality is debatable. In its essentials a "two Chinas" policy would mean that Washington continued its support of Nationalist China in Taiwan and the Pescadores while recognizing Communist China as the *de jure* government of the mainland. The offshore islands of Quemoy and Matsu might become a part of the People's Republic, and in any case such a policy would entail an effort to neutralize the Formosa Strait under international auspices, other Asian and Western states joining to guarantee the territorial integrity and political independence of the Republic of China as restricted to Taiwan and the Pescadores. In the United Nations a "two Chinas" policy would probably mean the seating of Peking as China's representative in all its organs and the election of Taiwan to membership in the world organization without a permanent seat in the Security Council.

For the foreseeable future, however, the fundamental problem is for the United States to *convince* Communist China that it *cannot* accomplish its major objectives through force or threat of force. Peking must recognize that it has more to gain in a genuine attempt to negotiate on the issues, to offer compromises, and to reach lasting agreements. Although the United States might be more flexible in its unofficial contacts (possibly even indicating under appropriate circumstances its acknowledgement of Peking's *de facto* control of the mainland), the principal initiative for a *détente* or a *modus vivendi* must come from the People's Republic. Unless it really believes in the need for negotiations, nothing can actually be gained through them, apart from demonstrating Chinese intractableness. Any broad settlement Washington makes should constitute, if possible, a package involving *de jure* recognition, representation in the United Nations, neutralization of the Formosa Strait, and participation by Western and Asian states in the defense of Taiwan and the free world in Asia.

It is important that the United States separate the question of seating Peking in the United Nations from that of recognizing Communist China. Although the General Assembly could have decided to seat the representatives of the People's Republic by a majority vote, it has concluded by a majority vote that the question was an "important" one necessitating a two-thirds majority. In the Security Council it is not established whether a veto could be used in connection with seating a member's representative. Is the matter procedural or substantive? The United States has shifted on its position, indicating on one occasion it would favor a ruling by the International Court of Justice and later asserting it could and would employ the veto.

Every effort must be made to prevent a humiliating setback for American diplomacy in the United Nations. If it appears that Peking is likely to be seated in the General Assembly, the United States should urge that the world organization insist on certain steps by Communist China that could be taken as purging it of its aggression in Korea. Peking's full participation in the United Nations ought to be made conditional upon some visible progress toward a Far Eastern settlement. But even if Communist China is seated without other arrangements and over American opposition, the United States should not reduce its loyalty to the world organization. The issue, although certainly important, is not one of overriding and overwhelming concern in world politics. When necessary, Washington can challenge Peking's policy in the United Nations, besides still refusing to recognize the People's Republic until favorable conditions obtain.

Over the next decade the United States must carefully watch and evaluate developments in relations between the Soviet Union and Communist China. If the ties of partnership continue to weaken over the period, Moscow obviously will have decreasing leverage on Peking and will be less and less able to exert any moderation on the latter's policy in Southeast Asia. Any sustained *détente* between the United States and the Soviet Union could work toward the isolation of Communist China. If "areas of overlapping interest" between Moscow and Washington emerge, the United States should exploit them. In the immediate years ahead, however, America must be prepared to cope with crises generated by a continuing Peking-Moscow axis, particularly along the vast periphery of the Sino-Soviet bloc with its neighbors.

In the military and strategic aspects of policy for Southeast Asia, Washington should continue its support for SEATO, moderately and gradually strengthening it as a holding operation; it should maintain its bilateral security ties with the Philippines and, if necessary, strengthen them; it should be flexible but resolute in support of Thailand and South Viet-Nam as they face Communist insurgency either in its latent or active manifestations; it should keep military assistance programs, adjusting them to changes in the threat and in the needs of the recipients. Washington should continue to oppose suggestions from Moscow for a mutual nonaggression pact of East Asian and Pacific countries whereby a "nuclear-weapons-free area" in Asia and the Pacific would be created. At the same time every effort should be made to close off "areas of vulnerability" in non-Communist Southeast Asia and to prevent a direct confrontation between Peking and Washington.

In longer-range terms, certainly well toward the end of the coming decade, and probably in subsequent years, the United States should seek to alter some of its basic military policies in Southeast Asia. In the light of changing circumstances the non-Communist countries of the region should undertake the obligations of a collective security pact wherein an armed attack on one in the treaty area is tantamount to an armed attack on all. They would, therefore, unite in resisting the common foe. This provision should apply to direct aggression from any power outside the area, and eventually, if not immediately possible, to aggression inside the region. Provisions for consultation at the request of any signatory should be inserted to meet a situation of danger to one or more participants or to the peace of the area apart from armed attack. The need for widespread cooperation in antisubversion measures should be adequately met.

The treaty should not prejudice the possible unification of Viet-Nam where a new government, created through free elections, should decide its attitude toward the alliance. Nor should it require the Philippines to relinquish its bilateral security ties with the United States, or the Federation of Malaya with Great Britain. The treaty area should include the territory of the signatories in Southeast Asia from the Philippines to Burma to Indonesia.

In accordance with the obligations of the members of the United Nations all the parties should undertake to settle disputes among themselves peacefully and not to threaten or employ force except in self-defense. Measures taken in the event of an armed attack should be reported at once to the Security Council. The treaty should affect neither the obligations of the signatories to the United Nations nor its responsibility in keeping world peace. At the same time the contracting powers through self-help and mutual aid should strengthen their single and collective capacity to withstand armed attacks and indirect aggression directed from outside. To implement the treaty a Southeast Asian Council, consisting of all the participants, should be established, meeting periodically but being organized in such a manner that it could convene at short notice. Further organizational steps could be taken as the needs develop. The treaty should be indefinite in duration although any signatory could cease to be a party upon a year's notice. In view of national sensitivities, the alliance might be termed an Association of Southeast Asian Nations (ASEAN).

India and Japan should be associated with the security pact as both have significant and growing interests in Southeast Asia. It has been pointed out that individually they can only serve as limited counterweights to the might of Communist China but together they can have a much greater impact. In the event of an all-out Chinese Communist offensive in the area, the two powers (though certainly not now but perhaps in the future) might be able and willing to help. The formula for associating New Delhi and Tokyo in the proposed security arrangement could be selected from a number of possibilities. Perhaps the best would be a formal pronouncement rather than a treaty commitment whereby India and Japan as friends with many common interests in the future of Southeast Asia would separately proclaim their support for ASEAN and their willingness upon request to assist the members resisting armed aggression from outside. The two large Asian powers would receive no reciprocal assurances from the Southeast Asian states or assume any formal obligations to each other. Although it is preferable that both New Delhi and Tokyo give the pledges, one would be better than none. With its interests in Southeast Asia, Pakistan might also be willing to take a stand similar to that of India and Japan.

The United States, though not a party to the proposed Southeast Asian security pact, could pledge that upon request it would be willing to use its armed forces in defense of the integrity and independence of the ASEAN members in the event of armed aggression in the treaty area from the outside. Washington, furthermore, might restrict its pledge of armed assistance to circumstances involving Communist aggression, thus not being obligated to participate in military measures involving non-Communist controversies. The best instrument would probably be a public law arising from a joint resolution of Congress at the request of the President. Under the law the chief executive would decide if action was necessary, and the employment of U. S. armed forces would conform to American constitutional practice and treaty obligations.

Even though the United States under this arrangement would not be a party to ASEAN, its willingness to help repel Communist armed aggression from the outside would necessitate a capability for limited war in the treaty area. At the same time the maintenance of a deterrent to total war, essential in dealings with the Sino-Soviet bloc, would not be lessened. As regards Communist subversion or indirect aggression in Southeast Asia, the formula under consideration for an American association with ASEAN does not have direct relevance. Yet there is no reason why Washington through preventive measures should not assist in building internal security forces and in providing economic and technical aid to reduce the appeals of communism. And the United States might even assert in its declaration that it would extend its offer of armed aid upon request to any state in the treaty area victim of open Communist aggression at the hands of another there, thus taking into account the possibility of successful Communist subversion.

It would be desirable if other Western powers with special interests in Southeast Asia—Australia, New Zealand, and Great Britain—assumed individually a position similar in fundamentals to that of the United States toward the suggested security pact. The three Commonwealth members would probably not want to qualify their obligations just to external aggression that is Communist in origin. Although the Asians themselves should have responsibility in the first instance for the defense of their homelands, an association linking them less directly with the United States, Great Britain, Australia, and New Zealand in the event of Communist armed attack can advance the national interests of all concerned. Military planning among the last four powers would be possible under conditions that might arouse less suspicion in Southeast Asia.

The question can logically be raised as to whether or not Communist China and the Soviet Union could be invited by the parties of ASEAN to pledge individually their willingness upon request to support the victims in the treaty area of armed aggression from the outside. The proposed multilateral treaty is basically directed against any external armed attack and each outside power gives unilateral assurances, restricting or not restricting them as it sees fit to Communist aggression. Yet in reality the source of any external armed attack would doubtless be Communist, and North Viet-Nam would not be a member of ASEAN. Nevertheless the provision that Viet-Nam upon unification after free elections should decide its attitude toward the security pact would introduce an element of flexibility into the situation. All aspects considered, there is no basic reason why Peking and Moscow should not give independent assurances like those projected for most other governments outside the treaty area. If the pledges could be expected, they would be factors in facilitating the approval of a Southeast Asian defense treaty in some capitals of the region. And the security arrangements are so drawn that they could go into effect even if the Communist bloc did not approve of them.

Along with the projected defense pact, other military issues involving the United States enter into the equation. Washington, its Western associates, Japan, India, Pakistan, and the Southeast Asian countries would still welcome effective U.N. participation in a crisis. Bilateral defense treaties already contracted, involving the Philippines and Malaya, would remain although their value might well be reduced if the proposed security arrangement worked. At the same time the United States would have a firmer basis for strengthening regional ties by working through the parties of ASEAN. Australia and possibly Japan could still be developed as producers of standard equipment and as major arsenals. The former could still provide sites for medium- and long-range missiles. The use of brinkmanship and other forms of risk-taking and alarms as well might be reduced.

Although the collective defense proposal as here presented may be desirable, its attainment is certainly not a foregone conclusion. In long-range terms Washington would have much to gain in such an arrangement since it places a premium upon the governments of Southeast Asia themselves, and is adjusted to the actual needs and emerging political climate in the area. But the United States cannot pressure the countries into a collective security pact; they themselves must be the arbiters of their own destiny. As for the suggested unilateral American assurances of aid, they could be forthcoming without very much difficulty. Yet if the proposed defense system or some similar arrangement never becomes reality, the United States can still fall back upon the setup currently in effect and make improvements when needed and possible.

Security involves far more than just military and strategic considerations. Diplomacy and defense, for instance, are two sides of a single coin. Through the exercise of "total diplomacy" in the political and ideological fields of policy Washington should be more effective in Southeast Asia over the coming decade. The role of the U.S. ambassador in promoting relations, a role far more complex than that prescribed in classical diplomacy, will become increasingly important. His is the task of encouraging political stability, of helping to keep the peace, and furthering U.S. interests. Modern communications have served to reduce his discretionary powers abroad, but his participation in policymaking at home has simultaneously been increased; moreover, extensive American aid enables the ambassador in an underdeveloped country under the "New Diplomacy" to influence the direction of modernization. The ambassador can personally make a vital contribution to the development of friendly relations between his government and the one to which he is accredited; in fact, his role is relatively more important than that in most Western capitals. In an environment where personal considerations are so important, an ambassador who does not command the confidence of, say, Sihanouk or Diem is severely handicapped.

The special importance of the personal element in Southeast Asian diplomacy necessitates the most careful selection of American ambassadors. The United States should send outstanding career officers of the Foreign Service, as well as certain other qualified people, to head the various missions in the region. All must be adept in coping with passionate local feelings, such as those manifest in Thai-Cambodian and South Vietnamese-Cambodian relations. In 1960 all American ambassadors in Southeast Asia were professionals, and it would be interesting, if it were possible, to compare the record of U.S. diplomacy in the area with one where all the ambassadors were political appointees. Although the Foreign Service does not necessarily bring the best individuals to the top, it can be argued that the chances of finding an excellent envoy are greater among career people than in the political selection of a person from the outside. But the important criteria are the qualifications of the individual; the ambassador should be neither a technician trained and skilled in the

Foreign Service Regulations nor a person whose claim to distinction arises solely from political considerations, but a man or woman who has the important human qualifications for effective work. The Kennedy administration has appointed some excellent ambassadors representing both career officers and political appointees in Southeast Asia.

At present the best use of the envoy's time presents more problems than his selection. The ambassador's responsibilities are increasing as official and unofficial relations with the Southeast Asian countries become more intensive and complex. As the country team which he heads embraces wider fields of activity, as his embassy staff expands in members and in duties, and as the unofficial community of Americans grows, the ambassador must guard against having to major in red tape and minor in cocktail parties. In any case, administrative responsibilities and social obligations weigh heavily, and the only solution lies in the establishment of embassy priorities, in judicious delegation to reliable subordinates, and in the careful budgeting of time. Despite any structural and functional reforms, the basic duties and over-all responsibility of the ambassador cannot be separated from his office; only the man in charge can measure up to the assignment.

It is essential that in his work the U.S. envoy stress contacts with Southeast Asians; the latter wish to be frequently consulted, the former needs the rapport that comes only from personal relations. This principle holds from the ambassador down through many members of his staff who work at lower echelons with local people of similar specializations. American private citizens abroad can also be of value here, for they often reach people reluctant to have extensive dealings with U. S. officials. The expansion of American public and private contacts at all levels of Southeast Asian society, so-called "diplomacy in depth," can lead to more effective representation and reduce the insulating tendencies of overseas "little Americas." As already noted, it is important that the United States maintain contacts not only with the ruling elements of today but also with those who will be in power tomorrow.

The diverse American activities in Southeast Asia need to be better coordinated. In a given state the ambassador and his country team should have an increasingly important function in the process of applying total U.S. resources and of integrating programs under a carefully considered plan. But coordination on an area-wide basis obviously calls for a broader and different approach. Efforts are being made to meet the needs: in the military field, the U.S. Commander in Chief, Pacific, has responsibilities for coordinating the entire American military effort in the Pacific; in economic and cultural matters, meetings are held of USIS or AID officials from a large area of Asia to discuss common subjects; and in the political field, annual conferences of the chiefs of U.S. missions in the Far East serve as a focus for the exchange of viewpoints and the evaluation of developments affecting common problems. In March 1962 a Regional Operations Conference of ambassadors, heads of MAAGs, chiefs of USIS, and administrators of AID missions, together with key officials from Washington, was held in Baguio. Yet these meetings and conferences cannot achieve over-all, permanent, and systematic correlation of policy. On the other hand, a Phoenix Park establishment under an American commissioner-general for Southeast Asia is scarcely necessary; there are substantial differences among U.S. operations in the various countries of the area, reflecting the diverse problems presented by various governments.

Coordination of American policy throughout Southeast Asia can best be done in Washington. The Secretary of State has a heavy responsibility for basic American policy in a given nation and region although, like the President, he does not have the sheer physical capability to handle the span of people associated with official duties. In order to improve supervision from Washington, the more effective use of existing channels and a better understanding of objectives, rather than the creation of many new organs, are needed.

Although the United States does not wage a campaign to sell democracy in Southeast Asia as the Soviet Union and the People's Republic of China propagandize communism, Americans living in the area (whether in official or private capacity) should remember that to Asians they *are* the United States and its democratic way of life. Americans cannot tell the leaders and peoples of Southeast Asia how to run their governments, but they can exemplify the moderate and constructive attitudes which must underlie any successful democratic society. At all times they should hold up the concept of democracy as an ultimate goal, reinforcing all conditions conducive to its eventual success. A doctrine of political development which embodies many of the principles of the Founding Fathers would have its place; the waves of dynamic ideas now breaking on the coasts of Asia and Africa cut deeper than the ripples of automobiles and refrigerators.

In the economic aspects of policy, Washington should vigorously seek to transform the "Decade of Development" from blueprint to reality. Although the obstacles are greater in Southeast Asia than in many other areas as a result of the direct and immediate challenge of the Sino-Soviet bloc, there are still time and opportunity for real achievement. The countries must have the means as well as the right to decide their future. If the Decade of Development fails in Southeast Asia, military measures by themselves will not prevent in the long run the extension of the Bamboo Curtain over the region. American technical and economic assistance, apart from meeting urgent needs, must be shifted toward long-term national programs of modernization, leading ultimately to self-sustained growth and social justice. The economic growth of the developing countries must also be related to the expansion of the international economy. This shift in emphasis will require even greater amounts of expertise and capital than in the recent past, and the importance of "good bookkeeping" should not bar imaginative thinking in Washington.

Although the overriding need for U.S. bilateral aid will remain, Washington should increase its attempts to associate other Western powers and Japan in a multilateral effort to assist in the orderly economic development of the less developed nations, including Southeast Asia. All the multilateral agencies working under U.N. auspices should be thoroughly utilized, and recent developments reflect a greater American emphasis in this area of activity. Promotion of multilateral aid programs on a regional basis should be pushed as opportunities offer. Apart from the intrinsic economic promise of the Mekong River and the Indus River projects, it is clear that such undertakings also strengthen essential regional ties. The Colombo Plan has proved to be a valuable approach in a given geographic area, and private sources can help to promote regional activities. Where regional cooperation helps to solve current national problems, the governments involved will display much greater interest in the future of regionalism. A challenging field is found, for instance, in a possible marketing arrangement between the rice-surplus and the rice-deficient countries of Southeast Asia. Current and future marketing conditions in the chemical fertilizer industry, in cotton textiles, and in iron and steel point up the need for cooperation in the Far East for mutual benefit.

Present instruments for national and multilateral assistance to the countries of Southeast Asia appear to meet the current needs; but better coordination is necessary and new emphases or approaches may be required in the future. The Colombo Plan might be used for economic and technical assistance more directed toward national defense. In the event of a broad Southeast Asian collective security treaty, economic aid might be channeled through one of its organs. A common market, a regional development bank with Western and Japanese participation, and a regional payments system may all eventually develop.

It has been suggested that the Soviet Union should play an important part in multilateral aid projects. But even if the U.S.S.R. is willing to associate itself with the "capitalist imperialists," Moscow would scarcely desist from its national objective of promoting its version of communism wherever possible, and Washington would not want to support any specific program that might advance Communist interests. Indeed, the two superpowers might in such a framework be forced into such competitive positions that the net value of the project to the Asian or African recipient would inevitably be reduced. Criticism has already arisen in Washington over the mixing of U.S. and Communist assistance by local Asians in some uncommitted countries. Congress would be reluctant to appropriate funds that might be deliberately manipulated in one way or another to promote the cause of international communism in multilateral aid projects; extremely stringent safeguards would be necessary.

Despite its large programs of economic and technical assistance in Southeast Asia, the United States should not neglect the importance of normal trade and private investment in the economic growth of the area. As Southeast Asia moves ahead in economic development, it will furnish an increasingly better market for more American products (provided they can meet other foreign competition), and the United States will import many raw materials and certain semiprocessed and processed goods from the region. Despite their high cost, private American technical skills will be in wide demand in the area for many years. The achievement of greater political and economic stability should also attract much greater U.S. private investment. Perhaps the problems of unstable export markets cannot be stressed too strongly. Washington will need in the coming decade to give continuous attention to the problems of stabilizing world prices for certain agricultural commodities and basic raw materials exported from Southeast Asia, and of the disposal of surplus American food products without upsetting the markets of the region. Yet the American businessmen cannot be expected simultaneously to put up with artificial prices for raw materials from abroad and to abandon research for cheaper substitutes.

As a means of explaining and supporting U.S. objectives and actions overseas, the information program of the United States is an important element in security policy. The development of sympathetic understanding by the Southeast Asians through the projection of a favorable image of the United States is essential. Ideas are intangible weapons in the arsenal of any country. To be effective the information aims of the U.S. government abroad must be geared to specific national policies; words not backed by policy and action are soon bound to lose their impact. Problems cannot be solved by propaganda, and psychological warfare must have realistic foundations.

In its information program in Southeast Asia Washington should stress objectives of reinforcing the independence of the countries of the region and of contributing to their own efforts to achieve economic and social progress; communism should be exposed for what it is, but more dividends will come from placing emphasis on the twin objectives mentioned. Abstract concepts of stability and security are difficult to explain. The best results for American information activities will be obtained by promoting the national interests of the Asians in terms of their own values, providing the United States can associate itself with them on grounds of common concern. Efforts under private auspices can also contribute to the official information program.

Greater cooperation of the Western powers in this field in Southeast Asia would produce a more impressive total impact. The elites of the area, the leaders of today and tomorrow, are currently the best targets of information programs; but the importance of the popular base is growing and should not be neglected.

Although a domestic matter, Americans should have a better understanding of the culture and problems of Southeast Asians. The events of the Pacific war and the Korean War have directed interest to Asian countries, but the attention span of the public is limited. Apart from Americans living or traveling in Southeast Asia (whose mere physical presence does not always guarantee insight), the citizens of the United States have very limited information on the area. To tourists, Southeast Asia is often Bali and Angkor Wat; to many Americans residing in the region, the city streets of Singapore or Saigon. The greater contributions in an effort to remedy this defect must come through nonofficial channels involving schools, colleges, and the intelligent use of mass media. The task is enormous, and the results will be slow and sometimes disappointing.

In turn, the confused and often distorted image of the United States in Southeast Asia should be improved. The current situation is not surprising: for one reason the Americans in the area, though few in relative numbers, are more conspicuous than in many Western countries. U.S. civilian officials, military officers, businessmen, missionaries, tourists, scholars, teachers, technicians, and journalists inevitably portray different segments of the American scene. U.S. goods through aid and trade have entered into the big cities as well as the hinterland. American motion pictures have created a concept of the nation not generally flattering, to say the least. Southeast Asians who have returned home after visiting the United States have various concepts of what it represents. To some the country is grossly materialistic, characterized by status seekers and victims of racial discrimination, while to others it represents an ideal to be emulated.

The United States Information Agency obviously faces great challenges in its work. As an independent entity operating in close liaison with the Department of State, its organization is generally satisfactory. Full recognition is given to the importance of presenting American objectives and policies abroad in their best possible light, of winning support for them, and of building international understanding. This recognition is often reflected in the quality of the staff recruited.

Nevertheless, a reconsideration should be made of the U.S. cultural program in Southeast Asia. A significant number of the intellectuals of the area are still anti-American, representing an important target group for international communism. These intellectuals clearly have a marked influence on youth through the schools and universities of the region, and thus condition the national leadership of tomorrow. The situation requires that the United States take prompt and concrete steps to improve its programs of cultural relations and educational exchange. In the first place, the U.S. cultural efforts should be divorced from the information program, for the Southeast Asian often fails to distinguish between the cultural affairs officer and the public affairs officer. Both individuals are interested in promoting friendly contacts between the United States and the particular country where they are working, but their approach is quite different; the cultural affairs officer is primarily concerned with education, the public affairs officer with publicizing U.S. viewpoints. Each of these people has an important job to do, but in justice to each, their work should be clearly distinguished. The cultural affairs officer should also be upgraded in importance and functions. He should not be, in effect, close to the bottom of the official list in a mission; to the contrary, he should be a member of the country team in some states of Southeast Asia. The importance of this position in such countries, furthermore, calls for a person of considerable professional stature, one who would be highly regarded by the president of a national university. Some cultural affairs officers have done excellent work, but others have looked upon their position as only another tour of duty.

Consideration should be given to the establishment of a government agency in Washington on cultural cooperation, especially with the underdeveloped areas. Such an agency should work under the auspices of the Department of State in close liaison with the United States Information Agency and other government organs, and with American universities and learned societies.

Cultural interaction that is more effective and extensive can go a long way in developing good relations between the United States and Southeast Asia. Educational institutes, seminars, and conferences of specialists can profit from both public and private support. A person-to-person program on a much broader basis can bring dividends, as the volunteers of the Peace Corps are proving so convincingly. The work of Medico, a voluntary nonprofit organization, in Laos and elsewhere, and of the People-to-People Health Foundation with the hospital ship, the S.S. *Hope*, in Southeast Asia has been important. In another aspect, English as a language of cultural exchange and diplomacy should be encouraged; here binational centers can help to avoid the dangers of so-called "cultural imperialism." On the other hand, the creation in the United States of one huge university where most foreign students would study, and where American youths who plan to work abroad would go, is not desirable, for much is gained when foreigners study in various parts of the United States and Americans attend foreign universities. At the same time the East-West Center at the University of Hawaii has a useful place in the total effort. Sending U.S. teachers and scholars to the Far East probably is preferable to bringing large numbers of Asian students to the United States, as the latter often become uprooted and some do not even want to return home. What is needed for the non-Communist Asian world is a Cultural Colombo Plan.

If the recent past is a measure of the future, the next ten years will bring marked changes in the American outlook on Asia. The United States has generally focused its foreign policy on Europe, but the coming developments in the Far East may well contribute to a gradual shift in orientation, thus fulfilling the prophecies of a number of prominent Americans long since dead. In the pattern that is emerging in world politics the United States will continue to need Asian friends and many states in the Far East will want the support of Washington. The United States must be willing and able to assist the Southeast Asians in measuring up to the manifold challenges of Communist China. With the possible help of Japan and India as Asian counterweights and with the support of Australia, New Zealand, and Great Britain as Western associates, the United States should eventually achieve a real measure of success in trying to create conditions where the countries of Southeast Asia, through their individual and collective efforts, will be able to develop into strong, stable, and responsible members of the world community.

Bibliographical Note

Although voluminous material on U. S. policy toward the countries and the problems of Southeast Asia exists in various government offices in Washington, publications based on these sources are far too few and often not adequate. Declassification will be necessary before the general reader can have before him a definitive study of the evolution of American policy in Southeast Asia since the Second World War. It may well be that the actual record of U. S. diplomacy in the area, when ultimately subjected to the description and analysis of scholars, will bear up better than many critics now assume.

For an unofficial policy study focused on the problems of the present as they have evolved and as they point to the future, current bibliographical aids published under governmental and nongovernmental auspices are adequate. Although for the most part they do not focus directly upon American policy in Southeast Asia, they provide the necessary milieu for comprehension, interpretation, and evaluation. As these publications are increasingly extensive, it is necessary to be selective and to choose the material most related to the study under consideration.

The Department of State Bulletin occasionally contains the texts of speeches by high-ranking American officials on U. S. policy in Southeast Asia. Signed articles and official statements contribute to the importance of the weekly as a basic official source. The *Treaties and Other International Acts Series* provides the texts of agreements indispensable for an understanding of legal obligations. Unfortunately the annual volumes of the *Foreign Relations of the United States,* focusing on diplomatic correspondence, are issued several years after the developments considered, and so American relations with the newly independent countries of Southeast Asia are not yet covered. The successive foreign aid agencies and the

United States Information Agency have issued public data, often of interest to the student of Asian affairs. *Problems of Communism,* for instance, is a USIA bimonthly publication.

Congressional documentation is proving to be an increasingly valuable source of information on the region. Some of the best academic and other talent outside the government has been on occasion marshalled in special studies published as committee prints under the auspices of the Senate Committee on Foreign Relations.

Statements of American officials in international organizations afford an opportunity for an expression of policy. The *Official Records* of the United Nations Security Council, General Assembly, Economic and Social Council, and Trusteeship Council provide material sometimes bearing upon U. S. policy in Southeast Asia. The *Yearbook of the United Nations* and the monthly *United Nations Review* are helpful, and various publications of the Economic Commission for Asia and the Far East merit particular attention. The *United Nations Treaty Series,* successor to the *League of Nations Treaty Series,* represents official decisions in policy. Outside the framework of the United Nations, the publications of the Colombo Plan and of the Southeast Asia Treaty Organization provide further data.

Documents on American Foreign Relations, a volume issued annually by the Council on Foreign Relations, and *Documents on International Affairs,* one published yearly by the Royal Institute of International Affairs, afford the reader two carefully selected collections of merit. Companion volumes of description and analysis are *The United States in World Affairs* and *Survey of International Affairs,* issued annually by the Council on Foreign Relations and Royal Institute of International Affairs respectively. A valuable aid in the study of American policy in Southeast Asia is the reports and letters of the American Universities Field Staff written by highly qualified men in the area.

Bibliographies on the region are comprehensive although many books and articles do not lend themselves to easy classification. The author in his book entitled *The Diplomacy of Southeast Asia: 1945-1958* (New York: Harper, 1958), xv, 584 p., attempted in Appendix D, pp. 520-566, to present a bibliography that broadly covered the international relations of the area. The Asia section in the American Universities Field Staff's *A Select Bibliography: Asia, Africa, Eastern Europe, Latin America* (New York: Vance Weaver Composition, Inc., 1960), ix, 534 p., contains a carefully chosen list of books on Southeast Asia, most of which are annotated and some of which are graded A or B. *Supplement 1961* (New York: Vance Weaver Composition, Inc., 1961), iv, 175 p., brings it further up-to-date. Professor D. G. E. Hall in his significant article "On the Study of Southeast Asian History" (*Pacific Affairs,* vol. 33, September 1960, pp. 268-281) thoughtfully surveys historical literature on the region including works concentrating on "current affairs or very recent history." The American Institute of Pacific Relations for some time kept up-to-date Bruno Lasker's revised *Books on Southeast Asia: A Select Bibliography* (New York: American Institute of Pacific Relations, 1960 [latest issue]), 70 p., the last supplement covering the period to April 1960. Two earlier bibliographies of particular merit are

John F. Embree and Lillian Ota Dotson, *Bibliography of the Peoples and Cultures of Mainland Southeast Asia* (New Haven: Yale University, Southeast Asia Studies, 1950), xxxiii, 821 p., plus addenda, and U. S. Library of Congress, Orientalia Division, *Southeast Asia: An Annotated Bibliography of Selected Reference Sources,* compiled by Cecil Hobbs (Washington, 1952), ix, 163 p. The latter is in the process of being revised and brought up-to-date. The *Behavior Science Bibliographies* of the Human Relations Area Files, Inc., dealing with different Southeast Asian countries, the bibliographies of the Southeast Asia Studies Program of Yale University in addition to the volume mentioned by Embree and Dotson, and the lists of accessions on the area previously issued by the Orientalia Division of the Library of Congress are helpful.

The annual bibliographies of *The Journal of Asian Studies* (formerly *The Far Eastern Quarterly*) provide an extensive and comprehensive though not annotated compilation of books and articles. Southeast Asia is included in *The Politics of the New States: A Select Annotated Bibliography with Special Reference to the Commonwealth* (London: Oxford University Press, 1961), xvi, 171 p., compiled by Francis Carnell. Each issue of the quarterlies, *The American Political Science Review* and *International Organization,* has helpful bibliographic references. The summaries of activities of international organizations are supported by footnotes largely from documentary sources. Henry L. Roberts, editor, in *Foreign Affairs Bibliography, 1942-1952* (New York: Harper, for the Council on Foreign Relations, 1955), xxii, 727 p., has presented a briefly annotated but comprehensive list of books, some of them having direct relevance to Southeast Asia.

U. S. POLICY IN SOUTHEAST ASIA

The evolution of U. S. policy in Southeast Asia within certain periods of time has been considered by only a handful of authors. Lawrence S. Finkelstein's revised edition of *American Policy in Southeast Asia* (New York: American Institute of Pacific Relations, 1951), 78 p., is followed by Miriam S. Farley's revised edition of *United States Relations with Southeast Asia, with Special Reference to Indochina, 1950-1955* (New York: American Institute of Pacific Relations, 1955), 81 p. In his *Southeast Asia in Perspective* (New York: Macmillan, 1956), xx, 309 p., John Kerry King has focused his attention on problems facing the United States in the area in the mid-1950s. More current is Oliver E. Clubb, Jr., *The United States and the Sino-Soviet Bloc in Southeast Asia* (Washington: The Brookings Institution, 1962), viii, 173 p.

A number of speeches or statements published in *The Department of State Bulletin* since the Second World War may be specifically cited as throwing particular light on American policy in Southeast Asia, although some of them may center on a certain crisis at a given time. Singled out for mention are John Carter Vincent's "The Post-War Period in the Far East" (*The Department of State Bulletin,* vol. 13, no. 330, October 21, 1945, pp.

[444]

644-648); Dean Acheson's "Crisis in Asia—An Examination of U. S. Policy" (vol. 22, no. 551, January 23, 1950, pp. 111-118); Dean Acheson's "United States Policy toward Asia" (vol. 22, no. 560, March 27, 1950, pp. 467-472); Dean Rusk's "Fundamentals of Far Eastern Foreign Policy" (vol. 23, no. 585, September 18, 1950, pp. 465-468); John Foster Dulles' "The Threat of a Red Asia" (vol. 30, no. 772, April 12, 1954, pp. 539-542); John Foster Dulles' "Policy for Security and Peace" (published in final form in *Foreign Affairs*, vol. 32, April 1954, pp. 353-364); John Foster Dulles' "Security in the Pacific" (*The Department of State Bulletin*, vol. 30, no. 783, June 28, 1954, pp. 971-973; Walter S. Robertson's "The United States Looks at South and Southeast Asia" (vol. 33, no. 843, August 22, 1955, pp. 295-298); John M. H. Lindbeck's "Communist China and American Far Eastern Policy" (vol. 33, no. 854, November 7, 1955, pp. 751-759); Kenneth T. Young's "The Challenge of Asia to United States Policy" (vol. 35, no. 896, August 27, 1956, pp. 340-352); J. Graham Persons' "The Developing Nations of the Far East: Their Relation to U. S. Security" (vol. 41, no. 1050, August 10, 1959, pp. 201-205); Howard P. Jones' "Is the Tide Turning in Asia?" (vol. 42, no. 1090, May 16, 1960, pp. 782-789); Dean Rusk's "A Plan for International Development" (vol. 44, no. 1148, June 26, 1961, pp. 1000-1008); and W. W. Rostow's "Guerrilla Warfare in the Underdeveloped Areas" (vol. 45, no. 1154, August 7, 1961, pp. 233-238). The last named article, in fact, despite its title, is an excellent statement of American foreign policy under President Kennedy toward areas like Southeast Asia. More recent is W. Averell Harriman's "What We Are Doing in Southeast Asia," *The New York Times Magazine*, May 27, 1962, pp. 7, 53-55. The longer the period of time from V-J Day, it may be noted, the greater has become the scope of U. S. policy in the region. Cordell Hull's *The Memoirs of Cordell Hull* (New York: Macmillan, 1948), vol. ii, especially pp. 1595-1601, is a far call from the articles just cited by Ambassador Jones, W. W. Rostow, and W. Averell Harriman.

Relatively little attention has been given in books and journals to the problems of limited and general war as specifically applied to Southeast Asia. The Royal Institute of International Affairs in *Collective Defence in South East Asia* (London: Oxford University Press, 1956), xiv, 197 p., published the findings of a Chatham House Study Group, stressing the "Manila Treaty and its implications" and affording valuable insights into the "strategic picture." A broad timely study is one produced for the Senate Committee on Foreign Relations by the Washington Center of Foreign Policy Research, The Johns Hopkins University, *Developments in Military Technology and Their Impact on United States Strategy and Foreign Policy* (Washington: GPO, 1959), x, 120 p. Townsend Hoopes has contributed a thoughtful article in his "Overseas Bases in American Strategy" (*Foreign Affairs*, vol. 37, October 1958, pp. 69-82).

The best analysis of U. S. military aid is found in the *Composite Report of the President's Committee to Study the United States Military Assistance Program* [Draper Report] (Washington, GPO, 1959), xvi, 197 p., with the *Annexes*, vii, 355 p., comprising vol. II. Attention should be directed to Annex A, "The Purposes of United States Military and Economic

Assistance," pp. 1-29, written "for the most part" by Paul H. Nitze. General W. B. Palmer in an address published as "The Military Assistance Program as a Tool for Peace with Honor" (*The Department of State Bulletin*, vol. 42, no. 1079, February 29, 1960, pp. 329-333) shows well the impact of the Draper Report. Colonel Amos A. Jordan, Jr., deals specifically with Southeast Asia in a thoughtful paper given at the annual convention of the Association for Asian Studies in 1960 entitled "Considerations in U. S. Military Assistance to Southeast Asia." Excellent is his *Foreign Aid and the Defense of Southeast Asia* (New York: Praeger, 1962), xvi, 272 p.

Official statistics for both American military and economic aid, including the countries in Southeast Asia, are given in Agency for International Development, Statistics and Reports Division, *U. S. Foreign Assistance and Assistance from International Organizations: Obligations and Loan Authorizations July 1, 1945-June 30, 1961* (Washington (?): GPO (?), 1962), ix, 130 p. Another aid is *Report to Congress on the Mutual Security Program for the Fiscal Year 1961* (Washington: GPO, 1962), 48 p., a publication prepared under the direction of the AID administrator and with help from the Departments of State and Defense. Particularly comprehensive for the approach of the Kennedy administration to foreign assistance is *An Act for International Development: A Program for the Decade of Development* (Washington: GPO, 1961), xxi, 189 p., which is a "summary presentation" for fiscal year 1962. Also helpful have been the operations reports of ICA and the brief fact sheets issued under its auspices on "Mutual Security in Action" in various Southeast Asian countries. Extensive in coverage is *Foreign Aid Program: Compilation of Studies and Surveys*, Senate Document no. 52, 85th Cong., 1st sess. (Washington: GPO, 1957), xiii, 1582 p.

Charles Wolf, Jr., in his *Foreign Aid: Theory and Practice in Southern Asia* (Princeton University Press, 1960), xix, 442 p., has made a major contribution to the literature on American assistance. John D. Montgomery has completed a significant study under the auspices of the Council on Foreign Relations on the politics of U. S. aid in Burma, Thailand, Viet-Nam, and Taiwan, entitled *The Politics of Foreign Aid: American Experience in Southeast Asia* (New York: Praeger, 1962), xv, 336 p. In *The New Statecraft: Foreign Aid in American Foreign Policy* (University of Chicago Press, 1960), xv. 247 p., George Liska has analyzed American assistance as a tool of statecraft. Lucian W. Pye has contributed a perceptive article in "Soviet and American Styles in Foreign Aid" (*Orbis*, vol. 4, Summer 1960, pp. 159-173).

Two items in *The Department of State Bulletin* throwing light on multilateral aid may be singled out for special attention: one is a speech by Henry Cabot Lodge, "Mutual Aid through the United Nations" (vol. 42, no. 1084, April 4, 1960, pp. 524-527), and the other, "Economic Assistance as a Cooperative Effort of the Free World" (vol. 43, no. 1104, August 22, 1960, pp. 289-295), consists of key excerpts from a report by the same name which was prepared by the State Department and other government branches at the request of Congress. Charles W. Adair, Jr., in his "Economic Interdependence in the Free World" (*The Department of State*

SOUTHEAST ASIA IN UNITED STATES POLICY

[446]

Bulletin, vol. 43, no. 1111, October 10, 1960, pp. 572-577) devotes attention
to broad aspects of American economic policy, including the encouragement of private investments and the expansion of exports. A frank appraisal of the problems ahead is found in Edwin M. Martin's "Trade and
Aid in the Sixties" (vol. 44, no. 1144, May 29, 1961, pp. 822-825). As for
the past, Charles E. Bohlen in his "Economic Assistance in United States
Foreign Policy" (vol. 42, no. 1083, March 28, 1960, pp. 495-501) has carefully traced the evolution of American aid to its present dimensions. Emphasizing trade, Robert J. Barr has edited *American Trade with Asia and
the Far East* (Milwaukee: Marquette University Press, 1959), xix, 317 p.

American "overseasmanship" has attracted the interest of a number of
people. William J. Lederer and Eugene Burdick in their novel *The Ugly
American* (New York: Norton, 1958), 285 p., attack the American Foreign
Service and U. S. policies in Southeast Asia and present their concept of
what the ideal American should be and do in the area. Harlan Cleveland,
Gerard J. Mangone, and John Clarke Adams in *The Overseas Americans*
(New York: McGraw-Hill, 1960), xv, 316 p., and Harlan Cleveland and
Gerard J. Mangone, editors, in *The Art of Overseasmanship* (Syracuse
University Press, 1957), xvii, 150 p., have given careful thought to the ed-
ucational preparation and problems of Americans overseas. Livingston
Merchant for his part in a significant article "Diplomacy and the Modern
World" (*The Department of State Bulletin*, vol. 43, no. 1115, November
7, 1960, pp. 707-713) presents a convincing argument on the continuing importance of bilateral diplomacy despite the growth of multilateral and of
public diplomacy.

One of the most thoughtful studies having widespread implications for
American officials and U. S. policy in Southeast Asia is a monograph prepared by the Center for International Studies at the Massachusetts Institute
of Technology for the Senate Committee on Foreign Relations, *Economic,
Social, and Political Change in the Underdeveloped Countries and Its Implications for United States Policy* (Washington: GPO, 1960), ix, 98 p.
An "extensive revision" of the monograph is found in Max F. Millikan and
Donald L. M. Blackmer, editors, *The Emerging Nations: Their Growth
and United States Policy* (Boston: Little, Brown, 1961), xiv, 171 p. *Asia*
(Washington: GPO, 1959), ix, 157 p., is a study prepared by Conlon Associates also for the Senate Committee on Foreign Relations. Guy J. Pauker
is the author of the section on Southeast Asia. Both the MIT and Conlon
Associates monographs should be read for suggestions on American policy
in Southeast Asia.

SEATO AND THE WESTERN POWERS

The literature on SEATO is limited but growing. Official publications,
somewhat chaotic for the bibliographer, reflect the evolution of the organization and its headquarters in Bangkok is now producing an increasing
number of items. A valuable official account of the Manila Conference of
1954 is *The Signing of the Southeast Asia Collective Defense Treaty, the*

Protocol to the Southeast Asia Collective Defense Treaty and the Pacific Charter: Proceedings (Manila: Conference Secretariat, 1954), vi, 91 p. This source may be followed with *The Bangkok Conference of the Manila Pact Powers, February 23-25, 1955* [organizational conference], Department of State Publication 5909 (Washington: GPO, 1955), x, 45 p.; the "First Annual Report of the Council Representatives of the Southeast Asia Treaty Organization" (*The Department of State Bulletin*, vol. 34, no. 872, March 12, 1956, pp. 403-408); and the "Second Meeting of SEATO Council: Communiqué of March 8 [1956]" (same, vol. 34, no. 873, March 19, 1956, pp. 447-449). Official pamphlets, though without place and source of actual publication, are *SEATO: The Second Year*, including in 20 pages the second annual report of the Council Representatives and the final communiqué of the third session of the SEATO Council held March 11-13, 1957, and *SEATO: Record of Partnership, 1957-58*, including in 32 pages the first annual report of the Secretary-General and the final communiqué of the fourth session of the SEATO Council held March 11-13, 1958. Following these are two publications of the South-East Asia Treaty Organization, SEATO Headquarters, *SEATO Record of Progress, 1958-59* (Bangkok: Author, 1959), no pagination, and *SEATO: Record of Progress, 1959-1960* (Bangkok: Author, 1960), 36 p., giving the annual report of the Secretary-General and the final communiqué of the fifth and sixth regular meetings, respectively, of the SEATO Council, held April 8-10, 1959, and May 31-June 2, 1960. *Report on SEATO, 1960-61* (Bangkok: South-East Asia Treaty Organization, 1961), 20 p., contains the annual report of the Secretary-General, while the text of the communiqué of the SEATO Council at its seventh meeting held March 27-29, 1961, is published in *The Department of State Bulletin*, vol. 44, no. 1138, April 17, 1961, pp. 549-550. *SEATO Report, 1961-1962* (Bangkok: South-East Asia Treaty Organization, 1962), 19 p., is the report of the Secretary-General for the period mentioned.

SEATO headquarters also issues a number of pamphlets for general consumption focusing on the organization or on communism. Directed much more toward the specialist are South-East Asia Treaty Organization, SEATO Headquarters, *The South-East Asian Round Table: A Symposium on Traditional Cultures and Technological Progress in South-East Asia* (Bangkok: Author, 1958), viii, 152, xiii p.; *Collective Security: Shield of Freedom* (Bangkok: Author, 1959), iv, 125 p.; and *Seminar on Countering Communist Subversion* (Baguio, Philippines: 1957) (no place of publication), 101 p. *SEATO Record* is published every two months at the headquarters of the organization.

Valuable information from the American viewpoint on the origins and rationale of SEATO is found in *The Southeast Asia Collective Defense Treaty, Hearing before the Committee on Foreign Relations, United States Senate, Eighty-third Congress, Second Session, on Executive K, 83d Congress, 2d Session*, Part 1, November 11, 1954 (Washington: GPO, 1954), iii, 40 p., and *The Southeast Asia Collective Defense Treaty, Report of the Committee on Foreign Relations on Executive K, Eighty-third Congress, Second Session*, January 25, 1955, Senate, Executive Report No. 1, 84th Cong., 1st sess. (Washington: GPO, 1955), iii, 19 p. In addition, many of the publications already cited with reference to the evolution of SEATO contain statements by high-ranking U. S. officials, especially Secretary of State John Foster Dulles, on the Manila Treaty.

A number of analyses of SEATO have been made by authors in different journals. Among them are Ralph Braibanti in "The Southeast Asia Collective Defense Treaty" (*Pacific Affairs*, vol. 30, December 1957, pp. 321-341), W. Macmahon Ball in "A Political Re-Examination of SEATO" (*International Organization*, vol. 12, Winter 1958, pp. 17-25), Norman J. Padelford in "SEATO and Peace in Southeast Asia" (*Current History*, vol. 38, February 1960, pp. 95-101, 109), August C. Miller, Jr., in "SEATO— Segment of Collective Security" (United States Naval Institute *Proceedings*, vol. 86, February 1960, pp. 50-62), and J. A. Modelski in "The South-East Asia Treaty Organization" (*The Australian Journal of Politics and History*, vol. 5, May 1959, pp. 24-40) and in "Indo-China and SEATO" (*Australian Outlook*, vol. 13, March 1959, pp. 27-54). Hamilton Fish Armstrong in "Thoughts along the China Border: Will Neutrality Be Enough?" (*Foreign Affairs*, vol. 38, January 1960, pp. 238-260) makes a careful evaluation of SEATO. A Russian viewpoint is presented in M. Markov, "SEATO's Future and the NEATO Project" (*International Affairs* [Moscow], June 1962, pp. 56-62).

In any attempt to place the Manila Pact in the alliance context of U. S. foreign policy, the volume edited by Arnold Wolfers, *Alliance Policy in the Cold War* (Baltimore: Johns Hopkins Press, 1959), ix, 314 p., can be read with considerable profit. Stress is placed on the theoretical side in George Liska, *Nations in Alliance: The Limits of Interdependence* (Baltimore: Johns Hopkins Press, 1962), x, 301 p. Also worthy of mention is Ernst B. Haas' "Regionalism, Functionalism, and Universal International Organization" (*World Politics*, vol. 8, January 1956, pp. 238-263). The literature on regionalism and regional organizations, it should be noted, is extensive, a fact well revealed in the issues of *International Organization*. Lincoln P. Bloomfield's *The United Nations and U. S. Foreign Policy* (Boston: Little, Brown, 1960), xi, 276 p., is a very challenging "new look at the [U. S.] national interest," with significance for Southeast Asia. Having particular importance for the future is Joseph J. Sisco's "A New Look at the United Nations: Political Assessment of the Organization for the Decade of the Sixties" (*The Department of State Bulletin*, vol. 45, no. 1152, July 24, 1961, pp. 158-163).

In Australia more attention has been given to the Manila Treaty than in most of the other signatory countries. At the official level *Current Notes on International Affairs*, a publication of the Department of External Affairs, contains timely information on SEATO as well as on Australia's entire foreign policy. A similar publication of merit is *External Affairs Review* issued by New Zealand's Department of External Affairs. *Friends and Neighbors* (East Lansing: Michigan State College Press, 1955), vi, 181 p., by R. G. Casey, at the time Australian Minister for External Affairs, is a comprehensive presentation of "Australia's outlook on the world," including chapters on ANZUS, SEATO, and Dutch New Guinea.

The Australian National University at Canberra has had a SEATO Project involving research in the Department of International Relations. George [J. A.] Modelski, director of the project, has published a carefully written article, "Australia and SEATO" (*International Organization*, vol. 14, Summer 1960, pp. 429-437), and he is the editor of *SEATO: Six Studies* (Melbourne: F. W. Cheshire, 1962), xxxiii, 302 p. Gordon Greenwood and Norman Harper, editors, in *Australia in World Affairs, 1950-55* (Melbourne: F. W. Cheshire, 1957), vii, 366 p., Norman Harper and David Sissions in *Australia and the United Nations* (New York: Manhattan Publishing Co., 1959), xiii, 423 p., and Werner Levi in *Australia's Outlook on Asia* (East Lansing: Michigan State University Press, 1958), 246 p., have added to the information on Australia's foreign policy. Fred Alexander's "Australia in World Affairs" (*Australian Outlook*, vol. 10, March 1956, pp. 5-19) and Norman Harper's "Australia and Regional Pacts, 1950-57" (same, vol. 12, March 1958, pp. 3-22) have thrown more light on the subject. Dean E. McHenry and Richard N. Rosecrance have dealt well with a delicate topic in "The 'Exclusion' of the United Kingdom from the ANZUS Pact" (*International Organization*, vol. 12, Summer 1958, pp. 320-329) while Norman J. Padelford in "Collective Security in the Pacific: Nine Years of the ANZUS Pact" (United States Naval Institute *Proceedings*, vol. 86, September 1960, pp. 38-47) has made a thorough survey.

F. L. W. Wood has written authoritatively in "The ANZAC Dilemma" (*International Affairs* [Royal Institute of International Affairs], vol. 29, April 1953, pp. 184-192) and in "New Zealand and Southeast Asia" (*Far Eastern Survey*, vol. 25, February 1956, pp. 23-27). Gwendolen M. Carter in "New Zealand, Dependable Ally" (same, vol. 21, February 13, 1952, pp. 28-32), W. F. Monk in "New Zealand Faces North" (*Pacific Affairs*, vol. 26, September 1953, pp. 220-229), and L. K. Munro in "New Zealand and the New Pacific" (*Foreign Affairs*, vol. 31, July 1953, pp. 634-647) have added to the literature of the Dominion's postwar foreign policy. A timely and worthy study is C. Hartley Grattan's *The United States and the Southwest Pacific* (Harvard University Press, 1961), 273 p.

British official policy in Southeast Asia is reflected in the *Treaty Series* issued under the auspices of the Foreign Office, in *Parliamentary Debates*, in *Parliamentary Papers*, in *Commonwealth Survey, A Record of United Kingdom and Commonwealth Affairs*, sponsored by the Central Office of Information, London, and in items issued by the Regional Information Office for the United Kingdom in South-East Asia, Singapore. Eventual volumes of *British and Foreign State Papers* may throw more light on the policy of the United Kingdom toward the countries of Southeast Asia as they have achieved independence. *Keesing's Contemporary Archives* (London), an unofficial publication, is a valuable tool for following domestic and foreign developments in Great Britain as well as in the other countries of the world. Guy Wint's *The British in Asia*, rev. ed. (New York: Institute of Pacific Relations, 1954), 244 p., can be read with profit. The Royal Institute of International Affairs in *British Security* (London: Author, 1946), 176 p., and in *The Pattern of Pacific Security* (London: Author, 1946), 73 p., considered various defense problems. In its publication *Collective Defence in South East Asia*, previously cited, it devoted attention to security in the light of major postwar developments in the Far East. A. S. B. Olver had previously traced for a specific number of years the evolution of the policy of the United Kingdom in his *Outline of British Policy in East and Southeast Asia, 1945-May 1950* (London: Royal Institute of International Affairs, 1950), 83 p. Kenneth Younger in "A British View of the Far East" (*Pacific Affairs*, vol. 27, June 1954, pp. 99-111) has written a perceptive article on the subject. Also helpful is Saul Rose's *Britain and South-East Asia* (Baltimore: Johns Hopkins Press, 1962), 208 p., while Evan Luard's *Britain and China* (Baltimore: Johns Hopkins Press, 1962), 256 p., has a bearing on the region.

The declining French role in Southeast Asia is reflected in the publications. The *Journal Officiel de la République Francaise* and *La Documentation Francaise* (Secrétariat Général du Gouvernement), *Direction de la Documentation, Notes et Etudes Documentaires* are helpful. Roger Levy, Guy Lacam, and Andrew Roth have contributed to produce *French Interests and Policies in the Far East* (New York: Institute of Pacific Relations, 1941), xi, 209 p., and John F. Cady has written *The Roots of French Imperialism in Eastern Asia* (Ithaca: Cornell University Press, 1954), xii, 322 p. More timely is "Présence de la France en Asie" (*France-Asie*, vol. 13, no. 125-127, October-December 1956), 475 p. Extremely frank is an address entitled "France and Southeast Asia" by Achille Clarac, French ambassador to Thailand, published for the most part in the *Bangkok World*, April 20, 1961.

THE TWO CHINAS AND THE SINO-SOVIET BLOC

The literature on Communist China and its foreign policy is growing though still insufficient for the importance of the subject. The news releases of the New China News Agency (NCNA), the *Peking Review* which has replaced *China Digest* and *People's China*, and publications of the Foreign Languages Press present the official viewpoint of the People's Republic. The American Consulate General in Hong Kong in its *Survey of the China Mainland Press, Extracts from China Mainland Magazines,* and *Current Background* series is providing a wealth of material for the reader. Publications on Communist China of the Union Research Institute in Hong Kong as well as of the U. S. Joint Publications Research Service are helpful. The *News Times* (Moscow) and *Current Digest of the Soviet Press* contribute to an understanding of Moscow's outlook and policy.

A. Doak Barnett in his *Communist China and Asia: Challenge to American Policy* (New York: Harper, for the Council on Foreign Relations, 1960), xi, 575 p., has made an excellent analysis not only of the Peking regime but also of its policy in Asia. Other books of merit are written by Peter S. H. Tang, *Communist China Today: Domestic and Foreign Policies,* 2d ed. (Washington: Research Institute on the Sino-Soviet Bloc, 1961), xviii, 745 p.; Walt W. Rostow and others, *The Prospects for Communist China* (Cambridge: Technology Press of Massachusetts Institute of Technology, 1954), xx, 379 p.; Ygael Gluckstein, *Mao's China: Economic and*

BIBLIOGRAPHICAL NOTE

[451]

Political Survey (Boston: Beacon Press, 1957), 438 p.; Richard L. Walker, *China under Communism: The First Five Years* (New Haven: Yale University Press, 1955), xv, 403 p., and Chang-tu Hu and others, *China: Its People, Its Society, Its Culture* (New Haven: Human Relations Area Files Press, 1960), xviii, 611 p. An "appraisal" and an "analysis" of "The First Decade" of Communist China by a number of well-known authors are found in the first issue of *The China Quarterly* (January-March, 1960, pp. 3-71).

Of value on unconventional warfare in Southeast Asia are Mao Tsetung's *On the Protracted War*, pp. 157-243, and *Strategic Problems in the Anti-Japanese Guerrilla War*, pp. 119-156, of his *Selected Works, Volume Two, 1937-1938* (New York: International Publishers, 1954), 296 p. Some of the methods of operations against the Japanese that he describes are still timely. Given the conditions of 1961 and 1962, it is not surprising that in Western circles particular attention was devoted to the subject of guerrilla operations. Among the many publications may be cited Otto Heilbrunn, *Partisan Warfare* (New York: Praeger, 1962), 199 p.; Peter Paret and John W. Shy, *Guerrillas in the 1960's*, rev. ed. (New York: Praeger, 1962), 98 p.; and Franklin A. Lindsay, "Unconventional Warfare" (*Foreign Affairs*, vol. 40, January 1962, pp. 264-274). Y. Dolgopolov's "National-Liberation Wars in the Present Epoch" (*International Affairs* [Moscow], February 1962, pp. 17-21) is very revealing.

The militancy of Peking has been pointed out by Ralph L. Powell in "Everyone a Soldier: The Communist Chinese Militia" (*Foreign Affairs*, vol. 39, October 1960, pp. 100-111). Also helpful to the author has been "Background Information on the Communist Threat to South and Southeast Asia," an unclassified American document, including in its contents such topics as "General Appraisal," "Military Manpower Potential," "Military Forces," "Military Capabilities," and the "Bloc Politico/Subversive Offensive." Alice Langley Hsieh has written a skillful article, "Communist China and Nuclear Warfare" (*The China Quarterly*, no. 2, April-June 1960, pp. 1-15); her *Communist China's Strategy in the Nuclear Era* (Englewood Cliffs, New Jersey: Prentice-Hall, 1962) xx, 204 p., is very much worth reading.

The relationship of the Chinese Communists to the international Communist movement in Southeast Asia is analyzed in Shen-yu Dai's *Peking, Moscow, and the Communist Parties of Colonial Asia* (Cambridge: Center for International Studies, Massachusetts Institute of Technology, 1954), 167 p. Commendable is Richard Butwell's "Communist Liaison in Southeast Asia" (*United Asia*, vol. 6, June 1954, pp. 146-151). A broader perspective is found in Malcolm D. Kennedy's *A History of Communism in East Asia* (New York: Praeger, 1957), ix, 556 p.; while in contrast are two monographs by Ruth Thomas McVey, *The Development of the Indonesian Communist Party and Its Relations with the Soviet Union and the Chinese People's Republic* (Cambridge: Center for International Studies, Massachusetts Institute of Technology, 1954), 97 p., and *The Soviet View of the Indonesian Revolution: A Study in the Russian Attitude towards Asian Nationalism* (Ithaca: Southeast Asia Program, Cornell University, 1957), iii, 83 p. A reference for comparative purposes is *World Strength of the Communist Party Organizations* published annually under the auspices of the Bureau of Intelligence and Research, Department of State. Evron M. Kirkpatrick has edited *Target: The World; Communist Propaganda Activities in 1955* (New York: Macmillan, 1956), xxiv, 362 p., and *Year of Crisis: Communist Propaganda Activities in 1956* (New York: Macmillan, 1957), xix, 414 p., showing the many similarities in Communist propaganda themes. A recent perceptive analysis of the international Communist movement in Asia is Robert Scalapino's "Moscow, Peking and the Communist Parties of Asia" (*Foreign Affairs*, vol. 41, January 1963, pp. 323-343).

The Overseas Chinese in Southeast Asia have occupied the attentions of many authors. Victor Purcell in *The Chinese in Southeast Asia* (London: Oxford University Press, 1951), xxxvii, 801 p., has written a comprehensive book of value on the subject. Among American scholars G. William Skinner has distinguished himself in his *Chinese Society in Thailand: An Analytical History* (Ithaca: Cornell University Press, 1957), xvii, 459 p., and *Leadership and Power in the Chinese Community of Thailand* (Ithaca: Association for Asian Studies, Cornell University Press, 1958), xvii, 363 p. In *The Dragon's Seed, Peking and the Overseas Chinese* (New York: St. Martin's Press, 1959), 319 p., Robert S. Elegant has produced a journalistic but helpful book.

The economic activities of the Sino-Soviet bloc in the underdeveloped nations have been the subject of increased attention in publications. *The Sino-Soviet Economic Offensive in the Less Developed Countries*, Department of State Publication 6632 (Washington: GPO, May 1958), vi, 111 p., *The Communist Economic Threat*, Department of State Publication 6777 (Washington: GPO, March 1959), 22 p., *Communist Economic Policy in the Less Developed Areas*, Department of State Publication 7020 (Washington: GPO, July 1960), 38 p., and *The Threat of Soviet Economic Policy*, Department of State Publication 7234 (Washington: GPO, October 1961), 25 p., represent a series of well-written studies. Allen W. Dulles in "Some Implications of Soviet Economic Development" (*The Department of State Bulletin*, vol. 41, no. 1068, December 14, 1959, pp. 867-874) has made a realistic analysis. Henry G. Aubrey in his "Sino-Soviet Aid to South and Southeast Asia" (*World Politics*, vol. 12, October 1959, pp. 62-70) discusses the subject in terms of conclusions for U. S. policy. Joseph S. Berliner's *Soviet Economic Aid: The New Aid and Trade Policy in Underdeveloped Countries* (New York: Praeger, for the Council on Foreign Relations, 1958), xv, 232 p., gives thorough attention to the topic. Especially good for Communist China is A. Doak Barnett's *Communist Economic Strategy: The Rise of Mainland China* (Washington: National Planning Association, 1959), ix, 106 p. "Communist China's Economic Relations with Southeast Asia" (*Far Eastern Survey*, vol. 28, January 1959, pp. 1-11) by Shao Chuan Leng is a sound article. In the cultural field, a subject of interest to both Peking and Moscow, Frederick C. Barghoorn's *The Soviet Cultural Offensive* (Princeton University Press, 1960), vii, 353 p., should be mentioned.

The foreign policy of the People's Republic of China since its formal establishment in 1949 is the subject of varied interpretations. Harold C. Hinton has made an analysis with reference to two countries in his *China's Relations with Burma and Vietnam: A Brief Survey* (New York: Institute of Pacific Relations, 1958), viii, 64 p. R. G. Boyd, a Research Fellow at the Australian National University, is the author of a carefully written study, *Communist China's Foreign Policy* (New York: Praeger, 1962), 147 p. He previously published "Foreign Policy of Communist China" (*Australian Outlook*, vol. 13, September 1959, pp. 193-210) and "China's Relations with Japan" (same, vol. 14, April 1960, pp. 50-68). E. Stuart Kirby in "The Foreign Policy of Communist China" (*International Journal*, vol. 15, Winter 1959-1960, pp. 1-13) has covered a broad topic in an interpretative fashion. Dr. Otto E. Guthe, Central Intelligence Agency, in his speech (mimeographed) entitled "Asian Studies and Our National Security," delivered at the Asian Studies Conference at Indiana University, November 12, 1959, has given attention to Peking's foreign policy in Asia. Richard L. Walker's *The Continuing Struggle: Communist China and the Free World* (New York: Athens Press, 1958), 155 p., considers aspects of Peking's international relations. Richard Harris in his "China and the World" (*International Affairs* [Royal Institute of International Affairs], vol. 35, April 1959, pp. 161-169) has made some thoughtful generalizations about Communist China. Still valuable is H. Arthur Steiner's "Mainsprings of Chinese Communist Foreign Policy" (*American Journal of International Law*, vol. 44, January 1950, pp. 69-99). A. M. Halpern's "The Chinese Communist Line on Neutralism" (*The China Quarterly*, no. 5, January-March 1961, pp. 90-115) and "The Foreign Policy Uses of the Chinese Revolutionary Model" ·(same, no. 7, July-September 1961, pp. 1-16) are penetrating, as is Howard L. Boorman's "Peking in World Politics" (*Pacific Affairs*, vol. 34, September 1961, pp. 227-241).

Relations between Peking and Moscow are receiving considerable attention although definitive analysis is obviously not possible. Perhaps the best background book, though now dated, is Howard L. Boorman and others, *Moscow-Peking Axis: Strengths and Strains* (New York: Harper, for the Council on Foreign Relations, 1957), xxi, 227 p. More recent is G. F. Hudson, Richard Lowenthal, and Roderick MacFarquhar, *The Sino-Soviet Dispute* (New York: Praeger, 1961), ix, 227 p., a volume of documents well analyzed. Allen S. Whiting has made significant contributions on the topic; his "'Contradictions' in the Moscow-Peking Axis" (*The Journal of Politics*, vol. 20, February 1958, pp. 127-161) and "The Logic of Communist China's Policy: The First Decade" (*The Yale Review*, vol. 50, Fall 1960, pp. 1-17) were written against the background of his major specialization. Klaus Mehnert in "Soviet-Chinese Relations" (*International Affairs* [Royal Institute of International Affairs], vol. 35, October 1959, pp. 417-426), Thomas Perry Thornton in "Peking, Moscow, and the Underdeveloped Areas" (*World Politics*, vol. 13, July 1961, pp. 491-504), and G. F. Hudson in his "Mao, Marx, and Moscow" (*Foreign Affairs*, vol. 37, July 1959, pp. 561-572) and his "Russia and China: The Dilemmas of Power" (same, vol. 39, October 1960, pp. 1-10) have carefully considered the subject. Very helpful, though more for Europe than for Asia, is Zbigniew K. Brzezinski's

The Soviet Bloc: Unity and Conflict, rev. ed. (New York: Praeger, 1961), xxii, 543 p. Two other books of merit are Donald S. Zagoria, *The Sino-Soviet Conflict, 1956-1961* (Princeton: Princeton University Press, 1962), xii, 484 p., and Kurt London, editor, *Unity and Contradiction, Major Aspects of Sino-Soviet Relations* (New York: Praeger, 1962), xii, 464 p. Philip E. Mosely's *The Kremlin and World Politics: Studies in Soviet Policy and Action* (New York: Vintage Books, Random House, 1960), viii, 557 p., gives an excellent perspective on Moscow's foreign policy.

Works on the relations between the United States and China focus on both Nationalist and Communist China. In *The United States and the Far East*, 2d ed. (Englewood Cliffs, N. J.: Prentice-Hall, 1962), 188 p., A. Doak Barnett wrote the section on "The United States and Communist China," pp. 98-157, Allen S. Whiting and Robert A. Scalapino, on "The United States and Taiwan," pp. 158-182, and Robert A. Scalapino, on "The United States and Japan," pp. 11-73. American official policy is well expressed in *The Republic of China*, Department of State Publication 6844 (Washington: GPO, 1959), 63 p.; John Foster Dulles' "Our Policies toward Communism in China" (*The Department of State Bulletin*, vol. 37, no. 942, July 15, 1957, pp. 91-95); and *Department of State Press Release No. 459*, August 11, 1958, 8 p., which contains a memorandum the Department sent U. S. missions abroad on nonrecognition of the Peking regime. Among the various unofficial articles dealing with U. S. relations with the People's Republic are Ernest A. Gross, "Some Illusions of Our Asian Policy" (*Far Eastern Survey*, vol. 26, December 1957, pp. 177-183); Quincy Wright, "The Chinese Recognition Problem" (*American Journal of International Law*, vol. 49, July 1955, pp. 320-338); and Chester Bowles, "The 'China Problem' Reconsidered" (*Foreign Affairs*, vol. 38, April 1960, pp. 475-486). Joseph W. Ballantine's *Formosa, A Problem for United States Foreign Policy* (Washington: Brookings Institution, 1952), 218 p., and John K. Fairbank's *The United States and China*, new ed., rev. and enl. (Cambridge: Harvard University Press, 1958), xvii, 365 p., are valuable. Sheldon Appleton has contributed *The Eternal Triangle? Communist China, the United States, and the United Nations* (East Lansing: Michigan State University Press, 1961), xiv, 274 p.; and Robert P. Newman has written *Recognition of Communist China* (New York: Macmillan, 1961), ix, 318 p.

SOUTH ASIA AND JAPAN

Indian policy in Southeast Asia is not the subject of an extensive literature, but considerable information is available on the general foreign policy of New Delhi. (*Foreign Affairs Record*, put out by the Ministry of External Affairs, and *Indiagram*, issued by the Embassy of India in the United States, contain concise official data. The unofficial publication, *Asian Recorder* (New Delhi), is especially helpful for information on Indian developments. J. C. Kundra has analyzed India's relations with the "Western bloc" in his *Indian Foreign Policy, 1947-1954* (Groningen: J. B. Wolters, 1955), xi, 239 p., and Werner Levi has written on the Asian aspect in *Free*

India in Asia (Minneapolis: University of Minnesota Press, 1952), 161 p. Heinrich Bechtoldt's *Indien oder China* (Stuttgart: Deutsche Verlags-Anstalt, 1961), 332 p., presents some interesting viewpoints of a West German observer.

Specific studies dealing with Indian relations with different Southeast Asian countries are W. S. Desai's *India and Burma* (Bombay: Orient Longmans, 1954), 111 p., which is better for background than for current analysis, and N. Raghavan's *India and Malaya* (Bombay: Orient Longmans, 1954), 137 p., a comparable study. Vidya Prakash Dutt and Vishal Singh in their *Indian Policy and Attitudes towards Indo-China and S.E.A.T.O.* (New York: Institute of Pacific Relations, 1954), 38 p., have dealt with a topic of considerable interest. Nilkanth Vithal Sovani has contributed *Economic Relations of India with South-East Asia and the Far East* (Bombay: Oxford University Press, 1951), viii, 142 p. On the subject of minorities C. Kondapi has written *Indians Overseas, 1838-1949* (New Delhi: Indian Council of World Affairs, 1951), xi, 558 p., and Usha Mahajani, *The Role of Indian Minorities in Burma and Malaya* (Bombay: Vora, 1960), xxx, 344 p.

Defence and Security in the Indian Ocean Area (New York: Asia Publishing House, 1958), x, 208 p., is the product of a study group set up by the Indian Council of World Affairs. Southeast Asia is given considerable attention in the book and an Indian approach to security is presented. K. M. Panikkar makes some stimulating observations in "Regional Organization for the Indian Ocean Area" (*Pacific Affairs*, vol. 18, September 1945, pp. 246-251) and in his *Problems of Indian Defense* (New York: Asia Publishing House, 1960), 138 p. Also valuable is K. M. Panikkar and others, *Regionalism and Security* (Bombay: Oxford University Press, 1948), vi, 73 p.

The speeches of Prime Minister Jawaharlal Nehru constitute an excellent source for understanding Indian foreign policy, a particularly useful volume being his *Independence and After: A Collection of Speeches, 1946-1949* (New York: Day, 1950), 403 p. In "India's Foreign Policy Today: Reflections upon Its Sources" (*World Politics*, vol. 10, January 1958, pp. 256-273), Adda B. Bozeman has written a challenging article. Acharya J. B. Kripalani in his "For Principled Neutrality" (*Foreign Affairs*, vol. 38, October, 1959, pp. 46-60) skillfully analyzes an important concept.

Indian relations with Communist China, especially since the hostility arose over the long boundary, have produced a large number of publications. For instance, B. C. Tewari and Urmila Phadnis have compiled a long list in their "India-China Border Areas' Dispute: A Selected Bibliography" (*India Quarterly*, vol. 16, April-June 1960, pp. 155-169). Special note should be made of H. Arthur Steiner's "India Looks to Her Northern Frontiers" (*Far Eastern Survey*, vol. 28, November 1959, pp. 167-173), and of *United Asia*'s entire issue devoted to "Geo-Politics of the Himalayan Region" (vol. 12, no. 4, 1960, pp. 305-402). Rosemary Brissenden in "India and the Northern Frontiers" (*Australian Outlook*, vol. 14, April 1960, pp. 15-29) and Helga Haftendorn in "Die Spannungen zwischen Indien und der Volksrepublik China" (*Europa-Archiv*, vol. 15, March 20, 1960, pp. 203-212) have given good bibliographic references. Francis Robert Moraes in his *The Revolt in Tibet* (New York: Macmillan, 1960), 223 p., and S. C. S. in "Indian Reactions to the Crisis in Tibet" (*The World Today*, vol. 15, June 1959, pp. 236-246) have written an account of Tibetan developments and have considered Indian responses.

For Indian-American relations, a joint effort is Phillips Talbot and S. L. Poplai, *India and America: A Study of Their Relations* (New York: Harper, for the Council on Foreign Relations, 1958), xviii, 200 p. William Norman Brown in *The United States and India and Pakistan* (Cambridge: Harvard University Press, 1953), 308 p., and Chester Bowles in *Ambassador's Report* (New York: Harper, 1954), 415 p., have written penetrating books. Selig S. Harrison edited *India and the United States* (New York: Macmillan, 1961), xii, 244 p., a book arising from a conference held in 1959. Richard L. Park has contributed "Bases for Political Accord between India and America" (*The Indian Year Book of International Affairs*, 1957, pp. 437-449). In view of the U. S. assistance program to India three titles may be singled out for note: John Kenneth Galbraith, "Rival Economic Theories in India" (*Foreign Affairs*, vol. 36, July 1958, pp. 587-596); Wilfred Malenbaum, "India and China: Contrasts in Development Performance" (*The American Economic Review*, vol. 49, June 1959, pp. 284-309); and *Economic Development in India and Communist China* (U. S. Senate, Committee on Foreign Relations, Subcommittee on Technical Assistance Programs, Staff Study no. 6, 84th Cong., 2d sess., Washington, GPO, 1956), v, 51 p.

Many of the references on India's foreign policy include a consideration of its relations with Pakistan. Keith Callard's *Pakistan, A Political Study* (New York: Macmillan, 1957), 355 p., is a solid appraisal, while President Mohammed Ayub Khan in "Pakistan Perspective" (*Foreign Affairs*, vol. 38, July 1960, pp. 547-556) and in "Essentials of Pakistan's Foreign Policy" (*Pakistan Horizon*, vol. 14, fourth quarter, 1961, pp. 263-271) has contributed authoritative articles. Charles Burton Marshall in "Reflections on a Revolution in Pakistan" (*Foreign Affairs*, vol. 37, January 1959, pp. 247-256) deals with the general background leading to the *coup d'état* of General Ayub Khan. Mohammed Ahsan Chaudhri in "SEATO and Pakistan" (*Pakistan Horizon*, vol. 7, September 1954, pp. 138-149) has given a Pakistani viewpoint on the Manila Pact. "The Fundamentals of Pakistan's Foreign Policy" (same, vol. 9, March 1956, pp. 37-50) is the product of a "group study" published in the journal of the Pakistan Institute of International Affairs.

The role of postwar Japan in Southeast Asia is more often considered in literature on the general foreign policy of Tokyo than in studies specifically focused on the area. *Japan Report* issued by the Japanese Consulate General in New York is a primary source of merit on current developments. Edward Augustus Ackerman in *Japan's Natural Resources and Their Relation to Japan's Economic Future* (Chicago: University of Chicago Press, 1953), xxv, 655 p., has made a contribution of significance for an understanding of the country's economic future. Jerome B. Cohen in *Japan's Postwar Economy* (Bloomington: Indiana University Press, 1958),

BIBLIOGRAPHICAL NOTE

[457]

xvii, 262 p., and George C. Allen in *Japan's Economic Recovery* (New York: Oxford University Press, 1958), 215 p., have proved themselves authors of distinction. Hugh Borton and others in *Japan between East and West* (New York: Harper, for the Council on Foreign Relations, 1957), xxii, 327 p., have produced an important volume on Nippon's position in the world. Shigeru Yoshida's "Japan and the Crisis in Asia" (*Foreign Affairs*, vol. 29, January 1951, pp. 171-181), written before the San Francisco peace settlement, might well be compared with I. I. Morris' "Japanese Foreign Policy and Neutralism" (*International Affairs* [Royal Institute of International Affairs], vol. 36, January 1960, pp. 7-20). Robert E. Ward has thoughtfully looked into the future in *The Position of Japan in the Far East and in International Politics, 1965-1970* (Santa Barbara: General Electric Company, Technical Military Planning Operation, 1958), 27 p.

The relations of Japan with Communist China and the Soviet Union are the subject of considerable research and some publication. Rodger Swearingen and Paul Langer in their *Red Flag in Japan: International Communism in Action, 1919-1951* (Cambridge: Harvard University Press, 1952), xii, 276 p., have covered their subject well. James William Morley has contributed *Soviet and Communist Chinese Policies toward Japan, 1950-1957: A Comparison* (New York: Institute of Pacific Relations, 1958), 46 p., while Shao Chuan Leng has written *Japan and Communist China* (Kyoto: Doshisha University Press, 1958), 166 p. Kumaichi Yamamoto in his "Trade Problems with People's Republic of China" (*Contemporary Japan*, vol. 25, September 1958, pp. 363-398) and Akira Doi in "Two Years' Exchange with China" (*Japan Quarterly*, vol. 5, October-December 1958, pp. 435-451) have added more information. G. F. Hudson has made a good analysis in his "India, China and Japan: The Emerging Balance in Asia" (*Orbis*, vol. 1, Winter 1958, pp. 474-488). U. Alexis Johnson has compared the three in "The Emerging Nations of Asia" (*The Department of State Bulletin*, vol. 46, no. 1176, January 8, 1962, pp. 53-59).

U. S. relations with Japan have been analyzed by a number of competent authorities. Edwin O. Reischauer in *The United States and Japan*, rev. ed. (Cambridge: Harvard University Press, 1957), xxiv, 394 p., has written an outstanding book. A much broader study is his *Wanted: An Asian Policy* (New York: Alfred A. Knopf, 1955), xii, 276 p. *Japan's American Interlude* (Chicago: University of Chicago Press, 1960), vii, 257 p., by Kazuo Kawai is a penetrating examination and interpretation of the subject. Douglas H. Mendel, Jr., has carefully written "Japanese Attitudes toward American Military Bases" (*Far Eastern Survey*, vol. 28, September 1959, pp. 129-134) and "Japanese Security and United States Policy," a paper delivered at the 1960 meeting of the Association for Asian Studies. His *The Japanese People and Foreign Policy: A Study of Public Opinion in Post-Treaty Japan* (Berkeley: University of California Press, 1961), xv, 269 p., is commendable. Concerning the Treaty of Mutual Cooperation and Security, signed by the United States and Japan on January 19, 1960, profitable reading on relations between the two powers is found in "Prime Minister Kishi Visits Washington for Signing of Treaty of Mutual Cooperation and Security between the U. S. and Japan; Texts of Joint Communique, Remarks, and Treaty and Related Documents" (*The Department of State Bulletin*, vol. 42, no. 1076, February 8, 1960, pp. 179-201) and *Treaty of Mutual Co-operation and Security with Japan, Hearing before the Committee on Foreign Relations, United States Senate, Eighty-sixth Congress, Second Session, on Ex. E, 86th Congress, 2d Session*, June 7, 1960 (Washington: GPO, 1960), 101 p. Edwin O. Reischauer's "The Broken Dialogue with Japan" (*Foreign Affairs*, vol. 39, October 1960, pp. 11-26) is an analysis of Japanese-American relations at a critical time.

The period of Nipponese expansion in Southeast Asia has been well covered in whole or in part by F. C. Jones in *Japan's New Order in East Asia: Its Rise and Fall, 1937-45* (New York: Oxford University Press, 1954), xii, 498 p.; Willard H. Elsbree in *Japan's Role in Southeast Asian Nationalist Movements, 1940 to 1945* (Cambridge: Harvard University Press, 1953), 182 p.; and Harry J. Benda in *The Crescent and the Rising Sun; Indonesian Islam under the Japanese Occupation, 1942-1945* (The Hague: W. van Hoeve, 1958), xiv, 320 p. Toshikazu Kase in "Japan's New Role in East Asia" (*Foreign Affairs*, vol. 34, October 1955, pp. 40-49), A. Fujiyama in "Southeast Asia and Japanese Economic Policy" (*Contemporary Japan*, vol. 25, April 1958, pp. 180-184), Saburo Okita in "South and Southeast Asia and the Japanese Economy" (*Japan Quarterly*, vol. 1, October-December 1954, pp. 8-18), and Saburo Okita and others in "Problems of Economic Development in South-East Asia" [a number of articles] (*Asian Affairs*, vol. 1, March 1956, pp. 1-49) have all dealt with postwar aspects. Other issues of *Asian Affairs* were devoted to articles on "Japan's Reparations and Economic Cooperation" (vol. 1, September 1956, pp. 219-289), "Economic Development of Asia and Japan's Collaboration" (vol. 2, September 1957, pp. 221-325), and "Financing Economic Development of Asia" (vol. 2, December 1957, pp. 349-426). Yoichi Itagaki has contributed an excellent article in "Reparations and Southeast Asia" (*Japan Quarterly*, vol. 6, October-December 1959, pp. 410-419). Shigeo Horie has written "Economic Relations between India and Japan" (*India Quarterly*, vol. 15, January-March 1959, pp. 53-64), and the Pakistan Institute of International Affairs has published "Japan's Economic Role in Asia: A Group Study" (*Pakistan Horizon*, vol. 11, September 1958, pp. 184-192).

SOUTHEAST ASIA—GENERAL

The literature on Southeast Asia having a bearing on American foreign policy may be divided into material relating to the area as a whole and to a given country. *Governments and Politics of Southeast Asia* (Ithaca: Cornell University Press, 1959), xvii, 531 p., edited by George McTurnan Kahin, consists of well-written chapters by specialists on Thailand, Burma, Indonesia, Malaya and Singapore, Viet-Nam, and the Philippines. Professor Kahin has ably written on Indonesia in another volume he has edited, *Major Governments of Asia* (Ithaca: Cornell University Press, 1958), xiii, 607 p. Lucian W. Pye's section "The Politics of Southeast Asia," pp. 65-152, in Gabriel A. Almond and James S. Coleman, editors, *The Politics of the Developing Areas* (Princeton: Princeton University Press, 1960), xii, 591 p., is an analysis of comparative politics in Southeast Asia. Rupert Emerson's *From Empire to Nation; The Rise to Self-Assertion of Asian and African Peoples* (Cambridge: Harvard University Press, 1960), x, 466 p., is a thorough study of decolonization. In *Representative Government in Southeast Asia* (Cambridge: Harvard University Press, 1955), vii, 197 p., Emerson considered the problems involved, while in "The Erosion of Democracy" (*The Journal of Asian Studies*, vol. 20, November 1960, pp. 1-8) he contributes a more up-to-date analysis. H. J. van Mook in his *The Stakes of Democracy in Southeast Asia* (New York: Norton, 1950), 312 p., writes against the background of his experience as former Lieutenant Governor-General of Indonesia. *The New World of Southeast Asia* by Lennox A. Mills and Associates (Minneapolis: University of Minnesota Press, 1950), ix, 450 p., is helpful though somewhat out-of-date. More timely is Richard Butwell's *Southeast Asia Today—and Tomorrow* (New York: Praeger, 1961), x, 182 p.

The most detailed history of Southeast Asia (omitting the Philippines, however) is D. G. E. Hall's *A History of South-East Asia* (New York: St. Martin's Press, 1955), xvi, 807 p., but a more condensed account including the Philippines is Brian Harrison's *South-East Asia: A Short History* (New York: St. Martin's Press, 1954), 268 p. Professor Hall in "Looking at Southeast Asian History" (*The Journal of Asian Studies*, vol. 19, May 1960, pp. 243-253) has presented a short perspective of value. Francis Carnell in his "Southeast Asia and the Modern World" (*India Quarterly*, vol. 13, April-June 1957, pp. 101-120) has written a penetrating article. K. M. Panikkar's *Asia and Western Dominance: A Survey of the Vasco da Gama Epoch of Asian History, 1498-1945* (New York: Day, 1954), 530 p., is a good though controversial book. Robert Heine-Geldern in his *Conceptions of State and Kingship in Southeast Asia* (Ithaca: Southeast Asia Program, Cornell University, Data Paper no. 18, 1956), ii, 12 p., has contributed to an understanding of the precolonial environment.

A number of solid books and articles by geographers have appeared on the area. Among them may be mentioned E. H. G. Dobby's *Southeast Asia*, 7th ed. (London: University of London Press, 1960), 415 p., which is a regional geography; Karl J. Pelzer's *Pioneer Settlement in the Asiatic Tropics: Studies in Land Utilization and Agricultural Colonization in Southeastern Asia* (New York: American Geographical Society, 1945), xviii, 290 p., which is a distinguished technical work; Jan O. M. Broek's "Diversity and Unity in Southeast Asia" (*The Geographical Review*, vol. 34, April 1944, pp. 175-195) which is a well-written analysis; and the section on Southeast Asia with its maps in *The Pattern of Asia* (Englewood Cliffs N. J.: Prentice-Hall, 1958), 929 p., under the editorship of Norton S. Ginsburg.

Cora Du Bois has contributed a thoughtful study in *Social Forces in Southeast Asia*, 2d print. (Cambridge: Harvard University Press, 1959), 77p., while Kenneth P. Landon has added to the literature in *Southeast Asia: Crossroad of Religions* (Chicago: University of Chicago Press, 1949), ix, 215 p. Bruno Lasker has written *Human Bondage in Southeast Asia*

(Chapel Hill: University of North Carolina Press, 1950), 406 p.; Erich H. Jacoby has published *Agrarian Unrest in Southeast Asia*, 2d rev. ed. (London: Asia Publishing House), xi, 279 p.; and Virginia Thompson, *The Left Wing in Southeast Asia* (New York: Sloane, 1950), xiv, 298 p.

Warren S. Thompson's *Population and Progress in the Far East* (Chicago: University of Chicago Press, 1959), ix, 443 p., represents long examination of the population problem. Virginia Thompson and Richard Adloff have carefully written *Minority Problems in Southeast Asia* (Stanford: Stanford University Press, 1955), viii, 295 p., while Leslie H. Palmier has contributed "Changing Outposts: The Western Communities in Southeast Asia" (*The Yale Review*, vol. 47, Spring 1958, pp. 405-415). In broader terms Francis O. Wilcox in "World Population and Economic Development" (*The Department of State Bulletin*, vol. 42, no. 1092, May 30, 1960, pp. 860-867) has soundly dealt with a complex problem.

Eugene Staley has written with distinction in *The Future of Underdeveloped Countries: Political Implications of Economic Development*, rev. ed. (New York: Harper, For the Council on Foreign Relations, 1961), xx, 483 p., and Zbigniew Brzezinski in his "The Politics of Underdevelopment" (*World Politics*, vol. 9. October 1956, pp. 55-75) has made a penetrating analysis. In a specific field of interest John Kerry King's "Rice Politics" (*Foreign Affairs*, vol. 31, April 1953, pp. 453-460) is useful.

Russell H. Fifield in *The Diplomacy of Southeast Asia, 1945-1958*, previously cited, focused his efforts on a consideration of the comparative foreign policy of the states in the area. Amry Vandenbosch and Richard Butwell have contributed *Southeast Asia among the World Powers* (Lexington: University of Kentucky Press, 1958), vi, 360 p., and Claude A. Buss has written *Southeast Asia and the World Today* (Princeton: Van Nostrand, 1958), 189 p. Guy J. Pauker's "Southeast Asia as a Problem Area in the Next Decade" (*World Politics*, vol. 11, April 1959, pp. 325-345) is a discerning article. Still helpful is Harold R. Isaacs' *New Cycle in Asia; Selected Documents on Major International Developments in the Far East, 1943-1947* (New York: Macmillan, 1947), xiii, 212 p., especially for Indochina and Indonesia. The position of the military in Burma, Indonesia, and Thailand is included in John J. Johnson, editor, *The Role of the Military in Underdeveloped Countries* (Princeton University Press, 1962), viii, 427p.

Southeast Asia in the Coming World (Baltimore: Johns Hopkins Press, 1953), xii, 306 p., edited by Philip W. Thayer, is dated but solid. Worthy too are Tibor Mende's *South-East Asia between Two Worlds* (London: Turnstile, 1955), 338 p., and Maurice Zinkin's *Asia and the West*, rev. ed. (New York: Institute of Pacific Relations, 1953), xii, 304 p. Claude A. Buss includes Southeast Asia in *The Arc of Crisis* (Garden City, New York: Doubleday, 1961), 479 p., his arc extending from Japan to Indonesia to Pakistan.

Asian neutralism has been considered both in terms of definition and of substance. Although the words neutralism, nonalignment, neutralist, and neutrality have varied meanings in different countries of Southeast Asia, the basic effect whatever the terminology is generally the same. William

Henderson has thoroughly considered the matter in "The Roots of Neutralism in Southern Asia" (*International Journal*, vol. 13, Winter 1957-1958, pp. 30-40), and Robert A. Scalapino in " 'Neutralism' in Asia" (*The American Political Science Review*, vol. 48, March 1954, pp. 49-62), has made an incisive analysis. Hamilton Fish Armstrong has contributed "Neutrality: Varying Tunes" (*Foreign Affairs*, vol. 35, October 1956, pp. 57-71), while Peter Lyon has written "Neutrality and the Emergence of the Concept of Neutralism" (*The Review of Politics*, vol. 22, April 1960, pp. 255-268). "Le Neutralisme Afro-Asiatique" (*Chronique de Politique Etrangère*, vol. 13, March 1960, pp. 179-224) by L. Vandeweghe is comprehensive.

Regionalism in Southeast Asia like neutralism has also been studied by various authors. One of the best articles is William Henderson's "The Development of Regionalism in Southeast Asia" (*International Organization*, vol. 9, November 1955, pp. 463-476). Milton W. Meyer gave attention to the subject in "Regional Cooperation in Southeast Asia" (*Columbia Journal of International Affairs*, vol. 3, Spring 1949, pp. 68-77). R. G. Boyd has written "The Association of South East Asian States" (*Australian Outlook*, vol. 14, December 1960, pp. 246-256) focusing on the Federation of Malaya, the Philippines, and Thailand. Although the Bandung Conference in 1955 has been analyzed by many authors, George McTurnan Kahin's *The Asian-African Conference, Bandung, Indonesia, April 1955* (Ithaca: Cornell University Press, 1956), vii, 88 p., stands among the best accounts. Another version is E. Zhukov's "The Bandung Conference of African and Asian Countries and Its Historic Significance" (*International Affairs* [Moscow], May 1955, pp. 18-32). A significant article on commerce is "Regional Trade Cooperation" (*Economic Bulletin for Asia and the Far East*, vol. 12, June 1961, pp. 1-29). Official documentation on the Colombo Plan is increasing; the annual reports of the Consultative Committee (command papers, for instance, in Great Britain) and the communiqués at the end of its yearly meetings (often published, for example, in *The Department of State Bulletin*) are very useful. A good analysis is found in Antonin Basch, "The Colombo Plan; A Case of Regional Economic Cooperation" (*International Organization*, vol. 9, February 1955, pp. 1-18). *The Colombo Plan, and Other Essays* (New York: Royal Institute of International Affairs, 1956), 89 p., by Frederic Benham is commendable. Creighton L. Burns has written a more recent analysis in "The Colombo Plan" (*The Year Book of World Affairs, 1960*, pp. 176-206).

The work of the United Nations has regional aspects in Asia. The Economic Commission for Asia and the Far East publishes annually the *Economic Survey of Asia and the Far East* and more frequently the *Economic Bulletin for Asia and the Far East*, while its yearly reports to the Economic and Social Council are comprehensive. C. Hart Schaaf has written a sound evaluation of ECAFE in "The United Nations Economic Commission for Asia and the Far East" (*International Organization*, vol. 7, November 1953, pp. 463-481) and P. S. Lokanathan has contributed "ECAFE—The Economic Parliament of Asia" (*The Indian Year Book of International Affairs, 1953*, pp. 3-26). A more recent article is A. M. James' "The UN Economic Commission for Asia and the Far East" (*The Year Book of World Affairs*,

1959, pp. 161-187). Especially helpful for the Mekong development scheme is a mimeographed bibliography entitled "Mekong Project Documentation" (ECAFE, May 10, 1961), 11 p.

Bloc voting in the United Nations has been analyzed by a number of authors. Among them Geoffrey Goodwin has carefully prepared "The Expanding United Nations, I—Voting Patterns" (*International Affairs* [Royal Institute of International Affairs], vol. 36, April 1960, pp. 174-187). C. Hart Schaaf has contributed a scholarly article on another aspect of the United Nations, "The Role of Resident Representative of the UN Technical Assistance Board" (*International Organization*, vol. 14, Autumn 1960, pp. 548-562). T. A. Pyman has published "The Significance of the United Nations 'Presence' for International Security" (*Australian Outlook*, vol. 14, December 1960, pp. 229-245).

A number of people have considered Asian nationalism in their research. W. Macmahon Ball's *Nationalism and Communism in East Asia*, 2d ed., rev. (Carlton: Melbourne University Press, 1956), 220 p., is still good. Rupert Emerson's "Paradoxes of Asian Nationalism" (*The Far Eastern Quarterly*, vol. 13, February 1954, pp. 131-142) is very perceptive. *Asian Nationalism and the West* (New York: Macmillan, 1953), viii, 449 p., edited by William L. Holland, contains a number of thoughtful studies on developments in Indonesia, Viet-Nam, and Malaya, while *Nationalism and Progress in Free Asia* (Baltimore: Johns Hopkins Press, 1956), xvi, 894 p., edited by Philip W. Thayer, adds to the information. Robert Strausz-Hupé and Harry W. Hazard have edited a volume bearing on nationalism, *The Idea of Colonialism* (New York: Praeger, 1958), 496 p. M. N. Roy has written "Asian Nationalism" (*The Yale Review*, vol. 42, Fall 1952, pp. 96-102). Self-determination has been considered by Philip C. Jessup in "Self-Determination Today in Principle and in Practice" (*The Virginia Quarterly Review*, vol. 33, Spring 1957, pp. 174-188) and by Clyde Eagleton in "Excesses of Self-Determination" (*Foreign Affairs*, vol. 31, July 1953, pp. 592-604).

Socialism has been thoroughly analyzed by Saul Rose in his book *Socialism in Southern Asia* (New York: Oxford University Press, 1959), 278 p. David J. Saposs has published "The Split between Asian and Western Socialism" (*Foreign Affairs*, vol. 32, July 1954, pp. 588-594), and M. N. Roy has written "The State of Socialism in Asia: Rangoon and After" (*Pacific Affairs*, vol. 26, June 1953, pp. 135-139). Frank N. Trager has edited and contributed to *Marxism in Southeast Asia: A Study of Four Countries* (Stanford: Stanford University Press, 1959), 381 p., the countries being Burma, Thailand, Viet Nam and Indonesia. J. H. Brimmell's *Communism in South East Asia: A Political Analysis* (New York: Oxford University Press, 1959), ix, 415 p., is commendable. Valuable articles are Harry J. Benda's "Communism in Southeast Asia" (*The Yale Review*, vol. 45, Spring 1956, pp. 417-429), Milton Sacks' "The Strategy of Communism in Southeast Asia" (*Pacific Affairs*, vol. 23, September 1950, pp. 227-247), and Geoffrey Fairbairn's "Since the Calcutta Conference" (*Australian Outlook*, vol. 13, September 1959, pp. 223-244). Also worthy of mention is Ruth Thomas McVey's *The Calcutta Conference and the Southeast Asian Uprisings* (Ithaca: Southeast Asia Program, Cornell University, 1958), 28 p.

Protracted Conflict (New York: Harper, 1959), 203 p., by Robert Strausz-Hupé and others is a penetrating analysis.

THE PHILIPPINES

Despite the ties between the Philippines and the United States both during and after the colonial period American scholars have given only limited attention to the former period. Joseph Ralston Hayden's *The Philippines, A Study in National Development* (New York: Macmillan, 1942), xxvi, 984 p., is a thorough account of genuine value; Grayson L. Kirk's *Philippine Independence: Motives, Problems, and Prospects* (New York: Farrar and Rinehart, 1936), 278 p., is a sound analysis. *The Philippine Story* by David Bernstein (New York: Farrar, Straus, 1947), xii, 276 p., includes an account of the Philippines at the conclusion of the Second World War. George A. Malcolm in *The Commonwealth of the Philippines* (New York: Appleton-Century, 1936), xviii, 511 p., and *First Malayan Republic* (Boston: Christopher Publishing House, 1951), 460 p., has written well from a background of long government service in the islands, and Robert Aura Smith in his *Philippine Freedom, 1946-1958* (New York: Columbia University Press, 1958), vii, 375 p., has published a work of merit. *Magsaysay of the Philippines* (Manila: Alemars, 1958), 266 p., by Carlos Quirino is the best biography of the late President. Raul S. Manglapus in "The State of Philippine Democracy" (*Foreign Affairs*, vol. 38, July 1960, pp. 613-624) gives an up-to-date analysis of the topic. A. V. H. Hartendorp's *History of Industry and Trade of the Philippines* (Manila: America Chamber of Commerce of the Philippines, 1958), xx, 743 p., is a sound account focused on the years 1945-1953 but broader than just a consideration of industry and trade. Frank H. Golay's work *The Philippines: Public Policy and National Economic Development* (Ithaca: Cornell University Press, 1961), xviii, 455 p., is a thorough analysis with an excellent bibliographical essay at the end.

Alvin H. Scaff in *The Philippine Answer to Communism* (Stanford: Stanford University Press, 1955), 165 p.; Luis Taruc in *Born of the People* (New York: International Publishers, 1953), 286 p.; Jesus Vargas and Tarciano Rizal in *Communism in Decline: The Huk Campaign* (Bangkok: South-East Asia Treaty Organization, 1957), 31 p.; and Sheldon Appleton in "Communism and the Chinese in the Philippines" (*Pacific Affairs*, vol. 32, December 1959, pp. 376-391) have given valuable insights into the Communist problem in the Philippines. David Wurfel's "Philippine Agrarian Reform under Magsaysay" (*Far Eastern Survey*, vol. 27, January, February 1958, pp. 7-15 and 23-30) has bearing on the situation.

Specific studies on U. S. relations with the Philippines include Garel A. Grunder and William E. Livezey, *The Philippines and the United States* (Norman: University of Oklahoma Press, 1951), xi, 315 p.; Shirley Jenkins, *American Economic Policy toward the Philippines* (Stanford: Stanford University Press, 1954), viii, 181 p.; and Sung Yong Kim, *United States-Philippine Relations during the Magsaysay Administration* (unpublished dissertation, University of Michigan, 1959), v, 328 p. David Wurfel's "Foreign Aid and Social Reform in Political Development: A Philippine Case Study" (*The American Political Science Review*, vol. 53, June 1959, pp. 456-482) is a perceptive analysis. "President Eisenhower Visits the Far East: Report to the People, Joint Statement and Communiques, Major Addresses" (*The Department of State Bulletin*, vol. 43, no. 1100, July 25, 1960, pp. 123-139), especially the items on his visit to the Philippines, is worth reading. *Republic of the Philippines*, Department of State Publication 6940 (Washington: GPO, 1960), 19 p., contains in its general survey a consideration of United States-Philippine relations.

Official sources in Manila giving information on Philippine foreign policy are found in the *Official Gazette, Department of Foreign Affairs Review*, and *Department of Foreign Affairs, Treaty Series*. Roger M. Smith's "The Philippines and the Southeast Asia Treaty Organization" and Mary F. Somers' "The Record of the Philippines in the United Nations" in *Two Papers on Philippine Foreign Policy* (Ithaca: Southeast Asia Program, Cornell University, Data Paper no. 38, 1960), 79 p., are up-to-date and well-documented studies. Martin Meadows in "The Philippine Claim to North Borneo" (*Political Science Quarterly*, vol. 77, September 1962, pp. 321-335) has written an article utilizing Philippine sources. Harold C. Conklin's "The Philippine National Self Image," a paper read at the annual meeting of the Association for Asian Studies in March 1959, is very instructive.

INDONESIA

Indonesia has received more attention in the postwar literature on Southeast Asia than the Philippines. George McTurnan Kahin's *Nationalism and Revolution in Indonesia* (Ithaca: Cornell University Press, 1952), xii, 490 p., is a thorough study of the subject. Alastair M. Taylor in *Indonesian Independence and the United Nations* (Ithaca: Cornell University Press, 1960), xxix, 503 p., has written a scholarly account of merit. Soetan Sjahrir's *Out of Exile* (New York: Day, 1949), xxii, 265 p., is important for the observations of the leading Socialist intellectual of the country. Willard A. Hanna's *Bung Karno's Indonesia* (New York: American Universities Field Staff, 1960), vii, 231 p., is a collection of 25 reports written for the American Universities Field Staff. Louis Fischer has published *The Story of Indonesia* (New York: Harper, 1959), 324 p., and Dorothy Woodman, *The Republic of Indonesia* (London: Cresset Press, 1955), ix, 444 p. Leslie H. Palmier has painted a portrait in his article "Sukarno, The Nationalist" (*Pacific Affairs*, vol. 30, June 1957, pp. 101-119) while his book, *Indonesia and the Dutch* (London: Oxford University Press, 1962), xii, 194 p., is timely.

Bernard H. M. Vlekke has published a good study in *Nusantara: A History of Indonesia*, rev. ed. (The Hague: W. van Hoeve, 1959), viii, 479 p., and W. F. Wertheim another in *Indonesian Society in Transition*, 2d rev. ed. (The Hague: W. van Hoeve, 1959), xiv, 394 p. Robert Van Niel in his

The Emergence of the Modern Indonesian Elite (The Hague: W. van Hoeve, 1960), ix, 314 p., has focused on the period 1900 to 1927. Benjamin H. Higgins' Indonesia's Economic Stabilization and Development (New York: Institute of Pacific Relations, 1957), xxii, 179 p., is commendable, and G. C. Allen and Audrey G. Donnithhorne in their Western Enterprise in Indonesia and Malaya (New York: Macmillan, 1957), 321 p., have written a book of careful comparison. Stanvac in Indonesia (Washington: National Planning Association, 1957), x, 118 p., prepared by the Center for International Studies of the Massachusetts Institute of Technology is a solid case study. Mention should also be made of James W. Gould's Americans in Sumatra (The Hague: Martinus Nijhoff, 1961), 185 p. Irene Tinker and Millidge Walker for their part have contributed "Indonesia's Panacea: 1959 Model" (Far Eastern Survey, vol. 28, December 1959, pp. 177-182).

Donald Hindley's "Communist Party Strategy in Indonesia, 1948-1959" (Australian Outlook, vol. 13, December 1959, pp. 253-271) is a well-written survey, as are Justus M. van der Kroef's "Communist Policy and Tactics in Indonesia" (The Australian Journal of Politics and History, vol. 5, November 1959, pp. 163-179) and Arnold C. Brackman's Indonesian Communism: A History (New York: Praeger, 1963), xvi, 336 p. Excellent is Guy J. Pauker's "The Soviet Challenge in Indonesia" (Foreign Affairs, vol. 40, July 1962, pp. 612-626). "Indonesia: Developments during the Past Two Years" (Current Notes on International Affairs, vol. 30, June 1959, pp. 293-313) is a comprehensive article covering a crucial period including the failure of the PRRI in Sumatra and Sulawesi. Vishal Singh has published "The Revolt in Indonesia in Retrospect" (Foreign Affairs Reports, vol. 8, January 1959, pp. 1-11). Benjamin and Jean Higgins in "Indonesia: Now or Never" (Foreign Affairs, vol. 37, October 1958, pp. 156-165) analyzed the Indonesian situation in the wake of the failure of the PRRI. Two excellent articles by Mohammad Hatta on Djakarta's foreign policy have appeared. "Indonesia between the Power Blocs" (same, vol. 36, April 1958, pp. 480-490) and "Indonesia's Foreign Policy" (same, vol. 31, April 1953, pp. 441-452). C. D. Cowan has written "Indonesia and the Commonwealth in South-East Asia: A Reappraisal" (International Affairs [Royal Institute of International Affairs], vol. 34, October 1958, pp. 454-468).

The West New Guinea controversy has been considered by many authors with various degrees of objectivity. One of the best studies is by Robert C. Bone, The Dynamics of the Western New Guinea (Irian Barat) Problem (Ithaca: Southeast Asia Program, Cornell University, 1958), x, 170 p. Justus M. van der Kroef has published The West New Guinea Dispute (New York: Institute of Pacific Relations, 1958), 43 p., while Charles A. Fisher's "West New Guinea in Its Regional Setting" (The Year Book of World Affairs, 1952 pp. 189-210) is comprehensive. The viewpoints of the Indonesian, Dutch, and Australian governments are well shown in the Official Records of the United Nations General Assembly when the controversy has come up for discussion, as well as in various items produced by The Netherlands Information Service and by the Indonesian government through its ministries at home and missions abroad. In terms of solution the text of the U. S.-supported Bunker Proposals is found in Press

[466]

Inquiries, Permanent Mission of the Netherlands to the United Nations, May 28, 1962, and of the subsequent Dutch-Indonesian agreement, signed August 15, 1962, in *United Nations Review*, vol. 9, September 1962, pp. 39-43. *Australia and the United Nations* by Norman Harper and David Sissons, previously cited, and *Friends and Neighbors* by R. G. Casey, also cited, contain insights relative to Australian policy in both western and eastern New Guinea. J. R. Kerr has written a careful article in "The Political Future of New Guinea" (*Australian Outlook*, vol. 13, September 1959, pp. 181-192). A. J. Rose's "Strategic Geography and the Northern Approaches" (same, vol. 13, December 1959, pp. 304-314) should be read with Peter Hastings' "New Guinea—East and West" (same, vol. 14, August 1960, pp. 147-156).

MALAYA

The Federation of Malaya and Singapore have received considerable attention in literature. Norton Ginsburg and Chester F. Roberts, Jr., have written *Malaya* (Seattle: University of Washington Press, 1958), xii, 533 p., a comprehensive and reliable book on the area. Charles Robequain in his *Malaya, Indonesia, Borneo, and the Philippines: A Geographical, Economic, and Political Description of Malaya, the East Indies, and the Philippines*, 2d ed. (New York: Longmans, 1959), xi, 466 p., has handled the subject well. Lennox A. Mills has made a good analysis in his *Malaya: A Political and Economic Appraisal* (Minneapolis: University of Minnesota Press, 1958), xi, 234 p. Also helpful is the volume by the International Bank for Reconstruction and Development, *The Economic Development of Malaya* (Baltimore: Johns Hopkins Press, 1955), xix, 707 p., the report of a mission sent to the area at the request of the London, Kuala Lumpur, and Singapore governments. T. H. Silcock's *The Commonwealth Economy in Southeast Asia* (Durham: Duke University Press, 1959), xvii, 259 p., focuses not only on the Federation and Singapore but also on North Borneo, Sarawak, and Brunei. Here it might be added that the Human Relations Area Files volume *North Borneo, Brunei, Sarawak (British Borneo)* (New Haven: Human Relations Area Files Press, 1956), xi, 287 p., contains good data.

Communism in Malaya has been the topic of a number of important studies. Lucian W. Pye has made a thorough analysis in *Guerrilla Communism in Malaya: Its Social and Political Meaning* (Princeton University Press, 1956), 369 p. Other works dealing with communism are Vernon Bartlett's *Report from Malaya* (New York: Criterion Books, 1955), 128 p.; Harry Miller's *The Communist Menace in Malaya* (London: Harrap, 1954), 248 p.; and John Bradstreet Perry Robinson's *Transformation in Malaya* (London: Secker and Warburg, 1956), 232 p.

Maurice Freedman has contributed a commendable article in "The Growth of a Plural Society in Malaya" (*Pacific Affairs*, vol. 33, June 1960, pp. 158-168). Victor Purcell's *The Chinese in Malaya* (New York: Oxford University Press, 1948), xvi, 327 p., is a sound study. Sir Donald MacGilliway has published "Malaya—The New Nation" (*International Affairs* [Royal Institute of International Affairs], vol. 34, April 1958, pp. 157-163),

BIBLIOGRAPHICAL NOTE

[467]

and J. Norman Parmer has skillfully written "Malaya's First Year of Independence" (*Far Eastern Survey*, vol. 27, November 1958, pp. 161-168). "The Malayan Elections of 1959" (*Pacific Affairs*, vol. 33, March 1960, pp. 38-47) by T. E. Smith is a solid study, while "Elections in Malaya" (*Current Notes on International Affairs*, vol. 30, September 1959, pp. 475-481) is worth reading. "Working Out Singapore's New Constitution" (*The World Today*, vol. 14, September 1958, pp. 406-414) by G. G. T. represents a thoughtful contribution. T. H. Silcock in his "Singapore in Malaya" (*Far Eastern Survey*, vol. 29, March 1960, pp. 33-39) has discussed the problems of the island area and its relationships with the Federation. A more recent article is William P. Maddox' "Singapore: Problem Child" (*Foreign Affairs*, vol. 40, April 1962, pp. 479-488). Looking toward the future, T. E. Smith has contributed "Proposals for Malaysia" (*The World Today*, vol. 18, May 1962, pp. 192-200).

VIET-NAM, CAMBODIA, AND LAOS

Viet-Nam has been the subject of considerable literature, especially in the postwar period. Virginia Thompson's *French Indo-China* (New York: Macmillan, 1937), 516 p., and Thomas E. Ennis' *French Policy and Developments in Indochina* (Chicago: University of Chicago Press, 1936), ix, 230 p., can still be read with profit. *The Emancipation of French Indo-China* (London: Oxford University Press, for the Royal Institute of International Affairs, 1961), xii, 445 p., by Donald Lancaster; *The Struggle for Indochina* (Stanford: Stanford University Press, 1954), xvii, 342 p., by Ellen Hammer; *Conflict in Indo-China and International Repercussions: A Documentary History, 1945-1955* (Ithaca: Cornell University Press, 1956), xxix, 265 p., edited by Allan B. Cole; and *Communist Revolutionary Warfare: The Vietminh in Indochina* (New York: Praeger, 1961), 175 p., by George K. Tanham all contribute to a better comprehension of the war in the area. Bernard B. Fall's *Street without Joy: Indochina at War, 1946-54* (Harrisburg, Pa.: Stackpole, 1961), 322 p., and "Post Mortems on Dien-Bien-Phu: Review Article" (*Far Eastern Survey*, vol. 27, October 1958, pp. 155-158) are worth reading. Joseph Buttinger's *The Smaller Dragon: A Political History of Vietnam* (New York: Praeger, 1958), 535 p., is a good general history, while Le Thanh Khoi's *Le Viêt-Nam, Histoire et Civilisation* (Paris: Éditions de Minuit, 1955), 558 p., is valuable though impaired by a Marxist orientation. Noteworthy is Philippe Devillers' *Histoire du Viêt-Nam de 1940 à 1952* (Paris: Éditions du Seuil, 1952), 471 p. Brian Crozier in "The International Situation in Indochina" (*Pacific Affairs*, vol. 29, December 1956, pp. 309-323) has described a complex situation existing at the time. Especially helpful in following many international developments in Indochina after the Geneva Conference of 1954 are the reports of the International Commission for Supervision and Control in Viet-Nam. Similar reports, when issued, are good as regards the International Commissions for Supervision and Control in Cambodia and Laos.

The Republic of Viet-Nam under President Ngo Dinh Diem has been thoroughly scrutinized by a number of authors. Wesley R. Fishel's "Free Vietnam since Geneva: Factors in the Rollback of Communism without War" (*The Yale Review*, vol. 49, Fall 1959, pp. 68-79) and "Vietnam's Democratic One-Man Rule" (*The New Leader*, vol. 42, November 2, 1959, pp. 10-13) are written from personal observation. J. A. C. Grant has contributed "The Viet Nam Constitution of 1956" (*The American Political Science Review*, vol. 52, June 1958, pp. 437-462). Other articles of note on South Viet-Nam include Bernard B. Fall's "South Viet-Nam's Internal Problems" (*Pacific Affairs*, vol. 31, September 1958, pp. 241-260), Roy Jumper's "Sects and Communism in South Vietnam" (*Orbis*, vol. 3, Spring 1959, pp. 85-96), and P. J. Honey's "Progress in the Republic of Vietnam" (*The World Today*, vol. 15, February 1959, pp. 68-78) and "The Problem of Democracy in Vietnam" (same, vol. 16, February 1960, pp. 71-79). Richard Wadsworth Lindholm has edited *Viet-Nam: The First Five Years; An International Symposium* (East Lansing: Michigan State University Press, 1959), xi, 365 p., and Wesley R. Fishel, *Problems of Freedom: South Vietnam since Independence* (New York: Free Press, 1961), xiv, 233 p. Timely is *A Threat to the Peace: North Viet-Nam's Effort to Conquer South Viet-Nam*, Department of State Publication 7308 (Washington: GPO, December 1961), Part I, vi, 53 p., and Part II, iii, 102 p.

The relations of the United States with the Republic of Viet-Nam have received publicity especially when attention is directed to the aid extended by the United States. *A Symposium on America's Stake in Vietnam* (New York: American Friends of Vietnam, 1956), 110 p., gives helpful insights. It includes a contribution on the topic by Senator John F. Kennedy. A comprehensive article by Leland Barrows, former director of USOM in Saigon, is "United States-Vietnamese Cooperation: The ICA Program since 1955" (*The Department of State Bulletin*, vol. 40, no. 1037, May 11, 1959, pp. 674-681). The published hearings and related data on Viet-Nam under the auspices of the Subcommittee on State Department Organization and Public Affairs, Senate Committee on Foreign Relations, are extensive.

The Democratic Republic of Viet-Nam has long been considered in the writings of Bernard B. Fall. His *The Viet-Minh Regime: Government and Administration in the Democratic Republic of Vietnam*, rev. ed. (New York: Institute of Pacific Relations, 1956), xi, 196 p., is expanded in his *Le Viet Minh, 1945-1960* (Paris: Librairie Armand Colin, 1960), xii, 377 p. Timely are his articles "North Viet-Nam's New Draft Constitution" (*Pacific Affairs*, vol. 32, June 1959, pp. 178-186) and "North Viet-Nam's Constitution and Government" (same, vol. 33, September 1960, pp. 282-290); also worth reading is Fall's "Crisis in North Viet-Nam" (*Far Eastern Survey*, vol. 26, January 1957, pp. 12-15). Theodore Shabad has contributed "Economic Developments in North Vietnam" (*Pacific Affairs*, vol. 31, March 1958, pp. 36-53). Prime Minister Pham Van Dong for his part has written "The Foreign Policy of the Democratic Republic of Viet-Nam" (*International Affairs* [Moscow], July 1958, pp. 19-22) and Bui Cong Trung, "The Democratic Republic of Viet-Nam on the Road to Socialism" (same, April 1959, pp. 53-58). A. Karpikhin's "The U.S.A. Sabotages the Geneva Agreements on Indochina" (same, August 1959, pp. 57-62)

BIBLIOGRAPHICAL NOTE

[469]

gives the Soviet interpretation. Very valuable is P. J. Honey's edited "North Vietnam" (*The China Quarterly*, no. 9, January-March 1962, pp. 2-111). Also revealing is General Vo Nguyen Giap, *People's War, People's Army* (New York: Praeger, 1962), xv, 217 p. *Viet Nam Information Bulletin*, News Service, Rangoon (Democratic Republic of Viet Nam) and *News from Viet-Nam*, Embassy of the Republic of Viet-Nam, Washington, D. C., present official contrasting viewpoints.

Modern Cambodia is beginning to receive more attention in the literature of Southeast Asia. David J. Steinberg and others in *Cambodia: Its People, Its Society, Its Culture*, revised for 1959 by Herbert H. Vreeland (New Haven: Human Relations Area Files Press, 1959), xiv, 351 p., have prepared a comprehensive handbook. "Présence du Cambodge" (*France-Asie*, vol. 11, no. 114-115, November-December 1955, 559 p.), gives a broad perspective of the Khmer kingdom. Martin F. Herz has written *A Short History of Cambodia from the Days of Angkor to the Present* (New York: Praeger, 1958), 141 p. *Réalités Cambodgiennes* is a Cambodian weekly paper in French that contains items often helpful in an understanding of the contemporary scene.

Prince Norodom Sihanouk has published an authoritative article in "Cambodia Neutral: The Dictate of Necessity" (*Foreign Affairs*, vol. 36, July 1958, pp. 582-586). V. M. Reddy's "A Study of Cambodia's Neutralism" (*International Studies*, vol. 2, October 1960, pp. 190-205) is commendable, as is Zoltan M. Szaz' "Cambodia's Foreign Policy" (*Far Eastern Survey*, vol. 24, October 1955, pp. 151-158). Roger M. Smith's "Cambodia Neutral: Dictate of Necessity" (unpublished draft seminar paper), 42 p., explains well Sihanouk's outlook. Malcolm MacDonald in *Angkor* (London: Jonathan Cape, 1958), 158 p., has expressed ideas of significance for the present. André Holleaux for his part has contributed "Le Gouvernement du Cambodge Contemporain" (*Politique Etrangère*, vol. 23, no. 4, 1958, pp. 414-426). Michael Leifer has carefully written "Cambodia and SEATO" (*International Journal*, vol. 17, Spring 1962, pp. 122-132), "Cambodia and Her Neighbors" (*Pacific Affairs*, vol. 34, Winter 1961-62, pp. 361-374), and *Cambodia and Neutrality*, Working Paper no. 1 (Canberra: Department of International Relations, Australian National University, 1962), 51 p. An excellent expression of the American attitude toward the Khmer kingdom is found in "U. S. Policy toward Cambodia" (Secretary Dulles to Foreign Minister Nong Kimny) (*The Department of State Bulletin*, vol. 34, no. 879, April 30, 1956, pp. 727-728).

Literature on the Kingdom of Laos, long a storm center in Southeast Asia, is still limited. *Laos: Its People, Its Society, Its Culture* (New Haven: Human Relations Area Files Press, 1960), xviii, 295 p., edited by Frank M. Le Bar and Adrienne Suddard, is a comprehensive account, while "Présence du Royaume Lao" (*France-Asia*, vol. 12, no. 118-120, March-May 1956, 1153 p.) adds to the general perspective. Joel M. Halpern has contributed *Aspects of Village Life and Culture Change in Laos* (New York: Council on Economic and Cultural Affairs, 1958), iii, 143 p., and "The Lao Elite: A Study of Tradition and Innovation" (a research memorandum working paper of the Rand Corporation dated November 15, 1960), v, 89 p.

Bernard B. Fall for his part has published a comprehensive article in "The International Relations of Laos" (*Pacific Affairs*, vol. 30, March 1957, pp. 22-34). Robert Gilkey has written "Laos: Politics, Elections and Foreign Aid" (*Far Eastern Survey*, vol. 27, June 1958, pp. 89-94) and E. H. S. Simmond's "A Cycle of Political Events in Laos" (*The World Today*, vol. 17, February 1961, pp. 58-68; Anne M. Jonas and George K. Tanham have contributed "Laos: A Phase in Cyclic Regional Revolution" (*Orbis*, vol. 5, Spring 1961, pp. 64-73).

The Situation in Laos, a publication of the U. S. Department of State in September 1959, iv, 23 p., focuses on the Communist movement in the kingdom and its international ramifications. *Report of the Security Council Sub-Committee under Resolutions of 7 September 1959*, S/4236, 5 November 1959, is a United Nations document giving the report of a subcommittee established to cope with the crisis in Laos that developed in the summer of 1959. Leo Gross in "The Question of Laos and the Double Veto in the Security Council" (*American Journal of International Law*, vol. 54, January 1960, pp. 118-131) and Marion K. Kellogg in "The Laos Question: Double What Veto?" (*Virginia Law Review*, vol. 45, December 1959, pp. 1352-1360) have dealt with the voting problem in the Security Council. Edwin F. Stanton has written "A 'Presence' in Laos" (*Current History*, vol. 38, June 1960, pp. 337-341). A significant statement on U. S. policy toward Laos a day after the start of the Geneva Conference in 1961 is found in Dean Rusk's "United States Outlines Program to Insure Genuine Neutrality for Laos" (*The Department of State Bulletin*, vol. 44, no. 1145, June 5, 1961, pp. 844-848). The "Declaration on the Neutrality of Laos," including a neutrality statement by the Royal Government made on July 9, 1962, and the "Protocol to the Declaration on the Neutrality of Laos," approved by the members of the Geneva Conference, July 23, 1962, are found in same, vol. 47, no. 1207, August 13, 1962, pp. 259-263. Congressional documentation on American aid to the Mekong kingdom has been forthcoming. Hearings, for instance, before a subcommittee of the Committee on Foreign Affairs, House of Representatives, and before another of the Committee on Government Operations, House of Representatives, have been published. A recent volume of interest written by a Laotian who has been active in the diplomacy of his country is Sisouk Na Champassak, *Storm over Laos, a Contemporary History* (New York: Praeger, 1961), x, 202 p.

THAILAND AND BURMA

The domestic and foreign policies of Thailand have not been the subject of an extensive literature. Wendell Blanchard and others have produced *Thailand: Its People, Its Society, Its Culture* (New Haven: Human Relations Area Files Press, 1958), xii, 525 p., a comprehensive survey of the country. Ruth Benedict previously wrote a valuable monograph in *Thai Culture and Behavior* (Ithaca: Southeast Asia Program, Cornell University, Data Paper no. 4, 1952), iii, 45 p. Virginia Thompson's *Thailand: The*

New Siam (New York: Macmillan, 1941), xxxii, 865 p., though dated, is still useful. Kenneth P. Landon's *Siam in Transition* (Shanghai: Kelly and Walsh, 1939), ix, 328 p., focuses on the *coup d'état* of 1932 and subsequent changes. Very perceptive is David A. Wilson's *Politics in Thailand* (Ithaca: Cornell University Press, 1962), xv, 307 p. Walter Francis Vella has rendered a good study in *The Impact of the West on Government in Thailand* (Berkeley: University of California Press, 1955), 93 p. Well presented is International Bank for Reconstruction and Development, *A Public Development Program for Thailand* (Baltimore: Johns Hopkins Press, 1959), xv, 301 p.

David A. Wilson and Herbert P. Phillips have written "Elections and Parties in Thailand" (*Far Eastern Survey*, vol. 27, August 1958, pp. 113-119) and Frank C. Darling has contributed "Marshal Sarit and Absolutist Rule in Thailand" (*Pacific Affairs*, vol. 33, December 1960, pp. 347-360), and he is critical of Washington in his "American Policy in Thailand" (*The Western Political Quarterly*, vol. 15, March 1962, pp. 93-110). "Political Changes in Thailand" (*External Affairs*, vol. 11, March 1959, pp. 53-56) is brief but helpful. Edwin F. Stanton, former U. S. Ambassador in Bangkok, has written two articles that should be singled out for particular mention: "Spotlight on Thailand" (*Foreign Affairs*, vol. 33, October 1954, pp. 72-85) and "Communist Pressures in Thailand" (*Current History*, vol. 38, February 1960, pp. 102-109).

Thailand, Department of State Publication 6296 (Washington: GPO, 1956), 15 p., is a general account but includes some data on U. S.-Thai relations. The latter is considered in more detail in U. Alexis Johnson's "Thai-United States Cooperation" (*The Department of State Bulletin*, vol. 42, no. 1095, June 20, 1960, pp. 1001-1006). Another helpful source is a statement in Bangkok by Ambassador Johnson "U. S. Rice Policy in Asia" (same, vol. 42, no. 1080, March 7, 1960, pp. 363-364). Attention should also be directed to "Vice President Johnson Visits Six Countries in South and Southeast Asia: Texts of Joint Communiques" (same, vol. 44, no. 1147, June 19, 1961, pp. 956-961), especially for the Thai-U. S. communiqué of May 18, as well as the Vietnamese-U. S. one of May 13. A subsequent highly important joint statement of Secretary Rusk and Foreign Minister Thanat Khoman, March 6, 1962, on U. S. obligations to Thailand is found in *Department of State Press Release No. 145* of the same date. A *White House Press Release*, May 15, 1962, contains a statement of the President on stationing U. S. forces in Thailand.

Literature on modern Burma is more extensive than for some other Asian countries. Hugh Tinker's *The Union of Burma: A Study of the First Years of Independence*, 3rd ed. (London: Oxford University Press, 1961), xiv, 424 p., is comprehensive and thorough, while Lucian W. Pye's *Politics, Personality, and Nation Building: Burma's Search for Identity* (New Haven: Yale University Press, 1962), xx, 307 p., is stimulating in its methodology. *Modern Burma: A Survey of Political and Economic Development* (Berkeley: University of California Press, 1942), ix, 381 p., by John L. Christian, though dated, is commendable. J. S. Furnivall's three books, *Colonial Policy and Practice: A Comparative Study of Burma and Nether-*

lands India (New York: New York University Press, 1956), xii, 568 p., *An Introduction to the Political Economy of Burma*, 3d ed. (Rangoon: People's Literature Committee and House, 1957), xxix, 255 p., and *The Governance of Modern Burma*, rev. ed. (New York: Institute of Pacific Relations, 1960), 165 p., are penetrating studies. John F. Cady has contributed *A History of Modern Burma* (Ithaca: Cornell University Press, 1958), xiii, 682 p. "Perspective of Burma," supplement (*The Atlantic Monthly*, vol. 201, February 1958, pp. 98-170) contains a number of good articles, including one by James Barrington, "The Concept of Neutralism: What Lies behind Burma's Foreign Policy," pp. 126-128.

In domestic politics Josef Silverstein has written "Politics, Parties and National Elections in Burma" (*Far Eastern Survey*, vol. 25, December 1956, pp. 177-184), "Politics in the Shan State: The Question of Secession from the Union of Burma" (*The Journal of Asian Studies*, vol. 18, November 1958, pp. 43-57), and "The Federal Dilemma in Burma" (*Far Eastern Survey*, vol. 28, July 1959, pp. 97-105). John H. Badgley has produced "Burma's Political Crisis" (*Pacific Affairs*, vol. 31, December 1958, pp. 336-351), and Frank N. Trager has written "Political Divorce in Burma" (*Foreign Affairs*, vol. 37, January 1959, pp. 317-327) and "The Political Split in Burma" (*Far Eastern Survey*, vol. 27, October 1958, pp. 145-155). Maung Maung contributed "Burma at the Crossroads" (*India Quarterly*, vol. 14, October-December 1958, pp. 380-388). Richard Butwell's "The New Political Outlook in Burma" (*Far Eastern Survey*, vol. 29, February 1960, pp. 21-27) should be read along with John F. Cady's "Burma's Military Regime" (*Current History*, vol. 38, February 1960, pp. 75-81). Richard Butwell and Fred von der Mehden have written together "The 1960 Election in Burma" (*Pacific Affairs*, vol. 33, June 1960, pp. 144-157). Hugh Tinker's "Nu, The Serene Statesman" (same, vol. 30, June 1957, pp. 120-137) is a good biographical article.

Maung Maung in *Burma in the Family of Nations*, 2d ed. (Amsterdam: Djambatan, 1957), xi, 243 p., has published a book with considerable emphasis on the Union's constitution. Frank N. Trager's "Burma's Foreign Policy, 1948-56: Neutralism, Third Force, and Rice" (*The Journal of Asia Studies*, vol. 16, November 1956, pp. 89-102) is a comprehensive preview of the subject. More recent is William C. Johnstone's *Burma's Foreign Policy* (Cambridge: Harvard University Press, 1963) ix, 340 p. The border dispute between Burma and Communist China has been well discussed by Hugh Tinker in "Burma's Northeast Borderland Problems" (*Pacific Affairs*, vol. 29, December 1956, pp. 324-346), by Richard J. Kozicki in "The Sino-Burmese Frontier Problem" (*Far Eastern Survey*, vol. 26, March 1957, pp. 33-38), and by Daphne E. Wittam in "The Sino-Burmese Boundary Treaty" (*Pacific Affairs*, vol. 34, Summer 1961, pp. 174-183). The items on foreign policy in the official *Burma Weekly Bulletin* have been useful.

Index

Acheson, Dean, 37
Administrators, 295-96, 298
Afghanistan, 118, 127
Africa, Communist influence, 62, 164
Afro-Asian bloc, 349, 372, 374, 385
Afro-Asian Solidarity Conference, 164
Agency for International Development (AID), 268, 271, 432
Aggression: "by proxy," 7; deterrents to, 80, 111; indirect, *see* Indirect aggression; local, 88-89; *see also* Wars
Agreements: bilateral, 100; Communist trade, 260; multilateral economic aid programs, 274-80, 411; *see also* Treaties
Agriculture, 247, 250-51: research programs, 139
Aid and trade programs, 43, 161: amounts, 256-59; Communist, 48, 251-61; Communist China, 49; Soviet Union, 59, 161, 375-76, 400-1; types of, 258; *see also* Economic aid programs, U. S., and Technical and economic assistance
Aidit, D. N., 57, 307-9
Air forces: Communist China, 70; Great Britain, 87; Indonesia, 77-78; Malaya, 77; Pacific, 84-85; South Viet-Nam, 76; Thailand, 75; U. S., 84-85
Air transport, 5; routes, 35
Albania, 61
Alejandrino, Castro, 172
Aleutians, 37
Algeria, 123
Ali, Mohammad, 41
All-China Federation of Trade Unions, 45
Allison, John M., 312
Ambassadors, 429-30: duties, 431; qualifications, 430-31

American citizens, role abroad, 431-32, 437-38
American Doctrine, 411-12
Annam, 7, 40, 286
Anti-American feeling, 324-25, 340, 405
Anticolonialism, 10-11
Anti-Fascist People's Freedom League (AFPFL), 56
ANZAM region, 328, 334, 343
ANZUS Treaty, 20, 26, 334, 337-38, 341-42, 353
Arakan territory, 371
"Asia for the Asians," 381, 385
Asian-African Conference at Bandung, 26
Asian Games, 366
Asian Solidarity Committee, 164
Association of Southeast Asia (ASA), 412
Association of Southeast Asian Nations (ASEAN), 426-30; Communist bloc membership, 428
Atoms For Peace, 267
Australia: ANZUS treaty, 20-21, 337-38, 341-42; Colombo Plan, 340; and, Communist China, 341; in event of war, 90-91; and Great Britain, 327-28, 335-38; and Indonesia, 351-53; and Japan, 401-2; military power, 86; neutralism, 415; and New Guinea, 336; and New Zealand, 337-38, 343; role in Southeast Asia, 326, 335-42; and SEATO, 28, 30, 119-120, 138-40, 154-55, 338-39, 342; and South Viet-Nam, 214; and Thailand, 142; trade, 336; treaties, 124; troops in Malaya and Singapore, 340; and United States, 119, 337-38, 340-41; West New Guinea controversy, 351-53

civil war, 17; diplomatic relations, 51; and India, 378; and Japan, 391-92, 400; KMT crisis in Burma, 225-33; Korean War, 19-20; military power, 79; seating of Red China in U.N., 64-65, 335; and SEATO, 125; and U. S., 20, 63-67, 123, 421
China, People's Republic of (Communist), 6-9, 57-63, 72: aid and trade programs, 48, 161, 400-1; aid to Communist parties, 45, 53-54; Bandung Conference, 41-43; boundary dispute with India, 14, 372-77; and Cambodia, 41, 149-50, 237-39; denunciation of SEATO, 8, 113, 119-20, 153; diplomatic relations, 45-49, 64, 421-22; economic aid from Soviet Union, 62-63; economic offensive, 254-56; and Federation of Malaya, 177; and France, 347-48; general war, 88-91; Geneva Peace conference, 23-25; ideological dispute with Soviets, 60-61; and India, 24, 41, 63, 358-59, 364-65, 370-77; and Indochina War, 7-8, 21-22; and Indonesia, 52-53; influence in Southeast Asia, 6-9, 40-67; instruments of policy, 21, 45-47, 162; intervention in Laos, 141, 178, 194-96; intervention in South Viet-Nam, 207, 213; invasion of Tibet, 371-73; and Japan, 358-59, 390-93, 395, 400-1; KMT crisis in Burma, 226; Korean War, 7-8, 18-21; limited war, 92-98; Militant nationalism, 43, 126; military power, 69-74; and New Zealand, 344; and North Korea, 8; and North Viet-Nam, 8, 22; nuclear capability, 7, 72-74, 91, 421; objectives in Southeast Asia, 6-9, 41, 405; Overseas Chinese, 44, 45-53; policy of attraction and coercion, 41; popular democracy, 58-59; "popular diplomacy," 47-48; population, 6, 63, 69-70; recognition of, 334-35, 340-41, 344, 347, 371; seating in U.N., 46, 335, 347-48, 371, 378, 421; and Soviet Russia, 57-63, 424; tactics, 41-45, 47-48, 169; transportation facilities, 71-72; and United States, 8, 48, 420-23; U.S. nonrecognition policy, 64-67, 340-41, 344, 347; visits of leaders to, 47-48
Chou En-lai, 25-26, 223, 239, 374: at Bandung Conference, 41-42, 46-47; Five Principles of Peaceful Coexistence, 363-65; personal diplomacy, 46-47
Churchill, Winston, 27, 33, 35, 343, 410
Collective security system, 26-32, 80, 105
Colombo Plan, 25, 27, 30, 224, 276-77, 340, 343-44, 401, 434-35: India, 363, 367; and Japan, 385, 387; members, 41
Colonialism, 3, 9-10, 218, 249, 349, 351, 361, 384, 404: Bandung Conference, 42-43; Communist charges, 169; elites, 292-93; U.S. opposition to, 37-38
Commander in Chief, Pacific (CINCPAC), 83, 85, 132
Commonwealth of Nations, 6, 327, 417
Commonwealth Strategic Reserve, 93, 122, 328, 330, 339-40, 342-43
Communications, 10, 85-86, 321-22
Communism in Southeast Asia, 6-9: attempts to capture nationalist movements, 17-18; attempts to control elections, 166, 173; countermeasures against, 169-216, 407; elites, 60; exploitation of economic grievances, 99, 160-61; extension of, 435; front organizations, 162-64; "hard core," 162; indirect aggression, 141, 158-216; international, 21-22, 160, 180, 194; "revisionism," 61; "revolutionary situation," 167; tactics, 44-45, 48, 323; "volunteer troops," 159, 181;

Publications of the Council on Foreign Relations

FOREIGN AFFAIRS (quarterly), edited by Hamilton Fish Armstrong.

THE UNITED STATES IN WORLD AFFAIRS (annual). Volumes for 1931, 1932 and 1933, by Walter Lippmann and William O. Scroggs; for 1934-1935, 1936, 1937, 1938, 1939 and 1940, by Whitney H. Shepardson and William O. Scroggs; for 1945-1947, 1947-1948 and 1948-1949, by John C. Campbell; for 1949, 1950, 1951, 1952, 1953, and 1954, by Richard P. Stebbins; for 1955, by Hollis W. Barber; for 1956, 1957, 1958, 1959, 1960, 1961 and 1962, by Richard P. Stebbins.

DOCUMENTS ON AMERICAN FOREIGN RELATIONS (annual). Volume for 1952 edited by Clarence W. Baier and Richard P. Stebbins; for 1953 and 1954, edited by Peter V. Curl; for 1955, 1956, 1957, 1958 and 1959, edited by Paul E. Zinner; for 1960, 1961 and 1962, edited by Richard P. Stebbins.

POLITICAL HANDBOOK AND ATLAS OF THE WORLD (annual), edited by Walter H. Mallory.

AFRICA: A Foreign Affairs Reader, edited by Philip W. Quigg.

THE PHILIPPINES AND THE UNITED STATES: Problems of Partnership, by George E. Taylor.

UNESCO: ASSESSMENT AND PROMISE, by George N. Shuster.

THE PEACEFUL ATOM IN FOREIGN POLICY, by Arnold Kramish.

THE ARABS AND THE WORLD: Nasser's Arab Nationalist Policy, by Charles D. Cremeans.

TOWARD AN ATLANTIC COMMUNITY, by Christian A. Herter.

THE SOVIET UNION, 1922-1962: A Foreign Affairs Reader, edited by Philip E. Mosely.

THE POLITICS OF FOREIGN AID: American Experience in Southeast Asia, by John D. Montgomery.

SPEARHEADS OF DEMOCRACY: Labor in the Developing Countries, by George C. Lodge.

LATIN AMERICA: Diplomacy and Reality, by Adolf A. Berle.

THE ORGANIZATION OF AMERICAN STATES AND THE HEMISPHERE CRISIS, by John C. Dreier.

THE UNITED NATIONS: Structure for Peace, by Ernest A. Gross.

THE LONG POLAR WATCH: Canada and the Defense of North America, by Melvin Conant.

Publications of the Council on Foreign Relations

ARMS AND POLITICS IN LATIN AMERICA (Revised Edition), by Edwin Lieuwen.

THE FUTURE OF UNDERDEVELOPED COUNTRIES: Political implications of Economic Development (Revised Edition), by Eugene Staley.

SPAIN AND DEFENSE OF THE WEST: Ally and Liability, by Arthur P. Whitaker.

SOCIAL CHANGE IN LATIN AMERICA TODAY: Its Implications for United States Policy, by Richard N. Adams, John P. Gillin, Allan R. Holmberg, Oscar Lewis, Richard W. Patch, and Charles W. Wagley.

FOREIGN POLICY: THE NEXT PHASE: The 1960s (Revised Edition), by Thomas K. Finletter.

DEFENSE OF THE MIDDLE EAST: Problems of American Policy (Revised Edition), by John C. Campbell.

COMMUNIST CHINA AND ASIA: Challenge to American Policy, by A. Doak Barnett.

FRANCE, TROUBLED ALLY: De Gaulle's Heritage and Prospects, by Edgar S. Furniss, Jr.

THE SCHUMAN PLAN: A Study in Economic Cooperation, 1950-1959, by William Diebold, Jr.

SOVIET ECONOMIC AID: The New Aid and Trade Policy in Underdeveloped Countries, by Joseph S. Berliner.

RAW MATERIALS: A Study of American Policy, by Percy W. Bidwell.

NATO AND THE FUTURE OF EUROPE, by Ben T. Moore.

AFRICAN ECONOMIC DEVELOPMENT, by William Hance.

INDIA AND AMERICA: A Study of Their Relations, by Phillips Talbot and S. L. Poplai.

JAPAN BETWEEN EAST AND WEST, by Hugh Borton, Jerome B. Cohen, William J. Jorden, Donald Keene, Paul F. Langer and C. Martin Wilbur.

NUCLEAR WEAPONS AND FOREIGN POLICY, by Henry A. Kissinger.

MOSCOW-PEKING AXIS: Strengths and Strains, by Howard L. Boorman, Alexander Eckstein, Philip E. Mosely and Benjamin Schwartz.

RUSSIA AND AMERICA: Dangers and Prospects, by Henry L. Roberts.

FOREIGN AFFAIRS BIBLIOGRAPHY, 1942-1952, by Henry L. Roberts.